At
9 No c 30A
6 Jan 30
7 Oct 30
7 Nov 30

STUDIES IN HISTORY
ECONOMICS AND
PUBLIC LAW

53

EDITED BY
THE FACULTY OF POLITICAL SCIENCE
OF COLUMBIA UNIVERSITY

VOLUME ONE HUNDRED AND EIGHTEEN

New York
COLUMBIA UNIVERSITY
LONGMANS, GREEN & CO., AGENTS
LONDON: P. S. KING & SON, LTD.
1925

CONTENTS

STUDIES IN HISTORY, ECONOMICS AND PUBLIC LAW

EDITED BY THE FACULTY OF POLITICAL SCIENCE
OF COLUMBIA UNIVERSITY

Volume CXVIII]   [Number 1

Whole Number 262

IMPRESSMENT OF AMERICAN SEAMEN

BY

JAMES FULTON ZIMMERMAN, Ph.D.

New York
COLUMBIA UNIVERSITY
SELLING AGENTS
NEW YORK: LONGMANS, GREEN & CO.
LONDON: P. S. KING & SON, LTD.
1925

𝕿𝖔

MY FATHER AND MOTHER

ACKNOWLEDGMENTS

RESEARCH on the subject of this dissertation was begun in September 1923. In the Spring of 1924 the materials collected were carefully examined by Professor John Bassett Moore, who not only offered suggestions for additional research, but also advised as to general literary form. Professor J. P. Chamberlain and Dr. Julius Goebel, Jr., have carefully read and criticized the manuscript, making numerous constructive suggestions both as to form and content.

Many individuals in the libraries consulted, and others acting in secretarial capacities rendered helpful service. To each one who gave assistance the author is deeply grateful. To Professors Moore and Goebel he is under lasting obligations.

7]   7

CONTENTS

CHAPTER I

INTRODUCTION

THE impressment of American [1] seamen by the British

During the Colonial Period the impressment of American seamen occurred, but the practice was not regularly resorted to, as was the case in the British Isles. The intense opposition of the colonists to the practice is seen in the case of the wholesale impressment of " sailors, ship-carpenters and labouring land-men" by Commodore Knowles in the port of Boston on November 17, 1747 (see Hutchinson, *History of Massachusetts,* vol. ii, pp. 386-390.) Hutchinson points out that the colonists were unaccustomed to the practice. This fact may explain the three days of rioting which followed, during which the Colonial Governor felt obliged to retire from Boston for safety. According to Hutchinson's account, "most if not all" of those impressed were afterwards released. The legal right to impress colonial seamen rested on the same principles that justified impressment of seamen of the mother country (see *supra,* pp. 13 *et seq.*). John Adams, in his defense of Michael Corbet in 1769, argued that impressment of American seamen was illegal. Corbet was charged with murder, for killing with a harpoon Lieutenant Panton, of the British frigate " Rose", while Panton was trying to impress Corbet and his companions from on board a brigantine belonging to Mr. Hooper of Marblehead, Mass., as she was coming in from Europe six or seven leagues from land. Adams cited 6 Anne, c. 37, s. 9, a statute exempting Americans from impressment, claiming that the statute was still in force. (For Adams' review of this case, see *Works of John Adams* (C. F. Adams, vol. ii, Appendix B, pp. 526-534.) The judge pronounced Corbet's act "justifiable homicide", and, according to Hutchinson's account, on the ground that neither Lieutenant Panton, nor his superior officers, were authorized to impress by any warrant or special authority from the Lords of the Admiralty. It would appear that the statute exempting Americans was passed in order to encourage trade from the colonies, and doubtless for this same reason the practice was not often applied to the colonists. It is also doubtless true that the British navy found it much easier to man ships by means of the use of press-gangs operating in Great Britain. Any doubt as to the continued operation of the statute referred to above, exempting Americans from impressment, was removed after 1769 by its repeal at the hands of Parliament. (See *Works of John Adams* (C. F. Adams), vol. ii, pp. 225-226.)

navy began shortly after the Revolutionary War, originating in connection with the practice of impressing British seamen into the service of the navy in time of war.

This practice, which was discontinued after the war of 1812, had been strongly relied on as a means of manning the British navy in all the wars in which that nation engaged during the seventeenth and eighteenth centuries.

The usual method of procedure consisted first of an order in council which authorized the Lord High Admiral or the Commissioners of the Admiralty to institute impressment proceedings. Such authorization was sometimes limited and specific, applying only to certain commands or ships; at other times it was general, applying to the entire navy. The Admiralty would then issue press-warrants to the officers of the navy based on the order in council.[1]

[1] A copy of such a press-warrant follows:

"By the Commissioners for executing the office of Lord High Admiral of Great Britain and Ireland, etc. and of all his Majesty's plantations, etc.

"In pursuance of his Majesty's order in council dated the 19th day of January 1742, we do hereby impower and direct you to impress or cause to be impressed so many seamen and seafaring men and persons whose occupations and callings are to work in vessels and boats upon rivers, as shall be necessary not only to compleat the number of men allowed to his Majesty's ship under your command, but also to mann such others of his Majesty's ships as may be in want of men; giving unto each man so impressed one shilling for press money; and in execution hereof that neither yourself nor any officer authorized by you do demand or receive any money, gratuity, reward, or other consideration whatsoever, for the sparing, exchanging, or discharging any person or persons impressed, or to be impressed, as you will answer it at your peril. You are not to intrust any person with the execution of this warrant but the Commission Officer, and to insert his name and office in the deputation on the other side hereof, and set your hand and seal thereto, This warrant to continue in force 'till the 31st day of December, 1743. And in the due execution of the same and every part thereof, all mayors, sheriffs, justices of the peace, bailiffs, constables, headboroughs, and all other of his Majesty's officers and subjects whom it may concern, are hereby required to be aiding and assisting you and those employed by you, as they tender his Majesty's service, and will answer the con-

The practice was by no means cheerfully submitted to in England, and at times even met with strong objection from leading naval officials.[1] It was, however, generally regarded as a prerogative of the crown and as having been established by immemorial usage, and for this reason needed no parliamentary sanction. The British courts were never called upon to decide specifically on the question of the legality of impressment, but in 1743 Sir Michael Foster, in King *v.* Alexander Broadfoot stated, " The right of impressing mariners for the public service is a prerogative inherent in the crown, founded upon common law and recognized by many acts of Parliament." [2]

trary at their perils. Given unto our hands and the seal of the office of the Admiralty the 31st day of January, 1742.

Jo. Cokburne
Geo. Lee
J. Trevor

By command of their
Lordships
   Thomas Corbett "

Note.—The above warrant was issued to Captain Hanway and published in connection with the well-known Broadfoot case. See *infra.*

[1] Montague Burrows, *Life of Admiral Lord Hawke* (London, 1883), pp. 133-136; Douglas Ford, *Admiral Vernon and the Navy* (London, 1907), pp. 248-49; Frederick Hervey, *Naval History of Great Britain* (London, 1779), vol. iii, p. 18.

[2] *Sessions of Oyer and Terminer and Gaol Delivery Held for the City of Bristol, and County of the same City on the 30th of August 1743* (Oxford, 1758).

Broadfoot was on trial for killing Calahan, a member of Captain Hanway's crew, who led a press-gang in an attempt to impress Broadfoot and his companions on board the " Bremen Factor." Calahan with the boat's crew had a general order to impress, which was expressly contrary to Captain Hanway's warrant from the Admiralty, which stipulated that only the Commission Officer could execute it. After deciding that Broadfoot was guilty of manslaughter, Foster entered into a discussion of the legality of pressing in general, because of " uncommon pains having been taken to possess people with an

Blackstone, although recognizing that impressment " had been a matter of some dispute, and submitted to with great reluctance " regarded it as a legal power of the crown, relying upon Sir Michael Foster's historical review of the subject in the Broadfoot case, which showed the practice to be of ancient date and to have been "uniformly continued by a regular series of precedents to the present time," and also upon the acts of Parliament exempting certain classes of seamen from impressment, which in his judgment strongly implied the legality of the practice. In his opinion, however, it was " only defensible from public necessity." [1]

opinion that pressing for the sea service is a violation of the Magna Charta, and a very high invasion of the liberty of the subject."

Foster's leading arguments in support of the legality of the practice may be briefly summarized:

1. The crown has the right to impress seamen on the ground of necessity for the preservation of the nation, just as the crown has the right to the services of every able-bodied man in cases of sudden invasion or insurrection.

2. Since it is too extravagant to mantain a strong naval force in time of peace, the crown must employ this emergency in time of war.

3. The fact that no statute has been passed by Parliament expressly empowering the crown to impress seamen does not make the practice illegal.

4. Copies of commissions issued to commanders of ships in earlier centuries authorizing them to " arrest and take up " mariners for the King's service indicate the long established basis of the practice.

5. Although no statute directly gives the crown the right to impress seamen, there are many statutes which recognize the practice, without disapproving it, which is evidence of usage if not tacit approbation.

6. Impressment is a restraint on natural liberty, but every such restraint is not *eo nomine* illegal. In this case it is for the good of the whole, and hence must be regarded as a private mischief which must be endured.

[1] Blackstone, *Commentaries on the Laws of England* (Cooley), (Chicago, 1872), vol. i, pp. 267-268.

" The power of impressing seafaring men for the sea service by the King's Commission, has been a matter of some dispute, and submitted to with great reluctance; though it hath very clearly and learnedly been shewn, by Sir Michael Foster (Rep. 154) that the practice of impressing, and granting powers to the Admiralty for that purpose, is of very ancient date, and hath been uniformly continued by a regular series of precedents to the present time: whence he concludes it to be part of the common law. (See also Comb. 245; Barr. 334). The difficulty arises from hence, that no statute has expressly declared this power to be in the crown, though many of them very strongly imply it. The statute 2 Ric. II. c. 4. speaks of mariners being arrested and retained for the King's service as of a thing well-known and practiced without dispute; and provides a remedy against their running away. By a later statute (2 and 3 Ph. and M. c. 16) if any waterman, who uses the river Thames, shall hide himself during the execution of any commission of pressing for the King's service, he is liable to heavy penalties. By another (5 Eliz. c. 5.) no fisherman shall be taken by the Queen's Commission to serve as a mariner; but the Commission shall first be brought to two justices of the peace, inhabiting near the sea coast where the mariners are to be taken, to the intent that the justices may choose out and return such a number of able-bodied men, as in the Commission are contained, to serve her Majesty. And, by others, (7 and 8 W. III. c. 21; 2 Ann. c. 6; 4 and 5 Ann. c. 19; 13 Geo. II. c. 17. 2 Geo. III. c. 13; 2 Geo. III. c. 38; 19 Geo. III. c. 75.) especial protections are allowed to seamen in particular circumstances, to prevent them from being impressed. And ferrymen are also said to be privileged from being impressed, at common law. (Sav. 14) All which do most evidently imply a power of impressing to reside somewhere; and, if anywhere, it must from the spirit of our constitution as well as from the frequent mention of the King's Commission, reside in the crown alone."

Christian, in his edition of Blackstone, says in a note in vol. i, p. 419, "The legality of pressing is so fully established, that it will not now admit of a doubt in any court of justice" and in proof cites Lord Mansfield in Rex *v.* John Tubbs. (See *infra*, p. 16.)

Very elaborate arguments against the legality of impressment are found in J. Almon, *An Enquiry into the Practice and Legality of Pressing by the King's Commission*, and *An Enquiry into the Nature and Legality of Press-Warrants* (London, 1770). The leading points in his argument may be summarized as follows:

1. If press warrants are legal why are those who commit murder during their execution never brought to trial?

2. If press warrants are legal as applied to mariners why are they not legal as applied to soldiers?

3. Impressment is not mentioned by writers on the King's prerogatives.

4. It is not a part of the common law or Lord Coke would have mentioned it.

5. Impressment has never been legalized by Parliament.

In 1776 Lord Mansfield wrote,[1] " The power of pressing

6. Blackstone gives rather weak support to the practice.

Most of these arguments were also presented in John Adams, *Inadmissible Principles of the King's Proclamation* (Boston, 1809).

There is, however, one very ingenious phase of Almon's argument which calls for elaboration. He sought to overthrow the entire historical position presented by Foster in the Broadfoot case, by an etymological discourse on the origin of the words *prest* or *imprest*. His theory is that the words came into use in feudal days, being first employed by the exchequer in describing the money advanced to those persons who agreed to serve the King in war. Such money was called *prest* or *imprest* money, the terms originating either from the French *prest* meaning *ready*, or from the Latin *praestitum* meaning *engaged*. The men thus engaged or ready could then be called to arms by the King's commissioners. Gradually they came to be spoken of as men pressed or impressed by the King's commissioners. The entire procedure was voluntary and it was not until much later, probably during the reign of Henry VIII., that the compulsory idea originated.

A law against vagrants, many of whom were seamen out of service, was passed during this reign, and magistrates were supplied with warrants for their arrest. Officers of the navy, supplied with the King's Commission, which up to this time had no compulsory force, soon found recruiting easy among the vagrants, who were probably willing to enlist in order to escape the penalty of the law against vagrancy.

This was the germ of the idea of compulsion, which without changing essentially the older form of the King's Commission, finally grew into the full-blown doctrine of impressment as a prerogative of the crown.

In support of the legality of impressment see also an essay on the *Legality of Impressing Seamen*, by Charles Butler (London, 1777).

[1] Rex *v.* John Tubbs, Cowpers Reports, p. 512. In this case Lieutenant Tait, having a press-warrant from the Admiralty in the usual form, impressed Tubbs from a ship in the Thames River. Tubbs brought suit on the ground that he, being a waterman of the Lord Mayor of London, was exempt from impressment, and produced a certificate of exemption signed by the water-bailiff.

The question as stated by Lord Mansfield was whether there was in this case a legal right of exemption from impressment, and it was decided in the negative, on the ground that watermen as a class had not previously been exempted either by act of Parliament or by action of the Admiralty, except as favors granted on application of those served by watermen. On the general question of impressment Lord Mansfield, without referring to King *v.* Alexander Broadfoot, said:

" I own I wished for a more deliberate consideration upon this subis founded upon immemorial usage," but he added that it could not be " vindicated or justified by any reason but the safety of the state."

During negotiations on the subject in 1806 Lords Holland and Auckland, the British Commissioners, inquired of Sir John Nicholl on what grounds impressment was claimed as a right. To this inquiry he replied on November 3, 1806, as follows:

His Majesty, by His Royal Prerogative, has a right to require the service of all his seafaring subjects against the enemy, and to seize them by force wherever they shall be found. This right is limited by the territorial sovereignty of other nations, and therefore his Majesty cannot seize his subjects, because he cannot perform any act of force within the territory of another state. But the high seas are extra-territorial, and merchant vessels navigating upon them are not admitted to possess a territorial jurisdiction, so as to protect British subjects from the exercise of His Majesty's Prerogative over them. This right, I apprehend, has from time immemorial been asserted in practice, and aquiesced in by foreign countries.[1]

A well-recognized authority [2] on the prerogatives of the

ject, but being prevented that, I am bound to say what my present sentiments are.

" The power of pressing is founded upon immemorial usage. If it be so founded, and allowed for ages, it can have no ground to stand upon, nor can it be vindicated or justified by any reason but the safety of the state: and the practice is deduced from the trite maxim of the constitutional law of England, that private mischief had better be submitted to, than public detriment and inconvenience should ensue. To be sure there are instances where private men must give way to the public good—in every case of pressing, every man must be sorry for the act, and for the necessity which gives rise to it. It ought therefore to be exercised with the greatest moderation and only upon the most cogent necessity, and though it be a legal power, it may like many others, be abused in the exercise of it."

[1] See the Report of the *Naturalization Commission of 1869*, Appendix i, pp. 32-33.

[2] Joseph Chitty, *A Treatise on the Law and Prerogatives of the Crown* (London, 1820), p. 46.

crown, after stating that his Majesty could not legally force anyone to serve in the army, added the following:

With respect, however, to persons who come within the description of seamen and seafaring men, the King may even in time of peace compel them to re-enter the navy, by forcibly impressing them. This prerogative of the crown, which has been much attacked, and is certainly a blot on English freedom, is founded on immemorial usage, recognized, admitted, and sanctioned by various acts of Parliament.

As long as the practice was confined to taking British seamen who were found in British territory, it was purely a national question, but following the independence of the United States and the phenomenal growth of that nation in the field of commerce, the British government began to give broader scope to the practice. Desertion from the British navy was often followed by entrance into the American merchant service, where wages were much higher than those paid in the British merchant service, or in the British navy itself. The inducements to desert, therefore, were twofold. First, the deserting seaman escaped service in the British navy; and, second, he acquired higher wages and better working conditions in general in the American merchant service. This practice of desertion became so prevalent as to endanger the efficiency of the British navy, and the practice soon arose of impressing deserters, not only when found in the territory of Great Britain, but also when found in ships of neutral nations in British ports, or on the high seas. The press-gangs who carried out the orders of the British government did not always make sure that they were getting *bona fide* British seamen, and in many cases American seamen, who were not easily distinguishable from British, on account of the similarity in language and manners, were impressed.

The claim of Great Britain that she was entitled to the services of her seamen was never challenged by the American government. Her practice of taking them from American vessels in the ports of Great Britain was reluctantly permitted, but the practice of taking them out of American ships on the high seas involved certain principles of international law, on which, at this time, there was definite disagreement between the two nations. The right of visitation and search of neutral merchant vessels on the high seas by a belligerent for certain specific purposes was generally admitted. On the basis of this right, Great Britain as a belligerent was entitled to visit neutral merchant vessels and to search them for goods of the enemy, or for contraband, or for persons in the military service of the enemy. In the execution of this right of visitation and search, Great Britain maintained that if British seamen were found on board such neutral merchant ships, they too could be seized and forced into her naval service.

The United States government, while not denying the right of visitation and search for enemies' goods, contraband and for persons in the service of the enemy, did deny that the exercise of that right warranted the belligerent in taking members of the crew of a neutral merchant vessel. Furthermore, it held that the practice was all the more objectionable because of the fact that the press-gangs often took American seamen either by mistake or by design. The position of the government of the United States was that, with the exception of contraband, enemies' goods and persons in the military service of the enemy, the flag of the neutral merchant vessel protected all persons sailing thereon.

The legal question involved was in substance that of the degree of jurisdiction of a nation over its merchant vessels on the high seas. The complete jurisdiction of a nation over its ships of war was pretty well recognized, and the

right of visitation and search had not, as a rule, been applied
to national vessels for nearly a century. The case of merchant vessels, however, stood on a different ground. According to one view, the merchant vessels of a nation were
regarded as a part of the territory of that nation while they
were on the high seas. In such a view, the jurisdiction of
the nation over its merchant vessels on the high seas should
be absolute, for the same reason that its jurisdiction over
its territory was regarded as absolute. This view of the
territoriality of merchant vessels was strongly disputed by
Great Britain. In fact, that nation went so far as to deny
it *in toto*, claiming that ships upon the high seas composed
no part of the territory of the state. This principle was expressed by Lord Stowell, when he said, " The great and
fundamental principle of maritime jurisdiction is that ships
upon the high seas compose no part of the territory of the
state. The surrender of this principle would be a vital surrender of the belligerent rights of this country." [1]

Concerning the non-territoriality of merchant vessels on
the high seas, Hall says, " The doctrine was not only maintained (by Great Britain) to the full, but in dealing with
impressment, it was pushed beyond its natural limits and
was converted into an assertion of concurrent jurisdiction,
not by way of a customary exception, but as a matter of
principle, independently of general consent." [2] Admitting
that this was an extreme position to take, Hall is inclined to believe that the insistence on this point of view
by Great Britain had much to do with driving the United
States into complete denial of the position, and the adoption of the opposite extreme, stated occasionally in Congress
and in diplomatic correspondence, and finally set forth with

[1] *Report in Impressment Papers (1804)* quoted in *Report of the Naturalization Commission, 1869,* Appendix, i, p. 32.

[2] W. E. Hall, *International Law* (Oxford, 1909), p. 247, footnote.

vigor by Webster in his correspondence with Lord Ashburton, August 8, 1842,[1] in which he maintained that the
merchant ships of a nation were an actual part of the territory of that nation, over which it had exclusive jurisdiction.
Such jurisdiction could hardly be claimed in the light
of certain acknowledged exceptions which were, and for
many years had been, generally admitted to be within the
belligerent's rights. On the other hand, the doctrine of
non-territoriality, if carried to its logical conclusion, would
have resulted in a completely divided jurisdiction that would
have rendered the principle of the freedom of the seas utterly
impossible of realization.

Another issue complicated the question at this time;
namely, that of the doctrine of indefeasible allegiance, which
was generally held in European countries. According to
this doctrine, citizens or subjects of a nation could not divest
themselves of that citizenship without the consent of the
nation. Allegiance to the nation began with birth and
ended only in death. This was the common-law doctrine
of Great Britain, and although it met with considerable
popular opposition in the United States, the courts often
accepted it implicitly at least during the entire period of the
impressment controversy.[2]

The Executive Department, although not uniformly consistent in its utterances on the subject, did not, until after
the controversy over impressment had ended, announce the

[1] For Webster's letter August 8, 1842, to Lord Asbhurton, and Lord
Ashburton's reply, August 9, 1842, see *Niles Register,* vol. lxiii, pp. 62-63.

[2] See Moore, *Digest of International Law* (Washington, 1906), vol.
iii, p. 552, where the following citations occur:

Kent's Comm. 49; 3 Story's Constitution, 3, note 2; Whart. State
Trials, 654; Whart. Confl. of Laws, para. 5; Lawrence's Wheaton
(1863), 918; Inglis v. Trustees of the Sailor's Snug Harbor, 3 Pet. 99;
Shanks *v.* Dupont, 3 Pet. 242, 246; The Santissima Trinidad. 7 Wheat.
283; Portier *v.* Le Roy, 1 Yeates (Penn.) 371. Contra, Alsberry *v.*
Hawkins, 9 Dana (Ky.) 178.

doctrine of voluntary expatriation in its broadest implications.[1]

Popular objection to the doctrine of perpetual allegiance is in large part to be explained by the manner in which that doctrine was related to the practice of impressment. It should be observed that the central point at issue was not the question of allegiance, but the practice followed by Great Britain of enforcing the British law of allegiance on board American vessels on the high seas.

The legislative departments of both nations enacted naturalization laws that were not altogether consistent with the doctrine of the courts on the subject of allegiance. The British Parliament in the reign of George II passed a law granting naturalization to foreign seamen who had served two years during war on board either British men-of-war or merchant ships. A law naturalizing foreign Protestants engaging in the whale fisheries and serving three years on board these vessels was passed in the reign of George III. In addition to these statutes, any person could be naturalized by act of Parliament. In all cases of naturalization by statute, however, those so naturalized were prohibited from being members of the Privy Council, or of either house of Parliament; from holding any civil or military office, and from receiving any grant of land from the King in Great Britain and Ireland.[2]

The American Congress at first offered naturalization to all foreigners on rather easy conditions, the length of resi-

[1] The right of voluntary expatriation in the full meaning of that term was first announced by James Buchanan when Secretary of State, and was embodied in the Naturalization Act of 1868. For full discussion of the doctrine of expatriation, see Moore, *Principles of American Diplomacy*, (New York and London, 1918), ch. vii.

[2] For a review of this legislation see *The Report of the Naturalization Commission of 1869*, Appendix i, (Naturalization and Allegiance Memorandum by Abbott).

dence required in the first law of 1790 being only two years.[1] British seamen who had become naturalized in the United States were placed on the same footing as native-born American seamen and were declared to be entitled to the same protection by the American government. Great Britain, however, insisted that her claim to the services of a native-born British seaman was prior to any claim involved in American naturalization. Hence, she would take from American merchant vessels on the high seas, in the same manner that she took her own subjects, all seamen who were born in Great Britain and naturalized in the United States. The doctrine of indelible allegiance is therefore seen to be the basis of Great Britain's claim to the service of all her natural-born subjects, even those who had been naturalized in the United States, to aid her in war against her enemies. In fact, it may be said that Great Britain fought the war of 1812 rather than modify this practice.

The British position was clearly stated from time to time during the controversy. Grenville, British Foreign Secretary, in correspondence with Thomas Pinckney, American Minister to Great Britain, in 1796 expressed it in the following language:[2]

It appears perfectly clear that the belligerent has a right to visit neutral vessels on the high seas and to take therefrom all goods belonging to such subjects of the enemy (a right inconsistent with every idea of territory) and to take the subjects of the enemy, found on board, as prisoners of war—it also has the right to take its own subjects found on board of a foreign vessel on the high seas, for all the purposes for which they are liable to be taken by any act of its legal power and discretion. . . .

[1] In 1798 the length of residence was increased to fourteen years, but in 1802 it was fixed at five years, and this remained the law throughout the period of the impressment controversy.

[2] S. F. Bemis, "The London Mission of Thos. Pinckey," *American Historical Review*, January, 1913, p. 240, quoted from *Foreign Office Records*.

He declared that this right was being exercised with caution and discretion. That Americans were occasionally impressed he admitted, but the remedy, in his opinion, must be found by devising a mode of identifying native citizens of the United States, which would be agreeable to both nations, thereby exempting them from impressment. He was emphatic in declaring that Great Britain would not relinquish the alleged right of impressment.

The statement of Sir John Nicholl in 1806 has already been quoted. Perhaps the most thorough-going official statement of the determination of the British government to adhere to the practice of impressment on the high seas is found in the King's Proclamation issued October 16, 1807.[1] The Proclamation declared that many British subjects had been enticed into the service of other nations, and it not only urged them to return, but made it the duty of the naval officers "to seize upon, take and bring" all those found in the service of foreign merchant vessels. It is also set forth in the Proclamation that the acceptance by British subjects of letters of naturalization and certificates of citizenship from foreign nations did not discharge them from the prior duty of allegiance to the crown.

After the outbreak of the war of 1812, efforts looking toward an armistice were made. During these negotiations, in which the American government made a settlement of impressment the *sine qua non* of an armistice, the Prince Regent in a Declaration dated January 9, 1813, again presented in clear terms the position of the British government, as follows:[2] "His Royal Highness can never admit, that, in the exercise of the undoubted and hitherto undisputed right of searching neutral merchant vessels in time of war,

[1] For Text of Proclamation see *American State Papers, Foreign Relations,* vol. iii, pp. 25-26.

[2] W. B. Lawrence, *Visitation and Search* (Boston, 1858), p. 13.

the impressment of British seamen, when found therein, can be deemed any violation of a neutral flag."

He repudiated the naturalization policy of the United States on the ground that it assumed the right to transfer the allegiance of British subjects. He could not recognize the validity of American naturalization acts and certificates of citizenship outside the territory of the United States on the ground that such a recognition would nullify the jurisdiction of the British crown over its natural-born subjects. If American seamen were impressed through error, on account of a similarity of language and manners to British seamen, that situation only made it more difficult for Great Britain to dispense with the right of impressment from American vessels. He suggested, as Grenville had done in the earlier stages of the controversy, that the British government regarded impressment as a subject for negotiations, but could not give up the exercise of the right without a satisfactory substitute.

The position of the United States was stated from time to time by the American Secretaries of State, especially those from Jefferson to Monroe. The most vital element of that position, consisting of a complete denial of the British claim to the right of impressment from American vessels on the high seas, has already been noticed. It was repeatedly insisted that the laws and regulations of Great Britain providing for the impressment of her own subjects had validity only in British territory, and hence could never be enforced in neutral merchant vessels on the high seas. The practice of taking non-British and American seamen occasioned exceptional protests, as did the custom of allowing British naval officers to determine for themselves the national character of the seamen on board American vessels, and their insistence on taking all those who failed to produce proof that they were not British subjects.

Throughout the controversy, the American government strenuously denied that American seamen engaged on American vessels could be required to carry certificates of citizenship as a safeguard against impressment. Although the United States persistently opposed the British claim to the right to take British seamen from its merchant vessels on the high seas, still, had the practice been limited to British seamen only, there would undoubtedly have been much less irritation on the subject and doubtless less intense opposition to it.

These conflicting legal views were always at the center of the prolonged controversy between the two nations over impressment. They constituted a part of the historic struggle for the establishment of the principle of the freedom of the seas.[1] The controversy over impressment constituted a major issue in the diplomatic correspondence of the two nations from 1792 to 1812, and indeed during most of that time it was the one outstanding issue. Proposals from the American government for its solution were kept almost continuously before the British government from 1792 to 1807. Combined with other more distinctly commercial issues, it brought on the war of 1812. Even at the close of the war, although the practice of impressment ceased, a definite settlement proved impossible, and for thirty years thereafter the issue emerged from time to time accompanied by arguments on both sides similar in content to those urged before the war. Indeed Great Britain never formally renounced the claim of impressment, but she never exercised it after the war of 1812, and in later years she has permitted the expatriation of her subjects.

Although only of historic interest to us today, the claim of impressment and the doctrine of indelible allegiance were vital issues during the last decade of the eighteenth century

[1] Moore, *Digest of International Law*, vol. ii, p. 987.

and the early years of the nineteenth century. In order, however, fully to understand the impressment controversy, one must look beyond its more definitely legal implications. Shortly after the beginning of its existence as an independent nation, the United States exhibited an interest in world trade and commerce which rendered her potentially a future rival of Great Britain. Before the adoption of the Constitution, the practice of impressment had involved the taking of American seamen in British ports, and was, at that early date, of sufficient importance to claim a place in the correspondence of John Adams.[1] Adams gave expression to a feeling which was probably general among Americans of that day, that Great Britain regarded the United States as a serious commercial rival, and that, because of her jealousy of American commercial growth, she desired nothing more than to see a decrease in the number of American ships and sailors. By the practice of impressment she not only augmented her own naval forces—the announced objective—but at the same time deprived the United States of large numbers of seamen.

The prevalence among seamen of the habit of deserting was vitally related to the matter of trade rivalry between the two nations. For example, the large carrying trade of the American merchant service between French West Indies and Europe attracted large numbers of British seamen into American vessels. Phineas Bond,[2] British Consul at Philadelphia, reported that entire crews deserted in American ports in order to escape service in the navy, encouraged no doubt by the high wages offered by the American shippers, which were often as much as one hundred per cent higher than the wages paid in the British service. The charge that American ships were asylums for British deserters had evident foundation in fact, although it was difficult at that date,

---

[1] See *infra*, p. 31, footnote.   [2] See *infra*, p. 44.

and is altogether impossible now, to present accurate statistical data on the subject.

On the other hand, desertion of American seamen in British ports was a common practice, encouraged in many cases by the high bounty offered by the British government. The number of seamen thus deserting from American vessels was probably small compared with the number of deserters from British vessels. But it may be conservatively stated that by impressment Great Britain gained a sufficient number of American seamen to offset her loss by the voluntary desertion of her own sailors. All efforts made to reach an agreement for the mutual return of deserting seamen were blocked, either by British lack of confidence in the disposition or ability of the United States to enforce such a plan, or by American insistence on the abandonment of the practice of impressment as a condition preliminary to such an agreement.

Furthermore, by a series of blockades and orders in council instituted by Great Britain beginning in 1806, the entire commerce of the United States was threatened with destruction. Great as was the evil of impressment, it could not be considered entirely apart from the gigantic issues of trade with which the United States, having practically no navy, found it all but impossible to cope.

In lieu of any satisfactory agreement on the main issue, the United States, almost from the beginning of the controversy, sought ways and means for protecting its citizens from impressment. Requests were frequently made that orders be given to British naval officers not to impress American seamen. The British government acceded to these requests, and from time to time issued such orders, but on account either of their direct violation, or of the difficulty of discriminating between British and American seamen, or both, the practice did not cease. Testimonials

of American citizenship secured in a variety of ways were
carried by many American seamen, but often these papers
were disregarded by the British either on the ground that
they had been fraudulently obtained, or because they were
regarded as inadequate.

Special agents were stationed in Great Britain and in the
West Indies by the American government, whose duties were
to protect American seamen from impressment and to obtain
the release of those impressed.   Despite the faithful work
of these agents, however, thousands of American seamen
were impressed, and efforts to secure their release were only
partially successful largely because of the rigid rules of
evidence required by the British Admiralty and the dilatory
procedure followed by that body in dealing with the subject.

The following chapters present an account of the important facts bearing on the practice of impressment and a
review of the legislative and diplomatic history pertaining
thereto.[1]

[1] There are two important contemporary reviews of the diplomacy relating to impressment. One, covering the period from 1792 to 1801,
was presented to Congress, July 6, 1812, by James Madison, and is published in American State Papers, Foreign Relations, vol. iii, pp. 573 *et.
seq.* The other, being a brief synopsis of the negotiations from 1800
to 1830, remains unpublished in the Miscellaneous Documents of the
Bureau of Indexes and Archives of the Department of State.

CHAPTER II

The Early History of Impressment to the Close of Pinckney's Mission

Immediately following the adoption of the Constitution in 1789, the problem of avoiding impressment became highly important to American seamen, due to the large number impressed in British ports during 1790 and 1791. There being no American consuls in British ports at this time to whom American seamen could go for protection, the custom of securing written evidence of their American citizenship before leaving the United States was very soon established. The nature of this evidence was the record of an oath of the seaman made before a notary public or a justice of the peace, and to this paper was given the name "protection." The following is a copy of one of these documents :—

"Portsmouth, Va., July 12, 1790.

I, Henry Lunt, do solemnly swear on the holy Evangelist of Allmighty God that I was born in Portsmouth in the County of Rockingham, State of New Hampshire and have ever been a subject of said State.

Sworn before me

Thos. Veale "[1]

J. P.

Shortly after the first instance of impressment in large

---

[1] *Miscellaneous Letters to Joshua Johnson, MS. Consular Despatches,* London, vol. v.

numbers in 1790[1] the United States appointed consuls to the leading ports in Great Britain and instructed them to protect American seamen while the press lasted. The correspondence of these consuls, especially that of Joshua Johnson, who was appointed Consul at London, throws light on the impressment question during those early years.[2]

British preparation for war with Spain in 1790, followed in 1791 by preparation for war with Russia, caused a general rise in the wages of seamen both in Europe and in the United States. In the United States this resulted in many " landsmen or half-seamen " entering the service. According to the reports of the American consuls, both instances were accompanied by the impressment in British ports of large numbers of American seamen. In some cases entire crews of American vessels were said to have been impressed in British ports by the British press-gangs. The

----

[1] An account of this impressment is given in a letter of Morris to Washington, May 29, 1790, *American State Papers, Foreign Relations*, vol. i, pp. 123-125. The occasion was the effort of Great Britain to secure enough seamen to enable her to punish Spain for the capture of two British vessels in Nootka Sound.

S. F. Bemis in *Jay Treaty* (New York, 1923), p. 55, footnote, refers to this as " the first instance of impressment of Americans by the British Navy." There were, however, earlier instances as is shown by the correspondence of John Adams and Lord Carmarthen in 1787 (see Adams to Lord Carmarthen, October 3, 1787, *Works of John Adams* by C. F. Adams, vol. viii, pp. 455-456.) in which Adams remonstrated against the "practice, which has been all too common, of impressing American citizens, and especially with the aggravating circumstances of going on board American vessels, which ought to be protected by the flag of their sovereign." Adams resolved to demand the release of every one impressed. (See Adams to Jay, September 22, 1787, *Works of John Adams* by C. F. Adams, vol. viii, pp. 450-451.)

[2] Johnson's correspondence is found in *Miscellaneous Letters to Joshua Johnson, MS. Consular Despatches, London*, vols. iv-vii. The correspondence of James Maury, American Consul at Liverpool, William Knox, American Consul at Dublin, and Robert W. Fox, American Consul at Falmouth is also important.

threatened wars failing to materialize, many seamen who had been impressed were shortly afterwards released by the British navy. This action resulted in a large over-supply of seamen in British ports, and American captains were not slow in discovering that they could secure regular seamen in these ports for one-half the price that they had agreed to pay to their crews, many of whom were inexperienced. Acting on this discovery, many American captains, regardless of contracts, abandoned their crews or large parts of them, and engaged regular seamen, refusing in most cases to provide for the needs of those abandoned, or for their return to the United States.

This condition of affairs added greatly to the general distress of American seamen in British ports, due to sickness, shipwreck and other causes, and resulted in an appeal to Congress to provide temporary relief for American seamen in those ports. An act was approved April 14, 1792, containing a provision making it the duty of American consuls to provide for the relief of destitute seamen in foreign ports, and allowing an amount not to exceed twelve cents to a man *per diem.* The act also required all masters and commanders of vessels belonging to citizens of the United States to transport seamen who were citizens of the United States free of cost or charge at the request of the consuls and vice-consuls, provided, however, that the seamen, if able, should perform duty on board according to their several abilities, and provided further that no captain or master should be obliged to take a greater number than two men to every one hundred tons burden of his ship on any one voyage. Refusal on the part of a captain or master to comply with the request of the consuls was made punishable by a forfeit of thirty dollars for each seaman so refused. The act also provided that in cases where vessels belonging to citizens of the United States were sold in foreign ports, unless the crew was liable to be discharged by contract, or consented to be discharged, the master should either send them back to the United States or furnish them with means which in the judgment of the consul would be sufficient for their return. Penalty for violation of this clause was to consist in the arrest of the person, ship and goods until the law was complied with, provided the law of the place of sale permitted. The difficulty of enforcing this provision of the act in foreign ports rendered it of little value. Furthermore, if the reports of the consuls are reliable, violation of other provisions of this act was the rule rather than the exception.[1]

The work of the consuls in behalf of seamen during these earlier years may be briefly described. First of all, they tried to prevent impressment. In this effort various methods were followed. One consisted in issuing papers called " general protections " to American captains, which stated on the word of the captain that his entire crew or a large part of his crew were American citizens. Another method consisted in issuing papers called " certificates of protection," or more simply, " protection," to individual seamen based on the affidavit[2] of American captains or seamen made

---

[1] The act was entitled, " An Act Concerning Consuls and Vice Consuls," *United States Statutes at Large,* vol. i, pp. 254-257.

[2] The following is a copy of the type of affidavit on which James Maury, American Consul at Liverpool, would issue a certificate of protection. It is taken from *MS. Consular Despatches,* Liverpool, vol. i, being enclosed with a letter from Maury to Pinckney, July 18, 1796.

" Port of Liverpool   }
   In the County of Lancaster } To Wit.

On this Day personally appeared before me *John Sparling Esquire one of his Majesty's justices of the Peace in and for the said borough.*

Joshua Hamilton Seaman born in New York.
Benjamin Thurston, Seaman born in Gloucester,
State of Massachusetts and Isaac McCarthy,
born in Colchester, State of Connecticut.

in the United States of America, and made oath. That *they severally were* resident in, or in the service of, the United States, at the time

either before the consul or before a British magistrate that they were American citizens.[1] A third method was to secure an affidavit substantiating the American citizenship of a seaman, and obtain a certificate of protection from a British mayor.[2] Finally, certain of the consuls granted

their Independence was acknowledged by Great Britain; and that they are citizens of the said United States of America, and of no other country.

<table>
<tr><td>Sworn at Liverpool
15th day of April 1796
Before
John Sparling</td><td>Joshua Hamilton
Benjamin Thurston
his
James X. McCarty"
mark</td></tr>
</table>

NOTE.—The words not italicized were the printed form.

Descriptions of each man were on the back of the affidavit.

[1] The following is a copy of a certificate of protection issued by Joshua Johnson, American Consul at London. It is found in " S. F. Bemis, The London Mission of Thos. Pinckney," *American Historical Review*, Jan. 1923, p. 237.

" Joshua Johnson, Esq. Consul to the United States of America for the Port of London, etc. etc. Witnesseth that the bearer hereof (a description of whose person is on the other side) to wit, *Richard Weaver, a black man*, appears by affidavit made this day by *William Bleu* before *James Robinson, Esq.* one of his Majesty's Justices of the Peace, and witnessed by *Lieutenant W. I. Stephens,* to be a subject of the United States of America, as such being liable to be called upon in the service of his country, must not, on any pretense whatever, be interrupted in his lawful business, by sea or land, either by Impress Masters, or any other Officers, Civil or Military.

London, 21 July, 1791, Joshua Johnson."

NOTE.—The words not italicized were the printed form.

A copy of such a certificate follows and is likewise taken from Bemis, *ibid.,* p. 237.

" These are to Certify to those whom it may concern *that Captain Samuel Chancery of the Ship Hercules of Portsmouth in New Hampshire* came before me *Paul Le Mesurier, Lord Mayor of the City* and voluntarily maketh oath and sayeth, to the best of his knowledge and Belief, that *Robert Darling* (the description of whose Person is at the Bottom) *is a Native and Citizen* of the United States of America, and that he is actually one of the crew of the American ship *Hercules* as a

certificates of protection to persons arriving in American vessels, upon their presentation of a note from the British custom-house saying that they were admitted as American citizens.[1] This action was warranted under the operation of the British regulation refusing to permit American vessels to land unless two-thirds of the crew were American citizens. In making this test every seaman on board was required to make oath regarding his citizenship before the British collector.

If certain available reports of Joshua Johnson, covering parts of the years 1791 and 1792,[2] may be taken as representative of the work of the American consuls during this time, it is evident that by far the larger number of protections granted were of the first or general type. Out of a total of 304 protections recorded, 233 are listed as " general protections " and only 71 listed as " protections." Whatever the exact facts in this connection may have been, there is no doubt that this general or group method of determining American citizenship was later a factor in producing British opposition to the consular practice of granting protections.

In order more clearly to visualize the situation with reference to the impressment of American seamen during this early period, certain concrete instances found in miscellaneous letters written by sailors themselves to Joshua

---

Seaman—Samuel Chancery. And the said *Robert Darling,* likewise maketh Oath and sayeth that he is a Native of America, and a Citizen of the United States of America and that to the best of his Knowledge and Belief, he was born in *Portsmouth* County in the State of *New Hampshire* and that he is one of the crew of the Ship *Hercules. Robert Darling* sworn before me, London, July 27, 1784, Paul Le Mesurier, Mayor."

NOTE.—The words not italicized were the printed form.

[1] For instances of this method see especially a letter of Maury to Pinckney July 18, 1796, *MS. Consular Despatches,* Liverpool, vol. i.

[2] See Memoranda of Joshua Johnson for 1791 and 1792, *Miscellaneous Letters to Joshua Johnson, MS. Consular Despatches, London,* vol. vi.

Johnson may be helpful. The greater number of these letters were written from the " Enterprise," a British man-of-war, which seems to have been especially devoted to the practice; although some sailors wrote from the " Tender," the " Santa Margarita " and the " Resolution." Many also wrote from the Gravesend on the Thames and from Spithead on the southern coast of England, rendezvous of the British navy. The common plea in all these letters is for release, and for " protections " from the Consul to aid them in obtaining their freedom. Many wrote that they had protections from American justices of peace, while others stated that their protections contained the seal of the consulate. Some told how their own captains who owed them wages had stolen their protections and turned them over to the British; while others reported that their protections were destroyed by the British. Some had found their protections of no value because their names were spelled incorrectly, and others because they were regarded as British subjects. The predominant tone of these letters was pathetic and calculated to arouse the sympathy and enlist the aid of the Consul. The testimony given in them was, however, not always reliable, occasional instances of outright perjury being discovered. Some claiming American citizenship were found to have previously made oath that they were British subjects.

Stories of a wife and children or of aged parents in the United States to whom the writers longed to return were frequent, but the effect of their pathos was occasionally diminished by the discovery of a legal wife in London or Liverpool.

Several letters from a sailor by the name of James Barnes [1] give one an idea of the relations between American captains

[1] See especially Barnes to Johnson, Nov. 15, 1793, *Miscellaneous Letters to Joshua Johnson, MS. Consular Despatches, London*, vol. vi.

and their crew, and indicate the part that the captains
doubtless often played in relation to impressment. Barnes
declared that his captain owed him fourteen months' wages;
had stolen all of his clothes, and that instead of helping him
out he allowed him to be impressed on the charge that he
was a British subject, despite the fact that he had a wife and
two children in America, was American-born and carried
a protection with the seal of the American consulate.

A group of six seamen wrote October 18, 1793, from on
board the " Enterprise," seemingly with the idea that they
could secure their release by threatening the Consul. After
declaring that they were all American-born, they continued:
" If you can do nothing to assist us, then why do you
allow any protections to be granted by American justices,
unless so as the unwary seamen belonging to your country
may not be imposed on by the public." They add that if
he cannot help them, then " Gen'l Washington and all the
heads in America must certainly know of your miscon-
duct." [1]

From such evidence, it is obvious that in addition to
their efforts to prevent the impressment of American seamen the consuls were faced with a difficult task in seeking
to obtain the release of those impressed.

At this time the British government, experiencing great
difficulty in enforcing its numerous regulations relating to
navigation, had assigned to its important ports certain
special officers called " regulating captains." These officers
had general supervision of the ports to which they were
assigned, and were responsible to the Board of Admiralty.
It was to these regulating captains that American consuls
at first made application for the release of impressed seamen, and the results of these applications were uniformly

[1] *Miscellanous Letters to Joshua Johnson, MS. Consular Despatches,
London*, vol. vi.

successful. Later, the power to approve these applications for release was withdrawn from the regulating captains and placed in the Admiralty office in London. Furthermore, the practice of receiving applications directly from each separate consul, adopted and for a time followed by the Admiralty Board, was later modified by a requirement that all such applications should pass through the hands of the United States Consul at London. Finally, before the close of Pinckney's mission in 1796, such applications were required to be made by the American Minister in London to the British Foreign Secretary (Grenville at that time) who presented them to the Admiralty through its Secretary. The development of this somewhat complicated machinery, which is referred to by all American consuls in British ports, took place after the outbreak of war between Great Britain and France in 1793. The British navy was then in desperate need of seamen, while many British seamen preferred service in American merchant vessels, and often sought by fraudulent methods to secure protections from American consuls. By the above regulations, the Admiralty sought to prevent fraud, and retain all British seamen for service in the British navy.[1]

There being no United States consuls in the West Indies during this early period, our only source of information concerning the facts of impressment there is the newspapers, and is in the form chiefly of letters or oral statements from masters and captains concerning their experiences. The Federalist papers as a rule gave very meager accounts of British outrages, but placed a great deal of stress on French depredations on American commerce. The Republican press, on the other hand, showed a disposition to minimize French aggressions, and to give full display to those of the

[1] For additional evidence regarding the development of these regulations see Pinckney to Jefferson, Sept. 25, 1793, *American State Papers, Foreign Relations*, vol. i, p. 243.

British. This intense partisanship was characteristic of the press in handling all questions previous to and during the war of 1812, and for this reason the newspapers of the entire period, while valuable as guides to the complex structure of public opinion, are not trustworthy, on the whole, as sources for historical facts.

During this early period numerous accounts of impressment in the various ports of the West Indies were circulated by Republican papers, and some of them were published in Federalist papers. Wide publicity was given, for example, to the activities of the British Captain Oaks, of the " Regulus," in the port of St. Jeremie during 1795 and 1796. Accounts of impressment by other British officers in this port were frequent. Thomas Webb, master of the brig " Nymph " of Philadelphia, who stayed at St. Jeremie from December 26, 1795 to February 18, 1796, gave out on his return an account of the impressment of twelve men from American vessels there. Most of these men he contended had protections from notaries in the United States. During this time there was one British officer, named Reynolds, a refugee from the United States, who made the threat on February 10, 1796, that " By God he would strip the whole of the American vessels that night of their men." Upon hearing of this threat the American captains in the port united, and upon attack from Reynolds repulsed him successfully with the loss of only one man, killing three and wounding several of Reynolds' men. On the day following, the American captains complained to Colonel Murry, the British Commandant, who " assured them that he should neither sanction nor permit an insult to the American flag; that he would prevent any British naval officer from impressing any American citizen, and that they might continue to do their business without molestation." [1] *The Columbian*

[1] *Jersey Chronicle*, April 2, 1796, and *Boston Independent Chronicle*, March 17, 1796.

Centinel (Boston), a Federalist paper, in its issue of March 16, 1796, gave the account of the fight, and of Colonel Murry's assurances, but said nothing of the actual cases of impressment which preceded the fight.[1]

In its issue of July 4, 1795, the *Jersey Chronicle* published an account by Captain Helm, who had just arrived from St. Jeremie, saying that the British frigate, " Success," had impressed two-thirds of the Americans in that port, and that one American vessel had all her hands taken.[2] The same paper on August 22, 1795 referred to the impressment of sixty seamen by the British frigate " Hermione " in the port of St. Jeremie, leaving only the captains, mates and a few unfit seamen to navigate the American vessels there. The editor of this paper, Philip Frenau, along with other Republican editors regarded impressment on such a large scale as the real cause of the great increase in seamen's wages.

Captain M'Ever of the brig " Amiable Creole " reported that Captain Oaks of the British ship " Regulus " while at Port Au Prince, where there were seventy American vessels, impressed all seamen from them who " could not produce printed certificates." [3]

Cape Nichola Mole was another West Indian port from which frequent stories of impressment came. On March 16, 1796, *The Argus* (New York) giving Captain Coward and the two Captains Duncan of Baltimore, just returned from that port, as its authorities wrote:—

The practice of impressing American seamen is continued with unremitting diligence in the British ports, and dragging them on board their detested men of war. Some of these unfortunate people are American born, and have wives and chil-

[1] See also *Boston Independent Chronicle*, March 28, 1796.

[2] See also *New Jersey State Gazette*, August, 1795 issues.

[3] *Boston Independent Chronicle*, March 28, 1796.

dren, whose existence, perhaps, depends on the welfare of a husband in slavery—a father in chains!

[Probably the largest number of instances of impressment in the West Indies is given in reports from Kingston, Jamaica. Captain Brown, of the " Nancy," is authority for the statement in the *Jersey Chronicle,* March 12, 1796, that of the 150 American vessels which touched that port during his stay there, most of them had many, and some of them all of their hands impressed.] He said the protections held by American seamen were destroyed, and that the men were dragged off by press-gangs without the least hesitation.] This story along with one by Captain Trefethen, telling of the impressment of fifty seamen from American vessels at Kingston, was carried in many of the Republican papers, and in some of the Federalist papers. The Republican papers usually carried such stories under general titles such as " Evidences of British Amity " or " More British Amity," " British Piracy ", etc. Two such stories, the first taken from the *New York Argus,* June 8, 1796, and the second from the *Boston Independent Chronicle,* June 2, 1796, are printed below.[1]

[1]   " Evidences of British Amity "
" Captain Figsby of the Brig Fau Fau who sailed from this port some time the beginning of April, with stock bound to Guadaloupe, was boarded on the 27th of April by a privateer from New Providence called the Sea Nymph, who after abusing him, and pressing two of his crew, and robbing him of a great part of his poultry, suffered him to proceed, though not without taking away his colours and damning the American Flag. He was in two days after boarded by his Britannick Majesty's ship of war, called the Unicorn, of 18 guns, who treated him at first very politely, but before they left the vessel robbed him of four sheep, three hogs, and the remainder of his poultry; and taking from him by force, another of his crew (Josh White) of Mass. and sending in his room two disabled American seamen who had been wounded in a late engagement, whom he landed in Philadelphia, and who informed him that the British expected a very warm reception from

Letters and oral statements from captains who had been in Bermuda, Grenada and Barbadoes occur frequently, giving accounts of impressments carried out with varying degrees of cruelty and insult, and often in disregard of American protections. One writer said his vessel was boarded by three British frigates, which impressed fifty of his people under "circumstances of great insolence and barbarity." Another had all his hands taken in addition to his sailing orders, invoices and bills of lading. A third, after telling of his treatment adds:—

Americans! can you remain calm and indifferent spectators of such a gross and flagrant insult to your flag? . . . Does it not awaken your indignation to see your seamen, when at the point of being welcomed by their relatives and friends, torn from their vessels and insultingly confined under the imperious flag of Britain?

A fourth had many seamen impressed all of whom had "regular protections" which were entirely disregarded by tht British naval officers.

These instances give us some general idea of what was going on in the West Indies in the matter of impressment

the French. The above Capt. Figsby is ready and willing to attest to this."
      " Evidences of British Amity "
          " Official Documents "

   " Wm. Atkinson, a lad about 17 years of age and a native of this town, was lately taken out of a vessel belonging to this port, then at Jamaica, by a frigate's press-gang, and detained as a British subject, notwithstanding the Master applied to the Captain of the frigate for his release, assuring him that he knew him to be a native of Salem, and even testifying to the same on oath before a magistrate. He was forced to leave him overwhelmed with distress at his unfortunate situation. This lad was the sole support of an aged female relative, who had stood him in place of a mother in his helpless years, and to whom he was now repaying the debt of gratitude. Thus does the British power and barbarity daily rend asunder those who are connected by the tenderest ties of nature and affection."

during these earlier years. Their number might be greatly increased. The reports from the United States Agent for Seamen, who arrived there in the summer of 1796, give us more authentic information for the years which follow, and greatly strengthen our belief in the general situation for the earlier period as outlined in the above newspaper accounts.

Having given an account of impressment during these early years, it is important to find out what steps were being taken by the governments of the two nations involved toward a solution of the difficulty.

While peace prevailed in Europe, the American government did not consider impressment a vital issue. The outbreak of war between France and England in 1793 brought the question at once to the front in diplomatic discussion. Indeed, it was the danger of war in the immediate future that caused Jefferson, Secretary of State, to deal with that topic in the instructions written June 11, 1792 [1] to Thomas Pinckney, the newly chosen Minister to Great Britain. In the event of war between France and Great Britain, Jefferson was confident that trouble would arise over Great Britain's " peculiar custom of impressing seamen." He wrote, " The simplest rule will be, that the vessel being American shall be evidence that the seamen on board her are such." Anticipating the objection that on this basis American ships would become floating asylums for deserters from the British navy, Jefferson made the suggestion that the number of men to be protected by an American vessel be limited according to tonnage. As a check on American vessels to test their observance of such a rule, he suggested that one or two British officers be allowed to go on board. But no press-gangs should be allowed to board American

---

[1] Jefferson to Pinckney, June 11, 1792, *American State Papers, Foreign Relations*, vol. iii, p. 574.

ships, until after it had been discovered that the vessel had more than the stipulated number, nor until the American master had " refused to deliver the supernumeraries (to be named by himself) to the press-officer who had come on board for that purpose; " and even then the American consul should be called in. Throughout Pinckney's mission, he urged this method of settlement upon the British government without success.

Grenville, the British Foreign Secretary, in dealing with the subject, sought the advice of Phineas Bond, British Consul at Philadelphia, who was supposed to be familiar with all problems relating to American commerce. Bond offered strong objections to Jefferson's plan on the ground that its operation would be most beneficial to the United States but most fatal to Great Britain.[1] This view was based on the fact of the numerous desertions from British crews in American ports even in time of peace. In time of war, Bond maintained that under the tonnage plan every British seaman who did not want to fight would desert to an American ship. He held that before Great Britain could give up the practice of impressing seamen from American vessels, the United States must adopt a more rigid test than the customary oath before a notary for determining the allegiance of American crews. He insisted that proofs of American citizenship be made satisfactory to the British consuls in the United States either by the attestation of the rector and church wardens of a parish, or on the oath of reputable witnesses. On the basis of such proof the British consuls would grant certificates which would protect from impressment all who held them.

Grenville presented to Pinckney this suggestion of Bond's

[1] Bond's letter to Grenville Feb. 1, 1793, "Letters of Phineas Bond," 1787-1794, *Report of Historical Manuscripts Commission* for 1896, pp. 524-527, *American Hist. Assn.*, 1896-1897—J. Franklin Jameson.

that all American seamen be provided with certificates of
citizenship before leaving American ports. To this suggestion Pinckney would not agree unless it was made reciprocal;
that is, unless the British supplied their seamen with similar
evidence of their citizenship.[1] Acting in accordance with
Bond's suggestions, Grenville, on March 17, 1794[2] informed Pinckney that the British government could not
agree to the proposal of the United States, because of the
fact that it would be so open to abuse that its operation
would harm Great Britain far more than impressment
harmed the United States. Pinckney's failure to obtain a
settlement of the question, which was a keen disappointment
to the American government, occurred just before the beginning of the special mission of John Jay, who was sent
to London in 1794 to negotiate the treaty which bears his
name.

Although impressment did not form an item in the instructions to Jay, he did not ignore the subject. Early in
his negotiations with Grenville he secured a promise that
the King would renew the instructions to British naval
officers not to impress American seamen.[3] Later he urged
that an article against impressment be added to Grenville's
project of a treaty. To this Grenville on that occasion
agreed, but no such article was included in the treaty.[4] It
is thought that Grenville's willingness to agree to a plan for
disposing of impressment ceased upon the receipt of assurances from Hammond, the British Minister to the United

[1] Pinckney to Jefferson, March 13, 1793, *American State Papers, Foreign Relations,* vol. iii, pp. 581-582.

[2] Grenville to Pinckney, March 17, 1794, *MS. Despatches England,*
vol. iii.

[3] Correspondence of Jay and Grenville, *American State Papers, Foreign Relations,* vol. i, pp. 481-482.

[4] Correspondence of Jay and Grenville, *ibid.,* pp. 492-493.

States, on the authority of Alexander Hamilton, that the
United States would not join another combination of the
Baltic powers.[1] It is known that such assurance was received about ten days before Jay presented his draft of a
treaty, and it is curious, when we consider the earlier negotiations, that not even this draft contained an article limiting
the practice of impressment. It did, however, contain an
article providing a method for the reciprocal return of impressed seamen. By this article, the magistrates of either
nation, on complaint being made that a subject or citizen had
been impressed, were to be authorized to issue writs of
habeas corpus to the officer in command of the ship of war
that had on board the impressed seamen. The seamen were
then to be brought before the magistrate who would try
the case on its merits, and either remand the seaman if the
complaint proved groundless, or discharge him if it were
well-founded. But even this article was not included in
the treaty in its final form.[2]

It is important to note that this article does not deal with
the question of right involved in impressment, which is

---

[1] This view is set forth in S. F. Bemis, *Jay Treaty*, pp. 246-247.

[2] *Ibid.*, p. 311. The text of the article, published by Bemis for the first
time is as follows:

"And all magistrates duly authorized to issue such writs on complaint that any subject or citizen of either of the said parties, other than
the one to whom the said man of war belongs, hath been impressed and
is unlawfully detained on board thereof, shall issue a Habeas Corpus
to the officer having the command of the said man of war, and thereby
order him to have such person or persons so said to have been impressed
before the said Magistrate, at a time and place therein to be specified,
which writ shall be obeyed—And the said Magistrate shall then proceed
to inquire into the merits of the case, and shall do therein as to him
shall appear to be just and right, either remanding the said person or
persons, if the complaint be groundless, or discharging him if it be
well founded—And in the latter case, the said Officer shall deliver
forthwith to the said person or persons, whatever arrears of wages
may be due, and whatever Effects or Property he or they may have
on board—All which shall be done uprightly and with good faith."

clearly seen to have been in Jay's mind when he took up the question with Grenville in July, 1794. At that time, he viewed impressment as a violence which in future should be abstained from. Furthermore, his comment on Grenville's project was to the effect that there should be an article against impressment, whereas his own draft as we here have it, does not stipulate against the practice, but simply sets forth a way whereby those impressed may be secured to their own country. It is in fact an article providing for the reciprocal return of impressed seamen, which is quite different from an article against impressment, the announced objective of Jay during the preceding negotiations.

The opposition to the Jay treaty in the United States was so intense and on so many of its provisions or omissions that one may easily overlook the definite and keen disappointment over its omission of an article on impressment. It was not explicitly mentioned in Jay's instructions, yet in later instructions to King, it is mentioned as a point left unadjusted by the treaty. The feeling expressed about the treaty by Madison in a letter to A. J. Dallas, Aug. 23, 1795, was not altogether partisan. He wrote: " By omitting to provide against the arbitrary seizure and impressment of American seamen, that valuable class of our citizens remains exposed to all the outrages, and our commerce to all the interruptions hitherto suffered from that cause." [1]

For a short while after the signing of the Jay treaty there appears to have been a decrease in the number of impressments, but from April 1795 to April 1796, during which time Pinckney was absent from London on a special mission to Spain, the practice was carried on vigorously both in Great Britain and in the West Indies. [2]

---

[1] Madison to Dallas, Aug. 23, 1795, *Madison Papers,* vol. v, p. 88.

[2] Pinckney to Secretary of State, Feb. 2, 1795, *MS. Despatches, England,* and S. F. Bemis, " London Mission of Thos. Pinckney," *American Historical Review,* Jan. 1923, pp. 238-239.

Until 1796 it appears that impressment was largely confined to British ports, but in that year the practice was extended to American vessels on the high seas, and the principle involved was discussed at length for the first time. What Pinckney regarded as the first clear case of impressment on the high seas occurred on Feb. 1, 1796. On May 14th of that year, he presented the facts he had bearing on this case in a letter to Lord Grenville.[1] The "Lydia," an American vessel, was boarded on the high seas by officers from his Majesty's ship "Regulus" and five seamen taken by force. These facts were admitted by both sides. The American captain made oath that his vessel was left with only three men and a boy to navigate her, while the commander of the "Regulus" claimed he left an adequate crew. The names of the impressed seamen were Ezra Burns, Edward Netta and John Hutchins, who according to the books of the "Regulus," ran away at Port Au Prince; John Levy, who was discharged on May 15 into his Majesty's ship "Alexander," and R. Howe, who was still retained on the "Regulus." The British officer reported that none took bounty, nor could they at any time " produce papers or anything to prove themselves American citizens."[2] The significant paragraph in Pinckney's first letter is as follows:

Mr. Pinckney, with a view of preventing the animosities arising from treatment so dangerous and injurious to the lives and property of a friendly power, earnestly solicits Lord Grenville to cause investigation to be made into this case, and if the seamen so impressed should not appear to be *bona fide* subjects of his Majesty, that they may be released and such measures adopted as will prevent similar conduct in future.

[1] Pinckney to Grenville, May 14, 1796, *MS. Despatches, England*, vol. iii.

[2] Commander of *Regulus* to Grenville, May 31, 1796, *ibid.*

Pinckney's last act as Minister was to deal at length with this case. He wrote Grenville again on June 16, 1796,[1] and in this letter carried the argument far beyond the position taken in his earlier letter on this subject, maintaining that even if the seamen involved were proved to be British subjects, Great Britain had no right to take them from American vessels on the high seas. In his effort to strengthen this position, he seems to have acquiesced in the practice of taking seamen from American vessels in British waters. If they were taken in ports or harbors, he argued, the

sovereign has the right to impose what conditions he pleases upon foreigners coming to his Dominions, and may, if he thinks it reasonable, determine (after due notice given) that if the subjects of any power choose to frequent his ports they shall bring with them such proofs of their belonging to the country of which they state themselves to be, as may satisfy him, and he may, for want of such requisites, subject them to the penalties he may think proper. These regulations may be impolitic to himself and unfriendly to the foreign nation, but he has still the right to impose them and foreigners, if they find the regulations oppressive, must either refrain from visiting the ports, or by imposing countervailing regulations within their dominions, endeavor to obtain more equitable terms of intercourse.

Pinckney's view was that if the offense took place in ports, then the offended nation could retaliate in its own ports, but if on the high seas, redress would be impossible. He said further:

No article of the existing treaty (Jay's) requires, neither does any Maxim of the Law of Nations impose upon Americans the hard condition of not being able to navigate the seas without

[1] Pinckney to Grenville, June 16, 1796, *MS. Despatches, England,* vol. iii.

taking with them such Proofs of their being Citizens of the United States as may satisfy the Officers of any Power who may judge it expedient to stop and distress their vessels on this account. And as it is a fair argument to illustrate a position by reversing it, it may be asked what sensations it would excite here if the commanders of American armed vessels should take upon themselves to stop British vessels on the high seas and impress into their service such of the mariners as had not with them full proof of their being His Majesty's subjects.[1]

To this Grenville replied as follows:[2]

It appears perfectly clear that the belligerent has a right to visit neutral vessels upon the high seas to take therefrom all goods belonging to such subjects of the enemy (a right inconsistent with every idea of territory) and to take the subjects of the enemy, found on board, as prisoners of war—it has also the right to take its own subjects found on board of a foreign vessel on the high seas, for all the purposes for which they are liable to be taken by any act of its legal power and discretion . . .

This right, Grenville went on to say, was being used cautiously and discreetly; it would not be relinquished. He then stated:

Instances . . . unquestionably have occurred of seamen being detained as British subjects, who were actually citizens of the United States but there is little doubt of their being but rare. If any mode can be devised by the mutual concurrence of both countries of identifying *native* (italics inserted) citizens of the United States, and thereby exempting them from impressment, His Majesty's Government will most cheerfully accede to it. In the meantime, until such an arrangement can be made, it will always be ready to receive with attention every application

---

[1] Pinckney to Grenville, June 16, 1796, *MS. Despatches, England,* vol. iii.
[2] S. F. Bemis, "The London Mission of Thos. Pinckney," *American Historical Review,* Jan. 1923, p. 240.

relating to the impressment of persons alleged to be Americans, and to liberate all such as may be proved of that description.

Pinckney had anticipated Grenville's position in a letter written to the Secretary of State, July 10, 1796,[1] in which he said that he was confident Great Britain would deny exclusive jurisdiction of the United States over their vessels on the high seas, but that in his opinion, the government of the United States was correct in claiming such jurisdiction. He added,

I own I cannot foresee the principles on which it will be contended that a man shall be liable to be taken from on board an American vessel on the high seas merely because he may not have with him the proofs of his being an American, while no testimony is offered of his being a British subject.

In this instance, the British unqualifiedly claimed the right to impress on the high seas. Pinckney left his task practically admitting Britain's right to impress in British ports; at least granting that it might be right to require foreign seamen to produce proof of their citizenship in those ports, but strenuously denying the right on the high seas, or the need for American seamen to carry proofs of citizenship while on the high seas.

Failure to reach a settlement of the main issue rendered more imperative some method of identifying American seamen that would prevent their impressment. Suggestions looking toward that end had been numerous. Before the appointment of American consuls to Great Britain, Gouverneur Morris, who, as the special agent of President Washington, was in London during the period of impressment in 1790, had suggested the idea of having the admiralty courts of the United States grant certificates of citizenship

[1] Pinckney to Secretary of State, July 10, 1796, *MS. Despatches, England,* vol. iii.

to American seamen which should, on the order of the British government, be regarded by British marine officers as evidence of American citizenship.[1] The plan was to be carried out in the United States by the executive through the several admiralty courts. The securing of such certificates was not to be compulsory, and it was stipulated that other evidence of American citizenship would not be excluded. This plan, however, was distinctly repudiated by Jefferson in his instructions to Pinckney.[2] In 1791, shortly after Johnson assumed the duties of Consul in London, he urged that Congress pass a law requiring every American captain to compile a complete list of his crew, giving names, age, place of birth and residence for every seaman; that one copy of this list be retained by the custom-house officers of the port in the United States from which he sailed, and that another copy be kept by the captain and deposited with the ship's register with the American consul in the foreign port until clearance from that port. Upon returning to the United States the captain would be required to produce this same list in the presence of the customs officials and render an account for every man missing. Johnson said these records should be carefully preserved by states and quarterly reports compiled from them. Unless some such system were followed, he felt sure Great Britain would continue to take American seamen.[3]

Knox, American Consul at Dublin, urged that Congress

[1] Morris to Washington, May 29, 1790, *American State Papers, Foreign Relations,* vol. i, p. 125, and Updyke, *The Diplomacy of the War of 1812* (Baltimore, 1915), p. 4. Updyke credits the British government with originating this suggestion.

[2] Jefferson to Pinckney, June 11, 1792, *American State Papers, Foreign Relations,* vol. iii, p. 574.

[3] This plan is set forth in Johnson to Jefferson, February 26, 1791, *Miscellaneous Letters to Joshua Johnson, MS. Consular Despatches, London,* vol. vii.

pass a law requiring all captains upon landing at a British
port to take their crew before a local British magistrate
and have them swear to their American citizenship. Since
few of the seamen were bringing protections from America,
he said this was the only thing to keep them from being impressed, or to obtain their release after impressment. Inci-
dentally he advised that all those who were born in British
territory sail in ships bound for non-English ports.[1]

The suggestion of Maury, American Consul at Liverpool,
was that all seamen be required to secure " regular testimonials of their citizenship " before leaving the United
States.[2]

It has been seen that the British plan to have such certificates issued by British consuls in the United States was
objectionable to the American government, except on the
basis that it be made reciprocal. Since the diplomats had
failed to reach an understanding on this point, Congress
thought it advisable to take some action looking toward
the better protection of American seamen from the constant
danger of impressment due to a lack of adequate proof of
their American citizenship.

The subject was initiated in the House of Representatives
by Murray (Md.), May 19, 1794, when he moved that a
Committee be appointed to report a bill that would " provide
such regulations as may enable American seamen to carry
evidence of citizenship for the purpose of protecting them
from impressment into foreign service." [3]   The motion was
carried, and Murray, who was made a member of the Committee, reported a bill on May 28, 1794.   The bill provided

---

[1] Knox to Jefferson, January 17, 1792, *MS. Consular Despatches,
Dublin*, vol. i.

[2] Maury to Jefferson, Aug. 30, 1792, *MS. Consular Despatches, Liverpool*, vol. i.

[3] *Annals of Congress, Third Congress, First Session*, 703.

that the collectors of districts who gave clearance to vessels keep books with the names, ages, place of birth and place of general residence of all American seamen " who may apply with well attested proof of the fact and circumstance of birth and citizenship." Collectors were to make a memorandum of this in each case in the clearance papers of the vessels, certifying that the memorandum was based on authenticated evidence. They were also to give to each seaman producing such evidence a certificate to be called a protection, which was simply a memorandum of the evidence given, attested by the collector under seal. All original papers were to be returned to the seaman in order that he might be able to obtain a protection in another American port in the event that he desired to embark at a distance from his home where the necessary evidence could not be easily obtained.

It was claimed for the bill that it would not only protect all American seamen who took advantage of its provisions, but that it would also cultivate the habit of registering, and would soon result in a complete register of American seamen who could be counted on in the event of war. When sailors and captains became accustomed to it, it was thought that Congress could then require all captains when returning from a voyage to give in a list of all returning seamen, and the causes of absence of all those who did not return. It was also held that the bill would render the municipal rights of citizens more secure in cases of intestacy.

To the contention of Fitzsimmons (Pa.), who opposed the bill, that under this plan all seamen without these certificates would be regarded as non-American, Murray made reply that since the bill made the securing of these certificates voluntary, those who did not get them could not be penalized as non-American. Besides he declared that since not more than one-half of American seamen were on shore, and since many remained at sea for years, it would always be very difficult to make a compulsory regulation on this subject. The bill, however, did not get beyond the preliminary stage, a motion for a second sitting of the Committee of the Whole being defeated June 6, 1794.[1]

In 1796, the question was taken up in earnest by Congress, when Livingston (N. Y.), on February 19 presented the following resolution in the House of Representatives:

Resolved that a committee be appointed to inquire and report whether any and what Legislative provision is necessary for the relief of such American seamen as may have been impressed into the service of any foreign power—and also to report a mode of furnishing American citizens with such evidence of their citizenship as may protect them from foreign impressment in future.[2]

The resolution was agreed to and a committee appointed, which on Feb. 25, 1796, submitted the following resolutions:

1. *Resolved,* that provision ought to be made for two or more agents to be appointed by the President of the United States by and with the advice and consent of the Senate; the one of which agents shall reside in such part of the kingdom of Great Britain, and the other at such places in the West Indies as the President shall direct; whose duty it shall be to inquire into the situation of such American citizens as shall have been, or hereafter may be, impressed or detained on board any foreign vessel; to endeavor by all legal means, to obtain their release, and to render an account of all foreign impressments of American citizens to the government of the United States.

2. *Resolved,* that proper offices ought to be provided, where every seaman, being a citizen of the United States on procuring evidence duly authenticated, of his birth, naturalization, or resi-

---

[1] For debate on bill see *Annals of Congress, Third Congress, First Session,* 772-774.

[2] *Annals of Congress, Fourth Congress, First Session,* 250.

dence within the United States and under their protection on the 3rd day of September 1783, may have such evidence registered, and may receive a certificate of his citizenship.[1]

The omission of any concrete instances of impressment furnished a target for some who opposed the resolution; Harper (S. C.), declaring during the debate on February 29, 1796, that it was not the habit of Congress to legislate merely on the basis of rumor and newspaper reports.

Many who favored the general objective of the resolution thought that the consuls were the logical ones to handle the problem, and Bourne (R. I.) moved an amendment stipulating that an agent be appointed for the West Indies only, where the United States had no consuls.

This amendment was opposed on the ground that consuls were unpaid, and that they could not give sufficient time to it to enable them to go into all the cases. It was argued also that the appointment of special agents would impress foreign powers with the idea that the United States would no longer tolerate such an evil, and therefore might have the desired effect of causing Great Britain to stop the practice.[2]

The debate on the resolution was concluded March 1, in Committee of the Whole, during which many speakers gave instances of impressment. Swanwick (Pa.) alone mentioned nineteen cases and gave details concerning Robert Norris who had been impressed by Great Britain, and after four months' enforced service on the frigate "Stagg" had escaped at the risk of his life and returned to the United States, confident that his companions were still in bondage. Livingston, Bourne, Smith (Md.) and others cited other instances. Bourne's amendment was finally defeated, 52 voting against it and 33 for it, and the original resolution

---

[1] *American State Papers, Foreign Relations,* vol. i, p. 532.

[2] For debate see *Annals of Congress, Fourth Congress, First Session,* 381-393.

carried. Those on the committee to bring in the bill were: Livingston, Bourne, Swanwick, S. Smith (Md.) and W. Smith (S.C.).[1]

[The act as passed gave the President power to appoint two or more agents whose duty was to inquire into the situation of such American citizens, or others sailing conformably to the law of nations, under the protection of the American flag, as had been or might thereafter be impressed or detained by any foreign power; to endeavor by all legal means to obtain their release, and to render an account of all impressments and detentions whatever, from American vessels, to the Executive of the United States.] The sum of $15,000 a year was authorized to compensate such agents and to defray their incidental expenses. [The act also provided that each district collector keep books in which he should at their request register the names of those seamen who could produce authenticated proof of their American citizenship. To all such seamen he was to deliver certificates in a prescribed form [2] and for each certificate he should receive from the seaman applying for the same the sum of twenty-five cents.] It was made the duty of the collectors to file and preserve the proofs of citizenship produced by the seamen.

It was also made the duty of the master of every ship or

---

[1] For debate see *Annals of Congress, Fourth Congress, First Session*, 395-400.

[2] Following is the form prescribed in the act:

"I, A.B., Collector of the district of D. do hereby certify that E.F., an American Seaman aged —— years, or there-abouts, of the height of —— feet, —— inches, (describing the said seaman as particularly as may be) has this day produced to me proof in the manner directed in the act entitled, "An Act for the Relief and Protection of American Seamen," and pursuant to the said Act, I do hereby certify that the said E.F. is a citizen of the United States of America. In witness whereof, I have hereunto set my hand and seal of office, this —— day of ————."

vessel of the United States, when any member of his crew was impressed or detained, either in foreign ports or on the high seas, immediately to make a protest stating the manner of such impressment or detention, by whom made, together with the name and place of residence of the person impressed or detained, distinguishing also whether he was an American citizen, and if not, to what nation he belonged.

Every such protest made in a foreign country was to be sent to the nearest American consul, minister or agent, if there were such in the country, and a duplicate sent to the Secretary of State.   Protests made in the United States or in a foreign country in which no consul, minister or agent of the United States resided, were to be transmitted to the Secretary of State.   The provisions of the act were to be transmitted to the collectors, who were required to make them known to all masters of vessels.   Before receiving entry each master was required to declare on oath whether any of his crew had been impressed or detained in the course of his voyage, and how far he had complied with the directions of the act.   Every master neglecting or refusing to make such a declaration or to perform the duties enjoined by the act was to forfeit the sum of one hundred dollars. Collectors were required to prosecute for any such forfeiture.

Finally it was provided that all collectors should send a list of the seamen registered under the act once every three months to the Secretary of State, together with an account of such impressments or detentions as appeared by the protests of the masters to have taken place.[1]

Those speaking for the bill were in agreement in holding that only by a treaty between the two countries would complete protection be given to American seamen, but they

[1] For text of act entitled "Act for the Relief and Protection of American Seamen," May 28, 1796, see *United States Statutes at Large,* vol. i, pp. 477-478.

thought that the bill would aid in that direction. They
agreed also that such a bill did not infringe on the power of
the Executive in foreign affairs, and would in fact aid
negotiations for a final settlement. There was considerable
disagreement, however, on many of the legal questions involved. Some thought the United States should seek to
protect alike American and neutral seamen. Madison (Va.)
was outspoken on this point. Others thought the government should first protect American seamen only. Even on
this point opinions differed, some claiming the right to protect all who had come to the United States since 1783, and
others insisting that Great Britain would never allow it.
Some declared that no nation had the right to take neutrals
off neutral ships, while others thought if Great Britain respected native American seamen more than she did neutral
foreigners, it would greatly increase the number of the former in service. Gallatin (Pa.) gave it as his opinion that
impressing American seamen was not only contrary to the
law of nations, but that it was also an act of hostility
which would have to be settled by negotiations or by war.
Since war was justifiable only when every pacific means had
been tried in vain, he felt it was the duty of Congress to
place such a mark on American citizens as would require
Great Britain to declare that she " will or will not respect
American citizens." [1]

Those speaking against the bill were Coit and Tracy of
Connecticut, who maintained that the first clause requiring
the President to appoint agents was unconstitutional on the
ground that it constituted legislative interference with the
President's authority. They claimed the Legislature could
appropriate money for such agents but could not direct the

---

[1] *Annals of Congress, Fourth Congress, First Session, 807.* During
the debate reference was made to the protections already being resorted
to by the merchants and sailors, and it was thought by the majority
that those provided for in this bill would be much better.

President to appoint them. Another objection to the bill was that the plan of obtaining evidence of American citizenship was too loose. It was maintained that any foreigner could get such a certificate if he could get one witness to swear that he was a citizen of the United States; and hence they would not be respected either at home or abroad. This bill passed 77 to 13.[1]

The Senate disagreed with that portion of the House bill which dealt with the types of certificates to be granted. The Senate, it seems, desired to issue three types of certificates, one to natives, one to foreigners who were in this country in 1783, and one to naturalized citizens. The House insisted that all should be included under the one head of American seamen. On this point the Senate yielded. On the point of proof required for certificates, concerning which the two houses also disagreed, the House yielded to the Senate's demand for more evidence. However, the clause bearing on the latter point was by some " unaccountable reason " omitted from the bill.

The outstanding weakness of the act resulted from the omission of the clause stipulating the manner of authenticating the proofs of citizenship. In order to strengthen the law on this point, the President incorporated the plan of the omitted clause in a letter of instructions to collectors. According to these instructions collectors were to issue certificates only to those seamen who could produce an extract from the register of births or baptisms, in the civil or religious society to which the applicant belonged, certified

---

[1] Those voting against it were:—Connecticut: Joshua Coit, Chauncey Goodrich, Roger Griswold, Nathaniel Smith, Zephaniah Swift, and Uriah Tracy; Maryland: Wm. Hindman and Wm. Vans Murray; Massachusetts: Samuel Lyman and Theodore Sedgwick. New York: Wm. Cooper and Henry Glen; Pennsylvania: Samuel Sitgreaves.

For final debate, March 28, 1796, see *Annals of Congress, Fourth Congress, First Session*, 802-820.

by the proper officer of such society, and supported by the affidavit of at least one credible witness, testifying that the applicant was born within the limits of the United States.[1]

As will be seen later, the British government did not regard the instructions as having the full force of law. Furthermore, the effect of the act was to weaken the validity of all other methods of establishing American citizenship, in the minds of the British, who took the position that this special and definitely authorized mode of certification should supplant all others.

The position taken by Rufus King a few years later that seamen would have been better off had this part of the law never been enacted, was probably not an unfair estimate of its ultimate value.

But Congress had acted in a manner which appeared to the majority to be the best solution then possible. The difficulty of enacting a law that would be either uniform or compulsory was a very real one, owing to the large number of seamen who were always out of the country, and also owing to the general practice, which had so long been followed, of securing certificates of citizenship from notaries, magistrates and other officers. Furthermore, the keen desire on the part of merchants and ship-owners not to lose the services of foreign seamen was doubtless an important factor in deterring Congress from enacting very rigid legislation on the subject.

[1] Wolcott's letter to Collectors, July 19, 1797, quoted in *MS. Letters, British Legation,* vol. ii.

CHAPTER III

THE DEVELOPMENT OF THE IMPRESSMENT CONTROVERSY DURING THE MISSION OF RUFUS KING

A. THE WORK OF THE AGENTS FOR SEAMEN

IN accordance with the provisions of the Act of May 28, 1796, two Agents for Seamen were appointed, one to reside in Great Britain and the other in the West Indies. Silas Talbot, who had served with distinction in the navy during the Revolutionary War, was assigned to the position in the West Indies. In the effort to administer relief and protection to American seamen throughout these islands he devoted two years of energetic and intelligent service under most arduous conditions.[1] Upon the expiration of his term as Agent for Seamen he re-entered the naval service with the rank of captain.

Lord Grenville, the British Foreign Secretary, at first raised objections to the residence of an agent for seamen in the West Indies, fearing that the relationship between such an agent and the British officers and seamen would undermine the discipline of the British navy.[2] This objection was not pressed, however, and Talbot began his mission with the full endorsement of Liston, the British Min-

---

[1] Extracts from Talbot's Correspondence are published in the *Annals of Congress*. The review here given is based, when not otherwise indicated, on the original correspondence, *MS. Consular Despatches, Jamaica,* vol. i.

[2] Notes on Conference of King and Lord Grenville, August 10, 1796. *Life and Correspondence of Rufus King* (Charles R. King), vol. ii, pp. 617-619.

ister to the United States, who, on July 7, 1796, sent a letter
to all governors and commanders in the West Indies urging
them to give Talbot a good reception and full cooperation
in his undertaking.[1] This letter, which was sent without
instructions from the British government, was regarded by
the American Secretary of State as an attempt to substitute
conciliation and good will for the former policy which con-
doned acts of cruelty and unkindness. It was believed that
this attempt would probably result in a rebuke to the Minister from the British Foreign Office.[2]

The task which Talbot encountered was especially difficult. His duties required him not only to keep in close touch
with the various admirals, captains, commanders and governors by correspondence, but in addition to travel from
port to port among the islands making direct personal appeals for the release and protection of American seamen.[3]

On certain occasions he met with unusual success, making
friends with governors and admirals, often securing from
them the promise not to impress Americans, and in some
cases the promise to release those who had already been impressed. On other occasions he incurred the intense hatred
and opposition of British admirals, and was defeated in
every effort made to carry out the humane object of his
mission.

Among the British officers in the West Indies there were
several who manifested a liberal attitude toward the United
States, particularly on the subject of impressment, as was
demonstrated in the personal and official assistance which
they rendered Talbot in securing the release of impressed

[1] MS. Letters, British Legation, vol. ii.

[2] Pickering to King, Aug. 31, 1796, MS. Instructions to United States
Ministers, vol. iii, p. 237.

[3] See also letters of instructions from Pickering to Talbot, June 9,
1796—Pickering Papers, xxxvi, 102-103.

seamen. Outstanding examples were Admiral Harvey, who commanded a British squadron at Martinique, and Admiral Bligh in charge of a small British squadron at Brunswick. The latter officer, according to Talbot's report, openly expressed opposition to the British practice of impressing neutral and American seamen from American vessels. He permitted Talbot, accompanied by one of his captains, to go on board every vessel under his command in order that they might identify and release American seamen. He also allowed American masters to board his ships along with Talbot, to testify to the American citizenship of seamen whom they claimed had been impressed from them.

The Governors of the Barbadoes and of Jamaica also rendered valuable aid to Talbot. Through the instrumentality of the Governor of Jamaica, Talbot succeeded early in 1797 in getting the local courts to issue writs of *habeas corpus* upon evidence submitted by himself and by American masters. With the aid of these writs many seamen were released.

Talbot's relations with Admiral Sir Hyde Parker, the British Commander-in-Chief in the West Indies, whose authority was final on all general policies affecting impressment in the islands, were, on the other hand, not so congenial. To Talbot's initial request that American seamen be not impressed and that those impressed be released, Admiral Parker replied that while he would regard the protections of American seamen, it was his duty to release seamen from the British service only on " incontestible proof ".

Despite the activity of Talbot to prevent further impressment, the practice was renewed with considerable vigor during the early months of 1797. He sent to Admiral Parker a list of the names of those whom he claimed were impressed, and repeatedly asked for their release without success. According to his report, British captains under

Admiral Parker frequently admitted that they had American seamen on board, but stated that they could not release them without the Admiral's approval. He charged further that Admiral Parker often refused to accept the testimony of as many as three witnesses to the effect that certain impressed seamen were born in the United States. Bitterness was injected into the correspondence between him and Admiral Parker, and on one occasion, after the Admiral had permitted vessels to leave port carrying a number of seamen whom Talbot claimed to be Americans, the latter wrote to the effect that if the United States adopted unfriendly measures, it would be because they had exhausted all friendly means. To this statement which he regarded as " menacing," Admiral Parker replied saying that the proofs offered were not sufficient " to authorize me to discharge the individuals from his Majesty's service ". He added that he would transmit his actions to the British ministers " to whom, only, I hold myself accountable for my conduct whatever may be the consequences ".

This controversy may be said to have reached a climax on May 8, 1797, when Admiral Parker issued to all his commanders and captains an order stipulating that in future they should not discharge any seamen in consequence of any writ of *habeas corpus* till such writ was referred to him as Commander-in-Chief.[1]

---

[1] The text of the order found in *MS. Consular Despatches,* Jamaica vol. i, is as follows:

" Whereas the discharging of men from His Majesty's ships and vessels under my command in consequence of writs of habeas corpus, is attended with the utmost inconvenience and disadvantage to the public service committed to my care—

You are hereby required and directed never in future to discharge any man from the ship you command in consequence of any writ of habeas corpus till such writ is referred to me as Commander in Chief (a rule observed by all the judges in England) and my orders given in consequence thereof."

The effect of this order in thus placing the action of British naval officers above and beyond civil court procedure, resulted naturally in the increase of impressment and in making the release of those impressed more difficult to obtain. According to Talbot's report, the tendency of naval officers to " consider themselves above the law " resulted in the impressment of many seamen who possessed regular American protections.

The continued futility of his efforts to obtain the release of impressed American seamen finally led Talbot to suggest that the matter be taken up by the diplomatic representatives of the two nations. He suggested that a plan be agreed upon whereby the British commanders would release all seamen on board their vessels who were registered in the ship's books as having been born in the United States. His personal examination of these books in certain instances had led him to believe that they were generally true, for the reason that it was not foreseen either by officers or men at the time of entry on these books that any advantage would be derived from a fictitious place of nativity. If this plan could not be obtained, he then favored the prohibition by the United States of all trade with the West Indies. This action he was confident would compel Great Britain to give up American seamen. Since in his opinion the inhabitants of those islands could not get along without American products, an embargo of this character would " scare them worse than a hurricane " and soon result in the release of all American seamen. Neither suggestion was adopted.

Any account of the mission of Talbot would be incomplete which failed to mention his attitude toward the French. While he did not charge them with impressment, he did charge them with treating American sailors in an almost inhuman manner, and he regarded them as little, if any, less blameworthy than the British. The justification for this

general condemnation seems to rest chiefly on the activity
of the French privateers whose operations in the area of the
West Indies were vigorously carried on during these years.
According to Talbot's reports, when the captains of these
privateers at any time found that they no longer needed the
services of American sailors who had become members of
their crews, they would rob them of all their possessions,
including their clothing, and leave them afloat in small
boats. In many cases the English would impress those thus
stranded, before they could reach land. Talbot charged also
that when French privateers were about to be captured by
the British, they would plunder all American members of
their crews, taking even their protections from them.

Talbot's views regarding the operation of the law of
Congress of May 28, 1796, are instructive. Throughout
his entire correspondence with the Department of State,
from his first letter to Pickering, February 5, 1796, to the
end of his mission, he urged that American masters cease
carrying out seamen who had no protections. He declared
that often whole crews of American vessels, all of whom
were American citizens, could not produce a single protection. In his opinion, this carelessness was due to some extent to the ignorance of the law on the part of masters and
seamen, and he recommended that collectors be required to
explain the law fully to them. This ignorance was shown
to his satisfaction by the fact that very few protests had
been sent to him, as the law required of the masters. In
addition he reported that certain collectors seemed ignorant
of the law, and as a result issued imperfect certificates.
The difficulty was augmented, he thought, by the weakness
of the act of Congress. That act required proofs to be
made to collectors upon evidence which was often impossible
for seamen to secure. If a sailor born in New Hampshire
was sailing from a southern port, he could not get the proof

required to establish his nativity. As a result, he would resort to the notary, or else go without any protection at all.

The great variety of ways in which protections could be secured made additional complications. In Talbot's correspondence there is revealed his familiarity with a large number of these protections issuing from a variety of sources. It should also be borne in mind that these methods continued after the passage of the Act of Congress in 1796 because that act was not compulsory. The more important sources of protections as listed by him were: (a) Notaries Public, (b) Justices of the Peace, (c) Judges of the General Courts, (d) Mayors of cities, (e) Secretaries of the various states, (f) Secretaries of the United States, (g) Consuls, (h) Governors of states, and (i) Collectors. There is considerable evidence that many of these protections were not treated with any too great respect previous to the Act of Congress, and Talbot declared that this act destroyed all respect for them. The British claimed that they could certify to 4000 instances of older protections fraudulently obtained, and they were inclined to insist that since a new law had been passed, it should be carried out.

Talbot's feeling that he had not been very successful, combined with pecuniary reasons, caused him to ask to be relieved at the end of two years. In his last letter to Pickering dated June 11, 1798, he gives his total expenses incurred in behalf of seamen as $2,497.54. Of this amount, about one-half was for legal fees and the other half for support of the sick and disabled.

Talbot's correspondence does not furnish complete data as to the number of seamen impressed, or as to the number released. He does make definite reference to a total of 113 for which he and Craig, who for a time assisted him at Martinique, secured release. In addition, he refers in other letters to having secured the release of "many" or "several". His conviction that many seamen were being retained in British vessels was often expressed but never accompanied by estimates as to the number involved.

[William Savage, a subject of Great Britain and a magistrate of Kingston, Jamaica, was appointed as Talbot's successor.[1]]The attitude of Admiral Parker on the question of releasing seamen became more and more uncompromising. On July 7, 1799, he notified Savage that the only ground on which he would release seamen was that of executive applications through the British minister to the United States, accompanied by proofs that they were natural-born subjects of the United States. Impressments also multiplied, all restraints of the civil law being ignored and Admiral Parker refusing to do anything to prevent them. Savage gave it as his opinion, Sept. 17, 1799, that there were two hundred and fifty impressed American seamen at Kingston alone.[2]

[1] The review of Savage's work is based on his correspondence found in MS. Consular Despatches, Jamaica, vol. i. Reasons for the appointment of a British subject to this office were not ascertained.

[2] Savage to Pickering, Sept. 17, 1799, MS. Consular Despatches, Jamaica vol. i. This letter also contained a copy of a Collector's Certificate—the only one found in the records of the agents in the West Indies, which follows:

"I, Joseph Whipple, Collector of the district of Portsmouth in the State of New Hampshire, do hereby certify, that Richard Carter, an American seaman, aged twenty-three years or thereabouts, of the height of about five feet ten inches, light complexion, light-brown hair, light-colored or blue eyes, was born in Kittery in the state of Massachusetts, has this day produced to me proof in the manner directed in the act, entitled "An act for the relief and protection of American Seamen;" and pursuant to the said act I do hereby certify, that the said Richard Carter is a citizen of the United States of America.

In witness whereof, I have hereunto set my hand and seal of office, this second day of December A. D. 1796.

L. S.

JOSEPH WHIPPLE, Coll'r"
(copy)

A true copy, Wm. Savage.

In 1800 Admiral Parker was succeeded by Admiral Seymour, who adopted a more liberal policy in regard to releasing seamen. He agreed to discharge them upon certificates granted by Savage upon proof that they were natural born American citizens. The proof especially recommended by Savage consisted of an affidavit by the nearest kin, sworn to before the Governor or Chief Justice of the state of birth, accompanied by a certificate granted either by the Secretary of State or by the British Consul General in the United States. Certificates issued under the law of 1796 were of little value according to Savage on account of their imperfections, many of them omitting place of birth and residence. The records do not contain any exact figures as to the number released, though Savage in a letter to Madison, Oct. 9, 1801, referred to " hundreds " which he had liberated.

The first appointee to the agency in London was John Trumbull, who is best known for his achievements as an artist. On account of his duties in connection with another commission Trumbull was unable to serve, and the task then fell on David Lenox, who had already served for a time as Comptroller of the Treasury. Lenox received his instructions from Pickering March 24, 1797.[1] It was set forth as his duty—

(1) To see that all American seamen who were released were provided with proper certificates which the British officers and impress-gangs would respect so that they would not again be exposed to impressment. He was to consult with King, Pinckney's successor as Minister to Great Britain, on the form of such a certificate and on the means of getting it recognized by the British.

[1] *American State Papers, Foreign Relations*, vol. ii, p. 146; for complete text of instructions see *Pickering Papers*, xxxvii, 87.

(2) To see that all other types of certificates were also respected.

(3) To obtain a more direct method of procedure with regard to the release of impressed seamen. Previous to his appointment, all applications for the release of impressed seamen had to be made by the American minister to Lord Grenville, who in turn presented them to the Lords of the Admiralty. From the Admiralty they were sent out through a secretary to the commanders of the various ships. Such a circuitous routing resulted in almost endless delays, and it was thought, in the actual loss of applications.

(4) To protect American seamen from impressment and to visit all European ports where impressments took place for this purpose.

Lenox landed in London May 31, 1797, and entered on his duties in a task which was to engage his labors for nearly five years.[1]

The presence of an American minister in London with whom Lenox was instructed to cooperate in certain important phases of his task, combined with the procedure with reference to impressment instituted and carried out by the Admiralty board in London rendered his work different in many respects from that of Talbot. He assumed all duties in relation to seamen formerly performed by the American consul in London. American consuls in other European ports, however, were instructed to continue their work in behalf of seamen, and to report to Lenox, who had general supervisory relations to the work in all European ports. Contrary to his instructions, he did not visit these ports for the reason that in his judgment he could be of no ser-

---

[1] His official title was: "Agent of the United States of America residing in Great Britain for the relief and protection of American seamen." The review of his work here given, is, when not otherwise indicated, based upon his Correspondence found in *MS. Consular Despatches, London*, vols. vii and viii.

vice to seamen in them on account of the attitude of the British commanders, who he said would not permit him to go on board their ships. He did, however, keep in touch by correspondence with all American consuls in Europe. At the outset, Lenox was able to accomplish something along the lines laid down in his instructions. For example, he secured a modification of the process of presenting applications for the release of impressed seamen. Instead of the long and cumbersome method followed heretofore by the consuls, he obtained an agreement whereby he was permitted to make application direct to the secretary of the Admiralty. Furthermore, he was successful, in some cases at least, in obtaining the release of seamen impressed in the port of London, by making application to the regulating captains of that port, apparently without the action of the Admiralty. This would indicate that there were cases of impressment, in which the American character of those involved was so clear that the regulating captains of the port were willing to release the seamen without reporting their cases to the Admiralty.

Lenox's correspondence during 1797 and 1798 gives ample evidence of his sincere conviction that the Admiralty board itself was disposed to act favorably on all legitimate applications. This conviction was based on the board's action in individual cases, which showed that seamen who had no documentary proof of their American citizenship were released upon the recommendation of British officers who were convinced that the seamen involved were Americans. Lenox was convinced that the refusal to release seamen, which had in many cases occurred, was due to the inadequacy of the documents presented, and not to " a wish to retain one of our seamen entitled to our protection ". In cases of refusal, therefore, he urged the seamen involved to write home for the necessary evidence, and in addition sent several lists of the names of seamen to the Secretary of State, requesting that they be published in the United States, in order that friends and relatives of the impressed seamen could supply them with evidence of their American citizenship.

The variety of sources of certificates of citizenship soon became a real source of difficulty, and on this point the experience of Lenox was similar to that of Talbot in the West Indies. He found it difficult to obtain the release of those whose only evidence of American citizenship was a certificate granted by American notaries. In addition to these, there were those who had taken bounty, those who had either married or settled in Great Britain, and those taken from French privateers by British ships-of-war, all of whom the Admiralty at all times refused to release.

During the year 1799 the reports from Lenox began to assume a more pessimistic tone. He experienced great difficulty in securing release for all impressed seamen who did not have collectors' certificates in accordance with the law of 1796, and he reported many instances where even this type of certificate was disregarded by British captains in acute need of men to man their war-ships. The fact that officers were allowed discretion in this matter in a situation which he characterized as "degrading to our citizens and insulting to our flag" often aroused his intense opposition. From the beginning of his services in 1797 to the year 1800 the correspondence of Lenox with the Department of State dealt almost exclusively with reports of actual cases of impressment. The few comments on the general issue between the two nations which did occur revealed a liberal attitude on the part of Lenox toward the procedure of the British Admiralty, and a very critical attitude toward the policy of American seamen in their failure to secure ample evidence of American citizenship. However, by the year

1800 he was moved to characterize impressment as " an evil not lessening in magnitude . . . which demands the most prompt and decisive interference of our Government ".

Abstracts of Lenox's reports giving statistical data on impressment were presented to Congress annually, during his term of office, and with the exception of two or three abstracts of quarterly reports all of them were published in annual installments in the Annals of Congress.[1]

[1] A complete statistical summary or abstract of the data on impressment compiled by Lenox is found in his final report to the Secretary of State. This report is found in *Applications for the Relief of Impressed Seamen,* vol. ii, David Lenox. Volumes I and II covering his entire mission are found in the Bureau of Rolls and Library, Library of State Department. For more detailed comment on this abstract, see Appendix.

This abstract, which was prepared by Lenox himself, is somewhat more detailed than those prepared by the State Department for presentation to Congress, but a comparison of the two shows clearly that there is substantial agreement. There is convincing evidence that the form followed in these abstracts originated with Lenox rather than with the State Department. In 1801 a circular was issued to the agents for seamen prescribing a standard form for reporting, but later reports give no evidence that this form was ever used. This circular found in *MS. Despatches to Consuls,* vol. i, p. 73 is as follows:

"Department of State,
Washington, July 22, 1801

Circular to the Agents of the United States
    for the Relief and Protection of American Seamen.
Sir:
You will be pleased to furnish the Department as soon as possible with a statement concerning impressed American seamen, that have come under your notice since your appointment as agent in ————— which shall contain the following particulars:

1. An annual and aggregate account of the number impressed

Citizens $\begin{cases} \text{native} \\ \text{naturalized} \end{cases}$ Aliens $\begin{cases} \text{British} \\ \text{Other than British} \end{cases}$

2. Number with protections: without protections
3. Number who enlisted after impressment
4. Number discharged
5. Number still detained

From June 26, 1797, to May 1, 1802, Lenox made application to the Admiralty for the release of 2,248 impressed seamen.[1] Of this number, 500 were actually discharged and 590 were " ordered to be discharged ".

In the last letter which Lenox wrote from London he estimated the total expense of his mission at £2500. This amount covered all his own expenses and the expenses of the American consuls in Great Britain, incurred for the relief and protection of American seamen. He regarded this as a reasonable amount. No distribution of the amount is given. Lenox landed in New York in August, 1802, after a fifty-seven day journey from London.

B. DIPLOMACY AND LEGISLATION

Pinckney, at the close of his mission in 1796, as has been shown, practically acquiesced in the policy of the British in impressing seamen from American vessels in the ports of Great Britain. He also stated, with definite precision, as the dominating element in the controversy, the problem of impressment from American vessels on the high seas. The instructions to Rufus King, Pinckney's successor, while adhering to the principle expressed in Jefferson's instructions to Pinckney in 1792 that the American flag should protect those sailing under it, laid special stress on the importance of reaching an early agreement with Great Britain which would guarantee the operation of that principle on

It is not expected that there will be entire precision in any detail which you can make; but a general and tolerably correct view of the subject is supposed to be attainable from the material in your possession, and this will suffice. The enclosed form embraces all the objects of this inquiry and you will observe it in making your return.

P. S. You will include those whose allegiance is unknown.

I am etc.

JAMES MADISON "

[1] This number included 401 applications made by Pinckney and King before Lenox reached England.

the high seas, and in the ports of the British Colonies, especially those of the West Indies.[1] Impressment in the Colonies usually resulted in detention of vessels for lack of seamen, which often meant the destruction of the detained vessels by worms, and the exposure of their crews to fatal diseases. Furthermore, the practice in the Colonies was attended with many abuses, which, because the supreme authority was so far away, became irremediable before redress could be obtained. This situation is clearly revealed in the experience of Talbot in the West Indies.

The American government was willing, however, to effect a settlement of the matter in Colonial ports, requiring every American master on his arrival in any one of these ports to report his crew at the proper office, and permitting the British officers to impress in the ports any British subjects added to the crews after such report. Impressment of British seamen from American vessels in the ports of Great Britain and Ireland was to be admitted, but regulations were to be obtained to prevent insults and injuries and to insure the release of all American seamen taken either by mistake or otherwise. The instructions to King contained comments on the matter of certificates of citizenship as approved by the Act of Congress and urged him to obtain a definite agreement that would admit other reasonable proof of the citizenship of seamen such as their own oaths, along with those of the masters, mates or other credible witnesses. It was thought also that the rolls of the crew or shipping papers, if authenticated by the collectors, should be admitted as of equal validity with the individual certificates provided for in the law.

After discussions with Grenville over the issue between the two nations on the basis of his instructions, King reached

[1] For text of Instructions see Pickering to King, June, 8, 1796, *American State Papers, Foreign Relations*, vol. iii, pp. 574-575.

the conclusion that Great Britain would ultimately make a reasonable settlement on impressment, but that while the war with France lasted, it would be very difficult to obtain any agreement that might involve the loss to Great Britain of any seamen in her navy, whether they were British or not.[1]

The negotiations for some time were centered on the question of certificates of citizenship. The question arose at the outset over the certificates which were granted by the American consuls in Great Britain. Grenville took the position that the granting of such certificates was not one of the " ordinary functions " of consuls. The practice had originated in response to the urgent appeal of American seamen who found themselves in foreign ports in danger of being impressed because of a lack of evidence of their citizenship. Although unauthorized in American law and not definitely stipulated in consular instructions, the practice had come to be regarded by the American government as a very important and necessary function of American consuls, especially of those in Great Britain.[2] Furthermore, it had been the ancient practice of consuls of maritime nations to grant such certificates *ex officio;* a practice which was still followed in some European countries. The British government maintained, however, that consuls had no such jurisdiction within British territory; that the practice was not sanctioned by the law of nations, nor by any treaty between the two nations. Moreover, it was regarded as injurious to the authority of the British government, being accompanied " by the unwarranted assumption of a power in the consuls to administer oaths to his Majesty's subjects and others resident within these realms, concerning the matter

[1] King to Pickering, Oct. 16, 1796, MS. Despatches, England, vol. v.

[2] Pickering to King, Oct. 26, 1796. *American State Papers, Foreign Relations,* vol. ii, p. 146.

of said certificates ".[1] The crux of the matter was the claim of Great Britain that American consuls granted these certificates on insufficient evidence, and often to British subjects. The discussion was brought to a head on Nov. 3, 1796,[2] by a note from Grenville to King requesting that American consuls be notified to abstain in future from granting certificates. In reply King proposed that in future all certificates granted by consuls should meet the requirements of the American law, both as to form and evidence. If this were done he believed that those not entitled to certificates would be unable to get them. He agreed to issue instructions to the consuls based on those given by the President to collectors, thus giving to consular certificates the same validity as collectors' certificates, and in return he asked the British government to instruct its naval officers to respect such certificates.[3]

This plan failed to meet the approval of the British government, based as it was on the law of Congress and on the instructions of the President, because of the nature of the evidence required as proof of American citizenship. Grenville maintained such evidence would not be admitted in any other case of the most trifling civil or political right, since practically no security against fraud was provided. He analyzed the required evidence in detail, asserting that papers required in every step of the procedure could be easily fabricated. For example, he held that a British sailor could apply to the collector at Boston for a certificate of citizenship, and furnish as evidence an extract from a pretended register of births in Georgia, purporting to be certified to by the proper officer of some religious society there.

[1] Grenville to King, Nov. 3, 1796, *American State Papers, Foreign Relations,* vol. ii, pp. 146-147.

[2] *Ibid.*

[3] King to Grenville, Jan. 28, 1797, *ibid.,* pp. 147-148.

This could be supported by an affidavit that he was the person mentioned in the extract, or by an affidavit that he was born in Georgia, and in either case his certificate would be issued. Since all of these documents could be easily fabricated, the validity of the whole plan rested solely on the single affidavit of birth, and such affidavits he maintained would be granted at the pleasure of American magistrates. To the numerous opportunities for fraud in securing the certificates was added that arising out of the fact of their transferability.[1] For these reasons he could not accept the plan. The refusal to permit American consuls in Great Britain to issue certificates of citizenship, on the same conditions as were required of collectors by American law, illustrates the widely divergent views on the question of how the seamen of the two nations were to be distinguished.

From the beginning of his mission in London in 1796, until the arrival of Lenox in the spring of 1797, King in addition to performing his function as Minister, had been acting in the capacity of Agent for Seamen. During these months he had made application for the discharge of 271 seamen. With few exceptions, he was convinced that all of these were American seamen. But the British Admiralty was convinced of the American character of less than one-third of the 271, if one may judge by the number released.[2] The whole issue was colored by the belief of Americans that Great Britain desired all of her own seamen and as many others as she could take and keep, and the belief of the British that the United States had designs on British seamen and was using the various methods of issuing certificates to obtain as many of them as possible. British testimony was offered to establish chicanery and fraud in

[1] Grenville to King, May 27, 1797, *American State Papers, Foreign Relations*, vol. ii, pp. 148-150.

[2] King to Pickering, April 13, 1797, *ibid.*, p. 146.

connection with all American certificates, even those granted by collectors, while American witnesses were loud in their testimony that Great Britain took and held American seamen in defiance of abundant evidence that they were Americans. On each side there was an utter lack of confidence in the integrity of the motives of the other. In the discussions above reviewed Grenville made it perfectly plain that Great Britain had no faith in any methods used in the United States to identify real American seamen. He particularly stressed that lack of confidence in the validity of the one method prescribed by act of Congress.

In other words, while the British government would not give full recognition to the plan set forth in the American law, it did very definitely discriminate against all types of certificates other than the one provided in that law. In view of these facts King recommended that the existing law either be repealed or amended so as to require all American seamen to obtain certificates from collectors. With a view of strengthening the law of 1796 in the matter of certificates, the House passed a bill on March 2, 1797, containing a copy of the provisions pertaining to evidence of citizenship which had been inserted in the President's instructions to collectors. On the following day, however, the Senate postponed action on this bill.[1]

During the next session, Harper (S. C.), who had previously pointed out the necessity of more than one affidavit in each case before a certificate was granted, urged upon Congress such an amendment of the law of 1796 as would prevent persons from receiving certificates who were not entitled to them. But for some reason not given in the record, the act approved March 2, 1799, contained no such amendment. It merely renewed the first three sections of

[1] *Annals of Congress, Fourth Congress, Second Session,* 1575 for Senate, and 2335 for House.

the act of 1796, and required the Secretary of State to present annual reports from collectors and agents for seamen.[1]
On the question of releasing seamen, in view of the
British distrust of American certificates, King was compelled to await in patience the decisions of the Admiralty
Board, based entirely upon their own rules of evidence. In
addition to this complex and apparently insoluble difficulty,
King was faced with the settled policy of the Admiralty of
refusing release to every seaman who had voluntarily entered on board British ships or who had married or settled
within British territory. King maintained [2] that such a
policy was altogether inconsistent with the policy of Great
Britain which insisted that all nations acquiesce in her law,
holding that a subject could never divest himself of his
natural allegiance. He pursued this topic with inexorable
logic, showing that if Great Britain was right in refusing
release to an American seaman on the ground that such
seaman had voluntarily entered to serve on board a British
ship, she was wrong in the practice of impressing British
seamen from American vessels, since all her seamen in
American service were there of their own choice.

The reason assigned by the Admiralty for refusing to
release American seamen was itself, according to King's
reasoning, a condemnation of the practice of British naval
officers in entering American ships and impressing British
seamen. Such logic was difficult to meet, nor was any
attempt made by Grenville to meet it. The truth appears
to be that the principle of natural allegiance was adhered
to by Great Britain only in so far as it served to safeguard
her own seamen. If she could retain the seamen of the
United States by disregarding that principle, she did not
hesitate to do so.

[1] For text of law see *United States Statutes at Large,* vol. i, pp. 731-732.
[2] King to Grenville, Nov. 30, 1796, *American State Papers, Foreign
Relations,* vol. iii, p. 582.

As a matter of fact, each nation was so engrossed with the idea of keeping all of its own seamen, that it refused often to consider seriously the just complaints of the other. If the United States had not been so resolute in its efforts to conserve all of its own seamen, a law might have been passed that would have given a reasonable guarantee to Great Britain that her seamen would not receive American certificates. The criticisms made by Grenville of the law of 1796 were of sufficient validity to warrant a modification of that law. Furthermore, the consuming desire for seamen in the United States arose primarily from commercial motives, whereas in Great Britain it was based in large measure on the need for naval support in a war which threatened the life of the nation. These considerations although not directly related to the legal issue involved in impressment, were vital factors in the formation of public opinion in the two countries.

During practically the entire year of 1799 King in his negotiations with Grenville concentrated his efforts in an attempt to reach an agreement on the main issue of impressment on the high seas. From time to time he reviewed the question in all of its phases, urging that a settlement was vital to the harmony of the two nations. On the question of certificates he insisted that Americans could not be required to carry them on the high seas to escape impressment, and denied Great Britain's right to question the validity of those granted in accordance with the law of 1796.

He reiterated his former argument against the policy of retaining American seamen who had voluntarily entered British service, and placed in contrast the naturalization policy of the United States, which then required fourteen years' residence, with that of Great Britain, which regarded as *ipso facto* naturalized every alien who served two years during war on a British merchantman, privateer or man-of-war.[1] [He condemned impressment as the effective denial by Great Britain of the right of other nations to naturalize aliens.] He reviewed the work of the agents for seamen, admitting that consistent " with the maxims and practice adopted and adhered to by Great Britain " a disposition had been shown to comply with the demands of Lenox. But he pointed out that Talbot had not had a fair deal in the West Indies, and that Savage, who succeeded him, had failed to obtain any satisfactory results, because of the attitude taken by Admiral Parker in refusing to release seamen except on applications made from the executive department of the United States through the British minister at Washington, accompanied by documents proving that the seamen were natural-born citizens of the United States. This policy, he declared, not only ended all hope of getting American seamen released in the West Indies, but also

prescribes a mode of interference for the relief of our seamen, circuitous, inconvenient, and for obvious reasons unfit to be employed, and, moreover, by direct inference, asserts through an officer of high rank, a right in Great Britain to take out of our ships, and to impress into her service all foreign seamen not British subjects, nor American citizens, and also all American citizens not natives of the United States.[2]

King declared that the United States had long tolerated the practice, but always in the constant expectation of an early settlement. He was sure that an order permitting American ships of war to treat British seamen in the same way that British ships of war treated American seamen

[1] For correctness of King's statement on this point, see Joseph Chitty, *A Treatise on the Law and Prerogatives of the Crown*, p. 14.

[2] King to Grenville, Oct. 7, 1799, *Life and Correspondence of Rufus King* (Charles R. King), vol. iii, pp. 115-121.

would bring immediate trouble. Throughout this elaborate argument King combined freely the various abuses accompanying the practice of impressment with the evils of the practice itself, as reason for its discontinuance, but it turned out that his judgment in the beginning of his mission that agreement would be difficult to obtain during the war, was correct. Indeed his note did not even elicit a response from Grenville.

The program of the British government during these years on the matter of adjusting the controversy, although in large part purely negative, contained one distinctly positive element, which was a plan for the reciprocal delivery of deserters. The task of negotiating such an agreement was committed to Robert Liston,[1] who was British Minister to the United States from 1796 to 1802. The plan presented by Liston to Pickering, February 4, 1800,[2] provided that no refuge or protection be afforded in the territories or vessels of either of the nations, to deserters from the crews of the vessels of the other, but that on the contrary such deserters should be delivered upon demand to the commanders of the vessels from which they had deserted, or to other duly authorized officers on proof that the deserters demanded were actually part of the crew of the vessel in question; the proof required being an exhibition of the register of the vessel or authenticated copies of the same.

For the effectual execution of this provision consuls and vice-consuls of both nations were to be given power to

[1] This plan had been presented two years before by Liston. It is also known that King was acquainted with the nature of this plan as early as 1797, for he urged strong objection to it on the ground that it made no provision for the abandonment of impressment. See King to Pickering, July 27, 1797, MS. Despatches, England, vol. v.

[2] For full text of plan see American State Papers, Foreign Relations vol. iii, p. 577 and MS. Letters, British Legation, vol. ii.

arrest and return deserters upon the presentation before the courts or proper officers of the required proof of their desertion, but it was also stipulated that the term "deserters" should not apply to sailors employed on the vessels of either nation who had in time of war or threatened hostility voluntarily entered into the service of their own nation, or who had been compelled so to enter according to the law and practice of the two nations. Finally, it was definitely stated that public ships of war should not be entered with a view to compel the delivery of deserters.

President Adams referred the proposal to his cabinet on Feb. 20, 1800, and during the next few months received written replies from the various members, all of whom agreed with the plan on condition that an article against impressment should be added.[1] On May 3, 1800, Pickering replied to Liston, expressing the desire to continue the negotiations on the basis of a counter-proposal, which contained essentially the same provisions regarding the delivery of deserters as were embodied in Liston's plan, but added an article against impressment by stipulating that all vessels should be exempt from entrance with a view to compel the delivery of deserters, whereas the Liston proposal exempted only vessels of war.[2] This modification did not meet the approval of the British Minister and consequently the negotiations ended without accomplishing any important results.

[1] See letter of Attorney General, Charles Lee, to Adams, Feb. 26, 1800, *American State Papers, Foreign Relations,* vol. iii, pp. 580-581. Also letter of Secretary of the Treasury, Oliver Wolcott, to Adams, April 14, 1800, *ibid.,* pp. 578-579. Also letter of Secretary of War, James McHenry, to Adams, April 18, 1800, *ibid.,* pp. 579-580. Also letter of Secretary of Navy, Benjamin Stoddard, to Adams, April 23, 1800, *ibid.,* p. 580.

[2] The full text of this counter-project is found in *American State Papers, Foreign Relations,* vol. iii, p. 578.

John Marshall, who succeeded Pickering as Secretary of State, was much concerned over the subject of impressment, and did not fail to give the subject the benefit of his legal attainments. His views are set forth at length in a letter to King dated Sept. 20, 1800,[1] in which he covered nearly every possible phase of the controversy. An original contribution consisted in a demand that Great Britain punish those who impressed American citizens, for said he, " The mere release of the injured, after a long course of service and suffering, is no compensation for the past and no security for the future." He set it down explicitly as a demand, that all American seamen who were not British subjects, whether born in America or elsewhere, be exempt from impressment. He denied that Great Britain had any right to impress even British subjects, and expressed doubt as to the difficulty of distinguishing American from British seamen, saying: " We know well that, among the class of people who are seamen, we can readily distinguish between a native American and a person raised to manhood in Great Britain or Ireland; and we do not perceive any reason why the capacity of making this distinction should not be possessed in the same degree by one nation as by the other." If the United States should impress Americans, and foreigners including British subjects from British merchant vessels, he was convinced that such a course of injury, unredressed, would not be permitted to pass unrevenged. His most original suggestion was that the United States might retaliate by authorizing American ships of war to recruit sailors on board British merchantmen. But he immediately added that in his opinion Great Britain would consider it more advisable to desist from an acknowledged wrong, than, by perseverance in that wrong, to excite the well-founded re-

[1] Marshall to King, Sept. 30, 1800, *American State Papers, Foreign Relations*, vol. ii, pp. 489-490.

sentment of America, and force the American government
" into measures which may possibly terminate in an open
rupture ".

Long before King received this able statement of Marshall, he had reached the conclusion that while the war
lasted it would be impossible for him to get a convention
entirely eliminating impressment.   He still thought he might
succeed when peace came to Europe.[1]   On March 10, 1801,
he submitted the following article to Lord Hawkesbury, the
successor to Lord Grenville in the Foreign Office.[2]   "Neither
party to impress upon the high seas seamen out of the vessels
of the other."   He told Lord Hawkesbury that while he
hoped to effect, upon the return of peace, a final settlement
that would secure to both parties, as far as practicable, the
service of their respective seamen, and which would put an
end to impressment, still a temporary and limited measure,
was, even at the time of his communication, necessary for
the safety of Americans who were then exposed to so much
greater risk by the practice of Great Britain.   Admitting
that impressment within territorial waters by either nation
to obtain its own seamen might be allowed, he denied that
impressment should be permitted on the high seas "where
the jurisdiction of all nations is equal ".   He declared that
recently every able-bodied seaman had been taken out of an
American ship by a British cruiser in American seas, and
replaced by boys and invalids, leaving ship, cargo and lives
of people exposed to the perils of the ocean.   He therefore
proposed this temporary article until " more comprehensive
and precise regulations can be devised." [3]

[1] King to Secretary of State, July 15, 1799, *MS. Despatches, England,*
vol. viii.

[2] *American State Papers, Foreign Relations,* vol. ii, p. 493.

[3] There is evidence of King's belief that Great Britain would be disposed at this time to favor the above article. See King to Secretary
of State, April 21, 1801, *MS. Despatches, England,* vol. ix.

It was the feeling of the new administration at Washington that the practice of impressment would stop at the close of war and that all impressed seamen would be released. But on April 30, 1802,[1] Madison wrote to King, citing a definite case of impressment after the close of the war, and adding this comment:

That Government cannot be made too sensible of the tendency of such flagrant abuses of power to exasperate the feelings of this country, nor be too much prepared for the reformation on the subject which will doubtless be insisted on by this country in case of the renewal of the war, or whenever another war shall take place.

In the meantime, King had appealed[2] to Erskine, who perhaps because of his personal ties strongly favored the United States in the controversy, to use his influence with Lord St. Vincent, then in charge of the Admiralty, whose opinion, it was believed, had great weight with the foreign secretary, in the effort to secure his approval of the temporary article against impressment on the high seas. Erskine responded to this appeal, urging a settlement in the interests of justice and harmony between the two nations.[3] When King, seeing that another war was unavoidable, renewed the negotiation, he found that Lord Hawkesbury would agree to any article on the subject which met the approval of Lord St. Vincent. After prolonged conferences, he secured Lord St. Vincent's approval of the following regulations:[4]

[1] Madison to King, April 30, 1802, MS. Instructions to United States Ministers, vol. vi, p. 33.

[2] King to Erskine, March 11, 1801, Life and Correspondence of Rufus King (Charles R. King), vol. iii, pp. 401-402.

[3] Erskine to King, March 12, 1801, ibid., pp. 402-403.

[4] King to Secretary of State, July 1803, American State Papers, Foreign Relations, vol. ii, p. 503.

1. No seaman nor seafaring person shall, upon the high seas, and without the jurisdiction of either party, be demanded or taken out of any ship or vessel belonging to the citizens or subjects of one of the parties, by the public or private armed ships or men of war belonging to or in the service of the other party, and strict orders shall be given for the due observance of this engagement.

2. Each party will prohibit its citizens or subjects from clandestinely concealing, or carrying away from the territories or colonial possessions of the other, any seamen belonging to such other party.

3. These regulations shall be in force for five years and no longer.

According to King's report, however, on that same night he received a note from Lord St. Vincent stating that on further reflection, he was of opinion that the "narrow seas"[1] should be expressly excepted, and with this correction, he had sent the proposed convention to Lord Hawkesbury. On this basis an American vessel intending to enter a Baltic port through the British channel would be in the "narrow seas" from the time of her making soundings until she reached the Categat. King therefore preferred

[1] The claim to a certain special jurisdiction over the seas surrounding Great Britain and Ireland to a considerable distance had been asserted by British Kings from early times. The most extensive area ever comprised in this claim included the English Channel, St. George's Channel, the Irish Sea and the North Sea, and the entire group was often referred to as the "narrow seas" or sometimes as the "English" seas. The claim comprehended the control of fishing in these waters and more especially the right to demand within them a salute to British ships of war from foreign vessels. While Holland and other nations reluctantly complied with this alleged right of salute, France consistently refused to do so, and after the early years of the nineteenth century Great Britain no longer demanded it. For discussion of the "narrow seas" see Henry Wheaton, *History of the Law of Nations,* pp. 154-157; W. E. Hall, *International Law,* pp. 144-147, and references cited by these authors.

no convention at all to one reviving the old doctrine of *mare clausum*.   While he greatly regretted the failure to put the matter on a satisfactory basis, still he thought the plan as limited would " be productive of more extensive evils than those it was our aim to prevent ".[1] King, like his predecessor, left the problem in 1803 no nearer a solution than it was when he entered on his duties in 1796.

[1] King to Pickering, March 10, 1804, *Life and Correspondence of Rufus King* (Charles R. King), vol. iv, pp. 368-369.

CHAPTER IV

The Leading Events Relative to Impressment During the Mission of James Monroe

George W. Erving,[1] who was serving as American Consul in London, began actively to deal with the work of relief and protection of seamen before the departure of Lenox in the year 1802. The official reports, however, remained in Lenox's name and it was not until after his departure that Erving received his commission as Agent for Seamen.[2]

His first task was to give assistance to the large number of American seamen who had been discharged from the British navy at the close of the war. Many of these were now in a destitute condition, being unable to secure employment, and also unable to pay their way back to the United States. Formerly, when wages were high, these destitute seamen could either ship to the United States or enter the British merchant service, but war being at an end, the English masters preferred their own seamen, and American captains discharged American seamen either because they did not feel the need to go so fully manned, or because they could get other seamen cheaper.

[1] Erving had been a loyalist during the Revolutionary War. After his service as Consul and Agent for Seamen at London, he was made Secretary of Legation to Spain, in 1804. In 1811 he was appointed Special Minister to Denmark, and in 1814 Minister to Spain, which position he held for four years. (See *Appleton's Dictionary of National Biography*.)

[2] Erving to Madison, July 21, 1802, *MS. Consular Despatches, London*, vol. viii. Note: The review of Erving's work is based on *MS. Consular Despatches, London*, vols. viii and ix.

Erving recommended that an annual appropriation of $5,000 to be administered by him be approved, and a law requiring all vessels before leaving British ports to secure the permission of the consuls. In this way he thought the seamen might be returned to the United States. He also urged that a plan be worked out giving these seamen a certificate of the amount of wages due them from the British navy, on which the United States government could advance them funds, up to a certain part or even all of the value of the certificate. Some months later he withdrew his earlier request for an annual appropriation of $5,000. Because of the dissolute habits of seamen, he thought they would soon claim all of it, if they knew there existed any definite sum for their relief. He repeated from time to time his request that Congress give consuls control over the departure of American vessels, a plan which he said would reduce the cost of relief by guaranteeing the return of large numbers of destitute seamen. He reported that Maury at Liverpool and other American consuls in Great Britain favored this plan. Under existing regulations, the masters of American vessels were all but independent of the consuls, and it was Erving's conviction that the agents of the American merchants in London desired this condition to continue, lest the consuls get some of their business.

On August 16, 1802, Erving presented a list containing the names of 101 discharged American seamen to Nepean, Secretary of the Admiralty. After conference it was agreed that Erving should issue a printed notice to American seamen telling them that all those discharged from the British navy and unemployed would be returned to the United States without expense to them, upon proof of their American citizenship, provided they had neither voluntarily enlisted nor received bounty for enlistment. Erving objected to the latter provision on the ground that many of the

American seamen never accepted bounty until long after they had been impressed, and that the acceptance of British bounty did not destroy their right to relief by the British government. He had granted certificates of citizenship to 250, but of that number the British would approve only sixty, and there is no evidence that more than that number ever got the benefit of this arrangement.

On March 21, 1803, Erving wrote to Madison saying that the quarrel between England and France had been renewed and that impressment had been revived.[1] According to his statement, those with " regular protections " who had not married or taken the bounty were discharged. Many were without certificates, which he supplied to those concerning whose American citizenship he was absolutely sure. This situation aroused Congress to a recognition of the inadequacy of the act of 1792 designed to provide relief and protection to distressed seamen in foreign ports, and the result was the passage of a supplementary act which was approved February 28, 1803.[2] The act required first, that before clearance was granted to any vessel bound on a foreign voyage, the master should deliver to the collector of the customs a list of the names of the crew, with places of their birth and residence to which the captain of the vessel would annex his oath of affirmation. A certified copy of this list was to be returned to the master who was required to give bond in the sum of $400 that he would exhibit the list on his return to the United States and produce the persons named therein. The bond was not to be forfeited for the loss of seamen discharged in a foreign country with the consent of the consul, signified in writing under his hand

---

[1] The British declaration of war against France occurred on May 18, 1803.

[2] For complete text of the act see *United States Statutes at Large,* vol. ii, pp. 203-205.

and official seal, or for those lost by death, desertion or impressment, provided that satisfactory proof in each case was exhibited to the collector.

The law also provided that when vessels were sold in foreign ports and crews discharged, or when any American seaman was discharged without his consent in a foreign port, the master should pay to the American consul three months' pay over and above the wages due for each seaman so discharged. Two-thirds of this sum was to be paid to the seaman when he engaged on any vessel to return to the United States, the other third was to be used to create a fund for destitute seamen, to provide relief and passage home for them. Masters were required, as before, to take seamen to the United States on the recommendation of the consuls. Two seamen for every hundred ton was the limit of obligation, but ten dollars was allowed a master for each seaman taken. Violation of this provision was to be punished by a forfeit of $100 in each case, and a certificate of the consul was made *prima facie* evidence of such violation. Provision was made for reimbursing consuls for amounts spent in excess of twelve cents a day for each man for relief, and allowing consuls fifty cents for every certificate of discharge in a foreign port, and 2½% of the receipts from the three months' additional wages payable on discharge. Finally the act contained a regulation against the issuing of passports or certificates of citizenship to aliens by American consuls or other agents, and the penalty for violation was made a fine of $1000.

The "certified list" of the crew provided for in section one of this act came to be regarded in the minds of many seamen and of some of the consuls as virtually identical with the collectors' certificates to individual seamen provided for in the law of 1796. As an aid to the conservation of seamen for merchant service the law of 1803 was a great improvement over that of 1792, but the "certified list" seems only to have added to the general confusion already existing over the validity of certificates of citizenship. Furthermore, the act as passed did not give to American consuls the control over the departure of American vessels from foreign ports which the consuls themselves regarded as essential to the protection of American seamen.

Despite these weaknesses, Erving regarded the act as a great advance over the earlier law. He was at first particularly gratified over the provision requiring a certified list of all seamen, which he represented to the British Admiralty as evidence that the United States did not desire to deprive other nations of their seamen.

In his efforts to obtain the release of impressed seamen, Erving met with the same difficulties which Lenox, his predecessor, had faced. Those with collectors' certificates who had not entered the British navy voluntarily, had not taken bounty, nor married and settled in British territory, were released in London. In other British ports, however, even the collectors' certificates were often no protection to American seamen.

King's effort to obtain a settlement failed, as has been seen, because of his unwillingness to except the "narrow seas" from the agreement.[1] Had he agreed to this limitation the high seas in general would have been free from impressment. But he did not regard the gain to be derived from such a concession as equal to the loss the United States would suffer by conceding the right of Great Britain to impress seamen in the large and important area known as the "narrow seas," through which virtually all American ships must pass on their way to European ports.

James Monroe was appointed by Jefferson as King's successor. The new administration desiring full information

[1] For discussion of "narrow seas" see *supra*, ch. iii, p. 89, footnote.

concerning impressment directed Albert Gallatin to interview King on that subject. As a result of the interview,
Gallatin reported [1] that King thought he might have been
able to secure some arrangement on impressment if he could
have remained longer in London. King later confided to
Pickering [2] the opinion that it would not be difficult for
the new administration to get an agreement that would protect American native seamen from impressment. He did
not think, however, that Great Britain would ever give up
impressing those of her seamen who were naturalized in the
United States. On the point of excluding all but native
seamen from American vessels, King seemed to feel that
such a regulation would be very hard on the Southern states
which could not carry on their trade without the aid of
foreigners. His advice was to leave it to the administration and its friends to obtain " what we were unable to accomplish".

During the first months of Monroe's mission, the American government expected that the British government
through its representative in Washington would open the
general question of neutral rights and thus afford an opportunity to deal with impressment. When this seemed
doubtful, however, it was determined no longer to delay
the commencement of a negotiation, and on Jan. 5. 1804,[3]
Madison sent to Monroe the plan of a convention, which
according to his explanation, postponed subjects less urgent
in order to hasten the adjustment of those that could not
" be much longer delayed without danger to the good understanding of the two nations".

[1] Gallatin to Jefferson, August 18, 1803, *Writings of Albert Gallatin*
(Henry Adams), vol. i, pp. 139-143.

[2] King to Pickering, March 9, 1804, *Life and Correspondence of Rufus
King* (Charles R. King), vol. iv, pp. 367-368.

[3] Madison to Monroe, Jan. 5, 1804, *American State Papers, Foreign
Relations*, vol. iii, pp. 81-83.

The plan included impressment of seamen, blockades, visit and search, contraband of war, trade with hostile colonies, and a few other subjects affecting the maritime rights of neutrals. Impressment was placed first and two projects were transmitted, one being the first proposal and the other the ultimatum on the subject.

Article one contained the first proposal on impressment, stipulating that no persons, except those in the military service of the enemy, should be impressed on the high seas, and read as follows:

No person whatever shall, upon the high seas and without the jurisdiction of either party, be demanded or taken out of any ship or vessel belonging to citizens or subjects of one of the parties, by the public or private armed ships belonging to, or in the service of the other, unless such person be at the time in the military service of an enemy of such other party.

The ultimatum contained the same stipulation, but added the following explanatory paragraph:

But it is to be understood that this article shall not exempt any person on board the ships of either of the parties from being taken therefrom by the other party, in cases where they may be liable to be so taken according to the law of nations, which liability, however, shall not be construed to extend in any case to seamen or seafaring persons being actually part of the crew of the vessel in which they may be, nor to persons of any description passing from one port to another port of either of the parties.

Article two contained a regulation against compulsory service on board public or private vessels, and provided for the release of all seamen serving against their will. The plan also contained a clause providing for the reciprocal delivery of deserters, substantially the same as that drawn by Pickering in 1800. There was also an article providing that each party would prohibit its citizens or subjects from clandestinely carrying away, from the territories or dominions of the other, any seamen or soldiers belonging to the other party.

The interest attaching to this plan, which Monroe was instructed to offer, did not lie in its originality, but rather in its comprehensive scope. Substantially, it was an effort to combine the article on impressment for which King had been struggling in London, with the article on deserters which Great Britain had been trying to obtain through Liston, her Minister to the United States. The only difference between this and Pickering's counter-project of 1800 was that while the latter sought to eliminate impressment by denying the right to take deserters from neutral vessels, the Madison plan inserted King's positive proposal against impressment on the high seas with a modification embodying an exception recognized in the law of nations.

In a detailed explanation of his plan,[1] Madison stated that the practice of impressment was becoming very menacing, particularly since it had been extended to American coasts, to neutral ports, to neutral territory and in some instances to American harbors. He confined his plan to the high seas, because in his opinion Great Britain would consider it dishonorable to stipulate anything regarding the other "enormities", and if the United States could once get impressment stopped on the high seas, the other more humiliating practices would doubtless be discontinued.

The elaborate argument presented by Madison in connection with this plan is perhaps the ablest contemporary statement of the American position. He maintained that a belligerent could find no justification in international law for the taking away of any persons from neutral vessels, except those in the military service of the enemy; that neither in

[1] *American State Papers, Foreign Relations,* vol. iii, pp. 83-87.

the law of nations nor in treaties could there be found any
language giving any sovereign the right to enforce his claim
to the allegiance of his subjects on board neutral vessels on
the high seas; that the practice of impressment was in defiance of reason and justice because it deprived those persons
impressed of a regular trial, leaving their destiny to the
arbitrary will of officers, who were sometimes cruel, often
ignorant, and generally interested in their own decisions.
He argued that if it were allowable that British subjects
should be taken from American vessels on the high seas,
the proof of their allegiance ought to be established by the
British; that certificates to American seamen were not meant
to protect them under their own flag on the high seas, and
failure to possess a certificate was no evidence that a seaman was not an American, and surely no evidence that he
was British.

Madison dealt with the inconsistency of Great Britain's
position on the questions of naturalization, voluntary entrance into service, marriage, and residence, covering the
ground so ably discussed by King in his letter to Grenville,
Oct. 7, 1799,[1] closing with these sentences: " She takes by
force her own subjects voluntarily serving in our vessels.
She keeps by force American citizens involuntarily serving
in hers! More flagrant inconsistencies cannot be imag-
ined." [2]

He pointed out the leading objections which the British
government would probably raise to any settlement, the
first being that there were large numbers of British seamen
engaged in American vessels, whose services in the British
navy were necessary. His answer to this objection was
that the number of British seamen thus engaged was much
smaller than was generally supposed; that a wrong could

---

[1] *Supra*, ch. iii, pp. 83-84.

[2] *American State Papers, Foreign Relations*, vol. iii, p. 85.

not be made right by consideration of expediency or advantage, and that the number of actual British subjects gained by the practice of impressment was of inconsiderable importance. In support of this he referred to the report to Congress on impressed seamen from June, 1797 to September, 1801, which he said gave the number of those detained as British subjects as less than one-twentieth of the number impressed. This made it highly probable that for every British seaman gained by this violent proceeding, a number of others, not less than ten for one, must have been its victims, and it was even possible that their number exceeded the proportion of twenty to one.

The plan made no distinction between natural born and naturalized seamen. In case difficulty should arise over American naturalization of British subjects since the treaty of 1783, Madison would have reply made that there could be only a few of these because of the rigid requirements of the naturalization law of the United States, which made it all but impossible for persons of seafaring character to comply with. Besides, if impressments were stopped, each nation would be able to enforce the allegiance it claimed within its national jurisdiction and in its vessels on the high seas, and double claims would arise only within a jurisdiction independent of both nations.

British pretensions to dominion over the "narrow seas" Madison pronounced as an obsolete and altogether indefensible claim. Of course, he said, there was a time when England claimed and exercised almost full sovereignty over the seas surrounding the British Isles, even as far as Cape Finisterre to the south, and Vanstaten, in Norway, to the north. But such usurpation rested purely on power and not right, and now no principle in the code of public law was better established than "the common freedom of the seas beyond a very limited distance from the territories washed

by them ". If Great Britain insisted on exempting the
" narrow seas " as in the King proposal, Monroe was instructed not to accept it for the same reasons that led King
to refuse it.

As a concession to the British position that American
vessels would become sanctuaries for deserting British seamen, Monroe was instructed to concur, if necessary, in the
modification embodied in the second proposal or ultimatum
of Article 1. This plan he said would, in all cases, guard
the crews of American vessels from being interfered with,
for, in referring to the law of nations, for an exception to
the immunity on board vessels it yielded no principle maintained by the United States, inasmuch as the reference
would be satisfied by the admitted exception of enemies in
military service. Should persons, therefore, other than
such, be taken, under pretext of the law of nations, the
United States would be free to contest the proceeding.
Finally, Madison referred to the bill then before Congress
as an indication that a remedy for the evil would soon be
demanded in tones which could not be disregarded.

This bill had been reported in the Senate on January 14,
1804,[1] by a committee of which S. Smith (Md.) was chairman. It expressed resentment on account of the renewal
of the practice of impressment and authorized the President
to prohibit by proclamation the giving of aid or provisions
to any vessel of war whose commander impressed seamen
from on board any vessel of the United States. It stipulated
also that if impressment occurred on board an American
vessel, the cargoes of ships of the aggressing nation might
be prohibited from being landed, and the ships of that nation
prohibited from taking in lading.[2] On February 29, action
on this bill was postponed to the next session by a vote of

[1] *Annals of Congress, Eighth Congress, First Session, 232.*
[2] For text of bill see the *Aurora,* February 7, 1804.

21 to 11. The House, it appears, took no action on this bill. However, on January 24, 1804, the House passed a bill, presented by Nicholson (Md.), January 10, 1804, intended " for the better direction of the collectors of the respective ports of the United States in granting to seamen certificates of citizenship ",[1] but this bill was not considered by the Senate.

Monroe, pursuant to his instructions, presented a project of a convention to Lord Hawkesbury, April 7, 1804, which, with slight modifications, was identical with the plan set forth by Madison. To the article against compulsory service on board public or private vessels, Monroe added a paragraph as follows:

A certified list of the crew, or protections from either government in such form as they shall respectively prescribe, showing that the person claiming under it is a citizen or subject of either power, shall be deemed satisfactory evidence of the same; and in all cases where these documents may have been lost, destroyed, or by casualty not obtained, and any person claims to be a citizen or subject of either power, such other evidence of said claim shall be received and admitted as would be satisfactory in a court of judicature.

The article on deserters was the same as the one in Madison's proposal except that the provision for giving aid and assistance in searching for, as well as in seizing and arresting deserters and detaining them in prison, was omitted.

Monroe later engaged in discussions on the project with Lord Harrowby, who had succeeded Lord Hawkesbury as Foreign Secretary. Great Britain's chief complaint continued to be that deserters from her vessels were never restored, while the abolition of the evil of impressment remained the chief desire of the United States. Lord Har-

[1] *Annals of Congress, Eighth Congress, First Session,* 877 and 942.

rowby expressed grave doubt as to the possibility of enforcing the provision for restoring deserters in the United States on account of popular opposition, but Monroe urged that as the price of a stipulation against impressment, the people of the United States would support that provision.

Lord Harrowby expressed great indignation to Monroe on account of the action of Congress. He particularly disliked the Senate bill proposed by Smith of Maryland on Jan. 14, 1804. Monroe assured him that no act of Congress indicated the executive mind on the subject, but insisted that the bills did show the temper of public opinion, and therefore indicated all the more reason for an early settlement.[1] Monroe seems to have regretted that these bills ever came up in Congress, especially since the Federalists used this occasion to defend the British by charging that many seamen taken were really British. This, he claimed, encouraged the continuance of the practice and lessened the disposition of Great Britain to arrange it by treaty. Still he did not blame the Federalists, for he said " it shows that the public mind is not altogether ripe for a rupture on that ground, since the quarter of the Union most injured by these acts not only do not complain, but vindicate them." [2]

The negotiations were suspended during Monroe's absence in Spain during the latter months of 1804 and the early part of 1805. Before his departure, however, he had another interview [3] with Lord Harrowby with no result except a promise that during his absence in Spain, Great Britain would act with moderation in the matter. Madison [4]

[1] Monroe to Madison, Sept. 8, 1804, *Monroe's Writings* (Hamilton), vol. iv, pp. 241-245.

[2] Monroe to Jefferson, Sept. 25, 1804, *ibid.*, p. 254.

[3] Monroe to Madison, Oct. 3, 1804, *MS. Despatches, England*, vol. x.

[4] Madison to Monroe, March 6, 1805, *American State Papers, Foreign Relations*, vol. iii, pp. 99-101.

approved Monroe's conduct, which he characterized as " winking at " the dilatory tactics of the British and " keeping the way open for a fair and friendly experiment on your return from Madrid."

As depredations on American commerce increased during the years 1804 to 1806, a tendency to unite the problems of protection of seamen and of commerce arose in the minds of leaders of Congress. The two problems were definitely combined in a resolution presented to the House by Crowninshield (Mass.), Jan. 23, 1805,[1] and on March 3, 1805 an act was approved which merged impressment with British aggressions in general.[2] The purpose of the act was " for the more effectual preservation of peace in the ports and harbors of the United States, and in the waters under their jurisdiction ", and its most important provision was as follows:

That whensoever any officer of an armed vessel commissioned by any foreign power, shall, on the high seas, commit any trespass or tort or any spoliation, on board any vessel of the United States, or any unlawful interruption or vexation of trading vessels actually coming to or going from the United States, it shall be lawful for the President of the United States on satisfactory proof of the facts, by proclamation to interdict the entrance of the said officer, and of any armed vessel by him commanded, within the limits of the United States.

Violation of this proclamation was made punishable in any competent court in the United States, the penalty being that the offender should never return to the United States, and, if he did, he would be liable again to indictment. The act also provided that when any armed vessel of a foreign nation entered American jurisdiction and refused to leave

[1] *Annals of Congress, Eighth Congress, Second Session,* 1006.

[2] For full text of act see *United States Statutes at Large,* vol. ii, pp. 339-342.

when ordered, the President of the United States should
have power to use the land and naval forces or militia to
compel its departure. It gave the President power to forbid
all intercourse with such vessel and every armed vessel of
the same nation; to prohibit all supplies and aid to such
vessel, and to refuse entrance to any vessel of that nation
so long as the armed vessel remained in defiance of public
authority. If any person offered aid to such vessel either as
to repair, furnishings for her or her crew, or if any pilot
assisted in navigating the armed vessel or any other, contrary
to the prohibition of the President's proclamation—unless to
carry her out of American jurisdiction—a fine of $1,000
on all such offenders should be imposed.

As an amendment to this bill, J. Clay (Pa.) proposed in
the House to make unlawful search or impressment of any
of the crew of a trading vessel coming to or going from
the United States, punishable by a fine of $1,000.[1] This
amendment was not adopted because the majority held that
the general language of the act made it possible to accomplish all that was intended by the amendment. This act
attracted the attention of the British ministers and doubtless had a bearing on the diplomatic negotiations.

On his return from Spain, Monroe, on July 31, 1805,[2]
addressed a note to Lord Mulgrave, who had succeeded Lord
Harrowby in the office of foreign affairs, drawing his attention to the project submitted to his predecessor, and urging
the necessity of a settlement, but it does not appear that any
consideration was given to his request, and during the remainder of Lord Mulgrave's administration, impressment
was superseded by other topics.

In February, 1806,[3] Monroe presented the case of im-

---

[1] *Annals of Congress, Eighth Congress, Second Session*, 775.

[2] Wait, *State Papers*, vol. vi, p. 200.

[3] Monroe to Fox, Feb. 25, 1806, *American State Papers, Foreign Relations*, vol. iii, p. 114, and Monroe to Madison, March 11, 1806, *MS.
Despatches, England*, vol. xii.

pressment to Fox, who succeeded Lord Mulgrave, but the later negotiations between them seem to have been centered exclusively on the question of the unlawful seizure of American property, and to have left in abeyance the impressment issue.

In the midst of diplomatic delays, the impressment of American seamen continued. The reports of American consuls and agents for seamen from 1803 to 1806 indicated that the practice was carried on with greater vigor than ever before, and that the percentage of those released was much smaller. Out of approximately 1500 cases reported by Erving from March 12, 1803 to the end of his term of service on May 18, 1805,[1] only 273 were reported to have been released, whereas Lenox had been able to secure the release of nearly fifty per cent of those for whom he made application. According to Erving's own statement, he made application to the Admiralty for the release of seamen on the following grounds:[2]

1. That the seaman had a certificate from a collector of the United States in accordance with the law of 1796.

2. That the seaman was included in the certified list of the crew in accordance with the law of 1803.

3. That the seaman had a certificate granted by an American consul. These certificates he regarded as necessary because of the fact that hundreds of American vessels were at sea when the war began in 1803, and their crews were not provided with certificates of any kind before leaving the United States.

He was confident that consuls did not grant certificates

[1] Report enclosed in letter from Erving to Madison, June, 10, 1805, *MS. Consular Despatches, London*, vol. ix.

[2] Erving to Monroe, Nov. 5, 1803, *ibid.*, vol. viii.

without careful examination and the assurance that the seamen involved were entitled to them.

4. That the seaman was taken from on board an American vessel.

This last ground for application for release he stated was seldom used, because in most cases he had stronger proof. He justified it, however, on the ground that the British had no right to take any seaman from an American vessel without positive proof that he was not an American.

According to Erving's reports, the British Admiralty refused release to all except those whose applications were supported by a collector's certificate in accordance with the law of 1796, and even with such certificates, release was refused if the slightest inaccuracy in the description of the seaman occurred, or if he had taken bounty or married and settled in British territory. These conditions governing the release of seamen were perfectly clear, but when Erving sought definite information from the Admiralty as to the grounds on which seamen were impressed, he declared that no reply was ever made to his inquiry.[1]

There is evidence in Erving's correspondence [2] with the State Department indicating that the action of American captains in some instances furnished a basis for the British Admiralty's lack of confidence in the certificates granted by the United States. In some cases, he reported, American captains expelled American seamen who had regular certificates, either to avoid payment of their wages, or to secure other seamen for lower wages. On the other hand he credited the British with having invented methods of their own to discredit American certificates, a notable ex-

[1] Erving to Monroe, Nov. 5, 1803, *MS. Consular Despatches, London*, vol. viii.

[2] Erving to Madison, Feb. 2, 1805, *ibid.*, vol. ix.

ample being a " game " in which they would find an American seaman whom they could bribe to make affidavit that he was in fact a British subject and had obtained his certificate by direct purchase or by some other fraudulent method.[1] Another practice of the British to which he referred was that of enlisting American seamen whom they had impressed under false names so that applications for their release would be of no avail.

Charges and counter-charges of fraud in these matters were frequent, and there seems to be no way of sifting the evidence so as to arrive at any just appraisal of the degree of their validity. The general character of the officers and seamen of this period might warrant the belief that there was considerable truth in many of them.

Savage, who continued to act as Agent for Seamen in the West Indies, until 1806, reported[2] that with the renewal of the war in 1803, impressments took place with greater frequency than ever before, and complained of the difficulty in obtaining the seamen's release. Admiral Dawes, who was at this time Commander-in-Chief of the British fleet in the West Indies, was exceedingly skeptical as to the validity of American certificates, due according to Savage's statement, to the fact that British seamen were obtaining them in New York and certain other American ports. Complaints were also made that the certificates were too old, and Savage offered the suggestion that all existing certificates be called in and new ones issued. The suggestion, however, was not adopted by the American government.

In 1805, James M. Henry was appointed to succeed Savage, but did not accept, and in 1806 Hugh Lennox took

[1] Erving to Madison, April 10, 1805, *MS. Consular Despatches, London,* vol. ix.

[2] Savage to Madison, June 2, 1803, *MS. Consular Despatches, Jamaica,* vol. i.

charge of the office at Kingston. According to Lennox's letters during May and June of 1806, impressments were numerous. He pointed out the same imperfections in certificates as were noticed in Savage's correspondence, and stressed the point that no natural-born British subject would be released under any circumstances. In a letter to Madison, June 17, 1806, he referred to the frequency with which American seamen accepted the bounty, saying that fifty guineas were offered from Jamaica to London. On August 8, 1806, he informed Madison that in his opinion many certificates were being bought and sold in the open market, a practice which lessened the value of all of them, and that the British officers there made sure that only those with well-authenticated certificates were released.

In the fall of 1806, Lennox was able to obtain a general agreement with Admiral Dawes that all *bona fide* Americans on British ships would be sent to Lennox when the ships came into port; the decision as to whether they were Americans being left, however, to the British captains. Lennox regarded this as a great gain, as his letter to Madison, August 16, 1806, indicates.[1]

The publication of facts regarding impressment had slowly aroused public opinion in the United States, and there was a group in Congress that insisted on viewing impressment as the outstanding crime against the nation. This group, led by Senator Wright (Md.), seems never to have surrendered the idea of direct retaliation against Great Britain for this offence. Wright, on January 20, 1806, introduced

[1] William H. Savage resumed the duties of commercial agent in 1808, with authority to look after seamen. He, however, sent little information until after the outbreak of the war of 1812 during which he labored for the release of impressed seamen without any apparent success. His letter to Admiral Sterling, September 16, 1812, and the Admiral's reply on September 19, bring out the fact that the British would transfer to prison ships those proving American citizenship to their satisfaction. All others were retained.

a bill in the Senate entitled "A bill for the protection and indemnification of American seamen", which provided that impressment be adjudged piracy, and that all persons impressing seamen on board any vessels bearing the flag of the United States on the high seas, or in port, should, on conviction, suffer death. It also made it lawful for an American seaman sailing under the flag of the United States to resist any attempted impressment either on the high seas or in port by shooting " or otherwise killing and destroying " the person or persons attempting to impress him, and as an encouragement to resist he was to receive a bounty of two hundred dollars. If corporal punishment or death were suffered by impressed American seamen, the bill authorized the President to retaliate by seizing subjects of the power inflicting the punishment.

Finally, the bill provided that every impressed American seaman receive sixty dollars a month for every month of his enforced service on board a foreign ship, which amount could be recovered by the seamen in a district court by attachment of private debts due from citizens of the United States to any subject of the government by whom he was impressed. Such sums as were thus attached were to be regarded as paid by the American debtor to his foreign creditor. That part of the treaty of 1794 with Great Britain which secured the inviolability of such private debts was declared not to be obligatory on the United States in so far as the provisions of the bill were concerned.

In his speech on the bill, Wright referred to the official reports of the Secretary of State as "The black catalogue of impressments ". He reviewed the acts of 1796 and 1799 in behalf of seamen, declaring that through these years impressment had kept pace with discharges, " so that instead of redressing the wrong, it was only inflicted in routine, thereby adding insult to injury ". He briefly referred to the diplomatic efforts, showing that no progress had been made toward a solution. He maintained that impressment was piracy by common law, by the Statutes of Elizabeth, and by the law of nations, and that it would do no harm for Congress to declare the fact. If, he reasoned, all have the right to kill a pirate, one should surely receive a bounty for killing the head of a press-gang, this " hostis humani generis, wearing the caput lupinum ".[1] On March 10th, this bill was postponed to the next session, the reason given being " in order to afford an opportunity for further negotiation of the subject ".[2]

The idea of direct retaliation contained in the Wright bill undoubtedly had some support, but in the minds of a vast majority in both Houses, the more moderate plan of uniting impressment and violations of neutral trade rights, and striving for a settlement through the joint agency of diplomacy and the Non-importation Act [3] was thought advisable.

In the debate on the Non-importation measure, which began on March 5, 1806, in the House,[4] there was scarcely a speech made which did not deplore the evil of impressment, though among those favoring the measure, the cry against the outrage was much louder than it was among the opposition. Many of the former dwelt at length on the number of seamen involved, the general presumption being that the number given in the reports of the Secretary of State was but a small proportion of those actually impressed. This opinion was based on what was said to be

---

[1] For text of bill and for Wright's speech see *Annals of Congress, Ninth Congress, First Session,* 55-67.

[2] *Ibid.,* 166.

[3] For brief discussion of Non-importation Act and other restrictive commercial legislation, see *infra,* ch. vii, p. 157.

[4] For debate see *Annals of Congress, Ninth Congress, First Session,* 537 *et. seq.*

the policy of the British navy, in changing men from ship to ship; in guarding the seamen so as to make it almost impossible for them to find any opportunity of applying to the government of the United States or any of its officers for relief. Several speakers gave it as their opinion that Great Britain held enough American seamen to man five ships of the line.

Many of the speakers vied with one another in describing the nature of impressment as a violation of American rights as men and as citizens of an independent nation. It was said to be far worse than the bondage inflicted on the three hundred American seamen taken captive in Tripoli for whose rescue the government had sent out extra frigates. Impressment was worse than "Algerine bondage" because those impressed were required to commit murder in fighting battles with nations with whom the United States was at peace. It was declared to be even worse than human slavery because while the slave had to labor for the planter, he was not forced to kill those who had given him no provocation, or to be killed himself, and furthermore, there was some chance that he might some day be redeemed.

Campbell (Tenn.) urged that direct measures be taken to stop impressment, independent of the action to be taken on behalf of neutral trade rights. He declared that

the outrages committed on our citizens have made an impression on the public mind that demands on our part the adoption of some decisive measure to correct the growing evil—What time can be more favorable than the present to resist them? Will it be when Great Britain has gotten into her possession a greater number of our seamen? When instead of near 3000 she will have gotten 6000, 8000 or 10,000?

In his mind the right of seamen sailing under the American flag was as perfect as the right of citizens to be protected

in their homes or on the nation's highways. " You ought,
therefore," said he, " never to abandon it on any pretense
whatever. Nay, sir, you cannot abandon it, in justice to
your citizens, unless indeed you are willing to surrender
your independence as a nation." In a similar tone, Sloan
(N. J.) appealed to the spirit of '76, saying, " May the
remaining sparks be rekindled and burn up the residue of
British tyranny." [1]

Although the Non-importation Act united the problem of
impressment with that of the destruction of neutral trade,
many from the West and South, especially, viewed trade
losses " as but a drop in the ocean " compared with the
3000 seamen held in miserable bondage. There seemed to
be no limit to the oratory of some in painting pictures of
" aged parents " in anxiety for the return of their " only
son ", and of the " disconsolate widow bathed in tears sur-
rounded by helpless orphans ". Perhaps the palm for this
type of oratory should go to Jackson (Va.). To his vivid
imagination, if only one case of impressment had occurred
under circumstances such as he pictured it, the government
would be justified in any measure that would stop it. He
characterized the policy of the government on impressment
in the following language: " It sits down and calculates
the cost of asserting its rights with the nicety of a ledger-
keeper, and decides in favor of a pusillanimous acquiescence,
because the balance of dollars and cents is struck in its
favor." [2]

The Randolph following was accused of keeping silent
on the impressment question out of fear of public opinion.
To this charge, Randolph replied with his usual acumen:
"Let gentlemen lay their hands upon their hearts and answer
sincerely if they do believe this resolution has the power to

[1] *Annals of Congress, Ninth Congress, First Session,* 704-705.
[2] *Ibid.,* 734.

take one American seaman out of a British ship of war." [1]
In his mind, Great Britain was compelled to practice impressment in order to maintain her navy, and he believed the United States would have to do the same if they ever built up a big navy. Macon (N. C.), the Speaker of the House, likewise had no faith in non-importation as a remedy for the evil of impressment. But he did not stop with this negative position. Among all the speakers who favored peace rather than war, he was the only one to offer a plan for the settlement of impressment. In introducing the subject, he recognized the magnitude of the evil, saying:

That man who shall devise a certain remedy for this evil, will deserve the thanks of his country; he will, indeed, be its greatest benefactor—But can gentlemen seriously believe that the adoption of this resolution will produce this effect? The means are not adequate to the end, I conceive; at least it remains to be shown that they are. I will, without hesitation, state what I believe to be the best remedy for the evil. [2]

His plan was for the United States to agree with Great Britain that neither country should employ the sailors of the other, and to agree also on the kind of proof of citizenship that would be required on both sides. He maintained that since Great Britain exercised the right, or rather the power, of impressing her sailors, and in time of war prohibited them from entering foreign service, it would be sensible for the United States to recognize this fact and agree not to employ her seamen at all, even with their consent as had been the custom, if in return she would agree not to impress American seamen. If merchants were not willing to support such a plan, then it was clear to his mind that they preferred to employ British sailors at the risk of having American seamen impressed.

[1] *Ibid.*, 596.
[2] *Ibid.*, 695.

He had been informed, he said, that American certificates of citizenship were sold in open market in various parts of the world, and that the market was pretty well supplied. He thought Great Britain would agree to this kind of settlement because it would be to her interest, and he would not rely on any other sort of agreement with her. He urged members to look at the problem as it really was; not as they desired it to be. They should recognize the complex nature of this problem and see the impossibility of legislating themselves out of a difficulty which could only be adjusted by patient negotiation. He understood negotiation was going on and hoped it would result in some such plan as he had suggested which would secure to American seamen their safety on the ocean.

No action, however, was taken on Macon's suggestion. It made no appeal to many of the enthusiastic Republicans who were prone to be anti-British. His charge of defection in the plan of granting certificates of citizenship was declared to be of British origin, and his plan branded him in the minds of some as an apologist of Great Britain. Jackson (Va.) declared that if an American seaman had a protection, Great Britain claimed it was a fraud, and that if he had none, she insisted that this was proof that he was not an American citizen. He regretted, indeed, that the law of 1796, requiring protections in certain cases, had ever been passed, saying that the United States, from the very first, should have asserted the right to protect every man sailing under the American flag, except the enemies of a belligerent nation.[1] Jackson was probably right, but the law which had now been in operation for ten years, continued in force, and without modification.

[1] *Ibid.*, 733.

CHAPTER V

IMPRESSMENT AN IMPORTANT PHASE OF THE EXTRA-ORDINARY MISSION OF MONROE AND PINKNEY

THE great increase in the number of impressments during the years immediately following the renewal of the war in Europe in 1803 intensified the desire of the American government for a permanent settlement of the issue. Furthermore, the conversations and correspondence between Madison and Anthony Merry, the British Minister at Washington from 1803 to 1806, revealed the extreme divergence of the views of the two nations on the subject. Merry declared [1] that the British crown had the right, asserted for ages, of reclaiming British subjects from foreign vessels whether found on the high seas or in British ports, and expressed the opinion that the practice of impressment founded on that right would never be relinquished. Madison, on the other hand, vigorously denied the existence of such a right, declaring that no American Administration would dare so far surrender the rights of the American flag as to accede to such a practice on the high seas. [2]

With this decided clash of views in Washington, and with the growth of the number of impressments which aroused Congress and the American public in general, it is

[1] Merry to Madison, April 12, 1805, *MS. Letters, British Legation,* vol. iii.

[2] Conversations with Merry reported in letter of Madison to Monroe, March 6, 1806, *American State Papers, Foreign Relations,* vol. iii, pp. 99-101.

not surprising that although Monroe's negotiations in London became so involved with other important issues as to exclude impressment for the moment, this fact did not lessen the determination of the American government to seek a settlement of that troublesome question. This determined attitude on the part of the American government resulted in the sending of an extraordinary mission to Great Britain in 1806 to deal with all the points of difference between the two nations, with special stress on impressment. Monroe was notified in a letter [1] from Madison dated April 23, 1806, of the appointment of William Pinkney, who was to share with him the difficult task of representing the American government in the negotiations. In Madison's letter of instructions to the two ministers, dated May 17, 1806,[2] he said of impressment:

The importance of an effectual remedy for this practice derives urgency from the licentiousness [3] with which it is still pursued and from the growing impatience of this country under it. So indispensable is some adequate provision for the case, that the President makes it a preliminary to any stipulation requiring a repeal of the act [4] shutting the market of the United States against British manufactures.

They were instructed to follow the plan contained in the

[1] Madison to Monroe, April 23, 1806, *American State Papers, Foreign Relations,* vol. iii, p. 117.

[2] Madison to Monroe and Pinkney, May 17, 1806, *ibid.,* p. 120.

[3] Madison doubtless had in mind also the activities of the British ships, " Driver," " Cambrian " and " Leander " in blockading the port of New York, and in searching and impressing seamen from all outgoing American vessels. Only two days later, John Pierce, an American seamen, was killed by a shot fired from the " Leander." This incident caused great indignation throughout the nation. For an account of these activities, see Henry Adams, *History of the United States,* vol. iii, pp. 199-203.

[4] The Non-importation Act is referred to.

instructions given to Monroe, January 5, 1804, but were given the privilege of modifying article one by substituting the older article which King had worked to secure. Pinkney arrived in London, June 24, 1806, and shortly afterward he and Monroe presented a plan for the settlement of impressment to the British Commissioners, Lords Holland and Auckland,[1] who, on account of the illness of Fox, the British Foreign Secretary, were appointed especially to deal with all matters pending between the two governments. This plan differed only slightly from the one that Monroe had presented. It contained a change in the proposal. regarding documentary proof of citizenship. Instead of specifying precisely what documents would constitute such, as Monroe had done, the new proposal provided only that due credit be given to such public documents as the two countries should grant for the protection of their seamen, and stipulated that such documents were to be granted only to persons justly entitled to them.[2]

To this plan the British Commissioners [3] first of all re-

[1] For text of plan, see *American State Papers, Foreign Relations*, vol. iii, p. 137.

[2] The full clause was as follows:

"In all questions which may arise within the dominions of either power, respecting the national character of any person who claims to be a citizen of the other power, due credit shall be given to such public documents as his government may have granted for his protection and where such documents may have been lost, destroyed or by casualty not obtained, and any person claims to be a citizen or subject of either power, such other evidence of said claim shall be received and admitted as would be satisfactory in a court of judicature. The high contracting parties engage that due care shall be taken that such documents shall be granted in their respective ports to such persons only as are justly entitled to them, and by suitable officers who shall be especially designated for the purpose."

[3] For an account of the negotiations see Monroe and Pinkney to Madison, September 11, 1806, and November 11, 1806, *American State Papers, Foreign Relations*, vol. iii, pp. 137-140.

peated the long-standing objection to giving up their claim
to the right to take their own seamen from American vessels
on the high seas, and offered anew the suggestion that
American crews carry authentic documents of citizenship,
the nature and form of which should be agreed upon by
treaty; such documents completely to protect all seamen who
had them. This they claimed would make a clear distinction which would always be respected, and while preventing
American seamen from being impressed, would allow Great
Britain to continue impressing her own seamen from American ships as before. Unless they could impress from
American ships, they argued that those ships would become
floating asylums for deserters from the British navy. More
specific objections to the American plan were that it gave
too narrow a meaning to the term "deserters", and that it
would not be effective in restoring British deserters. In
the American plan the term "deserter" was limited to those
who were part of the crew of the vessel from which they
deserted. An agreement was reached whereby the term was
enlarged so as to comprehend " seafaring people quitting
their service ".

The plan for delivering up these British deserters contained no provision relating to those who might, immediately
after desertion, enter American vessels and go to sea. To
strengthen this clause, Monroe and Pinkney agreed, upon
the request of the British Commissioners, to urge the passage of a law by Congress making it penal for American
commanders to take deserters from Great Britain under
such circumstances; the British government too was to en-
act a similar statute. It was also made the duty of each
government to restore such deserters upon their arrival in
its territory, upon suitable application and due proof of
their citizenship. In agreeing to these modifications in the
plan for restoring deserters, every concrete objection raised

by the British Commissioners was met, and the latter seemed altogether satisfied, agreeing to propose an article embodying the total plan of settlement to the British Cabinet.

The opportunity for a permanent solution of the whole impressment issue had never been brighter than at this stage of the negotiations. Men of the highest integrity and ability of both nations had in a spirit of conciliation formulated a plan that seemed to them to meet the essential demands of both nations. By it Great Britain was to relinquish the practice of impressing from American vessels on the high seas, and in return the United States was committed to a policy for the restoration of deserters which assured their return, at least in so far as such assurance seemed possible. It is difficult indeed to see how any more rigid plan for returning deserters could have been devised.

Of course the plan might have been defeated after its adoption by the negotiators by the refusal of Congress to pass such a law relative to the return of deserters. As it was, it met that fate much earlier through the intense opposition of the crown officers and Board of Admiralty of Great Britain. The crown officers opposed such a settlement on the ground that the right of impressment must be maintained. They declared that

the King had the right, by his prerogative, to require the service of all his seafaring subjects against the enemy, and to seize them by force whenever found, not being within the territorial limits of another power; that as the high seas were extra territorial, the merchant vessels of other powers navigating on them were not admitted to possess such a jurisdiction as to protect British subjects from the exercise of the King's prerogative over them.

The British Commissioners, in response to this pressure from above, presented to the Americans on November 5,

1806, a counter-project which provided that laws should be passed by both nations whereby it should be made penal for the commanders of vessels of each nation to impress citizens of the other on board its vessels on the high seas—and penal also for officers of either nation to grant certificates of citizenship to the citizens or subjects of the other without due proof of same.

The difference between the two positions may be more clearly seen by viewing the two projects in parallel columns.[1]

American Project.	*British Counter-Project.*
" Both parties to enact laws making it penal for commanders of vessels in the ports of one of the parties, or of a third power, to receive and carry away the sailors belonging to the vessels of the other. Sailors so deserting, and carried away to be surrendered on their arrival at a port of the Party to which the vessels so receiving them belong, on the application of the Consuls, supported by lawful evidence of their citizenship."	" Whereas it is not lawful for a belligerant to impress sea-faring persons not its subjects, and whereas, from similarity of language, it is difficult to distinguish between the subjects of the two states, each party to enact laws making it penal to impress native subjects of the neutral or others not subjects of the belligerent — and to grant any certificates of birth to seafaring persons without due proof of the same."

The American Commissioners, whose hopes of a settlement had run high, were deeply chagrined at the *volte face* of the British negotiators. They at once declared that acceptance of the British counter-project would be tantamount to an abandonment of America's rights. They stated that they would adopt no plan which did not allow American ships to protect their crews. The firm stand of Monroe and Pinkney resulted in a deadlock which lasted for some time. Each side being unwilling to yield, it was finally agreed to omit from the treaty any clause on the subject of impressment. Up to this time, the Americans

[1] *American State Papers, Foreign Relations,* vol. iii, p. 140.

had repeatedly said that unless impressment was settled, it was useless to deal with other questions. When the absolute deadlock was reached, however, the British were able to convince them that they should go ahead and make a treaty, leaving impressment out of it, each nation maintaining its rights and agreeing in future to act in such a manner as to prevent future complaints. Monroe and Pinkney asked for a written note on the subject, and after receiving it proceeded to make the treaty.

The note itself was presented on November 8, 1806. Embodying as it did the official position of the British government, we are justified in reproducing it in full, as follows: [1]

His Majesty's Commissioners and plenipotentiaries have the honor to represent to the Commissioners and plenipotentiaries of the United States:

That the project of an article on the subject of impressing seamen, together with the reasonings by which the Commissioners of the United States have urged the expediency of an arrangement on that subject, has been laid before his Majesty's Government, and has been considered with the same friendly and conciliatory disposition which has marked every step of the negotiation.

That his Majesty's Government has not felt itself prepared to disclaim or derogate from a right which has ever been uniformly and generally maintained, and in the exercise of which the security of the British navy be essentially involved, more especially in a conjuncture when his Majesty is engaged in wars which enforce the necessity of the most vigilant attention to the preservation and supply of the naval forces of his Kingdom.

That his Majesty's Government, animated by an earnest desire to remove every cause of dissatisfaction, has directed his Majesty's commissioners to give to Mr. Monroe and to Mr. Pinkney the most positive assurance that instructions have been given, and shall be repeated and enforced, for the observ-

[1] *American State Papers, Foreign Relations,* vol. iii, p. 140.

ance of the greatest caution in the impressing of British seamen; and that the strictest care shall be taken to preserve the citizens of the United States from any molestation or injury, and that immediate and prompt redress shall be afforded upon any representation of injury sustained by them.

That the commissioners of the United States well know that no recent causes of complaint have occurred, and that no probable inconvenience can result from the postponement of an article subject to so many difficulties. Still, that his Majesty's Commissioners are instructed to secure the interests of both states, without any injury to rights to which they are respectively attached.

That, in the meantime, the desire of promoting a right conclusion of the proposed treaty, and of drawing closer the ties of connection between the two countries, induce his Majesty's commissioners to express their readiness to proceed to the completion of the other articles, in the confident hope that the result cannot fail to cultivate and confirm the good understanding happily subsisting between the high contracting parties, and still further to augment the mutual prosperity of his Majesty's subjects and of the citizens of the United States.

A formal reply to this note from the American Ministers would have added to its importance, giving it the effect of an understanding or of an agrement, but Monroe and Pinkney chose to regard the note itself as possessing " a peculiar degree of solemnity and obligation ", and proceeded with the negotiations without a formal reply to it. In support of their point of view we may refer to their joint despatch addressed to Madison, November 11, 1806,[1] in which they justified their departure from instructions as follows:

Many strong reasons favor this course (accepting the British Proposal) while none occur to us of any weight against it.

---

[1] Monroe and Pinkney to Madison, Nov. 11, 1806, *American State Papers, Foreign Relations,* vol. iii, p. 139.

When we take into view all that has passed on this subject, we are far from considering the note of the British Commissioners as a mere circumstance of form. We persuade ourselves, that by accepting the invitation which it gives, and proceeding in the negotiations, we shall place the business almost, if not altogether, on as good a footing as we should have done by a treaty, had the project which we offered them been adopted. The time at which this note was presented to us, and the circumstances under which it was presented being when the negotiation was absolutely at a stand on this very question, and we had informed the British Commissioners that we could do nothing if it was not provided for, give the act a peculiar degree of solemnity and obligation. It was sent to us as a public paper, and intended that we should so consider it, and with the knowledge and approbation of the cabinet. It ought, therefore, to be held as obligatory on the Government, in its just import, as if the substance had been stipulated in a treaty.

The two Ministers claimed that the note contained everything which could be desired except the relinquishment of the principle and they thought it " fair to infer " that Great Britain meant in future to recognize the just claims of the United States on the entire question of impressment, though on account of public opinion in England it was not good policy at that time to relinquish the claim. They felt very strongly that they should be supported by the American government, but notified the British Commissioners that they had accepted the note entirely on their own responsibility.

In sending the completed treaty to Madison, January 3, 1807,[1] Monroe and Pinkney repeated their opinion that although the British government did not feel itself at liberty to relinquish formally, by treaty, its claim to the right

---

[1] Monroe and Pinkney to Madison, Jan. 3, 1807, *American State Papers, Foreign Relations*, vol. iii, p. 146.

of impressment, the practice would, nevertheless, be essentially, if not completely, abandoned. The British Commissioners, according to the Monroe-Pinkney report, repeatedly assured the Americans that in their judgment the note made the United States as secure against impressment as a treaty would have done. Monroe and Pinkney urged Congress to check desertion from the British service, so that a good understanding between the two nations might continue.

Madison, writing to them February 3, 1807,[1] declared that such a settlement was not acceptable to the American government, since it did not comport with Jefferson's views of the "national sentiment or the legislative policy ".   The President insisted, he said, that no treaty should be entered into with the British government which did not contain an article providing for impressment which " both in principle and in practice is so feelingly connected with the honor and the sovereignty of the nation, as well as its fair interests, and indeed with the peace of both nations ".   Madison added that if no satisfactory or formal stipulation on the subject of impressment could be attained, negotiations were to be terminated without any formal compact on any of the disputed questions whatever, " but with a mutual understanding, founded on friendly and liberal discussions and explanations, that in practice each party will entirely conform to what may be thus informally settled ".   If a satisfactory informal agreement of this kind could be reached, Monroe and Pinkney were instructed to give assurance that, as long as the arrangement was duly respected in practice by Great Britain, more particularly on the subjects of neutral trade and impressment, the President would earnestly, and probably successfully, recommend to Congress that the operation of the Non-importation Act, which was already

---

[1] Madison to Monroe and Pinkney, Feb. 3, 1807, *American State Papers, Foreign Relations*, vol. iii, pp. 153 *et seq.*

in suspension, be permanently postponed. If, previous to the receipt of this view of the President, a treaty not including an article relating to impressment had been concluded, and on the way, Monroe and Pinkney were instructed to notify the British Commissioners not to expect its ratification and to invite them to renew the negotiations on the basis of the renewed instructions.

Madison then proceeded to make a few observations on the contents of the despatches received from Monroe and Pinkney. To the statement of the British Commissioners that "no recent causes of complaint have occurred", he replied that although he did not know what Lyman's [1] books showed on the subject, he was sure that in the American seas including the West Indies impressments had "perhaps at no time been more numerous or vexatious".

Madison did not regard the British Commissioners' note of November 8, 1806, as the sort of " informal arrangement " he had in mind, for he contended that this note still left discretionary power in the hands of the British naval commanders, who, because of the ascendency of the British navy on the high seas, were tempted to violate neutral rights, especially those of nations who had no fleets. As long as they had this arbitrary power they were sure to use it in such a way as to test the patience of neutrals. He claimed, therefore, that the United States must have definite security against the propensities of British naval commanders which the British note failed to give.

He declared that the American plan aided by internal regulations of Great Britain would close all the avenues through which British seamen found their way into American service, and that hence Great Britain under it could only lose those now in that service; the number of which

---

[1] Lyman was Erving's successor as American Consul in London and Agent for Seamen.

would be reduced by some voluntarily leaving and others
found in British territory.   This loss would be small because the number of those who were British subjects had
always been small, the great mass being Americans or other
neutrals.

He again urged that the proposals of Monroe and Pinkney were altogether fair to Great Britain and would really
have been a gain to her.   He added:

> In practice, therefore, Great Britain would make no sacrifice
> by acceding to our terms; and her principle, if not expressly
> saved by a recital, as it easily might be, would in effect be so by
> the tenor of the arrangement; inasmuch as she would obtain
> for her forbearance to exercise what she deems a right, a right
> to measures on our part which we have a right to refuse; she
> would consequently merely exchange one right for another.
> She would also, by such forbearance, violate no personal right
> of individuals under her protection.

But if the United States should yield to Great Britain, he
maintained that they " would necessarily surrender what
they deem an essential right of their flag, and of their
sovereignty ".

Referring to the promise in the note of November 8,
that instructions would be reported for enforcing caution in
making impressments, Madison declared that if such instructions were to be ignored as those in the past had been,
the United States could not rely on them.   In this same
communication, he reminded Monroe of the old plan of
King, presented in 1803 when Lord Hawkesbury agreed to
prohibit impressments altogether on the high seas, and Lord
St. Vincent demanded exception of the " narrow seas ".
Madison seemed to believe that this abandoned plan might
now be successful and he accordingly urged that it be again
presented for consideration.

In a private letter to Monroe, dated March 20, 1807, Madison wrote:

But the case of impressments consists altogether of thorns. Considering that the public mind has reached a crisis of sensibility, and that this essentially contributed to the extraordinary mission, as well as to the Non-importation Act, there is every motive to seek in every mode an effectual remedy. For reasons already hinted, the promise in the note of Lords Holland and Auckland of November 8 is not such a remedy, in the view produced here by circumstances which could not be so well appreciated where you are.[1]

Monroe and Pinkney replying April 22, 1807, to Madison's communication of February 3, 1807,[2] insisted again that they were right in accepting the British note on impressment. They held that according to its provisions the United States were conceded the right to regard any single impressment on the high seas as an act of aggression, adding:

This right existed, undoubtedly independent of that note; but it seems, notwithstanding, to derive from it a new and high sanction favorable to its just effect; and certainly the sensibility and determination which have been manifested on this point by the United States . . . must have inspired this Government with the conviction that a perseverance in such outrages on their sovereignty and the rights of their citizens would be wholly incompatible with the peaceable relations of the two countries . . .

After careful consideration of the text of the treaty by the American Cabinet, Madison wrote Monroe and Pinkney, May 20, 1807,[3] saying that the President would not accept

[1] *MS. Madison Papers,* vol. vi, p. 77.

[2] Monroe and Pinkney to Madison, April 22, 1807, *American State Papers, Foreign Relations,* vol. iii, pp. 160-162.

[3] Madison to Monroe and Pinkney, May 20, 1807, *ibid.,* pp. 166 *et seq.*

any arrangement either formal or informal which did not
carry a provision against impressment on the high seas;
that he could not reconcile it with his duty to American
seamen or with the sensibility or sovereignty of the nation
to recognize a principle that would expose on the high seas
the liberty and lives of seamen to the capricious and interested sentences against their allegiance pronounced by officers of a foreign government, whom neither the law of
nations nor even the laws of England would allow to decide on the ownership or character of the minutest article
of property found in a like situation; that he was sure
Congress viewed the matter in this light by their action in
sending Monroe and Pinkney and in approving the Non-
importation Act.

He urged them to renew the negotiations without further
reference to the informal settlement mentioned in the note
of February 3, 1807. If every other plan failed to meet
the approval of the British they were authorized to admit the
following article:

It is agreed that, after the term of . . . months, computed
from the exchange of ratification, and during a war in which
either of the parties may be engaged, neither of them will permit any seaman, not being its own citizen or subject, and being
a citizen or subject of the other party, who shall not have been
for two years, at least, prior to that date, constantly and voluntarily in the service or within the jurisdiction of the parties,
respectively, to enter or be employed on board any of its vessels
navigating the high seas, and proper regulations, enforced by
adequate penalties, shall be mutually established for distinguishing the seamen of the parties, respectively, and for giving full
effect to this stipulation.

It was explained that this article did not comprehend as
British seamen those who had already been made citizens
of the United States. This position was justified on the

ground that by the legal requirements of the United States for naturalization the number of seamen actually, or likely to be naturalized, was too small to be of any importance, and furthermore on the ground that the judicial authority of Great Britain had laid down the right of British subjects to naturalize themselves in foreign trade and navigation.

If Great Britain desired to add that the United States should not only exclude her seamen from its service, but deliver them up to her, they were instructed to refuse this as being inconsistent with American principles. If this plan could not be obtained, Monroe and Pinkney were to transmit the result to the American government along with any explanations or overtures which the British might make with a view to final accommodation. They were not to break off negotiations.

Monroe writing to Madison more than a year later [1] sought to defend the action of Pinkney and himself in accepting the note of November 8, 1806, and proceeding with negotiations to the final agreement. In his opinion the note signed by the British Commissioners was a real concession in favor of the United States and imposed on Great Britain the obligation to conform her practice under it until a more complete arrangement could be reached. He maintained that American rights under it were reserved and not abandoned, as has been erroneously supposed; that negotiations on impressment were to be revived as soon as the general treaty was out of the way, and that in the meantime the practice of impressment was to conform essentially with the view of the United States. Impressment as theretofore practiced was, according to his view, to be abandoned and none to take place on the high seas " except in cases of an extraordinary nature, to which no general prohibition

[1] Monroe to Madison, February 28, 1808, *American State Papers, Foreign Relations,* vol. iii, pp. 173 *et seq.*

against it could be construed fairly to extend ". These
cases were those arising when seamen from a British ship
of war in port should desert to an American merchant vessel
in the same port and the latter sail with them. It was admitted that no general prohibition against impressment
could be construed to sanction such cases of injustice and
fraud. Monroe admitted that it was an informal understanding, but claimed that this in itself was not enough to
condemn it. He held that under the note if Great Britain
did trespass from it in the slightest degree, during further
negotiations on it, then the United States could break off
negotiations and appeal to force, and that such a position
was much stronger than the one in which the American
government would have been under the general agreement
authorized in the note of February 3, 1807.

Monroe, however, took a slightly different view of the
transaction in writing to Pickering, April 18, 1808.[1] In
this letter he admitted that the joint letter to Madison, November 11, 1806, was written in haste and did not " state
with precision everything that passed in our conference
with the British Commissioners relating to our powers ".
Later in this letter, the following language appears:

In reviewing this transaction with the British Commissioners,
it has occurred to me that it would have been advisable for
Mr. Pinkney and myself to have presented to them a paper in
reply to theirs of November 8th, stating what we verbally did
as to our powers. This would have placed us on more satisfactory ground with the British Commissioners, but between
the governments the case would have been the same as between
them the only question is what our powers were, not what we
told the British Commissioners.

Monroe and Pinkney in writing to Canning, then British

[1] Monroe to Pickering, April 18, 1808, *MS. Monroe Papers,* vol. iv,
p. 485.

Foreign Secretary, July 24, 1807,[1] referred to the special project on impressment suggested in Madison's letter of May 20, 1807, which they had sent him along with other alterations necessary to make the treaty suitable to the President of the United States.   In this letter they dealt with impressment as follows:

It was one of the primary objects of the mission of the undersigned to adjust with His Majesty's government, a formal and explicit arrangement relative to a practice by British ships of war, which has excited in a very great degree the sensibility of the American people, and claimed the anxious attention of their government.   The practice alluded to is that of visiting on the main ocean the merchant vessels of the United States navigating under the American flag, for the purpose of subjecting their crew to a hasty and humiliating inquisition, and impressing as British seamen such of the mariners as upon that inquisition the visiting officer declares to be so.   The effect of this practice is that the flag of an independent power is dishonored, and one of the most essential rights of its sovereignty violated; that American citizens . . . are forced from the quiet pursuits of a lawful commerce into the severe and dangerous service of a foreign military navy to expose their lives in fighting against those with whom their country is at peace; and that the merchant vessels of the United States are frequently thus stripped of so large a portion of their hands . . . as to bring within most imminent peril vessels, cargoes and crews.

After reviewing their negotiations on the subject with Lords Holland and Auckland previous to the receipt of the note of November 8, 1806, the American Ministers added:

It appears that the President of the United States considers this collateral proceeding upon a concern of such paramount importance as unsuitable to the nature of it, as well in the mode

[1] Monroe and Pinkney to Canning, July 24, 1807, *American State Papers, Foreign Relations,* vol. iii, pp. 194-195.

as in the terms.   In this opinion the President does but continue
to respect the considerations which heretofore induced him to
believe that an arrangement upon this point ought to stipulate
with precision against the practice in question.

When Canning on October 22, 1807,[1] replied to this note,
news of the " Chesapeake " and " Leopard " incident [2] had
reached London.   There is no evidence in his reply that
Canning was at all moved by this incident to make concessions.   He took the position that Jefferson's refusal to ratify
the treaty made further negotiations regarding that instrument impossible.   The promise made by Lords Holland and
Auckland in their note of November 8, 1806, that the subject of impressment should be taken up again at some
future time, was not in his opinion applicable to the American request for its inclusion in a modified treaty.   He was
ready at all times to hear their proposals on that subject,
but the negotiations on the treaty had been closed by the
United States and must so remain.

With the receipt of this note the mission of Monroe and
Pinkney terminated.   At the same time all negotiations on
the subject were practically suspended until the outbreak of
war in 1812.   The American government tried to combine
impressment with the case of the " Chesapeake ", but this
effort was bluntly refused, first by Canning in England
and later by Rose in Washington.   As far as the diplomacy
of the years from this until the outbreak of the war is concerned, the question of impressment is noticeably in the
background, although the American government never
yielded its claims in the matter, and kept it alive by frequent references to it, as will be seen in the following
pages.   It is not without significance that during all these

[1] Canning to Monroe and Pinkney, Oct. 22, 1807, *American State
Papers, Foreign Relations*, vol. iii, p. 198.

[2] For discussion of incident see *infra*, ch. vi, pp. 135-136.

years the American representatives in London were Monroe, for a short time, and then Pinkney, who served until the war. The clear difference in viewpoint between them and the Administration at Washington may explain in part why the subject was not more vigorously pressed.

On the other hand, had such a difference never existed, it is hardly probable that the subject of impressment would have gone on indefinitely holding the center of the diplomatic stage, especially after the rebuff administered by Canning. Besides, there were many other serious differences between the two nations which called for adjustment, any one of which was of sufficient importance to keep the American minister in London quite fully engaged. From its beginning in 1792, impressment had held a more prominent place in American diplomacy then had any other single issue, and it was held in a uniquely important status by the executive, long after it had been merged by Congress into the general subject of neutral commerce.

Canning's refusal to deal with the general subject of impressment at all in connection with the " Chesapeake " affair made impossible at that time the consideration of the plan for the mutual exclusion of seamen during war, and it was in fact never seriously considered until after the declaration of war in 1812. It would appear that if the chief desire of Great Britain had been the retention of her own seamen, she would at least have called for further negotiations along the lines laid down in this proposal of the United States. Furthermore, had the American government pressed this plan, or some form of it, during the years immediately preceding the war, the case against Great Britain on the score of impressment would have been even stronger than it was. However, in the conflict over many other vital issues which divided the two countries, the impressment issue for the next four or five years was pushed into the background.

CHAPTER VI

THE "CHESAPEAKE" AFFAIR AND THE PROBLEM OF DESERTION

THE "Chesapeake" and "Leopard" incident referred to in the previous chapter being the only instance of impressment from an American public vessel, occupies for that reason alone a unique position in the history of impressment. The bearing of the particular controversy to which this incident gave rise on the various questions relative to the desertion of seamen, a knowledge of which is necessary to a full understanding of the impressment issue, warrants special consideration of the so-called "Chesapeake" case and of the problems relating thereto. At the outset, a brief outline of the facts relating to the case seems advisable.

On March 7, 1807,[1] certain sailors made their escape from the British gun sloop "Halifax" lying in Hampton Roads to Norfolk, Virginia, where they enlisted on the American frigate "Chesapeake". One of these was an Englishman named Ratford who enlisted on the "Chesapeake" under the name of Wilson. The commander of the "Halifax" was unsuccessful in his effort to recover them. The British Minister complained that three deserters from the British ship "Melampus" had also enlisted on the "Chesapeake". It was later found that these three men were native Americans who had been impressed by the

---

[1] For a brief account see Moore, *Digest of International Law*, vol. ii, pp. 991-994. For a more detailed account see Henry Adams, *History of the United States*, vol. iv, pp. 1-26.

" Melampus ". This incident, together with other desertions from British ships in Chesapeake Bay, were reported
to Admiral Berkeley, the British Naval Commander at
Halifax, who, without waiting for authority from England, issued on June 7, 1807, an order to all the ships under
his command, in which it was stated that deserters from
seven British ships had entered the American frigate "Chesapeake " in the Chesapeake Bay. These deserters Admiral
Berkeley charged " openly paraded the streets of Norfolk
in sight of their officers, under the American flag, protected
by the Magistrate of the town, and the recruiting officer belonging to the above mentioned frigate . . . which refused
to give them up although demanded by his Britannic Majesty's Consul as well as the captains of the ships from
which the said men deserted." Admiral Berkeley therefore
ordered all captains under him if they met the " ' Chesapeake ' at sea and without the limits of the United States "
to show this order and search her for these deserters.
They were also ordered to observe a similar demand for
search by Americans for deserters from the service of the
United States " according to the custom and usage of civilized nations on terms of peace and amity with each other ".

This order was sent to Chesapeake Bay by the British
frigate " Leopard ", commanded by Captain Humphreys.
The " Leopard " on June 22, 1807, met the " Chesapeake ",
an American frigate commanded by Commodore Barron,
about ten miles off the coast of Cape Henry, and sought to
execute the order of Admiral Berkeley. As a result an
engagement took place, during which three men on the
" Chesapeake " were killed and eighteen were wounded.
The " Chesapeake " was also boarded and four men were
taken from her, three of whom were Americans and one
an Englishman; all of them having previously deserted
from the British ship " Melampus ". These men were

taken to Halifax where the Englishman was hanged, while
the three Americans were placed in prison.

This attempt to search an American warship for deserters
in time of peace, constituting as it did an act of war,
aroused public feeling to a state of intensity unparalleled
since the days of the Revolution.   On July 2, President
Jefferson issued a proclamation requiring all armed British
vessels to depart from American waters.   Monroe, the
American Minister in London, was instructed [1] to settle the
incident, and as for security for the future, to demand an
entire abolition of impressment from vessels under the
flag of the United States, on terms compatible with the instructions to him and Pinkney as an indispensable part of
the satisfaction.

Upon receipt of these instructions, Monroe wrote to Canning, the British Foreign Secretary, September 7, 1807,[2]
asking reparation for the outrage " and such an arrangement of the great interest which is connected with it as will
place the future relations of the two powers on a solid
foundation of peace and friendship".   Adequate reparation
for the outrage was to consist of (a) restoration of the
seamen taken; (b) punishment of the officer; (c) abandonment of impressment from merchant vessels, and (d) announcement of the reparation by a special mission to Washington.   His argument for uniting the two questions was
based in part on the similarity of impressment from ships
of war and of impressment from merchant vessels.   This

---

[1] Madison to Monroe, July 6, 1807, *American State Papers, Foreign
Relations,* vol. iii, pp. 183-185. For further indication of Jefferson's
attitude on this point see also Jefferson to Armstrong, July 17, 1807,
Jefferson's Writings (Mem. Ed), vol. xi, p. 284; and Jefferson to Paine,
Oct. 9, 1807, *Jefferson's Writings (Mem. Ed.)*, vol. xi, p. 378; and
Monroe to Armstrong, Oct. 10, 1807, *Monroe Papers,* vol. iv, p. 453.

[2] Monroe to Canning, Sept. 7, 1807, *American State Papers, Foreign
Relations,* vol. iii, pp. 189-190.

similarity was to be seen in the fact that the injury done to individual seamen was the same in either case and that the seamen's claim on the government for protection was the same in both cases. Monroe also argued that the two questions should be united because the " Chesapeake " affair exhibited the pretensions of the British government in their widest range, and had become identified with the general practice of impressment in the feelings of the people of the United States and in the mind of the American government.

In this communication Monroe reviewed the main arguments of the United States against the practice of impressment, and stated that he was authorized to offer a plan that would give equal security to Great Britain that her own interests would be safeguarded.

At this point it should be stated that before receiving instructions from Washington, Monroe, on receiving news of the "Chesapeake" affair, had written to Canning [1] expressing the hope of an immediate disavowal of the outrage, which he characterized as a " most unjustifiable pretension to search for deserters ". He referred also in this letter to other " examples of great indignity " committed by the British off the American coasts and harbors with which he felt it improper to mingle " the present more serious cause of complaint ".[2] In reply to Monroe's letter Canning had promptly disavowed [3] the pretension of a right on the part of the British government to search ships of war for deserters, but stated that Great Britain would consider the

[1] Monroe to Canning, July 29, 1807, *American State Papers, Foreign Relations,* vol. iii, p. 187.

[2] See Monroe to ———, July 13, 1808, *Monroe's Writings* (Hamilton), vol. v, p. 60 for statement that the above comment was not intended to separate the " Chesapeake " affair from the impressment question.

[3] Canning to Monroe, August 3, 1807, *American State Papers, Foreign Relations,* vol. iii, p. 188.

question of reparation when all the facts of the case were known.

Canning therefore, in reply to Monroe's letter of September 7,[1] in which his instructions were communicated, took advantage of the antecedent correspondence with Monroe and insisted that the case of the "Chesapeake" and that of impressment from merchant vessels were "wholly unconnected," and that Monroe himself before receiving his instructions had expressed this view. For nearly a century, he declared, the crown had forborne to instruct the commanders of its ships of war to search foreign ships of war for deserters, on grounds which were wholly inapplicable to ships in the merchant service. British deserters engaged in American war vessels had entered into a contract with the American government, whereas the government was not a party to a contract between British deserters and American shippers. In the former case the act was hostile to Great Britain, and some form of hostility was the proper redress, whereas in the latter case the redress must be what it had always been, viz., impressment. Since all attempts to settle impressment had failed, why, he argued, tie up the "Chesapeake" affair, which should be speedily settled, with a problem that was almost impossible of adjustment? He also took the position that if the government of the United States had been refusing to discharge British seamen from its warships previous to the "Chesapeake" affair, the fact would have material bearing on the question of reparation. Canning definitely refused to discuss impressment until a later date, notifying Monroe that if a special minister were sent to the United States in accordance with the request of the American government he would not be authorized to treat of that subject in connection with the "Chesapeake".

[1] Canning to Monroe, September 23, 1807, *American State Papers, Foreign Relations*, vol. iii, pp. 200-201.

Although Monroe persisted [1] in the effort to unite the two questions, Canning would not modify his position and the negotiations ended without resulting in any settlement of either issue. This was Monroe's last work in Great Britain. His efforts to adjust the difficult problem, which were put forth both on his own responsibility and jointly with Pinkney during their extraordinary mission, have been followed in detail.[2] For a time at least he was disposed to regard as successful the adjustment reached by him and Pinkney, which the American government refused to accept. Later, however, he seems to have acquiesced in the policy of the American government. A review of his further efforts on this subject during his term as Secretary of State under Madison, and still later during his term as President, will be given later.

The American government remained determined to deal with the "Chesapeake" affair on the basis that it was merely an extreme instance of impressment. Perhaps no one was better qualified to appreciate the relation of the "Chesapeake" affair to impressment than William Lyman, who succeeded Erving as Agent for Seamen in Great Britain, serving in that position and as American Consul in London from 1805 to 1810.[3] In his correspondence with the American Secretary of State he dealt with that subject and his views throw additional light on the problem. He gave it as his opinion that the merchants of England, as a general rule,

---

[1] Monroe to Canning, Sept. 29, 1807, *American State Papers, Foreign Relations,* vol. iii, p. 202, and Monroe to Madison, Oct. 10, 1807, *ibid.,* p. 192.

[2] *Supra,* ch. v.

[3] William Lyman was born at Northampton, Massachusetts, in 1753 and died in London, England, in 1811. He graduated at Yale in 1776, was a member of the Massachusetts Senate, 1789, and of Congress from 1793 to 1797. He was appointed Consul at London and Agent for Seamen in 1805 and held that position until his death in 1811. *Appleton's Cyclopaedia of American Biography.*

felt that Great Britain should make reparation to the United States, but they would not admit it to be at all proper for their country to give up the right of search and impressment. Lyman's own comment was as follows:

Thus you will see on what grounds by this event is placed this point of impressment, which heretofore and still does continue to produce, as documents from this office so fully evidence, such vexations to our commerce, and humiliating and intolerable injuries to our citizens. The time has come to claim and insist on their redress and prevention of this badge of inferiority and submission too degrading longer to be bourne.[1]

A few months later,[2] writing again on the "Chesapeake" affair, Lyman went at great length into the whole question of impressment. He declared that as soon as the outrage occurred there was a " steady and constant endeavor " on the part of the British government and her apologists to separate it from impressment, but in his mind the two were united and could never be separated. Continuing he said:

This government, or rather most of its officers, from a toleration in such an unrestrained and capricious exercise of power, seem now to claim it as a right, and in very many instances, particularly when in want of men, totally disregard every circumstance and evidence of citizenship or national character accompanied with the retort of a disdainful curse for both character and country; and in all cases the most frivolous pretexts or even " suspicions light as air are confirmations strong " to set aside the best founded claims. In short the instruments of this brief authority play such fantastic tricks as to " make the angels weep." Individuals who are impressed are often bound, starved and scourged into submission to a service abhorrent to

---

[1] Lyman to Madison, August 1, 1807, *MS. Consular Despatches, London,* vol. ix.

[2] Lyman to Madison, Oct. 23, 1807, *ibid.*

their feelings and repugnant to their duties. There is not at this time, I believe, a single ship of war in the British navy whose crew does not consist partly, and in some instances on distant stations, principally of American seamen.

He declared that there were at least 15,000 American seamen in the British navy, and that the British were doing all in their power to keep the whole subject in the background. It was this idea in their minds when they were proclaiming that they had practiced impressment from time immemorial. He continued: " But suppose the right is allowed, we have another right which is to insist that if, like Shylock (You will pardon the allusion) they insist on taking the flesh, they shall not take a drop of blood. The right to take their own does not involve the right to take our seamen."

Lyman charged the British with making it a rule to impress seamen under different names so that when fair applications were made for their release they could reply that they had no one by that name, and said it would " tire e'en Fabius " to relate all the causes given by the Admiralty for not discharging seamen. The whole situation, he believed, had been growing worse for the past twenty years and it should be stopped even if it required war to stop it. The latter part of this letter was very belligerent indeed. He marshalled many reasons why the United States should make war on Great Britain on the issue of impressment, and insisted that the "Chesapeake" case was simply the most flagrant illustration of that obnoxious practice.

But the British government determined to keep the question of desertion paramount in dealing with the " Chesapeake " incident, and in view of this fact a review of that question, which had its origin very early in the negotiations on impressment, now seems advisable. The practice of desertion in fact constituted one of the most difficult phases of the impressment question. Unquestionably the desertion of British seamen from the British navy was the most critical phase of the problem, and this form of desertion was perhaps the most prevalent. Desertions from the American navy were few in comparison with those from the British navy.[1]

Since no treaty between the United States and Great Britain relative to the subject existed at this time, neither nation was under legal obligation to return deserters from the naval vessels of the other. If such deserting seamen were returned the action was based on courtesy only.

Desertion from the merchant vessels of both nations was also prevalent and had been a source of difficulty from the very beginning of the impressment controversy. The first American consuls to Great Britain wrote of the wholesale desertion of American seamen from American merchant vessels in British ports, and of their inability to check the practice. Many of the consuls referred often to the refusal of the British authorities to assist them in their efforts to recover the deserting seamen. To their requests for aid the British magistrates would reply that there was no British law applying to the case of deserting foreign seamen.[2] In some cases the magistrates took the position that rendering such aid would constitute an interference with a contract made in a foreign country between foreigners, which was distinctly forbidden by English law.[3] Discussing this subject at some length in 1812 in his correspondence with Fos-

[1] On this subject see Monroe to Foster, June 8, 1812, *American State Papers, Foreign Relations*, vol. iii, p. 464.

[2] See letters written in 1790 and 1791 by Fox at Falmouth and Knox at Dublin to Johnson at London, Miscellaneous Letters to Joshua Johnson, *MS. Consular Despatches, London*, vol. iv.

[3] For references to this situation see Maury to Pickney, March 24, 1793, *MS. Consular Despatches, Liverpool*, vol. i. Also Maury to Madison, July 23, 1803, *ibid.*, vol. ii, and Maury to Monroe, August 13, 1807, *ibid.*

ter, the British Minister at Washington, Monroe said: "In Great Britain we know from experience that no provision exists for restoring American seamen to our merchant vessels." [1]

In the United States there was no federal law relating to the return of deserting foreign seamen. The earlier colonial laws provided in many cases for the return of deserters, and in some instances these laws were said to have been continued in force after the establishment of the national government.[2] Most of the state laws examined contained

---

[1] Monroe to Foster, June 8, 1812, *American State Papers, Foreign Relations*, vol. iii, p. 464.

The United States did have at this time an agreement with France, providing for the return of deserting seamen, contained in Article IX of the Consular Convention with that nation concluded November 14, 1788, as follows:

"The Consuls and Vice Consuls may cause to be arrested the Captains, officers, marines, sailors and all other persons being part of the crew of the vessels of their respective nations, who shall have deserted from the said vessels, in order to send them back and transport them out of the country; for which purpose the said Consuls and Vice Consuls shall address themselves to the courts, judges and officers competent, and shall demand the said deserters in writing, proving by an exhibition of the registers of the vessel or ship roll that those men were part of the said crews; and on this demand so proved (saving, however, where the contrary is proved) the delivery shall not be refused; and there shall be given all aid and assistance to the said Consuls and Vice Consuls for the search, seizure and arrest of the said deserters, who shall even be detained and kept in the prisons of the country, at their request and expense, until they shall have found an opportunity of sending them back; but if they be not sent back within three months, to be counted from the day of their arrest, they shall be set at liberty, and shall be no more arrested for the same cause." Malloy, *United States Treaties*, vol. i, p. 494.

Section I of an "Act concerning Consuls and Vice Consuls" passed April 14, 1792, made it the duty of district judges and marshals of the United States to give aid to the French consuls and vice consuls "in arresting and securing deserters from vessels of the French nation according to the tenor of the said article." *United States Statutes at Large*, vol. i, p. 254.

[2] Madison in a letter to Monroe, March 6, 1806, referring to official

provisions for the restoration of seamen abandoning the
service of merchant vessels, to which they were bound by
voluntary agreement.[1] Instances were not found, however,
where these laws were invoked to restore foreign seamen.
It is a matter of considerable interest to find that at least
two of the states did have laws providing definitely for the
return of deserting foreign seamen. The state of Virginia
had such a law passed January 19, 1805,[2] in the midst of

information received from Glasgow and Liverpool of the refusal to
restore American seamen deserting in British ports, said: " The laws of
many of the states have been left, without interruption, to restore British
deserters." *American State Papers, Foreign Relations,* vol. iii, p. 100.

[1] As examples see *Public Laws of South Carolina* (Grimke), 1790,
p. 313, and *Perpetual Laws of Massachusetts up to 1788* (Isaiah Thomas),
p. 267. These laws provided that when any seamen under agreement
or contract, deserted, the justice of peace was empowered, upon complaint of the master of the vessel or other officer, to issue a warrant and
bring the deserting seaman to trial. If convicted of desertion the justice
was required to commit him to prison to be delivered to the master.

[2] "An Act Concerning Seamen" passed January 19, 1805, *Virginia,
Statutes at Large, New Series,* vol. iii (1803-1808), pp. 128-29.
" Be it enacted by the General Assembly, That if any seaman or
mariner, not being a citizen of this Commonwealth, or of any of the
United States, who shall have signed a contract to perform a voyage on
board any merchant ship or vessels (either a ship or vessel of the United
States, or of any foreign nation whatsoever) shall at any port or place
within this Commonwealth, desert, or shall absent himself from such
ship or vessel without the leave of the master, it shall be lawful for any
Justice of the Peace of any county or corporation within this Commonwealth, upon the complaint of the master of such ship or vessel, or other
officer commanding in the absence of the master, to issue his warrant
to apprehend such seaman or mariner, and bring him before such Justice ;
and if it shall appear by due proof that such seaman or mariner has signed
a contract as aforesaid, and that the voyage agreed for is not finished,
altered, or the contract otherwise dissolved, and that the seaman or
mariner has deserted the ship or vessel, or absented himself without
leave, the Justice shall commit him to the jail of his county or corporation,
there to remain until such ship or vessel shall be ready to proceed on her
voyage, or till the master, shall require his discharge, and then to be

the impressment controversy, and on the statute books at
the time desertions in Norfolk were being most complained
of by the British in 1806 and 1807. It is probable, however, that the authorities in the port-towns of Virginia
found such a law somewhat difficult to enforce against deserting seamen. The law of North Carolina provided for
the return of deserting foreign seamen, even though such
seamen had become naturalized in the state.[1]

Passing from the legal phase of the question it is obvious
that in practice the situation was far from ideal. The effort
made by the British government in 1800 to obtain an agreement for the mutual restoration of deserting seamen has

delivered to such master or other officer commanding in the absence
of the master, he paying all the cost of such commitment."

Clause two provided similarly for apprentices, and clause three was
as follows:

" Provided always, That if any seaman, mariner or apprentice, shall
offer sufficient proof to satisfy the Justice of the Peace before whom he
may be brought, that he hath been cruelly or improperly treated while
on board any ship or vessel, by the master thereof, or that he hath good
cause to apprehend danger to his person from the master, should he be
compelled to remain on board such ship or vessel, it shall be lawful for
the Justice to discharge such seaman, mariner or apprentice from all
further confinement on account of such desertion or absence."

[1] Haywood, *Manual of the Laws of North Carolina* (1808), vol. ii,
pp. 109-110.

This law, passed in 1780, was still in force. The clause on deserters
was as follows:

" Where any sailor, seaman or mariner belonging to any vessel of such
state (who hath acknowledged or shall hereafter acknowledge the independence of the United States of America) within this state, shall
desert or enlist in the service of this state, or of the United States, or
be found wandering from his vessel, it shall be lawful for the master
of such vessel to reclaim such sailor, seaman or marine; notwithstanding
such sailor, seaman or marine may, in the meantime be naturalized in this
state: and any Justice of the Peace to whom the master may apply, shall
grant his warrant for taking and conveying such sailor, seaman or
marine, from constable to constable, to the said vessel: or on application
from the consuls, the governor, with the advice of the consul, may issue
such orders to any sheriff, constable, or military officer, who shall yield
due obedience thereto."

been reviewed.[1]   That plan as it related to deserters was not in itself objectionable to the American government, particularly as an agreement existed with France containing all the essentials of the British plan.   But the American government was unwilling to agree to the latter, not only because Great Britain would not agree to give up the practice of impressment, but also because the British plan by implication sanctioned impressment from merchant vessels.   From the date of the failure of that plan, one of the recurring complaints of the British ministers in Washington had been that American officers refused aid in the matter of restoring British deserters.[2]   At times it was also charged that American citizens encouraged British seamen to desert in American ports.

In the matter of the alleged encouragement given to deserters by citizens of either nation, there is little of an authoritative nature that can be said.   Neither nation had laws bearing on the subject, and if such laws had existed, evidence pointing to guilt in any particular case would probably have been exceedingly difficult to obtain.

The British probably suffered greater losses by desertion than did the United States, but they doubtless gained enough seamen by impressment to offset those losses.   Whatever the facts regarding desertion might have been, they did not warrant the order of Admiral Berkeley to search an American ship of war in time of peace for deserting seamen. They do, however, explain the origin of that order, and help us better to comprehend the position of the British government on this particular question, and indeed on the general issue of impressment.

The effect of the " Chesapeake " incident on the public

[1] *Supra*, ch. iii, pp. 84 *et seq.*

[2] For instances of complaints of this character see Thornton to Madison, October 16, 1802, *MS. Letters British Legation*, vol. ii.   See also Merry to Madison, April 12, 1805, *ibid.*, vol. iii.

mind in America was almost electric, momentarily uniting the entire nation against Great Britain. Indeed, it is quite probable that had the government of the United States immediately declared war it would have received the support even of the majority of the Federalists. However, the policy followed in seeking to unite the "Chesapeake" outrage with the problem of impressment from merchant vessels aroused the bitter opposition of the Federalists and resulted in almost endless partisan controversy, which was so characteristic of this period. The Republican press, supporting the Administration, contended that this outrage was the full fruition of the practice of impressment, and that whether the seamen taken were British or American really made no difference.[1] Some Federalist papers soon began to find mitigating elements in the outrage in the possibility that the seamen taken were deserters from the British navy, and charged the Administration with suppressing the real facts on this point. These papers took the position that Great Britain could not permit American national vessels to become asylums for her deserting seamen, practically justifying the attack on the "Chesapeake" as legal reprisal.[2] This seems to be consistent with the general position taken by all Federalist papers both before and following this affair, on the question of impressment from merchant vessels. Those papers generally took the stand that irrespective of whether or not Great Britain had the right to impress, she did have the power, and all the United States could do in the matter was to acquiesce and seek to render the conditions as palatable as possible.

While the more rabid Federalist press took advantage of the affair of the "Chesapeake" to condemn the alleged policy of the United States in encouraging desertion from the Brit-

---

[1] *National Intelligencer* and *Aurora*, July and August, 1807 issues.

[2] *Boston Repertory*, August 4, 1807.

ish service and used this to palliate the wrongs inflicted by
the British, the Federalist *New York Evening Post*[1] stood
by the government. Its editor held that in offering to agree
to the mutual return of all deserters, the government had
done all it could along that line. He refused to believe that
British seamen received more encouragement to desert in
the United States than American seamen received in Great
Britain. On the " Chesapeake " affair, he regarded Great
Britain as wholly in the wrong. He criticized severely certain Federalist papers that, in his opinion, were seeking to
uphold the right to search national vessels in time of peace.
He was strongly opposed, however, to combining the issue
with that of impressment from merchant vessels, because in
his view the United States should not oppose Great Britain
in the practice of taking her own seamen from such vessels.

While popular excitement and party feeling was running
high in the United States on account of the " Chesapeake "
affair, the British government increased the tenseness of the
situation by issuing the King's famous Proclamation re-
calling British seamen from the service of foreign nations.
This Proclamation, issued on October 16, 1807,[2] not only
ordered all British seamen engaged in foreign vessels to
return, but commanded all British naval officers " to stop
and make stay " all natural-born British subjects in the service of foreign states, and " to seize upon, take and bring
away " all those engaged in foreign merchant vessels. They
were to request the release of those found on foreign war-
ships, and in case of refusal were to transmit the information to their commander-in-chief, who should in turn transmit it to the British minister residing in the state to which
the foreign warship belonged. The Proclamation also set
forth that no letters of naturalization or certificates of citi-

[1] See issues of July and August, 1807.
[2] *American State Papers, Foreign Relations*, vol. iii, pp. 25-26.

zenship from foreign states would discharge natural-born British subjects from their allegiance to the crown.

The Proclamation, definitely disclaiming the right to search national ships, but expressly commanding impressment from foreign merchant vessels, had the effect of increasing the war sentiment in the United States that had been aroused by the "Chesapeake" affair. John Quincy Adams [1] felt that it gave a "new and darker complexion" to the old impressment controversy. He did not believe the "new encroachment" should be tolerated, yet at the same time he feared that opposition to it would mean war with Great Britain.

The Proclamation not only aroused intense bitterness of feeling among large portions of the people of the United States, but was a heavy blow to the pride of the American government, because for fifteen years the United States had sought to obtain the abandonment by Great Britain of the practice of impressment, and now in the face of an incident of unparalleled lawlessness, the British crown proclaimed impressment as the British policy in a manner which lent it greater force than the mere expressions of British ministers. [2]

The obvious result of the Proclamation was to give the United States the alternative of abandoning further negotiations on impressment or of going to war. The former policy was adopted. Negotiations at London were closed but there continued in Washington some communication upon the subject, although desultory and not directed toward

[1] See his letter to John Adams, December 27, 1807, *Works of John Quincy Adams* (W. C. Ford), vol. iii, pp. 169-171.

[2] Monroe and Pinkney reported that Canning, with whom they held conversation on the subject of the Proclamation, regarded the renouncement of the right to search national vessels of foreign nations as quite conciliatory, since according to his opinion the press and general public in England still regarded that claim as lawful. Monroe and Pinkney to Madison, October 22, 1807, *American State Papers, Foreign Relations,* vol. iii, pp. 196-197.

any specific plan for its solution. During the remainder of the year 1807 Madison made requests to Erskine, the British Minister at Washington, for the release of about one hundred impressed seamen. Judging from Erskine's replies, notice was given of the release of some of these, but in most of the cases they were retained, large numbers being held on the ground that they had taken bounty upon enlistment.[1]

The British government, however, manifested a desire to adjust the "Chesapeake" affair, by sending George Henry Rose, a member of the British Cabinet, on a special mission to Washington for that purpose. The policy of keeping that issue entirely separate from impressment from merchant vessels, which Canning had earlier announced to Monroe, was made mandatory in the instructions to Rose. He was furthermore instructed not to enter into any negotiation upon the "Chesapeake" incident until the proclamation of the President requiring British public vessels to leave American waters had been withdrawn.[2] The American government regarded the question of reparation as antecedent to any question regarding the proclamation and refused to withdraw the latter until the British Minister should indicate the nature of the reparation which he was authorized to make. Hence, after a few desultory conversations[3] between Rose and Madison regarding the mutual discharge of natural-born subjects from public ships and merchant vessels, the negotiations ended, and Rose took his departure, leaving the "Chesapeake" affair still unsettled.

Shortly after the departure of Rose, Madison wrote to Pinkney,[4] American Minister at London, stating that any

---

[1] *MS. Letters British Legation*, vol. iv.

[2] Rose to Madison, January 26, 1808, *American State Papers, Foreign Relations*, vol. iii, pp. 213-214.

[3] For review of these conversations see *Madison's Writings* (Hunt), vol. viii, pp. 2-4.

[4] Madison to Pinkney, April 4, 1808, *American State Papers, Foreign Relations*, vol. iii, pp. 221-222.

renewal of the negotiations on the subject of the "Chesapeake" must originate with the British government, and that such negotiations should take place preferably at Washington. However, if a proposal on the subject should be made at London, Pinkney was instructed to accept reparation on terms previously laid down in the instructions to Monroe, except that the demand for the abandonment of impressment from merchant vessels was to be omitted.

After more than a year of delay, David W. Erskine, the British Minister at Washington, in a letter to Robert Smith, then Secretary of State, April 17, 1809, proposed a settlement of the "Chesapeake" affair, including the restoration of the seamen taken, and provision for their families in addition to the disavowal of the act and punishment of the officers, which had been effected soon after the outrage occurred.[1] The punishment administered to Admiral Berkeley consisted merely in his transfer to another command.

The American Secretary of State accepted this arrangement[2] on the same day it was offered, but expressed disapproval of the degree of punishment administered to the commanding officer of the "Leopard" in the following words:

I have it in express charge from the President to state, that, while he forbears to insist on a further punishment of the offending officer, he is not the less sensible of the justice and utility of such an example, nor the less persuaded that it would best comport with what is due from his Britannic Majesty to his own honour.

Upon the receipt of this note, the British government abruptly terminated the negotiations relative to the "Chesapeake" and again the question was left unadjusted.

[1] Erskine to Smith, April 17, 1809, *American State Paper, Foreign Relations*, vol. iii, p. 295.

[2] Smith to Erskine, April 17, 1809, *ibid.*, pp. 295-296.

Erskine, who was recalled by his government, was succeeded by Francis Jackson, who on October 11, 1809,[1] offered to renew the negotiations on the basis of the proposal
of his predecessor. Being requested by the Secretary of
State for further details regarding his particular proposal,
Jackson on October 27, 1809,[2] presented a special memorandum on the subject. The proposal for the restoration
of the seamen taken was modified by the exception of such
as might be proved to be natural-born citizens of Great
Britain or deserters from the British service. Provision
for families of those killed on the "Chesapeake" was offered,
but with the exceptions stipulated in the proposal on restoring seamen. Such a plan was so objectionable to the
American government that no official reply was made to it.[3]

The character of the proposals which Jackson offered as
reparation for the attack upon the "Chesapeake" was in harmony with other negotiations conducted by him with the
American government. He seemed determined not to commit the error, with which Erskine, his predecessor, had been
charged, of being too conciliatory. Indeed, he so persistently manifested an unfriendly attitude that the American
government instructed Pinkney in London to request his recall, which was finally complied with after more than a
year's delay.

For over a year after Jackson's recall the British government did not send a minister to Washington, the only
representative there, during that time, being a *chargé
d'affaires*. In June, 1811, A. J. Foster was sent as British
Minister to Washington, with instructions to make repara-

[1] Jackson to Smith, October 11, 1809, *American State Papers, Foreign
Relations*, vol. iii, pp. 308-311.

[2] Jackson to Smith, October 27, 1809, *ibid.*, p. 316.

[3] Updyke, *The Diplomacy of the War of 1812*, p. 54.

tion for the attack upon the "Chesapeake". The negotiations on the subject were, however, delayed for several months by the situation which arose from the encounter between the United States frigate " President " and the British sloop of war " Little Belt " near Cape Charles, on May 16, 1811, in which one person on the " President " was wounded, while thirteen on the " Little Belt " were killed and many others wounded.[1]

The activities of the British navy preceding this incident included the capture of many American vessels bound for France and numerous cases of impressment by the frigates " Melampus " and " Guerriere ", lying off Sandy Hook. The " President ", in command of Commodore Rodgers, had been sent by the American navy to protect American commerce against such unlawful interference. The " Little Belt ", in command of Captain Bingham, according to the Captain's account, had come from Bermuda, and while searching for the "Guerriere", for which vessel she carried despatches, had on the morning of May 16 chased the "President" until she was able to identify that vessel as an American frigate. Commodore Rodgers thought he was hailing the " Guerriere ", and had in mind inquiring for impressed seamen. Accounts of the encounter were quite conflicting, and the American government instituted a searching inquiry in which every officer and seaman of the " President " gave evidence under oath supporting the account of Commodore Rodgers, which maintained that the " Little Belt " had fired the first shot, in response to his legitimate attempts to hail her. The British government accepted the report of Captain Bingham, which made the "President" responsible for the initial aggression, and the case rested in this manner without a settlement of any kind.

[1] For a detailed account see Henry Adams, *History of the United States,* vol. vi, pp. 25-45.

The " Chesapeake " affair had dragged on unsettled for many years, during which the continued British aggressions on American trade by means of illegal blockades and orders in council had greatly heightened American resentment against that nation. There was, in the United States, a general feeling that the " Little Belt " incident avenged the attack on the " Chesapeake " for which Great Britain had refused reparation. Foster's instructions providing for a settlement of that issue were of such a character as to prohibit the settlement of any of the other issues between the two nations. The " Little Belt " incident being allowed to pass without definite settlement, Foster on November 1, 1811,[1] again disavowed the act of Admiral Berkeley in attacking the " Chesapeake "; agreed to restore the impressed seamen and to provide for the wounded and for the families of those who had been killed. The American government accepted this proposal[2] and the negotiations on the subject which had continued over a period of five years were finally closed. But this solution of the difficulty was purely a diplomatic and technical one. The American people were not satisfied with the delayed reparation for such an attack upon national honor and independence, and this incident continued to be linked in the public mind with that of impressment from merchant vessels as one of the major offences of the British government against the government and the people of the United States.

[1] Foster to Monroe, November 1, 1811, *American State Papers, Foreign Relations*, vol. iii, pp. 499-500.

[2] Monroe to Foster, November 12, 1811, *ibid.*, p. 500.

CHAPTER VII

THE HISTORY OF IMPRESSMENT FROM THE "CHESAPEAKE" AFFAIR IN 1807 TO THE DECLARATION OF WAR IN 1812

In the previous chapter the "Chesapeake" controversy was followed to its termination in 1811, but in proceeding now to a review of the general subject of impressment for the years immediately following the "Chesapeake" incident we shall have occasion to point out the relation of that incident to the more general topic.

The American government, while definitely placing impressment in the instructions to William Pinkney, who succeeded Monroe as the United States Minister to England, nevertheless made his action on it conditional on a settlement of other issues. Madison wrote to Pinkney, April 4, 1808:

You are authorized, however, to continue your interpositions in behalf of our impressed or detained seamen, and in the event of a repeal of the British orders, and of satisfactory pledges for repairing the aggression on the Chesapeake, to enter into formal arrangements for abolishing impressment altogether and mutually discontinuing to receive the seamen of each other into either military or merchant service. . . . [1]

It was natural that when Madison became President he should choose to continue the policy authorized above. In fact, this is evident in the letters of Robert Smith, his Sec-

[1] Madison to Pinkney, April 4, 1808, *American State Papers, Foreign Relations*, vol. iii, p. 222.

156

retary of State, to Pinkney, during the years 1809 and 1810, instructing him to delay further negotiations on impressment until satisfaction had been given on the "Chesapeake" affair, and until the orders in council had been removed.[1]

[1] Smith to Pinkney, November 11, 1809, *MS. Instructions to United States Ministers,* vol. vii, p. 65, and Smith to Pinkney, January 20, 1810, *American State Papers, Foreign Relations,* vol. iii, p. 349.

The first of the orders in council referred to was issued May 16, 1806, and proclaimed the coast of the continent of Europe from the river Elbe to Brest to be in a state of blockade. Another issued January 7, 1807, forbade all vessels to engage in the coastwise trade of France and her allies or with ports closed to British vessels. On November 11, 1807, still another order in council proclaimed all the ports of France and of her allies, and of all countries closed to British trade to be in a state of blockade. It also declared unlawful all trade in goods produced in the blockaded countries, and stipulated that vessels engaging in such trade would be subject to capture and condemnation both of the vessels and of the goods. It was furthermore declared that any vessel carrying a certificate of origin issued by France would be regarded as good prize.—Note: Copies of all these orders in council are printed in *American State Papers, Foreign Relations.*

The British government justified this unusual system of orders and decrees restricting neutral commerce on the ground that they constituted a reasonable retaliation for the concurrent system of French decrees which were equally unusual. It will be sufficient for present purposes to state that the American government appropriately refused to admit the legality of the British orders in council and sought to resist them by various legislative enactments, and by diplomatic representations as well. The legislative enactments consisted first of the Non-importation Act of April 18, 1806, prohibiting the importation of a specified list of articles—(*United States Statutes at Large,* vol. ii, pp. 379-381). Second, the Embargo Act of December 22, 1808 (*United States Statutes at Large,* vol. ii, pp. 451-453) prohibiting all American vessels from leaving American ports, which remained in force until March 4, 1809, and was followed by the Non-intercourse Act of March 1, 1809 (*United States Statutes at Large,* vol. ii, pp. 528-533) which excluded all public and private vessels of Great Britain and France from American waters; forbade the importation of British and French goods, repealed the Embargo laws except as to Great Britain and France, and gave the President power to renew by proclamation trade with Great Britain or France, on condition that either should cease to violate neutral rights. Finally the so-called Macon Bill, May 1, 1810

Pinkney, therefore, regarded the order of procedure to be, first, the "Chesapeake"; second, orders in council, and third the commercial and other concerns embraced by the commission of 1806 to him and Monroe.[1] On this basis impressment would have come in the third stage of negotiations, and since he was unable to accomplish the settlement of either of the previous stages he naturally never reached the point where he could deal with it in accordance with his instructions. On October 19, 1810, at a time when the American government erroneously believed that Great Britain contemplated revoking the orders in council, Smith wrote to Pinkney[2] stressing the need of a settlement on impressment, but still insisting on the necessity of a previous settlement of the " Chesapeake " affair, and adding that since every admissible advance on that subject had already been exhausted on the part of the United States, it would

be improper to renew the subject to the British government, with which it must lie to come forward with the requisite satis-

(*United States Statutes at Large*, vol. ii, pp. 605-606) providing for non-intercourse with Great Britain and France, and stipulating that if either one of those nations should cease to violate the neutral commerce of the United States before March 3, 1811, while the other after three months refused to do so, this law and the Non-importation Act should be revived against the nation refusing so to act.

This last act was revived against Great Britain by presidential proclamation February 2, 1811, which action was confirmed by Congress March 2, 1811, along with an authorization to the President to suspend both acts with reference to Great Britain whenever that nation revoked her orders in council. This Great Britain refused to do until after the declaration of war. For a review of this legislation see Henry Adams, *History of the United States,* vols. iv and v.

[1] Pinkney to Smith, April 8, 1810, *American State Papers, Foreign Relations*, vol. iii, p. 356.

[2] Smith to Pinkney, Oct. 19, 1810, *ibid.*, pp. 369-370.

faction to the United States. You will, therefore, merely evince a disposition to meet in a conciliatory form any overtures that may be made on the part of the British government.[1]

Pinkney held consistently to this position up to the end of his mission. Upon the appointment in 1811 of A. J. Foster as Minister to the United States, to succeed Francis J. Jackson, whose recall the American government had demanded, Pinkney wrote, February 17, 1811,[2] to the Marquis of Wellesley, who succeeded Canning as British Foreign Secretary:

I presume that, for the restoration of harmony between the two countries, the orders in council will be relinquished without delay; that the blockade of May 1806 will be annulled; that the case of the " Chesapeake " will be arranged in the manner heretofore intended; and, in general, that all such just and reasonable acts will be done as are necessary to make us friends.

Again in his letter to Smith, February 24, 1811,[3] Pinkney stated that satisfaction to the United States would consist in a distinct pledge on the affair of the " Chesapeake ", and a manifestation of a disposition to settle all differences on principles of justice. The failure of the Pinkney-Wellesley negotiations was dwelt upon at considerable length in the Republican press of the United States, and in many cases the failure to settle impressment was given greater prominence than any other phase of the negotiations.[4]

Ibid., 370.

[2] Pinkney to Wellesley, Feb. 17, 1811, *ibid.*, p. 414.

[3] Pinkney to Smith, Feb. 24, 1811, *ibid.*, pp. 414-415.

[4] *New York Morning Post,* April 20, 1811, quoting *New York Gazette and National Intelligencer.*

Virtually nothing on the subject passed between the American government and the British representatives at Washington during 1810 and the first half of the year 1811. Only two or three letters each were written by Morier and Baker, representing the British government, to Smith and his successor, Monroe. These letters dealt with individual cases of impressment and consisted of the bare report of the Admiralty officers at Nova Scotia, Jamaica or Bermuda to the Secretary of State.[1]

The correspondence of Monroe, who succeeded Smith as Secretary of State, and Foster, the British Minister at Washington, covering as it did the last year preceding the war, dealt with impressment, but not with any definite effort to reach an agreement on that subject. In a letter to Foster, July 23, 1811,[2] Monroe, after prolonged discussion of the orders in council, added this concluding paragraph:

I conclude with remarking, that if I have confined this letter to the subjects brought into view by yours, it is not because the United States have lost sight in any degree, of the other very serious causes of complaint, on which they have received no satisfaction, but because of the conciliatory policy of this government has thus far separated the case of the orders in council from others, and because, with respect to these others, your communication has not afforded any reasonable prospects of resuming them at this time with success.[3]

Foster, on April 15, 1812,[4] complained that a British seaman was induced to leave his Majesty's service in consequence of encouragement from the inhabitants of Annap-

[1] MS. Letters British Legation, vol. v.

[2] Monroe to Foster, July 23, 1811, American State Papers, Foreign Relations, vol. iii, pp. 439-442.

[3] Ibid., p. 442.

[4] Foster to Monroe, April 15, 1812, ibid., p. 454.

olis, and intimated that he could cite many other similar cases. He spoke of this practice of United States' citizens as an " insult highly irritating ", adding that although it had unfortunately not as yet been found practicable for the governments of the two nations to agree to reciprocal arrangements on the subject, he hoped that the government of the United States might find some means to prevent a recurrence of similar irregularities on the part of its citizens. He also stated that whenever the American government claimed any person on board any of his Majesty's ships as native American citizens, no exertion should be wanting on his part to procure their discharge, and asked to be furnished with a list of all those claimed as such, in order that he might use every effort to obtain their immediate release.

On May 30, 1812,[1] Monroe replied to Foster's note of April 15, saying that no encouragement to desertion had been given by the United States or Maryland authorities and " if they received such encouragement from any of our citizens it is a cause of regret; but it is an act not cognizable by our laws, any more than it is presumed to be by those of Great Britain ". He then cited the case of an American seaman, who deserted and took refuge on a British ship of war, whom the British commander refused to surrender on request. He gave attention to Foster's proffered exertions to procure the discharge of native American citizens from on board British ships of war, stating, however, that it was impossible for the United States to discriminate between their native and naturalized citizens, and pointing out that the British government made no such discrimination itself.

Foster's letter to Monroe of June 1, 1812,[2] was his last communication relative to impressment. In this letter he

[1] Monroe to Foster, May 30, 1812, *American State Papers, Foreign Relations*, vol. iii, p. 454.

[2] *MS. Letters British Legation*, vol. vii.

complained that British seamen were being held in American ships of war against their will, estimating that twenty-eight were thus held on the " Constitution " and the " Wasp ". He expressed the belief that the United States had taken no part in their retention and would upon the receipt of the information take prompt and effective measures to correct the practice. Monroe regarded the use made of this charge in Foster's letter as an effort to render less culpable the acts of Great Britain. The following language contained in the Foster letter was the ground of Monroe's opinion:

The American government will perceive from this friendly communication that it is not on this side of the water alone that the inconvenience necessarily resulting from the similarity of habits, language and manners between the inhabitants of the two countries is productive of subjects of complaint and regret.[1]

This was Foster's final statement about impressment. Baker, who was left in charge, was instructed in particular to look after returning the surviving seamen involved in the " Chesapeake " affair.

To Foster's letter Monroe replied June 8, 1812,[2] saying that many of the seamen referred to might now be American citizens, and that Great Britain should not object to this, because she naturalized *ipso facto* all alien seamen who served two years on her ships of war. He set forth the contrast between the conduct of the United States and Great

[1] The documents presented by Foster to prove that these seamen were detained cover about fifty pages and contain complete life histories of the five or six seamen who made affidavit to them. The Lords Commissioners had urged Admiral Roger Curtis to get these documents from the men who had deserted from the " Constitution ". They had all originally entered voluntarily some American vessel. Some had married in the United States and had lived there many years. One testified that he received $20. bounty for entering the " Constitution ".

[2] Monroe to Foster, June 8, 1812, *American State Papers, Foreign Relations*, vol. iii, p. 464.

Britain at great length, which may be summarized as follows:

Regulations of the United States prohibited the enlistment of aliens in vessels of war, and Great Britain had no such regulation.

Enlistments by force, or impressments were contrary to the laws of the United States but were not only practised by Great Britain within her legal jurisdiction, but extended to foreign vessels on the high seas, " with abuses which aggravate the outrage to the nations to whom the vessels belong."

Most of the states of United States had laws for restoring seamen deserting merchant vessels to which they were bound by voluntary agreement, while Great Britain had no provision to restore seamen deserting from merchant vessels even to fulfill their voluntary engagements, and if deserters from American ships of war were ever restored, it was by courtesy of the naval officers and not from legal duty.

Deserters from public vessels were deemed malefactors, and no nation would return such without reciprocal stipulation.

The assurances which Foster had previously given that orders would be sent to naval officers not to detain American seamen, were held by Monroe to be inadequate. Nothing would serve as an adequate remedy now, declared Monroe, except orders to prohibit the impressment of seamen from American vessels at sea. He reviewed again in detail the standard arguments of the United States against impressment and concluded that in the light of all the facts, Foster had very small ground of complaint. This correspondence, which took place only a few days before the declaration of war against Great Britain, contained the last official discussion on impressment previous to that event.

The prevalence of the practice of impressment during these years when the subject was somewhat submerged in the diplomatic correspondence is revealed in the reports of

William Lyman from 1805 to 1810, and of his successor, R. G. Beasley, from 1810 to 1812, American Agents for Seamen in Great Britain. As early as 1807 Lyman had expressed the opinion that the British navy held 15,000 American seamen.[1] The total number impressed during his term as Agent for Seamen, according to his reports to the Secretary of State, the final one of which was dated September 30, 1810, was 3,791.[2]

The work of Beasley, who was the last American Agent for Seamen in Great Britain, extended from 1810 until the outbreak of war in 1812. During the period of approximately eighteen months covered by his services many important facts regarding impressment were reported by him. Concerning the number of seamen impressed, Beasley's reports are available for the year 1811 only, and they give a total of 802 applications for release.

Accompanying Beasley's letter to Monroe dated October 17, 1811,[3] is a copy of a circular which was being distributed in Great Britain by the British Admiralty. This circular, which is 24x30 inches, carried in big black head-lines the following: "Game going on in America for the purpose of crimping British seamen out of the British navy." It contained the affidavit of five British sailors setting forth that a certain David Read of East George Street, New York, had made them drunk on "milk punch"; promised them three months' wages in advance if they would serve on an American ship, and then turned them over to another man for the consideration of forty dollars apiece, out of which sum

[1] For a discussion of Lyman's work as Agent for Seamen see *supra*, ch. vi, pp. 140-143.

[2] *American State Papers, Foreign Relations*, vol. ii, pp. 776-798; vol. iii, pp. 36-79; also p. 348.

[3] Beasley to Monroe, Oct. 17, 1811, *MS. Consular Despatches, London*, vol. ix.

Read had advanced each of them money binding them to future service. The affidavit further charged that Read, who was himself armed, received the aid of armed officers, who drove the men on board the frigate " President," where they told their story to Commodore Rogers, who promptly released them and sent them ashore. Immediately upon setting foot on shore, however, they were arrested on the charge of having accepted money in advance under false pretenses, and by the time they had satisfied the legal or quasi-legal proceedings which followed, they found themselves compelled to go to work on American ships in order to earn a living.

That such a gang was operating in New York for profit and receiving the patronage of certain merchants and masters is altogether possible, although one would think it strange indeed if the Federalist newspapers of that period had overlooked such a situation, and careful search has failed to find in the papers any reference to David Read or to such procedure as was described in the affidavit.

The Secretary of the British Admiralty made complaint to Beasley that protections in duplicate and even in triplicate forms were being issued to American seamen, the originals of which were being sold by them to British seamen in open market.[1] Beasley admitted that duplicate protections were sometimes issued, declaring the practice to be necessary on account of the frequency with which the originals were lost, and also on account of the persistent practice of British captains of impressing every American seaman found without a protection, regardless of the plea that the document had been lost. He furthermore contended that American seamen were often retained by the British on the alleged ground that their protections were forged, and that

---

[1] Beasley to Croker, Secy. of the Admiralty, Jan. 10, 1812, *MS. Consular Despatches, London*, vol. ix.

in all such cases it was the duty of American collectors, when requested, to issue duplicate protections in the hope of convincing the British Admiralty that the seamen were entitled to be released. He admitted that these duplicates could be, and might actually have been used fraudulently, but countered this point by charging that in the London market much more important documents, even the ships' papers themselves, were being forged every day and sold. He admitted also that a few protections might be illegitimately obtained in the United States, but insisted that this practice could never be absolutely prevented. On the whole, he maintained that collectors were very careful and that he had never seen any convincing proof that a single protection had been fraudulently obtained. On this point, however, he expressed the wish that the Admiralty be cautious, since he was sure that the United States did not want to protect seamen who were not their own. Beasley then charged that the British Admiralty treated all cases of impressment as a unit, never giving to each separate case a fair and individual hearing. In the early days, after the passage of the American law providing for certificates signed by collectors, he maintained that the Admiralty refused to accept all other affidavits, and recognized only those of the collectors. Now, however, he charged, they were systematically refusing for superficial reasons to honor the certificates granted by the collectors.[1]

To this letter, Croker of the Admiralty replied January 15, 1812,[2] disclaiming any desire on the part of Great Britain to impress any *bona fide* American seamen, and asserting that certificates of citizenship and other satisfactory

---

[1] Beasley to Croker, Secretary of the Admiralty, Jan. 10, 1812, *MS. Consular Despatches, London,* vol. ix.

[2] Croker to Beasley, Jan. 15, 1812, *ibid.*

proofs of American citizenship were accepted at that time just as they had always been, but that frauds having become very numerous, great caution had become necessary. Without replying to the specific questions raised by Beasley as to duplicate and triplicate copies of certificates, he declared that the Admiralty were in favor of a full and fair adjustment of the entire impressment question, but were convinced that such a plan could not be formulated except through the diplomatic channels of the two governments.

A few months later Beasley informed the American government that there was no curtailment of the practice of impressment, criticizing rather severely the policy of the Admiralty. He charged that body with refusing to pursue the claim of any seamen who had gone on a British ship to any foreign station; with refusing to release all seamen whose claims originated in the Consular Office, and refusing at the same time to return to him any of the documents involved.[1]

More specifically Beasley charged that, at times, the Admiralty would release seamen who had valid documents, but at other times would refuse release regardless of the validity of the documents. That sometimes a seaman's oath as to his birthplace would be the determining factor in obtaining his release regardless of other documents, while at other times no attention would be paid to such an oath. He charged the Admiralty with refusing at times to release seamen either because of their alleged conduct previous to impressment, or because of certain circumstances accompanying their impressment, regardless of all other evidence. At times the Admiralty replied to his requests for release of seamen, saying that the men for whom he sought release were British subjects, but offering no proof, and at other

---

[1] Beasley to Croker, April 16, 1812, *MS. Consular Despatches, London,* vol. ix.

times the reply merely stated that the seamen in question should not be discharged, giving no reason at all for the decision. Under such conditions, with absolutely no guiding principle, how, asked Beasley, could anyone know what kind of evidence the Admiralty desired? The reply of the Admiralty to this letter was similar to that made to Beasley's January letter, viz., that they hoped for a diplomatic settlement of the question and were sure that Great Britain had no desire to impress American seamen.[1]

Although during these years the diplomatic controversy over impressment was in abeyance, the practice of impressment, according to the review just given, showed no signs of abating, and there was frequently abundant discussion of the subject in the newspapers and in Congress. The letter of John Quincy Adams to Harrison C. Otis, in which Adams sought to refute certain arguments of Timothy Pickering on this subject, was widely published in the papers of both parties.[2] One of Pickering's contentions was that since

[1] Barrow, Secy. of the Admiralty, to Beasley, April 18, 1812, *MS. Consular Despatches,* London, vol. ix.

NOTE: During Beasley's mission six cases of impressment occurred which called forth letters from Monroe to Foster, the British Minister at Washington. One of these letters written February 8, 1812, contained a request for the release of John and Charles Lewis, great nephews of George Washington. See *British Legation,* vol. ii (Notes from the Department, 1810-1828.) Notes from the Department from 1804 to 1810 are unfortunately missing. The index to this volume shows several letters on impressment in 1804 and 1805. Beyond that date the index gives only the dates of letters. This volume if available might contain some valuable data on the subject.

With the outbreak of war between the United States and Great Britain the services of Beasley as Agent for Seamen were discontinued, but he remained in London during the war as Agent for war-prisoners, rendering valuable aid to many impressed seamen who had been discharged, and even after peace was signed he assisted many of these unfortunate seamen in returning to their homes in the United States.

[2] *New York Evening Post,* May 13 and May 26, 1808 issues.

impressment had been claimed as a right and exercised for ages, it was a legal right by prescription. Adams pointed out that such a right had never been mentioned by writers on the law of nations, and insisted that impressment had never been a question between any other nations except Great Britain and the United States and that hence there could be no right of prescription.

To another of Pickering's contentions that the number taken was small and that these were returned on due proof, Adams replied that there had been four or five thousand impressed since 1803, and in his opinion every single instance was on a par with murder. He declared that if England should discharge every seaman impressed, such action would not constitute an adequate remedy for the wrong. His description of the practice and procedure in relation to impressment being one of the most graphic to be found, is given in full, as follows:

An American vessel, bound to an European port, has two, three or four native Americans impressed by a British man of war, bound to the East or West Indies. When the American Captain arrives at his port of destination, he makes his protest, and sends it to the nearest American Minister or consul. When he returns home, he transmits the duplicate of his protest to the Secretary of State. In process of time, the names of the impressed men and of the ship into which they have been impressed are received by the agent in London. He makes his demand that the men may be delivered up. The Lords of the Admiralty, after a reasonable time for inquiry and advisement, return for answer that the ship is on a foreign station and their Lordships can, therefore, take no further steps in the matter, or that the ship has been taken and that the men have been received in exchange for French prisoners, or, that the men had no protection (the impressing officer often having taken them from the men) —Or, that the men were probably British subjects, or that they have entered and taken the bounty; (to which the officers know how to reduce them), or, that they have been married, or settled in England. In all these cases, without further ceremony, their discharge is refused. Sometimes their Lordships, in a vein of humor, inform the agent that the man had been discharged as unserviceable. Sometimes, in a sterner tone, they say he was an imposter—or, perhaps by way of consolation to his relatives and friends, they report that he has fallen in battle, against a nation in amity with his country. Sometimes they coolly return that there is no such man on board the ship; and what has become of him, the agonies of a wife and children in his native land may be left to conjecture. When all these and many other such apologies for refusal fail, the native seaman is discharged —and when by the charitable aid of his government he has found his way home, he comes to be informed that all is as it should be—that the number of his fellow sufferers is small— that it was impossible to distinguish him from an Englishman —and that he was delivered up, on duly authenticated proof!

Enough of this disgusting subject. I cannot stop to calculate how many of these wretched victims are natives of Massachusetts and how many natives of Viriginia. I cannot stop to solve that knotty question of national jurisdiction whether some of them might not be slaves and, therefore, not citizens of the United States. I cannot stay to account for the wonder, why, poor, and ignorant, and friendless, as most of them are, the voice of their complaint is so seldom heard in the great navigating states. I admit that we have endured this cruel indignity through all the administrations of the general government. I acknowledge that Great Britain claims the right to seize her subjects in our merchant vessels, that even if we could acknowledge it, the time of discrimination would be difficult to draw. We are not in a condition to maintain this right by war, and as the British Government has been, more than once, on the point of giving it up of their own accord, I would still hope for returning justice to induce them to abandon it without compulsion. I would subscribe to any compromises of the contest, consistent with the rights of sovereignty, the duties of humanity, and principles of reciprocity: but to the right of forcing even her own subjects out of our merchant vessels on the high seas, I can never assent.

A brief review of the opinions regarding impressment expressed in some of the leading newspapers of the day, may help toward a better understanding of public opinion on that subject in the United States. Certain Republican papers, notably the *Philadelphia Aurora,* the *Boston Patriot* and the *Baltimore Whig,* took a thoroughly uncompromising attitude on impressment, agreeing with men like Wright of Maryland, who insisted on a settlement of this question as a condition of any settlement on matters of trade. Duane of the *Aurora,* and the editor of the *Boston Patriot* held that the embargo should never have been given up until impressment was settled.[1] Irvine, the editor of the *Baltimore Whig,* expressed his views in the following language:[2]

We are only sorry that after all our blustering about impressment and free trade, that the acts of Congress permitted the renewal of any communication with England until our seamen should have been restored to their freedom, their country and their friends. Their liberation ought to be the *sine qua non* of trade with Great Britain. I trust no treaty will be concluded, without their previous release and an agreement that the flag shall henceforth protect the seamen; short of these, we ought to be despised, for regarding trade as everything—honor and the blood of our citizens as nothing. Next Congress must act like men. We are still of opinion that no safe treaty can be made with England, but on such terms as will admit of a general peace.

The editor of the Federal *New York Evening Post,* Coleman, maintained that such sentiments from Duane and

[1] Quoted in *New York Evening* Post, April 24, 1809. See April 1808 issues of *Boston Patriot.*

[2] Quoted in *New York Evening Post,* April 24, 1809.

Irvine proved them to be the tools of France, and characterized them as " a pair of cut-throat French hirelings ".[1]

This editor [2] did not expect any settlement to follow the Erskine negotiations in 1809 because he feared the administration would " insist on protecting British seamen on board our merchant vessels " and he was confident Great Britain would never agree to give up the practice of taking them.

During the spring of 1809 a long address by John Adams directed against the King's Proclamation of October 16, 1807, was published in papers of both parties.[3]   In this address Adams aroused opposition among the Federalists by declaring that the royal proclamation " furnished a sufficient ground for a declaration of war ".   He regarded the proclamation as the most pernicious act so far committed against the United States by Great Britain.   To use his own language,

not the murder of Pierce, nor all the murders on board the Chesapeake, nor all the other injuries and insults we have received from foreign nations, atrocious as they have been, can be of such dangerous lasting and pernicious consequence to this country, as this proclamation, if we have servility enough to submit to it.

The command to the officers of the British navy to search neutral merchant ships and impress all British seamen on board without regard to naturalization, certificates of citizenship or contracts was in his opinion a plain violation of the law of nations, and was " a counterfeit foisted into that law, by this arbitrary fraudulent proclamation for the first

[1] April 24, 1809 issue.

[2] April 22, 1809 issue.

[3] This address has already been referred to under the title, *Inadmissible Principles of the King's Proclamation.* See *supra*, ch. i, p. 16, footnote.

time ". No law of England, he declared, could have any
force on the ships of the United States.

Federalist critics of this address claimed that the right to
search for deserters was the same as the right to search for
contraband. To this argument the *Boston Patriot* replied:
" Let us suppose a sailor to be a bar of iron or a cask of
gunpowder, and see if the King's Proclamation will apply—
if press-gangs of ' discreet and orderly conduct ' can get
them." [1]

The *New York Morning Post* claimed to be a non-partisan
paper. While strongly anti-French, this editor was outspoken against impressment, for which he was often denounced by Federalist editors as a " d—— Democrat ".[2]

As an offset to the rising tide of opinion against impressment in 1810, the Federalist papers published numerous
articles that sought to place the British in as good a light as
possible. The August issues of the *New York Evening Post*
carried installments of an article that was typical. The
writer claimed that nineteen-twentieths of all the cases of
impressment took place in the West Indies, and this was
due to the low and unprincipled character of the masters
and captains of vessels in that trade; the most respectable
merchants being engaged in trade with Europe and the East
Indies. He cited cases of American captains in Kingston
and other West Indian ports entering into agreement with
British officers to get their crews impressed in return for all
or part of the wage money due them. On their return these
captains would report that their men were impressed by a
British man-of-war. This writer also asserted that the
British always aided American captains in search of deserters in British ports, and that Great Britain always released Americans as soon as proper proofs were offered.

[1] April 29, 1809 issue.
[2] December, 1810 issues.

During the first half of 1811 the activities of the British in impressing seamen near American coasts seem to have increased greatly. Many instances were so flagrant as to arouse the opposition of the most rabid Federalist papers. This was especially true of the case of one Diggio, who was impressed from the American brig "Spitfire" by the British frigate " Pizzaro ". about eighteen miles off Sandy Hook. All papers agreed on the facts in this case, which were briefly that Diggio was impressed because he did not have a protection, despite his captain's own testimony as to his American character, and this too while he was engaged in coastwise trade. This was more than the *New York Evening Post* could stand even from the British, and that paper condemned the act in most outspoken terms.[1] This and many other instances similar in character furnished the background for the outburst of sentiment over the affair of the " Little Belt ".

Previous to and during the sitting of the twelfth Congress, pro-war editors never lost an opportunity to picture the evil of impressment in its most aggravating and abominable form. The *Aurora,* the *Lexington Reporter,* the *Baltimore American,* the *Albany Register,* and other pro-war journals insisted that impressment was the foulest stain on American character and had been neglected while the attention of the government had been centered on mercenary trade. These editors went so far as to advocate that Congress provide a plan for the holding of British hostages for every American seaman impressed.[2]

They insisted that a firm stand against Great Britain when the first impressments began would have put a stop to the practice, and that neither the " Tories ", the " Federalists ",

[1] May 4, 1811 issue.

[2] See especially Oct., Nov. and Dec. issues of the *Aurora* and the *Albany Register.*

nor the " Democrats " had ever been real friends of the seamen.   The *Lexington Reporter* seems to have taken the lead
in a concerted effort to unite the cause of impressed seamen
with that of the farmers on the western frontiers in their
struggle against the Indians.   After the battle of Tippe-
canoe in November, 1811, the editor of this paper declared
that the blood of the farmers on the Wabash and the blood
of impressed seamen were then equally before Congress.[1]

Niles' Register,[2] claiming to be non-partisan, always
placed impressment at the head of the list of British aggressions against the United States, and advocated war on this
issue alone.   *The National Intelligencer,* which was supposed
to be the Administration paper, did not stress impressment
during 1811 as much as many other Republican papers, but
in the issue of April 9, 1812, that subject was placed first
on the list of grievances against Great Britain.   *The New
York Morning Post,* a paper that opposed war until the declaration, was equally opposed to impressment.   In its issue
of May 5, 1812, this paper gave in full Cobbett's letter to
the Prince Regent, from the *Weekly Register* of February 1,
1812.   This letter urged upon the Prince Regent a change
of policy on impressment in order to avert war with the
United States.   Cobbett felt that the complaints of wives,
parents and children in the United States would soon demand
a war on this subject.

The Federalist papers, on the other hand, urged that impressment had never been and was not at this time a just
cause for war.   They continued to support the doctrine that
expatriation was not permissible, and that Great Britain had
the right to take her own seamen from neutral merchant
vessels.   The fact that, in doing this, she had taken some

[1] Quoted in The *Aurora,* Feb., 17, 1812.
[2] See issues of Nov. 2, 1811; Jan. 4, 1812; April 18, 1812 and June 27,
1812.

American citizens by mistake, was a just cause of complaint, but it was a matter that could be easily adjusted, if the United States would make a real effort to identify its own seamen.[1] Later, during the Foster-Monroe correspondence, the Federalist press asserted that Foster had expressed a willingness to restore all impressed American seamen, and that the further clamorings of the Republican press on this subject were solely for the purpose of arousing war sentiment. These editors often admitted that Great Britain did great injury to the United States by the practice of impressment, but held that since Washington, Adams and Jefferson had not seen fit to go to war on this issue, it did not now constitute a just cause for war. Furthermore, many of them held that in 1806 Great Britain had made a satisfactory offer on the subject, which the United States refused because the government never wanted to settle anything with that nation.[2]

The view of the subject held by John Quincy Adams, previous to the declaration of war, clearly repudiated the Federalist sentiment, yet urged a modification of the warlike attitude of the Republican press. In a letter to William Eustis, dated October 26, 1811, he wrote:[3]

The practice of impressment is the only ineradicable wound, which, if persisted in, can terminate no otherwise than by war; but it seems clearly better to await the effect of our increasing strength and of our adversary's more mature decay, before we undertake to abolish it by war.

For as I have no hesitation in saying that at the proper period I would advise my country to declare a war explicitly and distinctly upon that single point, and never afterwards make peace

[1] *New York Evening Post*, May 22, 1811.

[2] *Trenton Federalist,* June 1, 1812, and May 1812 issues of *Boston Repertory.*

[3] J. Q. Adams to Eustis, Oct. 26, 1811, *Works of J. Q. Adams* (W. C. Ford), vol. iv. p. 262.

without a specific article expressly renouncing forever the principles of impressing from any American vessel, so I should think
it best to wait until the time shall come, and I think it not far
distant, when a declaration to that effect would obtain the article
without needing the war.

There is some reason to believe that this was very close
to the view held by Madison himself at the time of the convening of the twelfth Congress.   His message to that body
November 5, 1811, which was not lacking in warlike sentiment, did not expressly mention impressment among the
long list of grievances pronounced against Great Britain.[1]
In view of the well-known temper of the people on the subject, the absence of it in the President's message may be
explained by his desire and that of his cabinet to tread softly
on that subject in order not further to excite the public
mind.   Such an explanation would be plausible, however,
only on the theory that the executive department hoped, at
this time, to avoid war.

The discussions in Congress over the rights of neutral
trade in wartime had, it is true, for several years over-
shadowed impressment.   The subject had also been in the
background in the diplomatic struggle ever since 1807, but
it is questionable whether impressment was ever relegated
to a secondary position in the public opinion of the nation.
It was impressment that, in the last analysis, gave the greatest impulse to the war sentiment.

Shortly after the " Chesapeake " affair and the King's
Proclamation in 1807, the embargo policy was recommended.[2]   Among those favoring the embargo, it was rep-

[1] *Richardson's Messages and Papers of the Presidents,* vol. i, pp. 491
et seq.   For comment on this point see Henry Adams, *History of the
United States,* vol. vi, p. 125.

[2] For reference to Embargo Act and other restrictive commercial legislation, see *supra,* p. 157, footnote.

resented as a measure that would, by keeping American seamen at home, protect them against the evils of impressment. To those opposing the embargo, that measure instead of keeping seamen at home and thereby saving them from impressment, was regarded as the means of driving them to Europe to seek employment, and thus rendering them ever more liable to impressment.

This contradictory view of the situation prevailed throughout the period of the operation of the embargo, each side making broad assertions as to the truth of its position, but neither offering any substantial evidence in support of those assertions. When in the closing months of 1808, debate on the repeal of the embargo became keen, Federalists like Lloyd and Hillhouse, who argued for its repeal, asserted that instead of protecting seamen it drove them into foreign countries for work, increasing their chances of being impressed. On the other hand, Republicans who favored retaining the embargo, maintained that the real American seamen had found work in the factories and on the farms, and that it was only the foreign seamen who were leaving for Europe.

The debates in 1809 on the Non-intercourse Act, and on the Macon Bill in 1810, revealed the interweaving of impressment with the question of trade and shipping, with the former, which was the oldest outrage, in the background. At times, however, feelings burst forth in the form of violent attacks by Desha, Anderson, Sawyer, Mumford, Johnson, Wright, Rhea and others in the House, who charged that submission to impressment was the cause of the later aggressions of both Britain and France, and charged also that the compromising measures of the administration were dictated by the interests of merchants who were selling the liberty and independence of the nation for gold.

Wright (Md.) urged in the House on February 23, 1811,

that any revocation of the Non-intercourse policy against Great Britain be conditioned in the following manner: " In case Great Britain shall make such an arrangement with the United States relative to the surrender of impressed seamen as shall be satisfactory to the President of the United States." [1] He moved this amendment, declaring that if something was not done, he would bring in a bill for the ransom of impressed seamen, and suggesting that the $7,200,000 held by British subjects in the United States Bank might well be used for that purpose. In his opinion, unless American seamen were released, it was high time for a revolution. His amendment, however, received only sixteen votes.

Again on February 26, 1811, he moved another amendment providing that the restrictions of the Non-intercourse Act be not revoked by the President unless by July 4th, 1811, Great Britain had made a satisfactory arrangement relative to the surrender of impressed seamen. He maintained that the plan to require only the revocation or modification of Great Britain's edicts against our commerce was to regard property as more dear than life or liberty. This time his amendment received 21 votes while 83 voted against it. [2]

It may be fairly said that after the renewal of war in Europe in 1803 the violations of American neutral trade rights assumed such importance in the minds of the majority in Congress, that it did not seem wise to them to single out impressment and make of it a definite issue. In following this course there was probably no conscious abandonment of the rights of sailors, but rather a normal tendency to give attention to those matters which seemed most important because of their relation to the most vocal element of American

[1] *Annals of Congress, Eleventh Congress, Third Session*, 998-999.
[2] *Ibid.*, 1033, 1035.

citizenship. The sailors did not constitute a large political influence. The crimes against them were not forgotten but were merged with other outrages which for the time at least assumed a preeminent place in the legislative thought.

With the convening of Congress in the fall of 1811, there were indications that the subject of impressment would receive independent consideration. The revival of opposition to the evil was plainly revealed in the language of the report of the committee on Foreign Relations in the House, November 29, 1811, and in the debates on that report in December. The position was taken in the report that while it was the duty of the nation to encourage and protect the legitimate commerce of its citizens, the duty to protect sailors was even greater, inasmuch as " life and liberty are more estimable than ships and goods ". Hence the committee deprecated the policy of permitting the pleas of wives, parents and children of impressed seamen to be " drowned in the louder clamors at the loss of property ".[1]

During the debates in the House in December 1811, indictments of Great Britain on this subject were numerous, some estimating the number of those impressed at 50,000. One speaker declared he would rather see "that fast-anchored isle, that protector of the liberties of the world, swept from the catalogue of nations than to submit that one American— one natural born citizen—should at her will be torn from his family, his country, and kept in a state of the most horrible slavery ".

The opinion expressed by Sheffey (Va.), held certainly by most of the Federalist minority, did not regard impressment as a cause for war so long as the United States sought to protect aliens and naturalized citizens on the high seas.[2] It has been seen that the idea of direct and independent

---

[1] *Annals of Congress, Twelfth Congress, First Session,* 375-376.

[2] *Ibid.,* 623 *et seq.*

legislation on behalf of impressed seamen was never entirely
given up by the minority of which Wright of Maryland was
the leader.   As a member of the Senate, he had in 1806
urged unsuccessfully a bill for the protection and indemnification of American seamen.   In the House, in 1810 and
1811, he worked for amendments to the bill, supplementing
the Non-intercourse Act with Great Britain by an agreement on her part to surrender impressed seamen.   He came
forward in the House on December 30, 1811, with a revised form of his bill of 1806 for protection and indemnification of seamen.   This time the proposed measure was entitled " A bill for the protection, recovery and indemnification of American seamen ".   By April 27, 1812, this bill
was engrossed for the third reading.   The bill provided that
after June 4, 1812, impressment of native American seamen
on the high seas or in port be adjudged an act of piracy;
that all persons convicted of the crime should suffer death,
and made it lawful for any seaman to kill any person or
persons attempting to impress him.   It gave the President
power to retaliate for impressment of American seamen by
seizing the subjects of Great Britain either on the high seas
or in British territory.   It provided that impressed American
seamen should receive the sum of thirty dollars a month for
the entire period of their impressment.   They were authorized to attach this sum out of the hands of any debtor of
any British subject, which action should be regarded as
payment to the creditor.   The bill authorized the President
to capture, by way of reprisal, as many British subjects as
there were impressed American seamen in the possession of
Great Britain and by a cartel to exchange the same.   Finally,
it authorized the President to prohibit by proclamation the
landing of vessels or goods of a foreign nation whose commanders impressed American seamen and to prohibit all aid
or provisions to any vessel engaging in that practice.[1]

[1] *Annals of Congress, Twelfth Congress, First Session,* 1343-1345.

In some sections of the country the press was strongly advocating this measure, and it appears that only the more vigorous war measure prevented its passage. It came up for final consideration before the Committee of the Whole on June 1, 1812, and at this time Clay, as speaker, suggested that since the stronger war measure was to come before them, a measure which if passed would supersede Wright's measure, further consideration of it should wait until the stronger measure was disposed of. In case the war measure failed for any cause, Clay agreed to support Wright's bill in principle, saying that some details which to him were objectionable would no doubt then be modified, and its passage be assured. Wright expressed a willingness to wait for the war measure, with the understanding that nothing would supersede his measure, which in his opinion would be a necessity even if war was declared. The actual declaration of war, however, and the events that followed, precluded any further consideration of the plan.[1]

This revival of opposition to the practice of impressment, manifested in the newspapers and in Congress, found expression also in the message of President Madison to Congress, June 1, 1812, which placed that issue first in the list of British aggressions that were so soon to be met by an appeal to arms. On that issue the President said in part:

The practice, hence, is so far from affecting British subjects alone that, under the pretext of searching for these, thousands of American citizens, under the safeguard of public law and of their national flag, have been torn from their country, and from everything dear to them; have been dragged on board ships of war of a foreign nation and exposed, under the severities of their discipline, to be exiled to the most distant and deadly climes, to risk their lives in the battles of their oppressors, and to be the melancholy instruments of taking away those of their own brethren.

[1] *Ibid.*, 1480-1481.

Against this crying enormity, which Great Britain would be so prompt to avenge if committed against herself, the United States have in vain exhausted remonstrances, and expostulations, and that no proof might be wanting of their conciliatory dispositions, and no pretence left for a continuance of the practice, the British Government was formally assured of the readiness of the United States to enter into arrangements such as could not be rejected if the recovery of British subjects were the real, and the sole object. The communication passed without effect.[1]

In response to the President's message, the Committee on Foreign Relations[2] of the House on June 3, 1812, presented a report recommending an immediate appeal to arms. After reviewing the depredations on commerce, this report declared that the impressment of American seamen was a practice which had been unceasingly maintained by Great Britain in the wars to which she had been a party since the Revolution. After reciting at some length the standard objections to that practice, the report declared that its continuance was unjustifiable, because the United States had repeatedly proposed to the British government an arrangement which would secure to it the control of its own people, and insisted that the exemption of the citizens of the United States from this degrading oppression, and their flag from violation was all that the United States demanded.[3]   The act declaring war was passed June 18, 1812, the Federalist minority in both Houses voting against it.[4]

The address to their constituents of the minority opposing

[1] *American State Papers, Foreign Relations*, vol. iii, p. 405.

[2] In the absence of Porter (N. Y.), the chairman of the Committee, Calhoun (S. C.) presented this report.

[3] *Annals of Congress, Twelfth Congress, First Session*, 1550-1551.

[4] For action in House, see *Annals of Congress, Twelfth Congress, First Session*, 1637 *et seq.*; for action in Senate, see *Annals of Congress, Twelfth Congress, First Session*, 297.

the war, signed by the Federalists and a few of Randolph's following from both Houses of Congress, expressed quite clearly the minority position on the subject of impressment as a cause of war. They sympathized with the unfortunate seamen, who were the victims of this abuse of power, but regarded the position of the United States in claiming that the flag of their merchant vessels should protect all mariners, as embodying a very broad and comprehensive principle, which was liable to abuse. The principle was claimed, although every person on board, except the captain, might be an alien. Before going to war for such a principle all means of negotiation should be exhausted, and every practicable effort made to regulate the exercise of the right so that injury to other nations should be checked if not prevented. The principle should not be used to cover the employment of British seamen in American vessels. They urged that the United States should cease employing British seamen in its merchant service. If these steps were taken they believed the question could be settled by treaty, and that it was, therefore, not a proper cause for war.[1]

A somewhat critical view of the action of the administration on the impressment question in relation to the declaration of war is expressed by Henry Adams, who, in what he characterizes as a " Federalist view ", thus summarizes the action of the American government on that issue:[2]

The matter of impressment then, in the Autumn of 1811, began to receive the attention which had never yet been given to it. Hitherto neither Government nor people had thought necessary to make a *casus belli* of impressments. Orders in council and other measures of Great Britain, which affected American prop-

[1] For copy of this document to which thirty-four signatures were attached, see *Annals of Congress, Twelfth Congress, First Session*, 2196 *et seq.*

[2] Henry Adams, *History of the United States*, vol. vi, pp. 116-118.

erty, had been treated as matters of vital consequence, but as late as the close of 1811, neither the President, the Secretary of State, nor Congress had yet insisted that the person of an American citizen was as sacred as his property. Impressments occurred daily. No one knew how many native-born Americans had been taken by force from the protection of the American flag, but whether the number was small or great, neither Republican nor Federalist had ventured to say that the country must at all hazards protect them, or that whatever rules of blockade or contraband the belligerents might adopt against property, they must at least keep their hands off the persons of peaceable Americans, whether afloat or ashore. President Madison had repeated, until the world laughed in his face, that Napoleon no longer enforced his decrees, and that, therefore, if England did not withdraw her blockade, war would result; but he never suggested that America would fight for her sailors. When he and his supporters in earnest took up the grievances of the seamen, they seemed to do so as an afterthought, to make out a cause of war against England, after finding the public unwilling to accept the cause at first suggested. However unjust the suspicion might be, so much truth existed in this Federalist view of Madison's cause as warranted the belief that if England in July, 1811 had yielded to the demand for commercial freedom, the Government would have become deaf to the outcry of the imprisoned seamen. Only by slow degrees, and in the doubtful form of a political maneuver, did this, the worst of all American grievances, take its proper place at the head of the causes for war.

The inaccuracy of this so-called "Federalist view" is obvious. In the first place, the preceding review of certain Republican newspapers is sufficient demonstration that this view was not exclusively a Federalist one. The most essential part of it was, in fact, a distinctive product of the pro-war Republicans, advanced for the purpose of urging on a Republican administration the necessity of war. Furthermore, the outstanding Federalist view, both preceding the war, which has already been shown, and during the struggle, was that impressment was not a sufficient cause of war. Rufus King, a leader of the Federalist party, as late as 1813 gave it as his opinion that the United States should never have gone to war over that issue,[1] and Pickering, another Federalist leader, was outspoken in 1813 in condemning the administration for making war on that issue, even defending the British position, contrary to his own expressed views when he was Secretary of State.[2]

It is true that the United States varied its position from time to time on minor phases of the impressment issue, more especially in the earlier years of the controversy, but the central principle which denied the claims of Great Britain, and refused to accept any settlement that recognized those claims, was consistently adhered to throughout the years. The inability of the government to obtain the recognition of this principle was never regarded as conceding the principle. The struggle against violations of neutral commercial rights had up to 1812 been equally unsuccessful, but the American government, on that account, did not for a moment yield those rights.[3]

[1] *Life and Correspondence of Rufus King* (Charles R. King), vol. v, appendix iii, pp. 544-547.

[2] *Pickering Papers*, vol. l, pp. 237-240; vol. lii, pp. 273-274 and vol. lv, pp. 307 *et seq.*

[3] For a brief but excellent exposition of the impressment issue see A. T. Mahan, *Sea Power in its Relations to the War of 1812* (Boston, Little, Brown and Company, 1905), vol. i, pp. 116-133.

CHAPTER VIII

THE PROBLEM OF IMPRESSMENT DURING THE WAR OF 1812

DISAPPOINTED by continued failure to adjust the difficulties between the United States and Great Britain, William Pinkney had, in the spring of 1811, returned to the United States, leaving the affairs of the American government in London in the hands of a *chargé d'affaires*. Unfortunately this situation, which rendered any settlement by diplomatic negotiations difficult, if not impossible, continued until the declaration of war, at which time Jonathan Russell was in charge of the American Embassy in London. Even after the declaration of war the American government cherished the belief that Great Britain would prefer a settlement of the differences between the two nations rather than enter into war against the United States. Acting on this belief, almost immediately after the declaration of war, Russell was authorized [1] to arrange an armistice if the orders in council, other blockades and impressment could be adjusted. As an inducement to the British government to discontinue the practice of impressment from American vessels, he was authorized to give assurance that a law would be passed (to be reciprocal) to prohibit the employment of British seamen in the public or commercial service of the United States. It had been almost exactly five years since a proposal of this character had first emanated from the American government.

[1] Monroe to Russell, June 26, 1812, *American State Papers, Foreign Relations*, vol. iii, pp. 585-586.

[2] See *supra*, p. 129.

A month later,[1] Monroe explained to Russell that the stipulation to prohibit by law the employment of British seamen in the service of the United States must depend on Congress, which body, it might reasonably be presumed, would give effect to it. He also stated that it was not necessary that the several points be especially provided for in the convention arranging the armistice, but that a clear and distinct understanding with the British government on the subject of impressment comprising in it the discharge of the men already impressed, and on future blockades, if the orders in council were revoked, would be all that was indispensable. It was to be stipulated in the armistice that commissioners be appointed to form a treaty which should provide by reciprocal arrangements for the prevention of the seamen of either nation from being taken or employed in the service of the other, for the regulation of commerce and for the adjustment of all other questions.

In accordance with these instructions, Russell on August 24, 1812,[2] presented to Lord Castlereagh the plan for an armistice contained in Monroe's letter to him dated June 26, along with favorable comments upon it. Castlereagh, however,[3] refused to discuss the proposal on the alleged ground that Russell did not have adequate power to negotiate. He expressed surprise that as a condition preliminary to a suspension of hostilities, the government of the United States should demand that the British government " desist from its ancient and accustomed practice of impressing British seamen from the merchant ships

---

[1] Monroe to Russell, July 27, 1812, *American State Papers, Foreign Relations,* vol. iii, p. 586.

[2] Russell to Castlereagh, August 24, 1812, *ibid.,* p. 589.

[3] Castlereagh to Russell, August 29, 1812, *ibid.,* pp. 589-590.

of a foreign state, simply on the assurance that a law shall hereafter be passed, to prohibit the employment of British seamen in the public or commercial service of that state." In accordance with precedent, he gave assurance that the British government was ready to receive from the government of the United States, and to discuss, any proposition designed either to check abuse in the exercise of the practice of impressment, or to accomplish in a more satisfactory manner the object for which impressment had hitherto been found necessary. His government could not consent, however, to suspend the exercise of the right of impressment until fully convinced that means could be devised, and would be adopted, by which the service of British seamen in the British navy would be effectively secured.

After the receipt of Monroe's letter of July 27th, and also after all his goods were aboard the " Lark " waiting to take him back to the United States, Russell presented [1] the modified plan for an armistice contained in Monroe's letter of July 27, which proposed that hostilities be suspended on condition that each party appoint commissioners with full power to form a treaty which should " provide by reciprocal arrangements for the security of their seamen from being taken or employed in the service of the other power, for the regulation of their commerce, and all other interesting questions now depending between them." Russell stated it as his conviction that such an arrangement would be more than an equivalent for any advantage Great Britain derived from impressment.

Castlereagh replied [2] that the proposal of September 12 was the same as that of August 24, only more " covert "

---

[1] Russell to Castlereagh, Sept. 12, 1812, *American State Papers, Foreign Relations*, vol. iii, p. 591.

[2] Castlereagh to Russell, Sept. 18, 1812, *ibid.*, p. 592.

and "disguised" and hence all the more "inadmissible." On the subject of impressment, he asserted that Russell was not authorized to propose any specific plan, with reference to which the suspension of that practice could be made a subject of deliberation, and had no instructions for the guidance of his conduct on some of the leading principles which such a discussion must involve. Russell's instructions on the subject of impressment were, in Castlereagh's opinion, altogether inadequate. On the contrary, Russell maintained that the proposals of August 24 and September 12 were different, in that, by the former the discontinuance of the practice of impressment was to be immediate, and to precede the prohibitory law of the United States relative to the employment of British seamen; whereas by the latter, both these measures were to take effect simultaneously at a later date. He also insisted that his instructions were adequate.

In his letter to Monroe, September 17, 1812,[1] Russell gave a full account of a private interview which he had with Castlereagh on September 12. In that interview, according to Russell, Castlereagh took the position that there had evidently been some misapprehension on the subject of impressment, and an erroneous belief entertained by the American government that an arrangement in regard to that subject had been nearer an accomplishment than the facts warranted. This error he thought had probably originated with King, who because he was so well received by the British government, misconstrued their "professions of a disposition to remove the complaints of America, in relation to impressments, into a supposed conviction, on their part, of the propriety of adopting the plan which he had proposed."

The difficulty of any settlement, Castlereagh maintained,

---

[1] Russell to Monroe, Sept. 17, 1812, *American State Papers, Foreign Relations*, vol. iii, pp. 593-595.

was especially seen in the negotiations of Monroe and Pinkney with Lords Auckland and Holland.   On that occasion
Lords Auckland and Holland were committed to a policy
that required them to do everything in their power for the
satisfaction of America relative to impressment, yet all their
labors were in vain.   If such was the result of a negotiation
carried on under circumstances so highly favorable, he saw
no reasonable ground for the expectation that anything in
the way of a satisfactory arrangement could be reached by
him and Russell.   He informed Russell that neither he nor
the American government were aware of the great sensibility and jealousy of the people of England on this subject
and that no administration could expect to remain in power
that should " consent to renounce the right of impressment,
or to suspend the practice, without the certainty of an arrangement which should obviously be calculated most unequivocally to secure its object."   He was doubtful if such
an arrangement were possible under any circumstances, and
was quite sure that Russell had no sufficient powers for its
accomplishment.

Russell finally suggested that the proposed arrangement
should be expressed in the most general terms, and that the
law to be passed after the discontinuance of the practice of
impressment

should prohibit the employment of the native subjects or citizens
of the one state, excepting such only as had already been naturalized, on board the private or public ships of the other; thus
removing any objections that might have been raised with regard to the future effect of naturalization, or the formal renunciation of any pretended right.

This proposition was not well received and Russell, upon
being asked if the United States would deliver up the native
British seamen who might be naturalized in America, re-

plied that such a procedure would be disgraceful to America without being useful to Great Britain, but that a reciprocal arrangement might be made for giving up deserters from public vessels.

Russell apologized to Monroe for having offered to exclude from American vessels British subjects who might later become citizens of the United States, saying, however, that in his opinion such an offer did not trespass against the spirit of his instructions, and that if the proposition had been accepted, he should not have been without hope that it might have been approved by the President, "as its prospective operation would have prevented injustice, and its reciprocity disgrace." In any event, he felt that the proposition afforded an opportunity of testing the disposition of the British government. Its refusal was, in his judgment, ample proof that the British government did not desire any settlement of the question.

At this point it should be stated that on June 23, 1812, the British government had conditionally revoked its orders in council in so far as they applied to the neutral commerce of the United States, on account of pressure from British manufacturers, to whom those orders were bringing disaster. Accordingly the orders were revoked before news of the American declaration of war had reached England. The British government felt that when a knowledge of their revocation reached Washington, the United States government would in all probability recall its declaration of war. To meet this situation, Admiral Warren, who commanded the British fleet in American waters, was authorized by the British government to offer terms of an armistice. He proposed an armistice to Monroe on September 30, 1812,[1] an offer which proved unacceptable to the American gov-

---

[1] Admiral Warren to Monroe, Sept. 30, 1812, *American State Papers, Foreign Relations*, vol. iii, pp. 595-596.

ernment because it contained no arrangement on impressment.[1] Monroe, in writing to Warren, October 27, 1812,[2]
expressed regret that the proposition made by Russell to the
British government in regard to impressment had been rejected, adding that " no peace can be durable unless this
object is provided for."

The United States, he stated, was willing to prohibit the
employment of British subjects in their service, and to enforce the prohibition by suitable regulations and penalties,
and " it cannot be conceived on what ground the arrangement can be refused."

But the suspension of the practice of impressment, pending an armistice, was regarded as necessary to the success
of the negotiations.

If [wrote Monroe] the British government is willing to suspend the practice of impressment from American vessels, on
consideration that the United States will exclude British seamen
from their service, the regulations by which this compromise
should be carried into effect would be solely the object of
negotiation. The armistice would be of short duration; if the
parties agreed, peace would be the result, if the negotiations
failed, each would be restored to its former state and to all its
pretensions by recurring to war.

Monroe concluded this long communication by saying that
if there were no objection to an accomodation of the impressment issue in the mode proposed, other than the suspension of the British claim to impressment during the
armistice, there would be no need of an armistice, but that
discussions and the arrangement of an article on impress-

[1] Another proposal for an armistice of the same character as that made
by Admiral Warren, offered by Sir George Prevost, Commander-in-
chief of the British forces in America, was also rejected, and for the
same reason.

[2] Monroe to Admiral Warren, Oct. 27, 1812, *American State Papers,
Foreign Relations*, vol. iii, pp. 596-597.

ment could be entered into at once. If this great question could be satisfactorily adjusted, the way would then be open for an armistice or any other course leading to a general pacification.

By this statement of the American position, the issue of impressment was in fact made by the American government the sole reason for continuing the war. Had the British government desired peace, even at this late date, the way was left open provided this one obstacle could be removed. Great Britain being unwilling to remove this obstacle, the negotiations ended, and the war continued.

This review of the diplomatic situation that arose immediately after the declaration of war, is an aid to the study of the next important step taken by Congress on this subject. After the publication of the conditional repeal of the orders in council, the American government was essentially left in the position of waging war on the sole issue of impressment. This had not, however, been the only issue leading to the war, although it contained all the elements of sentiment calculated to arouse the popular war spirit, and without this issue it is probable that the nation would not have given even the measure of support which it did to the war. In view of the fact that this issue had been supplying a great stimulus to war, to which the majority in the twelfth Congress was committed, the refusal of that body to enter into a reconsideration of it previous to the declaration of war is not difficult to understand. War being declared, however, and the orders in council having been recalled, it then devolved on the Executive first to outline more clearly the American position on impressment.

As has been seen, this actual posture of affairs was anticipated by the Executive, and in the letter that conveyed the declaration of war to Russell, Monroe, in the hope of an armistice, authorized him to give assurance to the British government that in the event of the orders in council and blockades being repealed, a law (to be reciprocal) would be passed to prohibit the employment of British seamen in the public or private vessels of the United States, if Great Britain would agree to discontinue impressment. He later qualified this assurance by pointing out that such a law would of course depend on Congress. This plan for an armistice failed, but there was in the language of Castlereagh a suggestion that if there had been on the statute books a law embodying the above principle, the plan might not have failed.

The subsequent diplomatic impasse on impressment constituted a genuine reason for a full reconsideration by Congress of its attitude on the subject of impressment. To both of the above causes should also probably be added the unfavorable events of the first months of the war. It is worth while to note that the action taken by Congress was exactly in line with the position suggested by the Executive. The idea of excluding British seamen from American ships had been suggested years before by the Executive Department, but it was a measure that required congressional action, and at no time previous to this had it ever been carefully considered by that body. Macon, and some of the Federalists, had suggested it, but there had been no disposition among the majority to treat it seriously.

On January 29, 1813, Grundy (Tenn.), Chairman of the Committee on Foreign Relations in the House, to which had been submitted that part of the President's message relating to foreign affairs, presented a report in which the subject of impressment was considered not only as one of the leading causes of the war, but as the sole issue preventing an armistice after the declaration of war. The report held that the war must be continued until the evil was removed; that such removal must constitute a part of any peace settlement, and that the omission of it in a treaty of peace would in effect be the same as an absolute relinquishment of the principle, against which the feelings of every American would revolt. If possible, the evil was painted in darker pictures than ever before, as degrading to the nation, incompatible with the sovereignty of the United States and subversive of the main pillars of American independence. This was the language of a war Congress. It was probably at this time the opinion of the Executive and of the vast majority of the nation, but it was by no means the final word on the subject.

The report closed by recommending the passage of an act making it unlawful after the termination of the war to employ on board the public or private vessels of the United States any person or persons except citizens of the United States or persons of color, natives of the United States, and also making it unlawful to employ naturalized seamen unless they could show a copy of the act whereby they had been naturalized. The act was, however, to apply only to those nations that prohibited the employment of American seamen in their ships.[1]

Grundy, who was Chairman of the Committee reporting the bill, opened the debate February 3, 1813. The proposed measure was meant to be a permanent law, he said, which would insure a livelihood to all native American seamen by eliminating the competition of foreigners. Furthermore, he argued, by means of it the nation, in times of war, would not be dependent on foreigners, but would have its ships in the hands of purely American seamen. In his opinion, the bill would have a good effect on the relations of the United States with foreign nations by demonstrating that the American government claimed nothing beyond its indis-

[1] For report of committee and text of bill see *Annals of Congress, Twelfth Congress, Second Session*, 932-940.

putable rights.   It would also give assurance to all Americans that their nation was carrying on the war only for its essential rights, and thus unite the country.   The Federalists, he said, had long been demanding such a law, so why not give it to them?   Grundy's chief reason for urging the bill seemed to be his desire to test the sincerity of British diplomacy.   As a matter of fact, he did not think it would bring peace, but rather that it would be ignored by Great Britain, thus embarrassing the Federalists and perhaps forcing them to a more hearty support of the war.

Wright (Md.) opposed the bill, first on the ground that in respect to naturalization it violated the Constitution, and secondly because he regarded it as an attempt to wrest the treaty-making power from the Executive.   Seybert (Pa.) also strongly opposed the bill, holding that Great Britain had not yet redressed former wrongs, in that American seamen were not yet restored, there being at least 15,000 of them still on board British ships of war.   The time for such action as this bill called for, he insisted, was at the end of the war, when its terms could be incorporated into the treaty of peace.   America had gone to war, placing impressment first in the list of causes, and that should be the final attitude until the war ended.   Since Britain had repeatedly refused to consider this idea when suggested in the diplomatic negotiations, he saw no good reason for incorporating it into a law.   Other Republicans also insisted that the passage of the bill would be truckling to Great Britain with a fourth offer, after she had refused to consider three previous diplomatic offers of a similar nature.   If such a law were necessary, they asked, why was it not thought of years ago?

Among those favoring the bill, there were some who, though they regarded it as yielding the principle of impressment to a certain degree, thought that it would prove to the world that the nation was not fighting merely to gain a few seamen. Those holding this view suggested that in permitting the employment of a few hundred seamen, to whom protection could not properly be extended, the United States had probably jeopardized thousands of native citizens, who were dragging out their lives in a slavery which to a freeborn mind was most detestable. Some went so far as to say that war would have been unnecessary had such a law been passed at an earlier date. It was thought that the bill would not endanger the supply of seamen, since from 1796 to 1812 only 1530 foreigners, naturalized in the United States, had registered as seamen.

Quincy (Mass.), for the Federalists, declared that he had always favored exclusion of British seamen, but had never before heard of total exclusion of foreign seamen. He accused the Republicans of having completely reversed their attitude on this question, and asked what would become of their famous doctrine of expatriation if this measure passed?

Two important amendments offered were lost, one by Wright to the effect that if any naturalized seaman was impressed after the passage of the bill, the President be authorized to seize any seaman from the nation impressing and hold him on an armed vessel of the United States until the return of the impressed seaman; and another, offered by Pitkin (Conn.), requiring that after the war three-fourths of all seamen on American vessels be native-born or naturalized, while during the war the United States should employ neither British nor French seamen, and that vessels not complying with these regulations be denied the privileges of United States' ships.

The vote in the bill was eighty-nine for and thirty-three against.[1] On February 25, 1813, this bill was postponed indefinitely in the Senate by a vote of fourteen to thirteen;

[1] For debate on the bill see *Annals of Congress, Twelfth Congress, Second Session*, 960-1055.

nevertheless, the next day Pope (Ky.) moved to reconsider
and his motion was agreed to. Later a motion by Lloyd
(Mass.) for indefinite postponement was lost fifteen to
seventeen, and on the same day, February 26, 1813, the bill
passed the Senate nineteen to thirteen, a complete reversal
of the stand previously taken.[1]

The act was entitled, " An act for the regulation of seamen on board the public and private vessels of the United
States." It provided that after the war it should be unlawful to employ on board any of the public or private
vessels of the United States, any person or persons except citizens of the United States, or persons of color,
natives of the United States. It should also be unlawful
to employ naturalized citizens unless they could produce a
certified copy of the act by which they were naturalized,
giving facts concerning their naturalization. Furthermore,
no seaman should be employed on board private vessels
bound for foreign ports unless his name appeared in the
crew list approved by the collector of the district from
which the vessel sailed. The act also provided that no foreign seamen should be admitted into a public or private
vessel of the United States in a foreign port without permission in writing from the proper officers of the country
of which such a seaman was a subject or citizen. For
violation of the act a fine of one thousand dollars was to be
imposed on commanders of public vessels and a fine of five
hundred dollars on commanders of private vessels.

The provisions of the act were not to apply to the employment of the seamen of any foreign nation which did not
by treaty or special convention with the United States prohibit, on board its public and private vessels, the employment
of native citizens of the United States, who had not been
naturalized by such a nation. Furthermore, the act was not

[1] *Annals of Congress, Twelfth Congress, Second Session,* 108.

to be construed as preventing any arrangement between the United States and any foreign nation which might take place under any treaty or convention made and ratified in accordance with the Constitution of the United States. Finally, it was made a felony falsely to make, counterfeit or forge any certificate or evidence of citizenship referred to in the act, or to pass, sell or use the same, and the penalty for violation of this portion of the act was three to five years' imprisonment or a fine of from five hundred to one thousand dollars.[1]   Since the act was not to go into effect until the end of the war, and then to apply only to those nations which by treaty would agree to exclude native American seamen from their public and private vessels, it produced no immediate change in the relation of the United States to other powers, and in particular none with Great Britain. It was thought, however, that it would at least strengthen the position of the American government in the negotiations on impressment at the conclusion of the war, but later events proved that even this hope was without just foundation.   It is also doubtful whether the act added materially to the support of the war in the United States, a claim urged in favor of its passage by many supporters.

Within a few days after the passage of this act, the Department of State, on March 7, 1813, received word from John Quincy Adams, the American Minister to Russia, that the Emperor of Russia had offered his mediation in promoting peace between the United States and Great Britain.[2] The government of the United States, March 11, 1813,[3] accepted the offer and the President appointed John Quincy

[1] For text of the act see *United States Statutes at Large*, vol. ii, pp. 809-811.

[2] Adams to Monroe, September 30, 1812 and October 17, 1812, *American State Papers, Foreign Relations*, vol. iii, pp. 625-626.

[3] Monroe to Daschkoff, Russian Minister at Washington, March 11, 1813, *ibid.*, pp. 624-625.

Adams, Albert Gallatin [1] and James Bayard, American plenipotentiaries to meet representatives of Great Britain at St. Petersburg to conduct the contemplated negotiations. Instructions which were prepared at the Department of State under date of April 13, 1813, were devoted chiefly to the subject of impressment.[2] According to these instructions, an agreement on this subject was preferred whereby each nation would exclude from its service the seamen of the other, by restraints to be imposed on the naturalization of seamen, excluding at the same time all seamen not naturalized. If this agreement could not be obtained, the representatives of the United States were instructed to agree to the exclusion from its service by each nation of the natives of the other, and the complete prohibition of naturalization of each others' seamen. Whichever rule was adopted should be made reciprocal; that is, if Great Britain naturalized American seamen, America should naturalize British seamen, and if America excluded all native British subjects, Great Britain should exclude all native American citizens.

The instructions were clear on the point that the first course, viz., restraints on naturalization, was preferred by the President, but that in order to secure the United States against impressment he was willing to adopt either. In any event, clear and distinct provision must be made against that practice. As a necessary incident to an adjustment, it was held that all impressed seamen must be returned and all those naturalized under British laws by compulsory service should be allowed to withdraw. The real principle to be gained, Monroe said, was " that our flag shall protect the

---

[1] Gallatin's appointment failed to receive the approval of the Senate on the ground that he could not act in that capacity while also holding the office of Secretary of the Treasury. Gallatin, however, had previously sailed for Europe and did not receive notice of the Senate's refusal to confirm his appointment for several months.

[2] *American State Papers, Foreign Relations*, vol. iii, pp. 695-700.

crew " and if this were agreed to the United States government would secure Great Britain against the employment of her seamen in the service of the United States. No repugnance was felt toward the plan to exclude British seamen from American vessels, because it was thought that the supply of American seamen would be adequate. An article for the reciprocal delivery of deserters, such as had been authorized heretofore, might also be agreed upon. The agreement, if reached, was to continue in force only for the duration of the European War.

In addition to setting forth in the instructions the above plan for a settlement, Monroe also recapitulated the leading American arguments against impressment. While we are already familiar with all of these arguments, it may be well simply to enumerate them at this point. They were, (1) That the practice was repugnant to the law of nations; (2) That it was not supported in any treaty; (3) That it had never been acquiesced in by any nation, and that the United States, in submitting to it, would abandon all claim to neutral rights and to all other rights on the high seas; (4) That it was not founded on a belligerent right; (5) That the claim could not arise from the fact of allegiance due by British subjects to their sovereign, and his right to their service, as the Prince Regent claimed [1] because allegiance was a political relation between a sovereign and his people and not binding beyond the dominions of the sovereign. The sovereign might have a right to claim the service of the subject, but he could not enforce that right in the territory of another nation, without the latter's consent; (6) That every nation had exclusive jurisdiction over its vessels; its law governed in them, and its flag protected everything sailing under it in time of peace, and everything

---

[1] "Declaration of Prince Regent," January 9, 1813, *Annual Register* (1813), p. 330.

in time of war except contraband, enemy-goods and persons
in the military service of the enemy.

The Prince Regent, in the declaration of January 9, 1813,[1]
had expressed his willingness to permit the United States
to take American seamen from British vessels, and on this
point Monroe also thought it advisable to comment. He
declared the proposal unfair, because it was well known that
such a practice was repugnant to the Constitution of the
United States. Hence for the British government to offer
to reciprocate on this matter was to offer nothing. Furthermore, Monroe held that even if the Constitution allowed the
practice, any attempt at its execution would place the United
States at the mercy of Great Britain's superior navy, whose
ships outnumbered those of the American navy by a ratio
of at least thirty to one. Why, he asked, should Great
Britain wait until the war to make such an offer for the
first time? If Great Britain had originally complained that
American employment of her seamen was injurious to her
and had proposed a reasonable remedy, which had been refused, then, argued Monroe, her acts of impressment might
have a little better foundation. But Monroe pointed out
that as a matter of fact Great Britain never made such a
complaint except in defense of the practice of impressment.

The prominent place given in these instructions to the
subject of impressment reflects the importance which was
attached to that subject both by the government and by the
people of the United States. It also indicates the belief
then held that impressment would be the dominant subject
in the negotiations for peace. But eighteen months passed
from the date of the preparation of these first instructions
until the actual commencement of negotiations at Ghent,
and during this time significant events transpired both in
Europe and in the United States, the effect of which was to

[1] *Ibid.*, and Lawrence, *Visitation and Search*, p. 13.

modify greatly these original instructions of the Secretary of State on the subject of impressment.

Not the least important of these events was the refusal of Great Britain to accept the mediation offered by the Russian Emperor. Knowledge of this refusal was first obtained by the American government in a despatch from John Quincy Adams, dated June 26, 1813.[1] The refusal of Great Britain was not finally communicated to the Russian government until September 1, 1813, and on account of an estrangement between the Emperor and Count Romanzoff, the Russian Minister of Foreign Affairs, the information did not become officially known to the American plenipotentiaries until February, 1814.[2] By this time, Gallatin and Bayard, who had reached St. Petersburg in July, 1813, having become very much exasperated by the delay, had, in fact, two weeks before left that city and proceeded to London. During their six months' stay in St. Petersburg, the American Commissioners, acting on the belief that they were preparing for negotiations under the mediation of the Russian Emperor, had prepared, at the request of the Russian Chancellor, an informal note addressed to Emperor Alexander on the question of impressment. Great Britain had given as a reason for refusing mediation the pretensions of the American government concerning impressment, and the Russian government not being familiar with the history of that issue had asked for the explanation. This note, dated August 14, 1813,[3] contained a proposal on impressment to the effect that each nation should engage that in time of war it would not employ on the high seas on board its vessels,

[1] Adams to Monroe, June 26, 1813, *American State Papers, Foreign Relations,* vol. iii, p. 627.

[2] Updyke, *Diplomacy of War of 1812,* pp. 163-164.

[3] *Writings of Gallatin* (Adams), vol. i, pp. 552-562.

any seaman not being its own citizen or subject, and being
a citizen or subject of the other, who should not have been
for two years constantly and voluntarily in its service or
within its jurisdiction.   During the continuance of such an
agreement, the practice of impressment on the high seas was
to be abandoned.   The opinion was expressed that this plan,
(which was essentially the same as the final proposal made
by Monroe and Pinkney in 1807) might have succeeded at
that earlier date had not the British refused to consider it
on the ground of the President's rejection of the treaty, and
that it might later have been adopted had not the " Chesapeake " and orders in council rendered any negotiation on
impressment impossible.

In this connection the importance of the Seamen's Act of
1813 was explained, and numerous reasons were given for
believing that negotiations on this subject would now be
successful. Chief among these reasons were, first, that
England had never refused to negotiate on the principle now
proposed, and had never rejected such a proposal; secondly,
that Russell's plan was rejected because it was made a preliminary condition of an armistice; thirdly, that the law of
March 3, 1813 (The Seamen's Act) indicated the willingness of the United States to exclude British seamen from
American vessels, and that this law could be modified, if
necessary, to conform to any treaty which could be agreed
upon, and finally, that the question of abstract right was
not to be discussed. The American Commissioners said
they were willing to insert in the treaty that the arrangement was purely conventional without effecting in any way
the respective rights of the two nations; the treaty to be
binding on Great Britain only so long as the United States
fulfilled her part of the conditions.

In the original instructions to the American Commissioners, a provision against impressment was made a condition

sine qua non, and the belief that Great Britain would not likely revive the claim after the war in Europe ended, prompted the American government at that time to give the Commissioners power to enter into an agreement on that subject which would terminate with the existing European struggle. The plan presented in the note of August 14, to the Emperor, provided that there should be no discussion of the question of abstract right, and only the suspension by Great Britain of the practice on the high seas in time of war. The arrangement was to be purely conventional and was to be binding on Great Britain only so long as the United States fulfilled her part of the conditions, which was to exclude British seamen from American vessels.

The formulation of this particular plan was chiefly the work of Gallatin, but it had the hearty approval of Bayard. The history of its origin and development will be briefly outlined. Shortly after the appointment of the American Commissioners, Bayard had expressed the opinion that an informal understanding on impressments was all that was desired.[1]

Monroe, in response to this attitude, agreed that the question of abstract right might be omitted from the treaty if only the practice were yielded for a fixed term of years,[2] agreeing also that the Commissioners should exercise " entire discretion " as to the " mode and shape of the provision " for the discontinuance of the practice. He was distinctly not in favor, at this time, of any treaty of peace that was silent on the subject which had essentially been the cause of the war, and " trusting to a mere understanding liable to doubts and different explanations." Monroe also informed

[1] Gallatin to Monroe, May 2, 1813, *Writings of Gallatin* (Adams), vol. i, pp. 539-540.

[2] Monroe to Gallatin, May 5, 1813, *ibid.*, p. 540.

Gallatin [1] that if there could not be obtained a clause in the
treaty providing for " the forbearance of the British practice, in consideration of the exclusion of British seamen
from our service " then it would be " infinitely better that
nothing should be done." With a definite slant at the
political outlook, Monroe added that a treaty without such
a clause " would not only ruin the present administration,
but the Republican party, and even the cause."

With this position, Gallatin at this time expressed [2] entire agreement, saying that Bayard alone held the view that
an informal agreement was sufficient, but that he (Bayard)
would work earnestly for a plan agreeing with their instructions.

Gallatin and Bayard sailed from the United States on
May 9, 1813. Soon after his arrival in Europe, Gallatin
entered into correspondence with numerous acquaintances
in the various countries in order to acquire the best possible
information regarding the questions likely to come before
the peace conference. While at Gottenburg, he wrote on
June 22, 1813,[3] to the Baring Brothers, in London, on whom
the American Commissioners were authorized to draw for
salaries and expenses, asking for any " intelligence connected
with our mission which you may deem important and which
you may feel at liberty to communicate." The full and
frank reply of Alexander Baring, July 22, 1813,[4] contained
important information on the subject of impressment. This
distinguished gentleman, friendly toward the United States,
stated that in his opinion it was utterly useless for the

[1] Monroe to Gallatin, May 6, 1813, *Writings of Gallatin* (Adams),
vol. i, pp.. 542-543.

[2] Gallatin to Monroe, May 8, 1813, *ibid.*, p. 544.

[3] Gallatin to Baring Brothers, June 22, 1813, *ibid.*, p. 545.

[4] Alexander Baring to Gallatin, July 22, 1813, *ibid.*, pp. 546-552.

American Commissioners to raise the question of abstract right in regard to impressment, since with Great Britain the practice was regarded as necessary to the existence of the navy. He continued by saying that if the United States was determined "to give us no better security than the act of Congress lately passed, I should certainly think your coming here or negotiating anywhere useless for any government purpose."

In conveying this information to Monroe, Gallatin expressed himself as confident that it contained an indirect communication of the views of the British government.[1] Before the receipt of the communication from Baring, Gallatin, convinced that Great Britain was determined not to yield her claims to the alleged right of impressment, and knowing that his own government would never submit to a treaty acknowledging that right, had formulated the plan embodied in the note to the Emperor of August 14, 1813. A letter to the Emperor almost a year later [2] indicated Gallatin's continued adherence to this plan. In this communication, he stated that if the United States should concede to Great Britain the right of visit and search in time of war for any purpose other than those of seizing enemy goods, or goods considered as contraband destined to her enemy, or persons in the service of her enemy, "there would no longer be any acknowledged line of demarcation which should prevent her from exercising an unlimited jurisdiction over the vessels of all other nations." After stating his proposal that Great Britain, without renouncing impressment, should agree to suspend the practice so long as America fulfilled her engagement not to employ British seamen,

---

[1] Gallatin to Monroe, August 28, 1813, *Writings of Gallatin* (Adams), vol. i, p. 568.

[2] Gallatin to Emperor Alexander, June 19, 1814, *ibid.*, pp. 629-631.

Gallatin, anticipating the possible refusal of even this limited agreement, added:

Should the proposal of the United States be rejected, the only apparent means to make peace is a postponement of the discussion of the subject to a more favorable time. Maritime questions seem to fall with the war, and it is above all desirable that the whole civilized world may breathe, and, without any exception, enjoy universal peace.

In this statement of Gallatin there is foreshadowed the exact outcome of the impressment negotiations. Gallatin wrote to Baring August 27, 1813, saying that he had no hope that either nation would abandon its rights or pretensions.[1] In another letter from Alexander Baring October 12, 1813,[2] Gallatin was frankly told that the British gvernment wanted peace, because the war was expensive and had no real object. In this communication also there occurs a statement concerning impressment, which is referred to as the " only question really at issue." Baring added that while the British government would never yield the right or at least the practice, it would not demand from the United States a recognition of the right.

After the refusal of the British government to accept the mediation of the Emperor of Russia, and while the American Commissioners were delayed at St. Petersburg, the British government offered a plan for direct negotiation with the United States,

for the conciliatory adjustment of the differences subsisting between the two states, with an earnest desire on their part to bring them to a favorable issue, upon principles of perfect

[1] Gallatin to Alexander Baring, August 27, 1813, *Writings of Gallatin* (Adams), vol. i, p. 567.

[2] Alexander Baring to Gallatin, October 12, 1813, *ibid.*, pp. 584-587.

reciprocity, not inconsistent with the established maxims of public law, and with the maritime rights of the British Empire.[1]

There was in this last sentence a strong hint of the unyielding attitude of Great Britain on the impressment issue. Nevertheless, the offer was accepted, and the President appointed John Quincy Adams, James Bayard, Henry Clay and Jonathan Russell to conduct the negotiations for the United States. Albert Gallatin was added later to the mission, when it became known that he was still in Europe.

Monroe informed the plenipotentiaries January 28, 1814,[2] that they were to deal with the question of impressment in accordance with the instructions issued April 15, 1813; except that American seamen were not only to be released as provided in those instructions, but also to be paid by the British government, wages they might have made in their own country for the time they had been impressed. The position was strongly maintained that " this degrading practice must cease; our flag must protect the crew, or the United States cannot consider themselves an independent nation." In the original manuscript of this letter there are several passages which are omitted from the printed forms. One of these contains the statement of the conviction of the American government that Great Britain refused mediation because of her fear that her position on impressment would not be viewed with approval by Russia.[3] Less than a month later [4]

[1] Castlereagh to Secretary of State, November 4, 1813, *American State Papers, Foreign Relations*, vol. iii, p. 621.

[2] Monroe to the American Plenipotentiaries, Jan. 28, 1814, *ibid.*, pp. 701-702.

[3] Monroe to American Plenipotentiaries, January 28, 1814; *MS. Bureau of Indexes and Archives, Unclassified Instructions to United States Ministers*, vol. viii. Quoted in Updyke, *Diplomacy of the War of 1812*, p. 181.

[4] Monroe to American Plenipotentiaries, February 14, 1814, *American State Papers, Foreign Relations*, vol. iii, p. 703.

and because of the expectation of peace in Europe, Monroe, writing to the American plenipotentiaries, stated that if peace were soon made in Europe the practical evil in regard to impressment would cease and the British government would probably have less objection to a stipulation against the practice for a specified term of years, than if war should continue. He therefore offered this modification of the earlier instructions, which provided for an agreement that was to continue only for the duration of the European War. Up to this time it is evident that the American government had not accepted Gallatin's view of this subject. Later on, however, in the summer of 1814,[1] after the news of the general pacification in Europe had reached the United States, the government substantially accepted the position of Gallatin, and Monroe instructed the American plenipotentiaries to agree to the omission of an article on impressment from the treaty of peace, in case Great Britain would not grant one, but to arrange for special later negotiations on impressment and commerce, reserving all American rights in the meantime.

The advent of peace in Europe changed radically the views of the American government on impressment. It was expected that the practice would be relaxed, and it was also clear that Great Britain would be able more effectively to prosecute the war against the United States when released from war in Europe. This change of view was justified by Monroe on the ground that the United States, having resisted by war the practice of impressment, and having continued the war until that practice had ceased by a peace in Europe, had essentially obtained their object for the present. If, he stated, the subject were not properly settled later and war should come to Europe again, the United

---

[1] Monroe to American Plenipotentiaries, June 25, 1814, *American State Papers, Foreign Relations*, vol. iii, pp. 703-704.

States could again go to war in case that practice were revived. In Monroe's despatch of June 25, the following
article on impressment was suggested:

Whereas, by the peace in Europe, the essential causes of the
war between the United States and Great Britain, and particularly the practice of impressment, have ceased, and a sincere
desire exists to arrange, in a manner satisfactory to both parties,
all questions concerning seamen, and it is also their desire and
intention to arrange in a like satisfactory manner, the commerce
between the two countries, it is, therefore, agreed that commissioners shall forthwith be appointed on each side to meet at
————, with full power to negotiate and conclude a treaty,
as soon as it may be practicable, for the arrangement of those
important interests. It is, nevertheless, understood that, until
such treaty be formed, each party shall retain all its rights, and
that all American citizens who have been impressed into the
British service shall be forthwith discharged.

In a despatch dated June 27th,[1] Monroe authorized the
American Commissioners to agree to the omission of any
article on impressment, but to prevent by some appropriate
declaration or protest every inference that the American
claim had been abandoned.[2] This despatch, as has been seen,
reached the American Commissioners at Ghent August 8,
1814, immediately following the first session of the conference. Ghent had been agreed upon as the place of meeting after Gottenburg, Sweden, the place first selected, had
been declared unacceptable to the British government, and
after much delay and inconvenience to the American Commissioners. The representatives of the British government
reached Ghent August 7, 1814, six weeks after the arrival
of the Americans. The acts of the British Commissioners,
Lord Gambier, Henry Goulburn and William Adams, who

---

[1] Monroe to American Plenipotentiaries, June 27, 1814, *American
State Papers, Foreign Relations*, vol. iii, pp. 704-705.

[2] For Cabinet discussions see *Writings of Madison* (Hunt), vol. viii,
pp. 280-281.

have not usually been regarded as men of exceptional ability, were, throughout the negotiations, completely controlled by the British Ministry.

It is not intended here to follow in detail the long and intricate negotiations leading up to the signing of the Treaty of Ghent on December 24, 1814. In following the history of the negotiations on the single issue of impressment it will, however, be necessary to consider briefly other phases of the negotiations.[1]

Castlereagh, the British Foreign Secretary, discussed [2] the subjects which might arise in the conference under four general heads:—first, the questions of maritime rights including the principle of indelible allegiance and service of British subjects in time of war; secondly, the protection of the Indians, as allies in the war, by agreeing on definite boundaries for them; thirdly, the regulation of the frontier between the United States and Canada, and fourthly, the question of the fisheries.

On the subject of impressment, Castlereagh stated firmly that "the right of search and of withdrawing our seamen from on board American merchant ships can never be given up, even for a time, in exchange for any municipal regulation whatsoever." If the Americans had any regulations to propose tending to check the abuse they complained of, the British government would "weigh them dispassionately, and with a desire to conciliate." He regarded a satisfactory arrangement as doubtful, and thought it would probably be desirable to waive this discussion entirely, if other points could be adjusted. In fact, he thought the return of peace "practically set at rest" this whole question. The British Commissioners were instructed to keep silent on the subject,

---

[1] For a review of the entire negotiations see Updyke, *The Diplomacy of the War of 1812*, chs. v-viii.

[2] Castlereagh to British Commissioners, July 28, 1814, *Letters and Despatches of Castlereagh*, vol. x, pp. 67-69.

unless the Americans raised it, and in case the Americans made a specific proposal regarding it they were not to discuss such a proposal until it had been referred to the British government.

The British Commissioners presented these subjects in accordance with their instructions immediately after the opening of the conference on August 8, 1814, and by thus introducing problems of peace and territorial settlement with the Indians, of boundaries, and of fisheries, which had not been considered as causes of the war, provided an agenda which, apart from impressment, gave the conference sufficient work to insure reasonably long and difficult negotiations.

In addition to the question of impressment, the American Commissioners had also been instructed [1] to obtain from Great Britain a precise definition of blockade; to secure, if possible, regulations regarding search for contraband goods, and articles of contraband; recognition of the rights of neutral commerce; exclusion of the British from the Indian trade and the unrestricted right of the United States to increase her navy on the Great Lakes. The American Commissioners were not instructed concerning the leading questions raised by the British, and refused even to consider the suggestion that the Indian Territory become a barrier between the British Colonies and the United States. Finding it impossible, after a short time, to proceed further with the negotiations, adjournment was taken and the Commissioners reported to their respective governments asking for further instructions.

Castlereagh promptly sent additional instructions [2] to the

[1] Monroe to American Commissioners, April 15, 1813, *American State Papers, Foreign Relations*, vol. iii, pp. 695-700.

[2] Castlereagh to British Commissioners, August 14, 1814, *Letters and Despatches of Castlereagh*, vol. x, p. 86.

British Commissioners, proposing that the Indian boundary fixed by the treaty of Greenville become a permanent barrier between the two nations. The Canadian frontier was to be adjusted, involving certain cessions of territory to Great Britain and their right to navigation on the Mississippi, and the United States was to agree not to maintain naval forces or land fortifications on the Great Lakes.

The demand for territorial cessions, in view of the fact that perhaps one hundred thousand American citizens had settled beyond the Greenville boundary, and the further demand for the right to navigate the Mississippi, convinced the Americans that no such agreement would be acceptable, but they reported the British demands to their government with the statement that they intended to refuse them.[1] The demand for the continuation of the privilege of navigating the Mississippi River was insisted on by the British Commissioners as an equivalent to renewing American privileges in connection with the fisheries, and these two questions were to consume much of the time of the peace Commissioners. After the despatch by the Americans, on August 24, 1814,[2] of a note to the British Commissioners which declared the Indian boundary and all other demands inadmissible, the negotiations remained practically stationary for about two months.[3]

In concluding the note of August 24, in which the American Commissioners had declared the British proposals inadmissible, they stated their willingness to make a treaty based on the *status quo ante bellum*. Such a treaty if made

---

[1] American Commissioners to Monroe, August 19, 1814, *American State Papers, Foreign Relations*, vol. iii, pp. 708-709.

[2] American to British Commissioners, August 24, 1814, *ibid.*, pp. 711-713.

[3] Concerning the note mentioned above, John Quincy Adams wrote in his diary August 25th, "It ... will bring the negotiations very shortly to a close." *Memoirs of John Quincy Adams*, vol. iii, p. 23.

would necessarily exclude the settlement of impressment, and leave both nations with regard to that subject in the same position which they maintained previous to the declaration of war. They therefore proposed the following article for inclusion in the treaty:

The causes of the war between the United States and Great Britain having disappeared by the maritime pacifications of Europe, the government of the United States does not desire to continue it in defense of abstract principles, which have, for the present, ceased to have any practical effect. The undersigned have been accordingly instructed to agree to its termination, both reserving all their rights in relation to their respective seamen.

The British government finally decided to yield the unreasonable demands previously made regarding peace and territorial adjustment with the Indians, and also in regard to armaments on the Great Lakes, and on October 8,[1] offered an article which provided only that the Indians be restored to their situation as existing before the war. The article was also made reciprocal, requiring Great Britain to treat in a similar manner Indians who had been at war with her. The acceptance of this article by the Americans was, however, made a condition of further negotiations. The article was accepted by the Americans subject to the approval of the United States government. It may be said that not until after this date did the negotiations warrant any great hope of a successful outcome. Up to this time the British government had hoped to be able by successful conquest in America to possess the territory which was desired, and with military success be enabled to secure concessions from the American government on many other points. To the disappointment over not gaining great military victories in

---

[1] British to American Commissioners, October 8, 1814, *American State Papers, Foreign Relations*, vol. iii, pp. 721-723.

America was soon to be added the complete failure of the British attempt to invade New York, and the victories of the Americans at Plattsburg and Baltimore. Opposition to the war among the British people was also growing, and the negotiations at Vienna which were in progress at this time were not proceeding in a manner satisfactory to the British. This general situation undoubtedly had a tendency to modify the British policy at Ghent, and make possible the treaty of peace which resulted.

There were still, however, many difficult problems to face. On October 21, 1814,[1] the British Commissioners proposed that maritime subjects, including impressment, be omitted from the treaty, and that fisheries and the boundary questions be settled on the basis of their first proposals. This meant the exclusion of Americans from the enjoyment of fishing rights within British territorial waters off the coasts of Canada and Nova Scotia which had been enjoyed since the treaty of 1783, and the acceptance of the principle of *uti possidetis* in regard to boundaries. The comment in this note on the subject of impressment was as follows:—

With respect to the forcible seizure of mariners from on board merchant vessels on the high seas, and the right of the King of Great Britain to the allegiance of all his native subjects, and with respect to the maritime rights of the British Empire, the undersigned conceive that, after the pretensions asserted by the Government of the United States, a more satisfactory proof of the conciliatory spirit of his Majesty's Government cannot be given than by not requiring any stipulation on those subjects, which, though most important in themselves, no longer, in consequence of the maritime pacification of Europe, produce the same practical results.[2]

[1] British to American Commissioners, October 21, 1814, *American State Papers, Foreign Relations*, vol. iii, pp. 724-725.
[2] *Ibid.*, p. 725.

To this note the Americans replied,[1] refusing definitely to accept the British position on the subject of boundaries, insisting again that they could not accept any plan which involved the cession of American territory, thus producing another serious crisis in the negotiations. During the three weeks following this crisis, the Americans at the request of the British proposed a complete projet of a treaty, which was presented to the latter on November 10.[2] In this projet, although they had on August 24 agreed to conclude a treaty omitting any adjustment of impressment, the Americans included a temporary article on that subject, explaining that it would not affect the rights of either country; that it was purely conditional and limited in duration, and bound each party only so far and so long as the other fulfilled its conditions. The article as submitted read:—

Each party shall effectually exclude from its naval and commercial service all seamen, seafaring or other persons, subjects or citizens of the other party, not naturalized by the respective governments of the two parties before the ——— day of ———.

Seamen or other persons, subjects of either party, who shall desert from public or private ships or vessels, shall when found within the jurisdiction of the other party, be surrendered, provided they be demanded within ——— from the time of their desertion.

No person whatever shall, upon the high seas and without the jurisdiction of either party, be demanded or taken out of any ship or vessel belonging to the subjects or citizens of one of the parties by the public or private armed ships or vessels belonging to, or in the service of the other, unless such person be at the time in the actual employment of an enemy of such other party.

[1] American to British Commissioners, October 24, 1814, *American State Papers, Foreign Relations*, vol. iii, p. 725.

[2] For text of the Projet of Treaty, *ibid.*, pp. 735-740.

This article shall continue in force for the term of ———— years. Nothing in this article contained shall be construed thereafter to affect or impair the rights of either party.[1]

While the Americans were preparing this projet of a treaty, affairs in Europe were not proceeding in accordance with the hopes of the British Cabinet. The Congress of Vienna was moving slowly; financial problems in Great Britain were causing grave concern, and the war in America was not accomplishing their purpose. The Cabinet, therefore, considered the advisability of sending the Duke of Wellington, then British Ambassador at Paris, to the United States, with full power to make peace or continue the war with renewed vigor in case peace were found impracticable. The reaction of Wellington to the suggestion was decidedly unfavorable. He not only felt that the danger of the renewal of war in Europe made it desirable for him to remain there, but expressed the opinion that success could never be gained in the American war until the British established naval supremacy on the Great Lakes. As to the negotiation in progress at Ghent, Wellington gave it as his conviction that the results of the war did not justify the British in demanding from the United States any cession of territory whatever. This position of Wellington caused the British government to relinquish all demands for territorial cession, and paved the way to the final conclusion of the negotiations.[2] The treaty as finally agreed upon provided for the submission of all disputed boundary questions to Commissioners for adjustment later.[3] It contained no

---

[1] Adams states that the inclusion of the article was at the urgent insistence of Clay, to whom he also credits authorship. Both Bayard and Gallatin opposed it, and Adams himself and Russell finally sided with Clay. See *Memoirs of John Quincy Adams*, vol. iii, p. 63.

[2] Updyke, *Diplomacy of the War of 1812*, pp. 303-306.

[3] Malloy, *United States Treaties*, vol. i, pp. 612-619.

article on impressment, the British Commissioners having declared inadmissible the article included in the projet of November 10, and the American Commissioners in a note to the British Commissioners on November 30, 1814,[1] having consented to the omission of any article with the understanding, however, that such an omission did not in any degree weaken the rights of either nation.

As a matter of fact, the subject of impressment, as has been seen, had not been one of major significance during the negotiations, despite its importance as a cause of the war. Discussions regarding boundaries, the navigation of the Mississippi, disarmament of the Great Lakes, and the fisheries had consumed most of the time. This situation, though sometimes regarded as unusual, is adequately explained by the fact that after the close of the war in Europe, the impressment issue lost its intensely practical character, since, for a time at least, Great Britain, enjoying peace, would have no reason to resume that practice. It was evident, in the note written to Emperor Alexander in 1813 [2] before negotiations began, that the Americans had no idea of endangering the chances of peace with Great Britain by holding out for an abstract right on this subject. And this attitude was all the more justified after peace had actually come to Europe. The American government adjusted its position to fit a practical situation, and accepted peace on the best terms it could obtain at the time. There was no disposition to obscure the fact that in the peace, the United States failed to secure by treaty the main object for which they had been fighting. On the other hand, they did not yield that object, and in the meantime the practice of impressment was in abeyance. In a very true sense, the United

[1] American to British Commissioners, Nov. 30, 1814, *American State Papers, Foreign Relations*, vol. iii, p. 741.

[2] See *supra*, pp. 204-205.

States, in the peace treaty, failed to obtain a final settlement of impressment, for the same reason that she had so often failed before; viz., because under all the circumstances she was unable to compel Great Britain to yield her claim of abstract right in the matter.

Had Great Britain revived the practice after 1814, it is highly probable that the United States would again have gone to war, and on account of the relative status of the sea power of the two nations during these years, more than one war might have been fought before the United States could have persuaded Great Britain to abandon the claim. As a matter of fact, Great Britain yielded nothing on any subject of a maritime nature either at Ghent or in the commercial treaty signed in London in 1815. The abstract principles relative to illicit blockades and orders in council, along with the claim of impressment, were all stubbornly adhered to by that nation.

This fact is not unimportant, however, viz., that the United States, with limited resources and a very small navy had challenged these pretensions of Great Britain; had followed that challenge with respectable military and naval resistance, and had secured a treaty of peace which did not recognize any of them as valid belligerent rights. Another fact of perhaps even greater significance is, that never after the war did Great Britain renew the practice of impressment or any of the other maritime practices against which the United States had so strenuously protested.

CHAPTER IX

THE DIPLOMATIC HISTORY OF IMPRESSMENT AFTER THE TREATY OF GHENT

WE now turn to the diplomatic history of this subject during the years following the treaty of Ghent. The failure of all attempts to settle this irritating question, running over a period of two decades, does not seem to have discouraged the United States government in the effort to obtain that objective. Immediately after the signature of the treaty of Ghent, Clay and Gallatin, who were later joined by John Quincy Adams, went to London to negotiate a convention for the regulation of commerce between the United States and Great Britain. Russell went to Stockholm to resume his duties as American Minister to Sweden; and Bayard returned to the United States. In the conferences of the Americans [1] with Messrs. Robinson, Goulburn and Adams, the British representatives, the general question of commercial intercourse was treated under two heads: first, regulations applicable to a state of peace, and second, regulations applicable to the situation when one party was at war and the other at peace.

Under the latter heading, impressment was regarded by the Americans as of first importance, especially because they thought a new war in Europe possible at any time. The Americans proposed not to discuss the question of right, since it was impossible for Great Britain to have stronger

[1] Clay and Gallatin to Secretary of State, May 18, 1815, *American State Papers, Foreign Relations*, vol. iv, pp. 8-9.

convictions on this point than the United States had, and suggested that " it was better to look to some practical arrangement, by which, without concession of right by either party, the mischiefs complained of on both sides might be prevented ".   Although Great Britain had never contended that America should prohibit the employment of foreign seamen in her merchant service, they represented America as willing to do so, as the law of March 3, 1813, indicated. If that law were properly executed, the Americans held that no ground would longer exist for the claim of impressment, and hence no objection to its abandonment.

While ready, as always, to receive propositions on the subject, the British Commissioners objected to this one on the ground of the reluctance of Great Britain to abandon the right of impressment, and also on the ground that the law of March 3, 1813, did not settle the question, Who were to be considered British subjects?   On this question they did not think the two countries would be able to agree. Hence no article on impressment was inserted in the commercial treaty which was concluded and signed July 3, 1815. At the close of the negotiations, John Quincy Adams remained at London as American Minister to Great Britain.

President Madison had, on February 25, 1815, sent a message to Congress recommending that a law be passed providing for the navigation of American vessels exclusively by American citizens, either native or naturalized.[1] This was an advance on the exclusion clause in the act of 1813, which not only permitted the employment of naturalized seamen, but also those who might be naturalized in future as well.   Madison's proposal limited the employment of foreigners to those already naturalized.   His reasons for advocating this measure were first, that since peace

[1] Richardson Messages and Papers of the Presidents, vol. i, p. 555; see also *Annals of Congress, Thirteenth Congress, Third Session,* 275.

had been made between the United States and Great Britain,
it was desirable to guard against incidents which, during
periods of war in Europe, might tend to interrupt it. He
believed that the navigation of American vessels exclusively by American seamen, either natives or such as were
already naturalized, would not only conduce to the attain-
ment of that object, but also increase the number of American seamen, and consequently render American commerce
and navigation independent of the service of foreigners,
who might be recalled by their government under circumstances most inconvenient to the United States. In the
second place, such a law would manifest to the world the
desire of the United States to cultivate harmony with other
nations. He felt that the example on the part of the American government would merit, and probably receive, a reciprocal attention from all the friendly powers of Europe.
Madison repeated his recommendation for such a law again
in his message December 5, 1815.

In the report on the subject presented to the Senate
March 7, 1816, by Senator Bibb (Ga.), of the Committee
on Foreign Affairs, it was maintained that the law of March
3, 1813, sufficiently demonstrated to the world the conciliatory spirit of the United States on this question, by agreeing to prohibit the employment, as seamen, of the subjects
or citizens of any foreign nation which would prohibit the
like employment of citizens of the United States. All that
was needed, the report held, to make that law effective was
for other governments to pass a similar law.[1]

Adams had, however, in the meantime seized upon the
President's recommendation and presented it to Castlereagh,
British Minister of Foreign Affairs, as a reason for Great
Britain's eliminating impressment, but Castlereagh took the

---

[1] *Annals of Congress, Fourteenth Congress, First Session,* 172-174.

position that if such a law were passed, there would be no reason to consider the subject, as there would then be no British seamen on American ships, and of course the practice of taking them would cease.[1]

With the idea of enlarging on the commercial convention adopted July 3, 1815, which was not regarded as ultimate or definitive by the United States, Adams wrote Castlereagh September 17, 1816,[2] setting forth the various problems still calling for adjustment. His proposal on seamen was " that neither the United States nor Great Britain shall employ in their naval or merchant service native citizens or subjects of the other party, with the exception of those already naturalized ". Adams held that since wages of American seamen were in peace times always much higher than those of British seamen, Great Britain would really get the advantage in such an agreement. All that the United States wanted, he insisted, was the abandonment of the practice of impressment.

Castlereagh replied [3] that even if Great Britain should make such an agreement it would not be regarded as implying or intending an engagement to renounce the practice of taking men from American vessels during a future maritime war. This statement closed the discussion, because Adams felt that without such a renunciation, or at least a tacit understanding that the practice of impressment would be abandoned, the United States would not agree to such an article.

Richard Rush, who in 1817 succeeded Adams as American Minister to Great Britain, held conferences with Castle-

---

[1] Adams to Monroe, January 31, 1816, *American State Papers, Foreign Relations*, vol. iv, p. 360.

[2] Adams to Castlereagh, Sept. 17, 1816, *ibid.*, p. 363.

[3] See Adams to Monroe, September 27, 1816, *ibid.*, p. 362.

reagh April 18, June 11 and June 20, 1818, on the subject
of impressment. The matter was discussed on April 18 on
the basis of a proposal of Rush involving mutual restrictions on naturalization of seamen, and the abandonment of
the practice of impressment. On June 20, Rush proposed
that each nation exclude altogether from its service the seamen of the other, both from public and from private ships,
and that impressment be renounced.[1] These proposals, as
has been seen, were embodied in the original instructions to
the American Commissioners, dated April 13, 1813, and
Rush had been instructed to follow them in dealing with the
subject, in case it should arise. In these conferences Castlereagh referred to the recent discussions of the British Cabinet on the differences between the two nations on the subjects of naturalization, allegiance, and territorial sovereignty,
which had ended in the refusal of that body to modify the
position of Great Britain on impressment. Rush inquired
whether the claim would be abandoned if the United States
should agree to exclude from their public and private ships
all natural-born subjects of Great Britain. Castlereagh answered that such a proposal would still not be sufficient to
warrant Great Britain in agreeing to conclude a treaty
abandoning her right to enter vessels of a foreign power to
look for her subjects. In fact, he declared that his nation
would not make such a treaty on any terms.

Castlereagh was only willing to agree to such regulations
of the practice of impressment as restricting the boarding
officers to those of a rank not below lieutenants, and giving
receipts for the men taken out. He would go no further.
Rush replied that the United States would never, by con-

[1] Rush to Adams, June 26, 1818, *American State Papers, Foreign
Relations*, vol. iv, pp. 373-374.

vention, concede the right to enter American vessels for the
purpose of impressment. Castlereagh, admitting the evil of
the practice, expressed the hope that it would never be revived. He thought that if the United States would exclude
British seamen from her service the practice would take
place with much less frequency.

While these discussions had been going on in London, a
definite change of sentiment had apparently taken place in
Washington. The anxiety over the settlement of the impressment question, which ever since the war had been keen,
had by this time subsided, to a large degree, on account of
the discontinuance of the practice, and was gradually giving
way to the desire to regulate more satisfactorily the commercial intercourse between the two countries. As a result
of this desire to secure advantageous modifications of the
commercial convention of 1815, which was to expire in 1818,
Adams, in a letter to Rush dated May 30, 1818,[1] stated
that the American government did not wish the success of
the approaching commercial negotiations endangered by any
of the more academic questions of neutral rights, such as
blockades, contraband, or even impressment.

This letter did not reach London, however, until after
Rush had already made the proposals above referred to.
After first rejecting both proposals, Castlereagh, according
to Rush's report [2] on August 15, indicated that the second
proposal might be acceptable if modified in two important
respects, as follows: first, that either party be allowed to
withdraw from the agreement after giving notice three or
six months in advance, and second, that in case a British
officer entering an American vessel for admittedly lawful

[1] Adams to Rush, May 30, 1818, *American State Papers, Foreign
Relations*, vol. iv, pp. 372-373.

[2] Rush to Adams, August 15, 1818, *ibid.*, p. 379.

purposes, should find thereon a seaman whom he thought to be a British subject, he should be allowed to record the fact and have the matter brought to the attention of the American government. Castlereagh stated that these were only his personal views, since the Cabinet had not yet considered the subject. He seemed, however, desirous that they be given careful consideration. The suggested modifications were referred to the American government.[1]

On August 16, Gallatin, who was now American Minister to France, arrived from Paris to join Rush in negotiations for the renewal and modification of the Commercial Convention of 1815. It was during the negotiations which followed with Rush and Gallatin, that on September 17, 1818, the British Commissioners brought forward a plan containing six articles on the subject of impressment. It is significant that this, the first complete plan ever presented by the British government on the subject, was brought up at a time when the United States government for the first time in many years was not especially eager for a settlement of that question, or, to say the least, was much more anxious to settle definite trade questions. The instructions to Gallatin and Rush contained in Adams' letter to Rush of May 30, as has been seen, omitted the subject of impressment in order not to embarrass the proposed commercial negotiations. The British plan presented September 17, being the first ever presented by that government, merits careful consideration.

Article one of the plan proposed that each nation immediately adopt measures for the effective exclusion of the natural-born subjects of the other from service in its public or private marine. Subjects or citizens of either power who

---

[1] Rush to Adams, August 15, 1818, *American State Papers, Foreign Relations*, vol. iv, p. 379.

had been naturalized previous to the signature of the treaty were to be excepted.

Article two provided that a list of the names of all persons in each nation to be excepted, according to article one, be prepared and delivered each to the other within twelve months from the ratification of the treaty. This list should also give place of birth and date of naturalization.

Article three reserved to both nations the power to authorize and permit their subjects or citizens to serve in the public or private marine of the other. When such permission should be granted by either nation, the other nation could admit the performance of such service, until notified of the withdrawal of said permission, whereupon the exclusion clause of article one would become operative the same as if no permission had been promulgated.

Article four provided that in consideration of the previous stipulations neither party should, during the continuance of the treaty, impress from the vessels of the other on the high seas on any plea or pretext whatsoever. It definitely excepted the ports and territorial waters from the agreement, thus permitting the continuance of impressment in them.

Article five provided that the term of the treaty should be ten years, but that either party might abrogate it upon giving six months' previous notice to the other.

Article six provided that if the treaty expired, or was abrogated, or if war began between the two countries, then each party should stand as to its rights and principles as if no such treaty had ever been made.[1]

The chief objections urged by Rush and Gallatin to the British plan may be summarized as follows: In the first place, they urged that the period prior to which the citizens

[1] For text of the proposal, see *American State Papers, Foreign Relations,* vol. iv, pp. 389-390.

of each nation should have been naturalized in order to be included in the exception provided in article one should be the exchange of ratifications instead of the signature of the treaty. They objected to that part of the second article which required the preparation of a complete list of naturalized citizens. They held it impossible for the United States, and also regarded it as unnecessary. They favored a milder form of enforcing the regulation contained in article three regarding the exclusion of seamen of one nation from the marine of the other after their recall by the nation of which they were citizens, and finally, they objected to the clause in article four providing that naturalized citizens of one nation should be withdrawn from the vessels of the other within its ports or jurisdiction.

The most strenuous objections were urged against the second article, and in a memorandum dated October 12, 1818,[1] Gallatin and Rush declared their unwillingness to assent to that article for the following reasons:

1. It was impracticable for the United States to secure complete lists of naturalized seamen because

(a) Prior to 1790 aliens were naturalized by state laws.

(b) Since 1790 all aliens had been naturalized according to the laws of the United States, but the actual procedure had taken place in state as well as federal courts, and would involve records from hundreds of sources.

(c) All minor children of naturalized persons living in the United States became also, *ipso facto,* naturalized.

(d) The state courts might refuse to make abstracts covering thirty years, and were not bound to obey the general government in such a matter.

(e) If the courts did comply and such a list were compiled, there would be no way of telling who were seamen, because no occupational record was made.

[1] *American State Papers, Foreign Relations,* vol. iv, pp. 393-394.

(f) From 1790 to 1795 no designation of birthplace was required to be recorded.

(g) The collectors' records, based on the law of 1796, were the only other source, and they were very imperfect because first of all the law was never fully complied with, and secondly, the names of natives and naturalized citizens were not kept separate.

2. If the United States agreed to such an article it would mean that aliens naturalized prior to the treaty would by a retrospective, and hence unconstitutional act be deprived not only of political privileges, but of the right to exercise their chosen profession or calling.

3. Such an article was unnecessary.

4. It was directly contrary to American instructions because it discriminated against naturalized seamen.

On October 13, 1818, the British brought forward new articles on impressment containing the following provisions:[1]

1. Adoption of measures excluding from public and private marine, the natural-born subjects or citizens of each other except those who had been naturalized by either party previous to the signature of the present convention.

2. Delivery to each other within eighteen months from the ratification of the present treaty of a list of all naturalized seamen, giving places of birth and date of naturalization, and that no person who is not on this list should fall within the above exception.

3. Either party might at any time notify the other that it no longer insisted on the exclusion of its natural-born subjects from the public and private marine of the other, and upon decision to recall or return to that policy notify the other party, who would use its utmost endeavor to enforce the original article, the same as if it had always stood.

[1] *American State Papers, Foreign Relations*, vol. iv, pp. 395-396.

4. During the period of this treaty neither to impress or forcibly withdraw subjects from the vessels of the other on the high seas or upon the narrow seas, provided this should not apply to natural-born subjects or citizens, not falling within the exception mentioned in the preceding articles within the ports or ordinary jurisdiction, or provided the right of search in time of war established by the law of nations was not impaired.

5. The treaty to last ten years, but might be abrogated by either party on six months' notice.

6. When this convention ceased for any reason to be operative, then the parties should be as to their rights and principles as if no convention had been made.

Since the articles did not take account of the leading objections presented by the Americans, they were definitely rejected by them on October 19, 1818.[1] Negotiations proceeded on the other subjects under discussion, but no further reference was made to impressment. While there had been substantial agreement on the more difficult questions of principle, except the one proviso that seamen could be withdrawn in ports in the ordinary maritime jurisdiction, there had been radical disagreement on the means to be used in executing the plan. This disagreement was manifested on the question relating to the period of time which should govern the exclusion of naturalized seamen; on the preparation of lists of naturalized citizens, and on the time at which exclusion of seamen should begin anew after the recall of citizens by either nation from the marine of the other. The failure of this negotiation seems disappointing indeed, but it should be remembered that the American Commissioners had specific instructions not to permit this subject to interfere with other more important commercial interests. The peaceful conditions which prevailed the world over had brought about a state of mind in the United States in which

[1] *American State Papers, Foreign Relations*, vol. iv, p. 397.

the subject of impressment had lost much of its former significance. Seamen were not being impressed, and commercial interests were in a position to make unparalleled progress, if certain trade advantages could be realized. These points seem at this time to have been uppermost in the minds of the leaders of the American government. When, however, the government learned of Castlereagh's views on the subject, upon receipt of letters from Rush giving the terms first suggested by Castlereagh as modifications of Rush's proposal, new instructions were sent by John Quincy Adams to Gallatin and Rush under date of November 2, 1818.[1] In these instructions objection was made to the idea of the right of denouncing the agreement on three or six months' notice, and two years' notice was suggested instead. If this could not be obtained, Gallatin and Rush were instructed to set up the impressment clause independent of the rest of the treaty and let it be in force four years. It was also thought desirable to have the date for beginning the exclusion as of October 1, 1820, so as to give plenty of notice to merchants and seamen affected by it. There was strong objection to the idea of giving lists of crews to British officers entering American vessels, and to those officers having the right to remonstrate in case they thought there were British seamen on board. But these instructions did not reach Rush and Gallatin until after the negotiations were ended, and had they done so it was the opinion of these gentlemen that they would not have changed the final result.

Rush expressed the opinion [2] that Great Britain's unwillingness to meet the American demands on this occasion was due in part to the error, which he thought had always pre-

[1] J. Q. Adams to Gallatin and Rush, Nov. 2, 1818, *American State Papers, Foreign Relations*, vol. iv, pp. 399-401.

[2] Rush, *Memoranda of a Residence at the Court of London* (Philadelphia, 1833), pp. 445 *et seq.*

vailed in that country, viz., that of supposing that the United States was in reality dependent on Great Britain for a large number of seamen. Despite this difficulty, however, Rush believed that if Lord Castlereagh had remained in London [1] the negotiations on impressment would not have failed, because " He (Castlereagh) saw that the great principle of adjustment had at last been settled; and I can scarcely think that he would have allowed it to be foiled by carrying too much rigour into details."

The development of opposition to impressment in Great Britain had made a deep impression on Rush's mind. He referred especially to the public opposition of the London ship owners, and of Sir Murray Maxwell, a prominent officer in the British navy, adding that he also had information as to opposition "derived from private intercourse of a high kind ". [2]

After the failure of this negotiation, the British government never again offered a proposal on the subject, and never again entered into serious negotiations upon it. The government of the United States made no further attempt at a settlement until 1823, when in proposing a convention on maritime and neutral rights with special emphasis on regulations relative to privateering, looking toward its total abolition, articles on impressment were included. Article twelve of this project of a convention provided [3] that whenever a war should break out between either of the contracting parties and a third party, in which either party should be neutral, no natural-born subjects or citizens of the belligerent party, unless naturalized by an authentic public act be-

[1] Castlereagh was directing important negotiations in Aix la Chapelle.

[2] Rush, *Memoranda of a Residence at the Court of London*, p. 448. For discussion of the negotiations, see *ibid.*, pp. 436-450.

[3] Full text of these articles is found in *House Executive Document*, no. III, pp. 13-14, *Executive Documents, First Session, Thirty-third Congress*, vol. xiii.

fore the outbreak of the war, should be employed on board the public or private vessels of the neutral party. Article thirteen stipulated against the impressment of any person on any pretext " upon the high seas, or anywhere without the ordinary jurisdiction of either power ", except those in the military service of the enemy, as acknowledged by the law of nations.

Adams, Secretary of State, authorized Rush in a letter of instructions dated July 28, 1823, to agree if necessary to the exclusion of persons who might be naturalized after the ratification of the treaty, rather than endanger the agreement. This agreement was not to be of a temporary character such as that offered in 1818. Adams also expressed the belief that it would be impossible to avoid a war with Great Britain in the event of the renewal of the practice of impressment.[1] Rush regarded impressment as most vital of all maritime questions under consideration save alone that of privateering, and on his own initiative refused to treat on general maritime questions other than privateering unless impressment were included. The British plenipotentiaries, W. Huskisson and Stratford Canning, took the position that the articles gave no adequate guarantee for the exclusion of natural-born British subjects from the service of the United States and on the basis of this objection refused to agree to them.[2] The entire negotiation, in fact, was unsuccessful, and no agreement was reached on any of the subjects under discussion.

Having waged war against the practice of impressment, which involved the search of neutral merchant vessels in time of war, the American government objected after that

[1] Adams to Rush, July 28, 1823, *ibid.*, pp. 9-10.

[2] Rush to Adams, August 12, 1824, *ibid.*, p. 31. Also Protocol of the 13th Conference of the American and British Plenipotentiaries, April 5, 1824, *ibid.*, pp. 33-34.

war to the practice of searching merchant vessels in time of peace for any purpose. The position of the government on this subject is illustrated during the years following the treaty of Ghent, when the United States and Great Britain entered into negotiations regarding plans for the abolition of the slave trade, to which they were pledged by article ten of that treaty. John Quincy Adams, Secretary of State, announced the attitude of the American government on this subject in a letter to Gallatin and Rush, November 2, 1818,[1] in which he took the position that any effort to abolish the slave trade, which sought to introduce the right to visit and search merchant vessels in time of peace, would be unacceptable to the United States. If Great Britain should propose an agreement including such a principle, the American Ministers in London were instructed to reject it. Adams regarded such a step as the introduction of a new principle into the law of nations " more formidable than the slave trade itself." [2]

On March 13, 1824, Rush for the United States, and W. Huskisson and Stratford Canning for Great Britain, concluded a convention for the suppression of the slave trade,[3] article one of which provided for the mutual right of visit and search " on the coasts of Africa, of America, and of the West Indies ". In approving the convention the United States Senate expunged the words " of America ", and as a result Great Britain refused to ratify the convention.

Article ten of the convention of 1824 above referred to conceded the right of detaining, visiting, capturing and de-

[1] Adams to Gallatin and Rush, November 2, 1818, *American State Papers, Foreign Relations*, vol. iv, pp. 399-401.

[2] *Memoirs of John Quincy Adams*, April 29, 1819, vol. iv, p. 354.

[3] For text of Convention, see *American State Papers, Foreign Relations*, vol. v, pp. 319-322.

livering over for trial those merchant vessels engaged in
the African slave trade, but upon the insistence of Rush, the
American Minister, this right was declared to be " exclusively grounded on the consideration of their having made
that traffic piracy by their respective laws ".   The right was

not to be so construed as to authorize the detention or search
of the merchant vessels of either nation by the officers of the
navy of the other, except vessels engaged or suspected of being
engaged in the African slave trade, or for any other purpose
whatever than that of seizing and delivering up the persons and
vessels concerned in that traffic for trial and adjudication by
the tribunals and laws of their own country, nor be taken to
affect in any other way the existing rights of either of the
high contracting parties.[1]

In the later negotiations regarding the abolition of the slave
trade, the question of impressment did not become a subject
for discussion.

The next statement of the American government which
bore on the impressment controversy was made in 1826.
Henry Clay, who was then Secretary of State, on June 19
of that year wrote to Gallatin, then Minister to Great Britain,[2] reviewing the endeavors of the United States to obtain
a satisfactory settlement of impressment both in peace and
in war, and stating that the inquiry made of Rush in 1824,
on the question of securities for the efficient exclusion of
British subjects from the American service, seemed to imply
an obligation on the part of the United States to provide
such securities.   He made it clear to Gallatin that no such

[1] See text of Convention, *American State Papers, Foreign Relations,*
vol. v, p. 321.

[2] Clay to Gallatin, June 19, 1826, *House Executive Document,* no. 111,
pp. 35-36, *Executive Documents, First Session, Thirty-third Congress,*
vol. xiii.

obligation would be acknowledged by the United States; that, on the contrary, the United States denied *in toto* the right of impressment as applied to them, even that of British subjects not naturalized, from American vessels at sea or in port, and that when such subjects were naturalized the United States denied the right of impressment either on land, at sea, in the British jurisdiction or out of it. He furthermore instructed Gallatin that since all efforts at settlement had been repelled by Great Britain, the United States would make no further proposal on the subject, but would rely on their right under the law of nations to be exempt from the application of the British claim. Gallatin was, however, to receive any proposal which Great Britain might offer, and to be guided in the negotiations upon such a proposal by the instructions given to Rush in 1823. The instructions to Gallatin embodied other questions of a maritime nature, including privateering, blockade and contraband.

During the negotiations which followed, Stratford Canning, then British Foreign Secretary, in July, 1827, adverted to the subject of impressment by asking Gallatin what guarantee the United States could offer for the exclusion of British subjects. To this Gallatin replied that they could offer no guarantee except their good faith in performing their engagements. As a consequence of this reply, no further negotiations on the subject resulted.

Pursuant to a resolution of the House of Representatives, calling for complete information on impressment of seamen from American vessels on the high seas or elsewhere by commanders of British or other foreign vessels since 1815, Henry Clay, Secretary of State, reported January 15, 1827, that only three cases were known to the Department of State. Two of these were reported to have been impressed by Captain Clavering, of his Majesty's ship "Red Wing", from the American brig "Pharos" of Boston, in the harbor of

Freetown, Sierra Leone, on the coast of Africa. One was reported to have been released after ten days' detention, while the other had been held as a British subject. The British contended that both seamen volunteered to enter their service, but that one being a native of Norway, with an American protection, was returned, while the other, being a British subject, was retained. Charles Richard Vaughan, the British Minister at Washington, maintained that they were not, in fact, cases of impressment at all, saying, " I am not aware of any act being now in force in this period of peace which justifies the impressment of British subjects by his Majesty's forces." [1]

On June 13, 1828, Clay, in writing to James Barbour, Gallatin's successor as American Minister in London, called his attention to the instructions to Gallatin on the subject of impressment, and stated that the President still thought it advisable for the first move toward the settlement of that question to come from Great Britain. He gave it as his opinion that while peace continued, no difficulty was likely to arise; but in case war should break out and any attempt again be made to apply the practice of impressment to the United States, Barbour was instructed to inform the British government that the United States could not and would not submit to it. [2]

By the year 1831, impressment was regarded by the United States government as " A question of no present im-

[1] For report of Secretary of State and Correspondence of Clay and Vaughan, see *American State Papers, Foreign Relations*, vol. **vi**, pp. 368-371.

[2] *House Executive Document*, no. 111, pp. 37-38, *Executive Documents, First Session, Thirty-third Congress*, vol. xiii. For statement of strong objections to any revival of the practice, see also Clay to Barbour, January 26, 1829, *MS. Instructions United States Ministers, Great Britain*, vol. xii, p. 186, quoted in Moore, *Digest of International Law*, vol. ii, pp. 998-999.

portance, but of the most grave influence on our future peace ".[1]   The definite intention not to tolerate the practice again was expressed by Livingston in this same communication in the following language:

With the means now at our command of avenging insult and resisting aggression, the spirit of the people will no longer brook a practice consistent only with a state of actual vassalage; and the first well authenticated act of aggression of this kind unatoned for will be the signal for arraying the maritime force of the United States with that of the enemy with whom Great Britain may then be contending.

The American government had again decided to take a positive attitude toward the issue, perhaps on account of certain alleged instances of impressment in 1828 and 1829, and to this end Van Buren, who had been named American Minister at London, was instructed to inform the British government what results to expect as the inevitable consequences of future aggression of this kind. Such a statement, however, was to be tempered by references to the many controversies already settled; to the growth of commercial intercourse between the two nations; to the increase of friendly feeling, the community of language, literature, manners and religion which formed a natural bond of union between the two countries. The time was regarded as favorable to end once and for all this " one germ of discord " remaining, and Van Buren was to use his " highest exertions " to obtain the following agreement:

No person whatever shall, on the high seas, and without the jurisdiction of either party, be demanded or taken out of any ship or vessel belonging to citizens or subjects of one of the parties, by the public or private armed ships belonging to or in

[1] See Livingston to Van Buren, August 1, 1831, *MS. Instructions to United States' Ministers, Great Britain*, vol. xiv, pp. 106-112.

the service of the other, unless such person be, at the time, in the military service of an enemy of such other party.

Nor shall any person be taken out of such vessel belonging to one party, when within the jurisdiction of the other, unless by due process of law; nor shall any person, being a citizen or subject of one of the parties, and resorting to, or residing in, the dominions of the other, be in any case compelled to serve on board any vessel, whether public or private, belonging to the other party.

It was insisted that the law of 1813 would effectively exclude British seamen from American vessels, but the former request that the United States furnish a list of all naturalized British seamen was declared inadmissible. Van Buren was, however, instructed to agree to exclude native-born seamen from national or private ships except such as had been legally naturalized, or had given notice of their intention to become naturalized; to agree also to limit the convention to eight or ten years, the notice of termination by either party to be made not less than eighteen months in advance, and to agree to the usual article for surrendering deserters.

In conclusion, Livingston wrote: " It is repeated that the President considers this as the most important subject connected with your mission. . . . It is therefore to be presented unconnected with any other matter which is to be arranged between the two nations."

As had so often been the case before, however, the time regarded by the United States as propitious for a settlement proved not to be the appropriate time for the British government. Not only was Lord Palmerston, who was the British Minister of Foreign Affairs, occupied with more vital diplomatic problems, affecting immediately the entire European situation, but the entire British government was greatly concerned over the Reform question, which agitated and divided the nation. In the midst of these unfavorable circumstances, Van Buren and Palmerston thought it wise to postpone the negotiations regarding impressment.[1]   In the meantime, Van Buren received word that his appointment as Minister had failed to receive the approval of the Senate, and he returned to the United States without renewing his efforts for a settlement of the issue.   Aaron Vail, in charge of the United States Legation in London, in 1833, in a letter to McLane,[2] then Secretary of State, reported a conversation with Lord Palmerston to the effect that the King's Ministers in 1831, " owing to the pressure of business and the then existing circumstances of the country ", found it inconvenient to accede to the proposal made by Van Buren.   Lord Palmerston was said by Vail at that time to be ready to receive and consider any plan " likely to form the basis of an arrangement ".   The American government, however, did not see fit to offer such a plan at that time.

During the years 1833 and 1834, members of the British Parliament on several occasions expressed keen dissatisfaction with the practice of impressment as a method of recruiting for the navy, giving the impression that the practice was becoming very unpopular in that country.

On August 15, 1833, Mr. Buckingham, in the House of Commons, moved for a resolution looking toward a plan that would secure an adequate supply of seamen for the navy without recourse to impressment.[3]   A similar resolution was also debated March 5, 1834.[4]   In these debates, the practice of impressment applied to British seamen was bitterly denounced, being characterized as " unjust, cruel, inefficient and unnecessary " and as a " blot upon the escutcheon of

[1] See *Autobiography of Martin Van Buren*, edited by John C. Fitzpatrick, pp. 452-453.

[2] Vail to McLane, December 6, 1833, *MS. Despatches, England*, vol. xli, Number 101.

[3] *Hansard, Parliamentary Debates*, vol. xx, p. 636.

[4] *Ibid.*, vol. xxi, p. 1063.

our country's glory which every true patriot must be anxious
to see speedily wiped out ". The impressment of foreign
seamen in the past, particularly American seamen, was unfavorably commented upon, and especially the former practice of keeping impressed American seamen on board British
ships in foreign stations in order to prevent them from
having an opportunity to prove their American character
and be discharged.

The resolution of August 15, 1833, was defeated by a
majority of only five votes,[1] while that of March 4, 1834,
was lost by a substantial majority.[2] They were both opposed by the First Lord of the Admiralty, Lord Althrop,
who offered no justification for the practice save that of
necessity, but urged that before the method was definitely
abandoned the plan for registering seamen, already begun,
should be given a thorough trial. This cautious sentiment
seemed conclusive for the majority, yet there were numerous
indications that an effort to revive the practice would meet
with strong opposition in many sections of England. More
than one speaker urged that any future attempt to impress
seamen should be openly resisted by the seamen themselves.[3]

The growing opposition to impressment in Great Britain
was communicated to the American government,[4] and this
fact may account for the very definite language on the subject used by Daniel Webster, during his negotiations with

---

[1] *Hansard, Parliamentary Debates,* vol. xx, 694.

[2] *Ibid.,* vol. xxi, p. 1113.

[3] For references to Parliamentary action, see also McClane to Sir
Charles R. Vaughn, March 31, 1834, vol. v, *Foreign Relations—Notes to
Department of State.* See also Vail to Livingston, March 30, 1833,
MS. Despatches, England, vol. xl, no. 59.

[4] See especially Stevenson, American Minister at London to Forsyth,
Secretary of State, April 7, 1837, *MS. Despatches, England,* vol. xliv,
no. 22. Stevenson believed that Great Britain was preparing to abolish
impressment.

Lord Ashburton in 1842,[1] the next and last occasion in which impressment was considered an issue in diplomatic negotiations between the two nations. Webster set forth briefly the history of the long controversy, saying that despite all the efforts made to settle the question it " stands at this moment where it stood fifty years ago ". According to Webster's view, impressment was based on English law alone, and could not apply to a merchant vessel on the high seas which " is rightfully considered as part of the territory of the country to which it belongs ".

In the closing paragraphs of his letter of August 8, 1842, to Lord Ashburton, the position of the United States is set forth in no uncertain language:

The American government, then, is prepared to say, that the practice of impressing seamen from American vessels cannot be hereafter allowed to take place. . . . In the early disputes between the two governments on this so long contested topic, the distinguished person to whose hands were first entrusted the seals of this department declared that " the simplest rule will be, that the vessel being American shall be evidence that the seamen on board are such."

Webster also declared in this letter that fifty years of experience had fully convinced the American government that the above was not only the simplest and best, but the only rule, which could be adopted and observed consistently with the rights and honor of the United States and the security of their citizens. " That rule announces, therefore," said Webster, " what will hereafter be the principle maintained by their government. In every regularly documented American merchant vessel the crew who navigate it will find their protection in the flag which is over them."

---

[1] Webster to Lord Ashburton, August 8, 1842, *Niles Register*, vol. lxiii, pp. 62-63.

Lord Ashburton in reply stated that the object of his mission was limited to " existing subjects of difference ", and that " no differences have or could have arisen of late years with respect to impressment, because the practice has since the peace wholly ceased and cannot, consistently with existing laws and regulations for manning her Majesty's navy, be, under present circumstances, renewed." He expressed an earnest desire that " a satisfactory arrangement respecting it may be made, so as to set at rest all apprehension and anxiety ".[1]

In his message transmitting the Treaty of Washington to the Senate, August 11, 1842,[2] President Tyler referred to impressment as a subject likely to bring on renewed contentions at the first breaking out of a European war. Then, referring to Webster's letter, he said:

The letter from the Secretary of State to the British Minister explains the ground which the government has assumed and the principles which it means to uphold. For the defense of these grounds and the maintenance of these principles the most perfect reliance is placed on the intelligence of the American people and on their firmness and patriotism in whatever touches the honor of the country or its great and essential interests.[3]

During a debate in the United States Senate in 1846, the treaty negotiated in 1842 by Webster and Lord Ashburton was severely criticized. Among other things, it was stated that the situation regarding the impressment issue had not been improved in any way. Webster, in a reply[4] defending the treaty, insisted that the negotiations preceding the con-

---

[1] For Lord Ashburton's reply, August 9, 1842, see *ibid.*
[2] *Richardson Messages and Papers of the Presidents*, vol. iv, p. 169.
[3] *Ibid.*, p. 169.
[4] *Works of Daniel Webster*, vol. v, p. 145.

clusion of the treaty, especially his letter of August 8, 1842, to Lord Ashburton, had essentially modified the status of the impressment question and had " placed the true doctrine in opposition to it on a higher and stronger foundation ". That subject, in his opinion, would never again be deemed a proper subject for treaty stipulation. Referring to his statement in the correspondence with Lord Ashburton, that henceforth the crews of American merchant vessels would find their protection in the American flag, Webster said: " This declaration will stand. . . . We shall negotiate no more, nor attempt to negotiate more, about impressment."

Without seeking to detract from Webster's evaluation of his own services in this connection, it should be stated that the long years of peace in Europe following the defeat of Napoleon, combined with the subsequent establishment by Great Britain of a voluntary system for manning her navy,[1] contributed largely to the prevention of a revival of the practice of impressment. It should also be said that immediately following the treaty of Ghent, and during all the years from then until 1842, the government of the United States kept constant watch for any tendency of the British government which might seem to be directed toward the revival of the obnoxious claim. This watchful spirit was demonstrated in the Slave Trade Convention of 1824, and in the direct opposition to impressment voiced by John Quincy Adams, Clay and Livingston, in language practically as forceful as that used by Webster himself.

---

[1] By the " Naval enlistment Act " of 1835, the voluntary enlistment of seamen was encouraged by limiting the term of service to five years, and by requiring, at the end of such a term of service, certificates of discharge which exempted the holder from service for a period of two years. (The *Revised Statutes*, vol. v, p. 684.) Volunteer acts were later passed in 1853 and 1859 which, by creating large reserve forces, subject to actual service in case of national emergency, rendered the practice of impressment unnecessary. (*The Revised Statutes*, vol. ix, p. 120, and vol. x, p. 201.

It is true, however, that after the Webster-Ashburton conference in 1842, the subject of impressment ceased to be a matter of discussion or dispute between the two nations. Great Britain, though never formally renouncing the claim, never again sought to revive a practice so out of harmony with the principle of the freedom of the seas. Furthermore, in 1870,[1] Parliament legalized expatriation, and thus by abandoning the doctrine of indelible allegiance, yielded the principle which had not only furnished the pretext for the claim to the right of impressment, but which had rendered impossible any solution, by appropriate legislation, of the problem of desertion. A few years previous to the passage of this act, in dealing with the case of Mason and Slidell, the British government, to quote the language of John Bassett Moore, " impliedly affirmed that the taking of persons from a neutral vessel, under cover of the belligerent right of visit and search, could not be justified by a claim to their allegiance ".[2]

[1] See Naturalization Act of 1870, *The Revised Statutes*, vol. xii, p. 681.

[2] Moore, *Digest of International Law*, vol. ii, p. 987.

CHAPTER X

CONCLUSION

THE impressment of American seamen constituted for half a century an important problem in American politics. Perhaps no other single topic, affecting so small a proportion of the nation's population, has ever aroused keener national interest, or held that interest during so long a period. The more distinctly human element involved in impressment alone explains the unique position which it always held in the popular mind among all the difficult maritime issues confronting the nation during its formative period. The American government, as has been frequently shown, was not unmoved by this human element, at times mingling somewhat sentimental considerations with legal arguments against the practice.

In concluding this subject, a brief résumé of the legal positions regarding it, held by the United States and Great Britain, and an estimate of the merits of their respective positions will first of all be attempted. On the question of the indefeasible allegiance of her subjects, and of her consequent right to the services of her seamen, Great Britain, throughout the controversy, stood on unimpeachable legal ground. Furthermore, the right to impress British seamen into the service of the navy was well established in English law. It was the chief contention of the United States that the municipally legal right to impress could not be regarded as an international right, into which it was expanded, whenever seamen were impressed from neutral merchant vessels on the high seas. Great Britain without expressly denying

248   [248

the contention of the United States, sought to escape its results by asserting that as an incident to her legal right of search as a belligerent she had a right to take her seamen from neutral merchant vessels when found thereon. That such had been the previous practice must be admitted, but its continuance in an age that was realizing progressively the meaning of the freedom of the seas could not be justified. John Bassett Moore [1] has expressed the American view on the subject in the following language:

From time immemorial the commanders of men-of-war had been in the habit, when searching neutral vessels for contraband or enemy property, of taking out and pressing into service any seamen whom they conceived to be their fellow subjects. The practice was essentially irregular, arbitrary, and oppressive, but its most mischievous possibilities were yet to be developed in the conditions resulting from American independence.

During the first half of the nineteenth century the right of impressment was maintained by some British authorities in international law, and as late as 1839 Manning wrote, " We have a full right to take such of our subjects as are found by us during the lawful exercise of our right of search." [2] American authorities [3] have been unanimous in condemning the practice as having no legal justification, while many of the well-recognized British authorities of the present day omit any reference to the subject, and by their silence convey their unbelief in the validity of the formerly alleged right of their own nation. Halleck, who does mention impressment, speaks unfavorably of it as an attempt of

[1] *Principles of American Diplomacy*, pp. 112-113.

[2] *Law of Nations* (London, 1839), p. 371.

[3] See Wheaton, *Elements of International Law* (Dana) para. 108 and 109 and note 67. Also Woolsey, *Introduction to the Study of International Law* (5th Ed.), p. 394; and Hyde, *International Law* (Boston, 1922), vol. i, p. 421.

the British government " to engraft (it) upon the right of visitation and search".[1]   It must, therefore, be concluded that on the major legal issue involved in impressment the position of the American government was correct.

The subject of impressment does not, however, hold a place of importance in American diplomatic history because of the significance of the legal question involved.   In this connection it should also be said that impressment was not vitally related to any of the major principles of American diplomacy.   The doctrine of expatriation in the fulness of its expression, meaning " that naturalization in the United States not only clothes the individual with a new allegiance, but also absolves him from the obligations of the old ",[2] was never stated by the American government until 1848, after the impressment controversy had ended.   There was much criticism of the British doctrine of perpetual allegiance and a tendency to place naturalized American seamen in the same status as those born in the United States, but a review of the entire controversy makes it clear that the central objection to impressment was not made on the ground that it violated the principle of expatriation, but on the ground that it was a perversion of the legitimate belligerent right of search carried out by means of enforcing the British law of allegiance on board neutral vessels on the high seas.

The above statement of the major American objection to impressment is sufficient to show also that the controversy over that subject was not related to the principle of exemp-

[1] Halleck, *International Law* (4th ed.), vol. ii, p. 302.   For other British authorities regarding impressment from neutral merchant vessels on the high seas as illegal, see T. J. Lawrence, *The Principles of International Law* (Boston, 1900), p. 207; and Phillimore, *Commentaries*, pt. iii, ch. xviii.

[2] Moore, *Principles of American Diplomacy*, p. 276.   See also, *supra*, ch. i, p. 22, footnote.

tion of vessels from visit and search on the high seas in time of peace, a principle which owes its present universal recognition in no small measure to the constant and successful advocacy of the American government.

While impressment was for many years inextricably associated in the minds of Americans with the various violations of neutral trade rights, still it cannot be said to have any direct legal relation to any of them. Its relation to commercial questions consisted chiefly in the practical bearing which it inevitably had on the number of seamen engaged in American shipping, and on the actual status of the crews of American vessels, which were often depleted by the practice.

But while impressment cannot be viewed as a major problem in international law, nor as having direct relation to the cardinal principles of American diplomacy, still the unusual prolongation of the controversy and the remarkable influence it exerted over the thought of the American people as a whole, insure it an important place in American diplomatic history. In this connection the causes of the continued failure of negotiations throughout the years should be briefly summarized. There was one fundamental difficulty which almost continuously operated as an obstruction to successful negotiation. This difficulty was the result of a complex situation involving the lack of an adequate plan for manning the British navy, the prevalence of the habit of desertion on the part of British seamen, and the naturalization policy of the United States. It is a matter of history that when Great Britain established an adequate system for enlisting seamen, a return to the system of impressment, which was not only unpopular but inefficient, was never again seriously considered. Desertion became less and less prevalent when the length of service was limited and when the terms of the sailors' contract became in general more liberal. The Volunteer Acts in particular now provide seamen for the navy, always ready in cases of emergency.

But this system of recruiting seamen seemed impossible to Great Britain during the years when the impressment controversy was at its height, and the loss of her seamen by desertion to United States' vessels not only seemed unfair, but was looked upon as a positive danger to the maritime welfare of the nation, which was being encouraged by the liberal naturalization policy of the United States. As long as this view of things prevailed in the thought of the British nation as a whole, it is possible to understand why no British government was disposed to agree to the abandonment of the practice of impressment without holding out for some guarantee that would insure to Great Britain the services of her own seamen. The nature of the guarantee proposed by the American government, which varied at different times, was never acceptable to the British government. Whether it took the form of a reciprocal agreement to return deserting seamen, or of mutual restrictions on the policy of naturalization, or of the mutual exclusion of each others seamen from the vessels of the two nations, there was always something which failed to satisfy the British government. The execution of all such proposed agreements would have required the passage and enforcement of appropriate legislation, and the British government, lacking other more plausible objections, did not hesitate to express a lack of confidence either in the willingness or in the ability of the American government to insure the execution of the agreement by the necessary legislation. In the only proposal ever offered by the British government, impressment was to be abandoned in return for the mutual exclusion of the natural-born seamen of each nation from the vessels of the other. The phrase " natural-born " was intended to counteract the naturalization policy of the United States as applied to

British seamen. The proposal also involved practical requirements relating to seamen already naturalized, with which the United States refused to comply.

On three occasions during the controversy there was every indication that a settlement of the vexing question would be finally achieved. The first of these was in 1803, when the only obstacle to agreement was the revival by Great Britain, at the very close of the negotiations, of the doctrine of *mare clausum*, with the demand that British ships be permitted to impress from American vessels in the "narrow seas". The second occasion when a settlement seemed probable was in 1806. The American and British plenipotentiaries engaged in this negotiation had, after long and patient endeavor, reached an agreement in which impressment was to be abandoned, and the return of deserters insured on a basis requested by the British negotiators themselves. On this occasion, the British Board of Admiralty and the crown officers summarily rejected the plan. The third time at which an agreement seemed likely to be reached was in 1818, when the British presented a plan, when, as has been seen, the article regarding naturalized seamen proved objectionable to the United States. The United States also objected to the article in this plan permitting impressment within territorial waters. It is obvious that at this time the British government was ready to sign an agreement eliminating impressment from the high seas. Since this had been the chief objective of the United States government previous to the war of 1812, it may seem strange at first that the British plan was not accepted. One effect of the plan, however, would have been to create discrimination against a particular class of naturalized American citizens, and it is difficult to see how this could have been harmonized with the principles of the American constitution. Furthermore, the practice of impressment was in abeyance at the time this plan was under consideration and had been ever since the war; and there was some reason to doubt that it would ever be revived in the future. With these facts in mind, the American rejection of the British plan in 1818 may be more clearly understood.

Little more need be said in explanation of the causes producing continuous diplomatic failures to adjust the impressment issue. As time advanced, the American government continued to express its thoroughgoing objection to any possible revival of the practice, while the British government, finding other means of securing seamen for the navy, did not resort again to the method of impressment. It was in this fashion that the prolonged controversy finally ended, when the period of British abstention from the practice seemed sufficiently long to warrant American abandonment of diplomatic protest.

It was, of course, during the years preceding the war of 1812 that the question of impressment held such an important place in the public opinion of the United States. From the very beginning of the practice it seemed to touch every element of human sentiment and national pride calculated to arouse the warlike spirit of a nation. The calm statesman might view it merely as an unwarranted perversion of a belligerent right, but to the popular mind it was spontaneously associated with stealing, piracy and slavery. Popular indignation was undoubtedly greatly augmented by memories of the Revolution, and the willingness on the part of many to believe that Great Britain still hoped for the reestablishment of control over the nation. The sentimental appeal contained in the impressment issue was unquestionably used at times by commercial organizations, and by politicians as well, for the purpose of advancing their own interests, but on the whole the vast majority of American citizens viewed the practice as humiliating and degrading, both to the people and to the government of the United States. Without the stimulus of this sentiment, which, with the exception of New England, was practically universal throughout the nation, it is difficult to believe that war with Great Britain would have been declared.

The intense popular hatred of impressment and the validity of the American objections to its continuance must finally be considered in the light of the large number of American seamen who suffered as a result of the practice. Of course, if the principle of impressment was wrong, then the magnitude of the evil can not be estimated in terms of the numerical frequency of the practice. The impressment of ten American seamen or even of one deserved the same condemnation as the impressment of a thousand. Nevertheless, the large number of seamen impressed rendered more vivid the realization of the evil during the years preceding the war of 1812, and merits our attention at this time.

From the beginning of the war between Great Britain and France in 1793 to the Peace of Amiens in 1802, the American agents for seamen reported a total of 2,410 American seamen impressed, many of whom were held in British ships over long periods of time. The records of Lenox, the American Agent for Seamen at London, however, warrant us in believing that probably all of these seamen were finally released. The most distressing period of impressment was that from 1803, the date of the renewal of the struggle between France and Great Britain, to the outbreak of war between Great Britain and the United States in 1812. According to the most conservative estimates based on the agents' reports, the number of seamen impressed during those years must be given as 6000, probably not more than one-third of whom were released at the outbreak of war in June, 1812. Contemporary estimates of the number impressed made by members of Congress, by newspapers and by public speakers ranged all the way from 10,000 to 50,000. John Adams, in a letter to Monroe dated February 23, 1813,[1] estimated that Great Britain had 40,000 foreign seamen in her merchant service alone, and that nine-tenths of them were American. As to American seamen impressed in British ships of war, Lyman, during his term as American Consul and Agent for Seamen at London in 1807, estimated the number at 15,000.[2] In presenting the final report on the subject to Congress, January 16, 1812, Monroe, Secretary of State, gave 6,257 as the total number impressed since 1803, but referring to the difficulty of supplying accurate data on the subject Monroe said:

But it may be proper to state, that from the want of means to make their cases known, and other difficulties inseparable from their situations, there is reason to believe that no precise or accurate view, is now or ever can be exhibited of the names or number of our seamen who are impressed into and detained in the British service.[3]

In fact, the statistics relating to impressment were found to be so confusing that a special effort was made to present in considerable detail the various phases of this problem, after carefully reviewing all the data available on the subject. The results of this effort are printed in the appendix. It will be sufficient here to say that during the three or four years preceding the war of 1812 there were at least from 750 to 1000 American seamen impressed annually.

[1] *Works of John Adams* (*C. F. Adams*), vol. x, pp. 32-33.

[2] Lyman to Madison, Oct. 23, 1807, *MS. Consular Despatches, London,* vol. ix.

[3] This report is found in a miscellaneous collection of Executive Documents of the Twelfth Congress and is entitled " Message from the President of the United States transmitting a report of the Secretary of State on the subject of impressment."

The American reaction to this continued injustice was at first expressed in terms of indignation, and later of bitter enmity toward Great Britain. The accounts of American parents, wives and children bereft of sons, husbands and fathers in order that the British navy might be maintained, were extremely humiliating to loyal American citizens of that day, and indeed after the passing of a century it is not so very easy for an American to review the subject without some degree of patriotic indignation. For the United States, the significance of the impressment issue throughout its history was not to be found so much in legal arguments as in the more subtle realm of feeling and sentiment related to delicate considerations of national honor and pride.

APPENDIX

STATISTICS RELATIVE TO IMPRESSMENT

DURING the years immediately preceding the war of 1812, there was much discussion of the question of the number of American seamen impressed by Great Britain. The subject can best be understood by considering first the number impressed previous to 1803. In the letter of Madison to Monroe, dated January 5, 1804,[1] the question is reviewed from the earliest years of the difficulty down to the peace of Amiens, and the total number of those impressed is given as 2,059. As late as 1831 Livingston, then Secretary of State, in a letter to Van Buren dated August 31, of that year,[2] used this same figure, which would indicate that it was regarded as authoritative. The figure 2,059 was derived from the final report of Lenox,[3] covering the period from January 1, 1799, to May 1, 1802.[4] In that report the total number of " original applications " for release is given as 2,248. There were, however, 189 " renewed applications," which if deducted from 2,248 gives 2,059. Of these 500 were reported as " discharged " and 590 as " ordered to be discharged," but on his departure from London, Lenox left the names of only 579 seamen with

---

[1] Madison to Monroe, Jan. 5, 1804, *American State Papers, Foreign Relations,* vol. iii, pp. 81-83.

[2] Livingston to Van Buren, Aug. 31, 1831, *MS. Instructions to United States Ministers, Great Britain,* vol. xiv, pp. 106-112.

[3] See *infra,* p. 262.

[4] The figures given Jan. 1, 1799 included the entire number impressed up to that date.

his successor, Erving, requiring further proof for their release, giving it as his opinion that most of them had in fact
already been released.

The very small number of those who were "detained as
British subjects" calls for special comment. In the diplomatic correspondence at various times the argument is put
forth that if the same proportion of British and American
seamen obtained in the unadjusted cases as did in those
which were adjusted, considerably less than 200 British seamen had been recovered in all those years, and that hence
for every British subject recovered more than ten Americans
were torn from their country and later discharged on full
proof of that fact.

In addition to the 2,059 reported by Lenox, there were
351 cases of impressment in the West Indies reported by
Savage. The reports from Talbot in the West Indies referred to many seamen who were released, but no record of
the number impressed was found. Combining those reported by Lenox and Savage, a total of 2,410 for the entire
period preceding 1803 is reached.

The unprejudiced attitude of Lenox, which is revealed in
all his work as the Agent for Seamen, and the great care
with which he seems to have prepared each quarterly report,
and each annual report as well, inspire confidence in the
essential accuracy of his figures. He arranged every list
of seamen alphabetically, making duplication impossible, a
practice which was unfortunately not followed by the agents
for seamen after the year 1803. He kept a complete record [1]
of individual cases which contained the following items:
1. Date of application; 2. To whom made; 3. Name; 4. Ship
whence taken; 5. Captain's name; 6. States of which they

---

[1] See *Impressed Seamen,* vols. i-ii, which cover his entire mission.
These volumes are in manuscript form in the Bureau of Rolls and
Library, Library of State Department.

were citizens and natives; 7. Date of Impressment; 8. Ships where carried; 9. Captain's name; 10. Evidence of Citizenship; 11. Result of application.

A glance at this record reveals the fact that numbers 4, 5 and 9 were usually blank. He was unable in most cases to give the name of the ship or of its captain from which they were impressed. The name of the British ship into which they were taken was nearly always given, though very rarely was the captain's name recorded. The date of impressment is given in only about one-fourth of the cases, and the state is listed in about fifty per cent of them. Under "evidence of citizenship" he recorded in at least fifty per cent of the cases: "His letter of —— (date)." The evidence in many cases, however, is quite lengthy and involved, as is seen from the record of William Ingraham [1] a native of Massachusetts, who had been impressed in October 1799, and discharged September 21, 1800.

Abstracts of Lenox's reports were presented to Congress annually, and with the exception of two or three quarterly reports all of them were published in annual instalments in the *Annals of Congress.*

As an illustration of the work which he did along this line, an abstract of his final report is herewith reproduced.[2]

---

[1] This record, reproduced from *Impressed Seamen,* vol. i, p. 99 is as follows:

"Certificate of his birth under the hand of Chas. Spaulding, town clerk, Chelmsford, 10 May —— Certificate to the same effect with a description of his person, by Joseph and May Ingraham of Boston, his parents . . . . . . Certificate of baptism by Hezekiah Packard, Pastor of Chelmsford, 8 May —— Deposition of Ebenezer Bridge and William Adams both members of the State Legislature to the truth of the certificates of the clerk and Pastor, and also deposition of the father and mother to the truth of their certificates which oaths are in the form of an attestation by Samuel Gardner J. P. for the County of Suffolk 6th of June and authenticated by the British Consul for the New England States, 16 of same month 1800."

[2] This abstract is taken from *Impressed Seamen,* vol. ii.

Date of Abstracts	Number of original applications	Renewed applications	Cases unanswered at last abstract	Discharged	Ordered to be discharged	Detained for want of documents	Entered and received bounty	Detained as British subjects	Not on ships represented	Made their escape	Not answering description in certificate	Detained as prisoners of war	On board ships on foreign stations	Sent on board by the civil authority	Dead	Killed in action	Detained on ship on suspicion of being concerned in mutiny on the Hermione	No order to leave the service after having requested my interference	On board the La Bertin on date when she foundered	Unanswered cases at the date of abstract
1799																				
January 1	651			173	99	172	93	29	22	17	2	8	3	1	1					31*
March 1	111			9	5	28	18	5	4	3			5		1					33
June 1	78		33	8	11	22	9	10	1	2		2								45
August 1	79		45	8	39	23	4		7	4	2					1				38
November 1	192	21	38	35	48	37	22	4	8	6		2		1	1					85
1800																				
January 1	106	27	85	37	31	41	8	19	8	9		2								61
April 1	109	3	61	22	33	29	12	6	2	6	1	19						1		42
July 1	125	9	42	39	31	42	6	5	4	3										45
October 1	133	9	45	32	46	34	8	4	6	2		2						1	1	32
1801																				
January 1	142	21	52	33	36	78	6	6	15	4	5		3		1					12
April 1	83	28	12	11	24	33	3	2	6	2	3	1	1		1					12
July 1	130	6	33	21	39	43	4	6	7	2	1	2								33†
October 1	176	41	42	40	74	55	7	11	9	3			6		2					42
1802																				
May 1	133	24	51	31	54	69	10	5	13	7	1		7		1					7‡
	2248	189	539	500	590	706	210	112	112	71	15	38	25	2	8	1	1	3	1	2 & 3

* These 31 cases were on the 16th of January. Are in the return March 1st and the subsequent abstract.

† One invalid.

‡ One invalid and two on board the foundered La Bertin.

The real statistical difficulty concerning the number of impressments, however, arises in reviewing the period from 1803 to 1812.   On April 1, 1806, the Secretary of State reported that a total of 2,798 had been impressed since the renewal of the war in 1803.   From this date to September 30, 1810, the numbers are recorded serially beginning with the figure 2,799.   The last detailed report which was found was the final one made by Lyman covering the period from April 1, 1809, to September 30, 1810.   It began with the number 4,500 and ended with that of 6,057, making a total of 1,558 cases for that period.   An abstract compiled from this report is given as an illustration of the manner in which the reports were kept during the period from 1803 to 1812. The abstract follows: [1]

[1] This report is found in a miscellaneous collection of Executive Documents of the Twelfth Congress, and is entitled " Message from the President of the United States transmitting a report of the Secretary of State on the subject of Impressments—Jan. 16, 1812."   Reports issued previous to April 1, 1809, are printed in *American State Papers, Foreign Relations*.   No later report was found except a brief final summary of the record of the London Consulate, in which was given a total of 802 cases for the year 1811.

Abstract from the Returns or Lists of American Seamen and Citizens Impressed from April 1, 1809, to September 30, 1810

	April 1, 1809–June 30, 1809	July 1, 1809–Sept. 30, 1809	October 1, 1809–Dec. 31, 1809	Jan. 1, 1810–March 31, 1810	April 1, 1810–June 30, 1810	July 1, 1810–Sept. 30, 1810	Total
Discharged and ordered to be discharged	51	71	60	55	94	70	401
Duplicate applications	2	....	....	....	....	....	2
Having no documents	6	43	5	9	12	32	107
Said to be born in England, Scotland, Ireland or Wales	20	31	34	86	30	28	229
Being a native of the West Indies	....	1	5	5	2	1	14
Being a native of Africa	....	1	1	1	....	1	4
Being a native of Sweden	1	....	1	....	....	....	2
Being a native of Prussia	....	....	....	....	....	1	1
Not being an American	6	1	....	....	....	2	9
Being ignorant of America	....	1	....	....	....	4	5
Said to have been married in England, Scotland, Ireland or Wales	....	2	3	2	11	3	21
Having formerly belonged to the British Navy	....	1	....	....	1	....	
Being exchanged as British subjects from enemy prisons	....	2	2	....	2	....	6
Having voluntarily entered and taken bounty (9 only)	10	9	8	4	4	14	49
Having been taken in enemy's privateers	4	11	....	9	13	6	43
Having attempted to desert	....	....	1	1	....	....	2
Being deserters or said to be deserters	2	4	1	2	1	1	11
Having fraudulent protections	2	8	7	4	6	3	30
Protections being irregular—dated May 29, 1806, in United States and June 6, 1806, in England	....	....	1	....	....	....	1
Being released from prison at Gottenburg by British Consul	....	....	3	....	....	....	3
Said to be imposters	....	....	1	2	....	2	5
Not answering the description in their protections	14	12	17	10	9	13	75
Being a native of Italy	....	....	1	....	....	....	1
No reason assigned	2	5	9	1	....	2	19
	120	203	160	191	185	183	1042

Abstract—*Continued*

	April 1, 1809–June 30, 1809	July 1, 1809–Sept. 30, 1809	October 1, 1809–Dec. 31, 1809	Jan. 1, 1810–March 31, 1810	April 1, 1810–June 30, 1810	July 1, 1810–Sept. 30, 1810	Total
Protections from Consuls and Vice Consuls.	15	16	9	13	11	14	78
Notarial and other affidavits made in United States	6	11	3	7	9	9	45
Notarial and other affidavits made in England	....	2	1	....	1	3	7
Discharged from British ship of war as American citizen	1	....	....	3	1	....	5
Collectors' protections	2	....	....	2	5	2	11
Admiralty protections	1	....	....	....	....	1	2
Documents from the Department of State..	1	4	6	2	6	10	29
Indentures	1	....	....	1	2	1	5
Marriage certificate	....	....	1	....	....	....	1
	27	33	20	28	35	40	183
Not on board the ship as stated	3	7	12	12	15	9	58
Not known where or on what ship these men are serving	....	....	2	4	12	13	31
Deserted	3	11	9	3	6	7	39
Drowned or dead	1	....	....	....	1	4	6
Killed	....	....	....	....	....	1	1
Invalided	6	11	4	10	3	8	42
Said to be on board ships which are not in commission	1	1	....	2	1	....	5
On board ships in foreign stations	18	14	20	4	30	59	145
Unanswered	....	....	3	....	2	1	6
	32	44	50	35	70	102	333

Total Number Impressed 1,558
Total Number Discharged 401

According to the published reports of the agents for seamen in London from 1803 to September 30, 1810, 6,057 seamen made application for release from impressment. Since the names of seamen given in these reports were not arranged alphabetically, duplications occurred which must be taken into account.

While the American peace commissioners were in London, they made request for a report on the total number of impressed seamen recorded in the London Consulate at that time for the years 1803 to 1812, and during the absence of Beasley this information was prepared by Irving and is found in a letter written by him to Gallatin, dated June 3, 1814.[1]

The total given for the entire period ending with December 31, 1811, is only 5,987, and this includes those for the last quarter of 1810 and the entire year 1811 which were not included in the previous reports, although those reports as has been seen, gave a total of 6,057. This report gives the total by years for 1809, 1810, and 1811 only. That for 1809 is 792, for 1810, 921, and for 1811, 802. The report issued by Lyman gave 868 as the number of applications from January 1 to September 30, 1810; whereas Irving's final report gave only 921 for the entire year. It is possible that duplications and additional information later received reduced the totals given by Lyman. In an effort to estimate the number of duplications and thus arrive at some basis for judging the accuracy of the figure 5,987, an alphabetical list was made of the entire 1,558 names in the final report made by Lyman covering the period from April 1, 1809 to September 30, 1810. It was found that thirty-one names occurred twice, with different addresses in all but three instances; four names occurred three times; three names occurred four times, while one name, " John Smith," occurred six times; all having different addresses. This gives altogether only fifty-three duplicates out of a total of 1,558 names, without making any allowance for the possible contingency of two or even more seamen having the same name.

[1] Irving to Gallatin, June 3, 1814, *MS. Consular Despatches, London*, vol. x.

It would not seem, therefore, that the discrepancy involved could be accounted for solely on the ground of duplication. Furthermore, all abstracts from 1803 to 1809 carried a column marked " duplicate applications." If the 802 for 1811 be added to 6,057, a total of 6,859 would be reached, not including any figure for the last quarter of 1810 as against the total of 5,987 given in the later report of 1814.

It was found that the newspapers of 1812 took the figure 6,057, which was the last serial number in the report of Lyman on September 30, 1810, and after adding to it 200 cases which were listed by the Secretary of State as having been reported directly to the Department of State during that period, the grand total of 6,257 was reached, and this figure was continuously displayed during the early months of 1812 in large black letters in the columns of the pro-war Republican papers. These figures became a standing symbol of national degradation, and their size and position on the pages was usually a pretty good indication of the actual war sentiment of the editors.

If one should take the more conservative figure for the years 1803 to 1812; namely, 5,987, and add to it the figure for the period previous to 1803; namely, 2,410, a grand total of 8,397 would be reached. Furthermore, in the reports of the Secretary of State from 1796 to 1812, there are listed 1,594 cases of impressment as having been reported directly to the Secretary of State by masters and collectors. It has been seen that 200 of this list reported between April 1, 1809, and September 30, 1810, were treated by the news-papers as being additional to those reported from the London office. If they should all be regarded as additional to those reports, a grand total of 9,991 could be justified by statis-tical count. Furthermore, it should be noted that no figures were found covering the period from January 1, 1812, to the date of the declaration of war, during which some cases of impressment are known to have occurred.

Contemporary estimates made by members of Congress, newspapers, and public speakers ranged all the way from 10,000 to 50,000. John Adams, in a letter to Monroe dated February 23, 1813,[1] estimated that the British had 40,000 foreign seamen in their merchant service, and that at least nine-tenths of them were American. Cobbett, in his letter to the Prince Regent, quoted in the *National Morning Post*, May 5, 1812,[2] gave 14,000 as the estimate made by Lyman, while he was American Consul and Agent for Seamen in London. However, the actual estimate which Lyman made, as is shown in his correspondence, was 15,000, and referred solely to American seamen in the British navy.

As to the number of those impressed who were later released, it may be conservatively stated that previous to 1803 all or practically all impressed seamen were eventually released. In Irving's report made in 1814, only 1,995 of those reported as impressed from 1803 to 1812 were listed as "discharged" and "ordered to be discharged." The same report listed 680 as having been discharged and sent to depots as prisoners of war from the beginning of the war to March 1, 1814. The Secretary of State later reported at least 1,500 who were imprisoned during the war because of their refusal to fight against their own country. Only partial information concerning the final disposition of these and of others remaining unaccounted for in the final reports of the agents could be found.

It was frequently charged by the Federalists that the number of impressed seamen was greatly exaggerated. A report was issued in 1813 by the Massachusetts House of Representatives[3] which held that duplication of names occurred

[1] *Works of John Adams (C. F. Adams)*, pp. 32-33.
[2] See *supra*, ch. vii, p. 175.
[3] Report of Committee of House of Representatives of Massachusetts on Impressed Seamen (1813).

in the report of January 16, 1812,[1] the same name being
"reckoned three and four times." The report also contained the testimony of fifty-one ship owners including that
of William Gray [2] a Republican and the largest ship owner

[1] This was Lyman's report from April 1, 1809, to Sept. 30, 1810.

[2] Gray's testimony, which was undoubtedly significant, is given in full.
It is found on pp. 41-44 of the report.

"I, William Gray of Boston, in the County of Suffolk, Esquire, do
depose and say, that I have been engaged in commerce and navigation
for forty or fifty years, and have for the last fifteen or twenty years
employed about three hundred seamen annually upon an average.

"I recollect the following cases of impressments and detentions of
my seamen. In the year 1811 while one of my vessels, the Rachel, was
at Leith in Scotland, two of my men, to wit, Samuel Tuck, and I think
Israel Foster, were impressed from the vessel. one of them I under--
stand escaped from the man of war, and reached my vessel before she
left Leith; the other I also understood effected his escape with the
aid of a waterman at Liverpool. I cannot recollect any further cases
of impressments by the British from my vessels; but from the multiplicity of my business, it is almost impossible for me to remember
individual cases. I have no doubt that the aforenamed Tuck had a
protection.

"I recollect no cases of impressments and detentions by the French,
except the three Swedes taken soon after the affair of the Chesapeake,
and which are stated in my letter to Col. Pickering in the year 1808.

"I have had whole crews taken in my vessels when they have been
captured, both by the English and French; but I do not mean to say,
that the men in these cases were impressed or detained by these
nations.

"The other cases within my knowledge, are four men belonging to
Salem, which were taken in the Cynthia, John H. Andrews, master,
about 1806. I made application myself for one of them (Samuel Shepherd) and he was released. I do not recollect hearing what became
of the other three.

"Another case, about the year 1807, was that of four fishermen, belonging to the Northfields in Salem, who were taken off Halifax, by a
British ship; the British officer, as I understood, assigned as a reason,
that they had no protections; to which they replied, that it was not
customary for fishermen to have them. I was concerned in sending
evidence of their citizenship to Halifax, by the vessel hired for the
purpose, and they were released upon application. I think their names
were Symonds and Skerry.

in New England. Only thirty-five cases of impressment

"I have lately received a copy of a letter from the supercargo of the ship Pekin, belonging to Philadelphia, on which I am an underwriter; the letter is dated the 15th of July, 1812, at Calcutta, and states, that in February preceding, while he was at or near Batavia roads, the men of war, that had been ordered on an expedition, impressed every seaman belonging to the vessel; the letter gives no account of what has become of the men since.

"The most recent case in my knowledge, is that of the barque Mary, (belonging to my brother Samuel Gray.) On her passage from Boston to Savannah, in November or December last a lad belonging to Beverly was impressed (by the Southampton I think); the lad was a Portuguese or Spaniard by birth, which was the reason assigned when he was impressed; and I understood that he had a protection, and was bound as an apprentice in Beverly.

"I think I can recollect three or four cases more, in which I have been requested to apply for the discharge of men impressed, generally from Salem. I recollect one other Salem man, named Thomas Driver, who was killed in the battle of the Nile; but from the circumstances, that a sum of money passed through my hands, for the benefit of his family, which I think was a part of the subscription money, raised at Lloyd's coffee house in London, I am inclined to think he had entered the British service, but I do not know how the fact was.

"I do not recollect any other information on the subject of the present inquiry.

WILLIAM GRAY

Suffolk, ss. Feb. 16, 1813
  Sworn to before
    Alexander Townsend, Justice of Peace."

Addition to Hon. Mr. Gray's Deposition

"I can now add to the foregoing, the following cases. James Coburn of Easton, Maryland who was taken by the Sword-fish, American privateer, when she captured an English vessel lately. He had been impressed, as his brother states in a letter to me, about nine years ago. His last protection (which his brother forwarded to me) I find is dated, June 4, 1804. He was allowed by the Marshal to go upon his parole, before I received the letter from his brother, and the Marshal has not seen him since, but will discharge him when he appears.

"Two of the seamen, also, that were taken in the Macedonian some time since applied to me for employment; they said they were Americans, and that they had sailed in my employ, I did not know them. They said they had been impressed.

could be remembered by the entire group, and of these only
twelve were Americans, nine of whom had been discharged,
while one had escaped.   It is obvious from the analysis of
this report already given [1] that the charge of duplication,
though warranted, did not effect the essential trustworthi-
ness of the report as a whole.

The testimony of the fifty-one ship owners, although on
first thought very striking, upon reflection appears less
significant.   It is possible that ship owners employing from
200 to 300 seamen annually might have had very little
definite information about them.   Conceivably the exact
personnel could have been changed with each voyage without
the knowledge of the ship owner.   It will be readily admitted that the testimony of fifty-one masters or captains
on this subject would be of much greater significance than
that of the owners.   In any case the testimony served well
the purpose of the Massachusetts Legislature, which was to
discredit the Republican Administration.   It is a matter of

"I have understood that nine of the seamen taken in the Guerriere,
are impressed Americans, and have been discharged by the Marshal,
since she was captured.

"Two men have been landed from the Constitution, that were taken
by her in Java, in the late battle; they are Americans as I am informed,
and have been discharged as such, and had been impressed.   The proportion of foreigners in the merchant service of the United States
varies much in different places.   In Massachusetts proper, I should
think the proportion would be including foreigners of all nations, from
fifteen to twenty per cent.; of British subjects, I should think not more
than five per cent.

"The Protest of the captain of Pekin, (the ship above mentioned)
does not make mention of the impressment of the crew, which is stated
in the above letter.

WILLIAM GRAY

Suffolk, ss. Feb. 19, 1813.
        Sworn to before
            Benjamin Weld, Justice of Peace."

[1] See *supra*, p. 266.

record, and at this late day should by no means be altogether discounted.

The varying contemporary estimates regarding the extent of impressment were encouraged by the lack of accurate data concerning the number of American seamen employed during these years. The total number registered from 1796 to 1812 under the act of Congress of 1796 was 106,757.[1] There were probably never more than 60,000 to 65,000 seamen in the merchant service of the United States at any one time during these years, and during much of the time the number was probably much less. The *Boston Centinel*, in its issue of September 24, 1808, estimated 65,000, with 48,000 of those coming from New England and New York. There being no exact data from year to year on this subject the above estimates are valuable only as furnishing a general notion of the numbers involved.

Concerning the actual number of those impressed, the view expressed by Morison,[2] that this information was difficult to obtain in 1812 and impossible now, is doubtless correct. There seems to be good reason, however, for much greater faith in the validity of available statistical data such as has been presented, than Morison was willing to exercise. This author regarded the report of the Massachusetts Legislature of 1813 as destroying the validity of the government's figures, although he conceded that the Federalist calculations were much too low.[3] In presenting the report of January 16, 1812, Monroe, Secretary of State, referring to the difficulty of supplying accurate data on the subject said:—

[1] Seybert, *Statistical Annals of the United States* (Philadelphia, 1818), pp. 315 *et seq.*

[2] Samuel Eliot Morison, *Maritime History of Massachusetts* (New York, 1921), pp. 196-197.

[3] *Ibid.*

But it may be proper to state, that from the want of means to make their cases known, and other difficulties inseparable from their situations, there is reason to believe that no precise or accurate view, is now or ever can be exhibited of the names or number of our seamen who are impressed into and detained in the British service.[1]

Impressment by the French has not been given separate consideration for the reason that very little information on that subject was found. That some American seamen were impressed by the French there can be no doubt. The reports of the State Department list about fifty cases of impressment by the French and even a few by the Dutch. Newspapers and other sources report several other cases by the French, but the total number involved was insignificant compared with the number impressed by the British. We may be sure that had there been contemporary evidence of large numbers impressed by the French, such evidence would have found its way into the Federalist press and have become a matter of record. Certain flagrant cases were published which make it impossible to regard the subject as exhaustively treated until more careful research in this field has been made. It is not to be supposed, however, that such a study would reveal anything entirely new bearing on the general practice of impressment. The complications arising because of the presence of American seamen in French vessels captured by the British, and in British vessels captured by the French, have been considered. On this subject, Monroe, in the final report above referred to, said:—

It is equally impossible, from the want of precise returns, to make an accurate report of the names or number of citizens of

[1] This report is found in a miscellaneous collection of executive documents of the Twelfth Congress, and is entitled, "Message from the President of the United States transmitting a report of the Secretary of State on the subject of impressment."

the United States who have been compelled to enter into the French service, or are held in captivity under the authority of that government, whether taken from vessels captured on the high seas or seized in rivers, ports or harbors; the names of a few only, greatly below the number believed to be so detained, being within the knowledge of this department. A detail is therefore not attempted with respect to this part of the call of the House of Representatives.

The proportion of foreigners engaged in American commerce during these years was estimated as being about one-sixth [1] of the total number. The absence of data makes it futile to attempt to verify this calculation. Of the 106,757 seamen registered from 1796 to 1812, only 1,530 were naturalized.[2] Some contemporary writers, however, estimated the number of foreigners in figures almost as large as those given for the whole number of seamen in the American service. The habit of desertion among seamen of all nations during these years was so common that exact figures on this point will always be impossible to secure. Doubtless a large proportion of the foreign seamen engaged were British, but on this point there are no reliable figures.

It would be interesting indeed to know just how many British seamen were voluntarily engaged in the American service, and also how many Americans were engaged in the British service, both voluntarily and because of impressment. It is held by some that by encouraging British desertion the United States secured as many British seamen as Great Britain secured from the United States by impressment. It is significant that of the thousands of applications acted on by the British Admiralty, less than 400 seamen are reported

[1] Seybert, *Statistical Annals*, p. 316, quoting letter of Secretary of Treasury, Jan. 26, 1816, gave the proportion for 1807 as "nearly one sixth."

[2] Seybert, *Statistical Annals*, p. 315.

to have been "retained as British subjects." The conclusion
would seem to be warranted that the large majority of those
retained by the British were either American, or at least
non-British seamen. But this conclusion, if valid, does not
prove that other British seamen were not engaged in the
service of the United States, because American merchants
were fully warned, and probably heeded the warning, not to
ship British seamen to British ports. Thomas Barclay, in
a letter to Lord Hugh Seymour dated September 23, 1801,[1]
expressed the belief that where Great Britain had one American seamen, America had fifty British. This statement,
however, was deplored as unreasonably extreme by the
British Minister at Washington. Professor Channing
thinks that contemporary British reports claiming that the
United States held thirty or forty thousand of their seamen
were greatly exaggerated.[2] The estimate of the British
Admiralty was 20,000.[3]

In closing this statistical review of the number of impressments and of data bearing indirectly on that subject,
a feeling of dissatisfaction with the results obtained is freely
expressed. It is believed, however, to be based on the best
sources available, and to have a distinct value in giving a
more comprehensive view of the scope of the practice of impressment than could otherwise be obtained.

[1] *Correspondence of Thomas Barclay* (Rives), vol. i, p. 132.
[2] *The Jefferson System* (New York, 1906), p. 172.
[3] *Report of the Naturalization Commission* (1869), appendix p. 35.

INDEX

STUDIES IN HISTORY, ECONOMICS AND PUBLIC LAW

EDITED BY THE FACULTY OF POLITICAL SCIENCE OF
COLUMBIA UNIVERSITY

Volume CXVIII]   [Number 2

Whole Number 263

EXTRATERRITORIALITY:

Its Rise and Its Decline

BY

SHIH SHUN LIU, Ph.D.

New York
COLUMBIA UNIVERSITY
SELLING AGENTS
NEW YORK; LONGMANS, GREEN & CO.
LONDON: P. S. KING & SON LTD.
1925

𝕿𝖔

THE MEMORY OF

MY GRANDFATHER

IN AFFECTIONATE AND GRATEFUL ACKNOWLEDGMENT OF THE
COUNTLESS KINDNESSES HE LAVISHED UPON ME
DURING MY CHILDHOOD AND YOUTH

PREFACE

THE present thesis is not an exhaustive treatise on the vastly complicated subject of extraterritoriality. It does not pretend to deal with the legal intricacies of this peculiar institution, on which numerous works of unsurpassable value and insight are in existence. All it attempts to do is to present briefly the historical development of the system of consular jurisdiction as a whole, to show how it arose, how it later grew in importance, and how finally it has in recent years declined. It is the author's firm conviction that most aspects of international law have or ought to have their *raison d'être* somewhere in the cumulative experience of centuries gone by, and his belief seems to be borne out by the history of extraterritoriality. Though the latter is an institution essentially incompatible with modern conceptions of territorial sovereignty, on which the science of international law is founded, the story of its rise and decline will nevertheless serve to demonstrate the continuity of legal development.

In making this study, the attitude adopted by the author is one of impartial investigation. His sole obligation is to bring to the light of day all the salient facts connected with the rise and decline of extraterritoriality, and to draw such conclusions as the facts warrant. He advocates nothing, and suggests nothing. He presents no practical solution of the as yet unsettled problems arising out of the existence of extraterritoriality, but he has sought to furnish the background of historical fact, which is the first condition to a philosophical as well as a practical approach to these problems.

As to the material used, the author has relied chiefly upon the treaties, diplomatic correspondence and other state papers published from the archives of the leading countries of the world. Secondary works have been employed only as clues to the sources, and many of them have been of unusual assistance to the author. Such works as Miltitz's *Manuel des consuls* and Martens's *Das Consularwesen und die Consularjurisdiction im Orient* are indispensable aids to every student of the development of the consular office. The author's indebtedness to them can hardly be measured by the references made in the body of the thesis.

This monograph was written under a Fellowship awarded by the Carnegie Endowment for International Peace. Part of the manuscript was submitted to the criticism of Professor John Bassett Moore, whose example and inspiration have not infrequently kept the author from faltering in the face of the innumerable obstacles confronting a research student at every step. Professor Moore's retirement from Columbia University left the author to finish his work with Dr. Julius Goebel, Jr., to whom he is under the heaviest obligations. Dr. Goebel has not only read and re-read the manuscript with the care of a discerning scholar, but has suggested many alterations and emendations, which have added much to the work. Acknowledgment should also be made of the assistance rendered by Mr. Edward R. Hardy in reading some difficult mediaeval documents. To Dr. Edward M. Earle, of the Department of History, who read the sections on the Near East, the author is indebted for a number of helpful hints and suggestions. Finally, thanks are due to Chang Wei Chiu, a fellow student as well as a close friend, for assistance in proofreading.

SHIH SHUN LIU

COLUMBIA UNIVERSITY
  NEW YORK CITY
    MARCH, 1925.

CONTENTS

PART I

THE RISE OF EXTRATERRITORIALITY

CHAPTER I

IN EUROPE

PART II

THE DECLINE OF EXTRATERRITORIALITY

CHAPTER V

ANNEXATION

CHAPTER IX

UNILATERAL CANCELLATION

CHAPTER X

DIPLOMATIC NEGOTIATION

INTRODUCTION

It is a recognized principle of modern international law that every independent and sovereign State possesses absolute and exclusive jurisdiction over all persons and things within its own territorial limits. This jurisdiction is not qualified by differences of nationality, and extends to the persons and property of subjects and foreigners alike.[1] Nowhere is this principle of territorial jurisdiction more effectively pronounced than in the case of *The Schooner Exchange* v. *M'Faddon & Others,* where Chief Justice Marshall gave his opinion in this oft quoted passage:

The jurisdiction of the nation within its own territory is necessarily exclusive and absolute. It is susceptible of no limitation not imposed by itself. Any restriction upon it, deriving validity from an external source, would imply a diminution of its own sovereignty to the extent of the restriction, and an investment of that sovereignty to the same extent in that power which could impose such restrictions. All exceptions, therefore, to the full and complete power of a nation within its own territories, must be traced up to the consent of the nation itself. They can flow from no other legitimate source.[2]

In this passage due allowance is made for the limitations upon the main principle; and in practice there are a number of well-known exceptions to the general rule.[3] One of the

---

[1] Hall, *A Treatise on International Law* (7th ed., Oxford, 1917), p. 49; Phillimore, *Commentaries upon International Law* (3rd ed., London, 1879-89), vol. i, p. 443.

[2] 7 Cranch 116, 136.

[3] For the immunities of foreign sovereigns, diplomatic agents, military

most important of these exceptions is the system of extraterritoriality.

The word " extraterritoriality " is often used interchange-
ably with the word " exterritoriality " to denote the special
status of foreign ambassadors, who enjoy the right of exemption from the local jurisdiction. By a confusion of
ideas, the persons to whom this immunity is attached are
deemed to be legally removed from the territory in which
they actually reside,[1] and consequently, it has been maintained by some writers, foreign ambassadors may exercise
civil and criminal jurisdiction over their suite.[2] This theory
is now found to be inconsistent with the facts and is dis-
carded by the most competent writers on international law.
After discussing the extent and nature of the immunities

forces and public vessels, see Hall, *op. cit.*, pp. 179-209; Phillimore, *op.
cit.*, vol. i, pp. 475-481, vol. ii, pp. 139, 140, 141; *The Schooner Exchange*,
7 Cranch 116. The whole system of private international law is an
important exception to the exercise of territorial jurisdiction, but being
founded in international comity and constituting, in fact, a part of
municipal law, it does not fall within the province of public international law. See Phillimore, *op. cit.*, vol. iv, pp. 1 *et seq.;* Westlake, *A
Treatise on Private International Law* (6th. ed., London, 1922), p. 1.

[1] Under the section " the rights of *exterritoriality* and inviolability,"
Lorimer says: " An English ambassador, with his family and his suite,
whilst abroad in the public service, is domiciled in England, and his
house is English ground." *Institutes of the Law of Nations* (Edinburgh
& London, 1883-84), vol. i, p. 248. *Cf.* Wheaton, *Elements of International Law* (Dana's edition, Boston, 1866), p. 300, where the American
jurist says: " To give a more lively idea of this complete exemption from
the local jurisdiction, the fiction of *extraterritoriality* has been invented,
by which the minister, though actually in a foreign country, is supposed
still to remain within the territory of his own sovereign."

[2] " It follows from the principle of the extra-territorality of the minister, his family, and other persons attached to the legation, or belonging to his suite, and their exemption from the local laws and jurisdiction of the country where they reside, that the civil and criminal jurisdiction over these persons rests with the minister, to be exercised
according to the laws and usages of his own country." Wheaton, *ibid.*,
p. 302.

enjoyed by foreign ambassadors, etc., Hall declares that " it is clear that the fiction of exterritoriality is not needed to explain them, and even that its use is inconvenient." [1] For this reason, he has avoided the expression throughout his discussion of the subject. Today, the term " extraterritoriality " is generally employed to describe the condition of law existing in certain Oriental countries, under which foreigners are exempt from the local jurisdiction and are subject to their national authorities, by virtue of well-established usage or treaty arrangement.[2] In the present treatise, an attempt is made to examine into the rise and decline of the system of extraterritoriality in all the countries in which it has existed or still exists.

[1] *Op. cit.,* p. 210. *Cf.* Moore, *A Digest of International Law* (Washington, 1906), vol. ii, pp. 774-779.

[2] *Cf.* Moore, *ibid.,* p. 593: " Owing to diversities in law, custom, and social habits, the citizens and subjects of nations possessing European civilization enjoy in countries of non-European civilization, chiefly in the East, an extensive exemption from the operation of the local law. This exemption is termed ' extraterritoriality.' "

PART I
THE RISE OF EXTRATERRITORIALITY

CHAPTER I

In Europe

I. RELIGIOUS BASIS OF EARLY LAW

THE principle of territorial sovereignty as stated in the epoch-making opinion of Chief Justice Marshall in the case of *The Schooner Exchange* mentioned above was unknown in the ancient world. In fact, during a large part of what we usually term modern history, no such conception was ever entertained.[1] In the earlier stages of human development, race or nationality rather than territory formed the basis of a community of law. An identity of religious worship seems to have been during this period a necessary condition of a common system of legal rights and obligations. The barbarian was outside the pale of religion, and therefore incapable of amenability to the same jurisdiction to which the natives were subjected.[2] For this reason, we find that in the ancient world foreigners were either placed under a special jurisdiction or completely exempted from the local jurisdiction. In these arrangements for the safeguarding of foreign interests we find the earliest traces of extraterritoriality.

Under the reign of King Proteus of Egypt, in the thirteenth century, B. C., Phoenician merchants from the city of Tyre were allowed to dwell around a special precinct in Memphis known as the " camp of the Tyrians," and to have

---

[1] Maine, *Ancient Law* (3d Am. ed., New York, 1888), p. 99. *Cf.* Moore, *op. cit.*, vol. ii, p. 761.

[2] *Cf.* Twiss, *Law of Nations* (2d ed., Oxford, 1884), vol. i, p. 444.

a temple for their own worship.[1] Seven centuries later,
King Amasis (570-526, B. C.) permitted the Greeks to establish a factory at Naucratis, where they might live as a
distinct community under their own laws and worshipping
their own gods.[2] In his work on *The International Law
and Custom of Ancient Greece and Rome,* Dr. Coleman
Phillipson says: " The Egyptians often allowed foreign merchants to avail themselves of local judges of their own
nationality in order to regulate questions and settle differences arising out of mercantile transactions, in accordance
with their foreign laws and customs;—the Greeks especially
enjoyed these privileges on Egyptian territory." [3]

In Athens and in other Greek cities, the institution of
proxenia existed, the *proxenus* being appointed either by the
foreign government which he represented or by the State
in which he resided.[4] The choice was made from among
the citizens of the latter State, and had to be approved by
them.[5] The office of the *proxenus* was similar to the
modern consulate and is even regarded by some as its earliest
prototype.[6] It is said that nearly all the Greek republics
had *proxenoi* in Egypt.[7]

[1] Herodotus, bk. ii, ch. 112. Sir Travers Twiss also mentions "that
the merchants of Tyre who were strangers to the religion of Egypt,
were nevertheless permitted in the Twelfth Century before Christ to
establish trading factories in three different cities on the Tanitic branch
of the Nile, where they were allowed the privilege of living under their
own laws, and of worshipping according to their own religious rites."
Op. cit., vol. i, p. 444.

[2] Herodotus, bk. ii, ch. 178.   *Cf.* Twiss, *op. cit.,* vol. i, p. 445;
Pardessus, *Collection de lois maritimes antérieures au XXVIIIe siècle*
(Paris, 1828-45), vol. i, p. 21.

[3] Vol. i, p. 193.

[4] Phillipson, *op. cit.,* vol. i, p. 150. The earliest evidence of the existence of *proxenoi* dates from the middle of the fifth century, *ibid.,* p. 148.

[5] Pardessus, *op. cit.,* vol. i, p. 52; Hautefeuille, *Histoire du droit maritime international* (2d ed., Paris, 1869), p. 96, n. 1.

[6] Phillipson, *op. cit.,* vol. i, p. 149; Miltitz, *Manuel des consuls* (London
and Berlin, 1837-41), vol. i, p. 11.

[7] Hautefeuille, *ibid.*

Of more interest to us is the special system of jurisdiction for foreigners, which, in ancient Greece and Rome, received its most remarkable development. On this, Dr. Phillipson says:

In Greece special magistrates ξενοδίκαι (a general term, for which special names were substituted in different localities), were instituted for trying questions in which foreigners were involved. Sometimes such magistrates were appointed on the initiative of the particular national government in question, sometimes provisions were arranged to that effect by means of special conventions between States. In some cases these judges exercised full judicial power in pronouncing decisions as to the matters in dispute, in others they appear to have merely investigated the points at issue, and submitted their results to the ordinary magistrates who were to deliver the final verdict.[1]

The writer goes on to enumerate instances of such special judges, all of which go to prove the immiscibility of the alien in the ancient world, so far as his judicial status was concerned.

Somewhat like the *xenodikai* in Greece was the Roman magistrate, *prætor peregrinus*, whose influence on the development of international law is universally recognized. The name of this officer, as it appears in the present form, is, according to Mommsen, an incorrect one, deriving its popularity from mere usage. The full title of the Roman magistrate designated by the abbreviated form *prætor peregrinus* was, under the Republic, *prætor qui inter peregrinos jus dicit,* and under the Empire, *prætor qui inter cives et peregrinos jus dicit.*[2] The office was established about 242 B. C., in addition to that of the *prætor urbanus,* which was already in existence. The competence of the peregrine

[1] *Op. cit.,* p. 192.

[2] Mommsen et Marquardt, *Manuel des antiquités romaines* (Paris, 1888-1907), vol. iii (Mommsen, *Le Droit public romain,* vol. iii), p. 225.

prætor, as his full title suggests, extended to disputes between peregrines and between them and Roman citizens.[1] The connotation of the word *peregrini* is described by Girard as follows:

The peregrines, *peregrini,* formerly *hostes,* were not, in developed Roman law, true foreigners. The most ancient of them were certainly foreigners bound to Rome by treaties. But the development of the Roman power made them, like the others, members of the Roman State. They were subjects of Rome, the free inhabitants of the empire, who were neither citizens nor Latins.[2]

Outside of the peregrines, the foreigners who did not maintain treaty relations with Rome enjoyed no legal protection and were not amenable to Roman justice.[3] It was the peregrines who were placed under the jurisdiction of the *prætor peregrinus,* and it was to them that he administered the *jus gentium,* for even the foreigners of allied nationality, who later became subjects of the Roman State, were not amenable to the *jus civile,* which was applicable to a very restricted number of Roman citizens and Latins.[4] With the extension of Roman citizenship to all the provincials of the Empire under Caracalla, in 212 A. D., however, the office of the *prætor peregrinus* disappeared from the judicial system of Rome.[5]

It is true that the *prætor peregrinus* of Roman times was merely a Roman officer administering the *jus gentium,* which

[1] *Ibid.,* p. 252.

[2] Girard, *Manuel élémentaire de droit romain* (6th ed., Paris, 1918), p. 113.

[3] Mommsen et Marquardt, *op. cit.,* vol. vi, pt. ii (Mommsen, *op. cit.,* vol. vi, pt. ii), p. 216.

[4] For the jurisdiction of the *prætor urbanus* over the Latins, see Mommsen, *op. cit.,* vol. vi, pt. ii, p. 221; Girard, *op. cit.,* p. 112.

[5] Mommsen et Marquardt, *op. cit.,* vol. iii, p. 260, n. 3.

was municipal law, to foreigners resident in Rome, and that his competence bears little or no resemblance to the modern system of extraterritoriality, under which the consul or other authority invested with the exercise of the jurisdiction, is appointed by the State which he represents and administers his national law. But the fact that the Romans made a discrimination against the subjects of non-treaty Powers and that even those of the treaty Powers were subjected to a special jurisdiction serves to show the extralegal status of the foreigner in ancient times, out of which most probably extraterritoriality drew its impetus in its early development.

The germs of extraterritoriality were, however, not entirely absent in the Roman Empire. In the first century of the Christian era, Emperor Claudius (41-54, A. D.) accorded to the merchants of Cadiz the privilege of choosing magistrates, who were given the jurisdiction of the tribunals established by Caesar in Baetice.[1] Under the rule of Justinian (483-565, A. D.), the Armenians were granted the benefit of the same laws on certain subjects as those by which the Romans were ruled; but questions of marriage, succession to property, and personal status generally, were left to be settled either by the Armenians themselves or by a magistrate named by the Emperor to administer Armenian law.[2]

II. THE MEDIAEVAL THEORY OF THE PERSONALITY OF LAWS

In the absence of any views of territorial sovereignty, there developed in mediaeval Europe a complete system of personal jurisdiction, which has left in its wake many interesting survivals extending to modern times, and which has undoubtedly exercised an immense influence upon the development of extraterritoriality. In the days which fol-

[1] Miltitz, *op. cit.*, vol. i, p. 15.

[2] Pears, *Fall of Constantinople* (New York, 1886), p. 148.

lowed the downfall of the Roman Empire, as in the days of ancient Greece and Rome, but in a much more marked degree, racial consanguinity was treated as the sole basis of amenability to law. Thus, in the same country—and even in the same city at times—the Lombards lived under Lombard law, and the Romans under Roman law. This differentiation of laws extended even to the various branches of the Germanic invaders; the Goths, the Franks, the Burgundians, each submitted to their own laws while resident in the same country. Indeed, the system was so general that in one of the tracts of the Bishop Agobard, it is said: " It often happens that five men, each under a different law, would be found walking or sitting together." [1]

As an example of the prevalence in mediaeval Europe of the theory of the personality of laws, we may cite the retention of Roman law in the old provinces of Rome. Savigny shows that in the Burgundian laws and in the Constitution of Chlotar, the validity of Roman law in cases involving Romans was fully recognized. [2]

In the same way, the principle of the personality of laws was applied and carried out by the invaders themselves in their relations with one another. The laws of the Visigoths contain the remarkable provision that " when foreign merchants have disputes with one another, none of our judges shall take cognizance, but they shall be decided by officers of their nation and according to their laws." [3] Theodoric the Great (493-525), the first of the Ostrogothic rulers,

---

[1] Savigny, *Geschichte des Römischen Rechts im Mittelalter* (Heidelberg, 1834-51), vol. i, p. 116.

[2] *Ibid.*, p. 126. *Cf.* Jenks, *Law and Politics in the Middle Ages* (London, 1913), p. 14.

[3] " *Dum transmarini negotiatores inter se causam habuerint, nullus de sedibus nostris eos audire presumat, nisi tantummodo suis legibus audiantur apud telonarios suos.*" *Leges Visigoth.*, lib. xi, tit. iii, cap. ii, Pardessus, *op. cit.*, vol. i, p. 152.

instituted special judges or courts (*comtes*) to decide litigations between Goths and, with the assistance of a Roman jurisconsult, to decide cases between Goths and Romans.[1] In the first half of the eighth century, the Lombards in France were tried according to Lombard law and at least partly by judges who were Alamanns, the latter having once been Lombards and lived under Lombard law.[2] The oldest part of the *Lex Ribuaria* (tit. 31) is found to contain a passage which ensures to the Frank, Burgundian, Alamann or any other, the benefit of his own law.[3] In the Capitularies of Charlemagne and of Louis I, recognition was given to the applicability of Roman and other foreign laws to cases involving the respective foreign subjects.[4]

It is noteworthy that under the régime of personal jurisdiction, the law applied was that of the defendant, except in cases of serious crime, in which the law of the injured party or plaintiff prevailed.[5] A connection might be established between this rule and the principle *actor sequitur forum rei,* one of the basic formulae of modern extraterritorial jurisdiction, under which the plaintiff follows the defendant into his court.

III. EARLY MARITIME CODES OF EUROPE

In the maritime codes of the European cities in the Middle Ages, the influence of the principle of the personality of laws was clearly discernible. It is said that one of the cardinal principles of the celebrated Hanseatic League was the absolute independence of its members of all foreign jurisdiction wherever they resided and traded.[6] In the

[1] Miltitz, *op. cit.,* vol. i, p. 24.

[2] Savigny, *op. cit.,* vol. i, p. 124.

[3] Jenks, *op. cit.,* p. 16.

[4] Savigny, *op. cit.,* vol. i, p. 127.

[5] *Ibid.,* pp. 167-8.

[6] Pardessus, *op. cit.,* vol. ii, p. cxxvij.

twelfth century, Lübeck enjoyed such exemption in Wisby, and acquired the right to transfer the privilege to other cities.[1] From about the same time, the German merchants and other inhabitants of Wisby on the island of Gothland in the Baltic enjoyed similar privileges in the Republic of Novgorod in Russia.[2]

In the Statute of Gaeta, M. Pardessus finds a chapter on foreign consuls, which he dates back to the thirteenth century, where it is laid down that foreign consuls had sole jurisdiction over their nationals in all civil cases, and that their competence in such cases could not be transferred to any other authority.[3]

That the Amalfitan Tables provided for extraterritorial jurisdiction is evidenced by the fact that as early as 1190 the city of Amalfi was permitted to maintain consuls in the neighboring town of Naples to decide disputes between Amalfitan merchants.[4] Even in the fourteenth century, the maritime statute of Ancona, which bore the date of 1397, required all merchants of Ancona trading abroad to elect their own consuls and to submit to them their disputes, the penalty for resorting to any other tribunal being a fine of fifty pounds.[5]

Finally, in 1402, a Florentine consul resided at London. The statutes of that consulate, collected and approved in 1513, provided that the consul, assisted by two counsellors, should decide all contests between the subjects of the republic resident in England; those who resorted to any other court were liable to a pecuniary fine, and in order to bring those who were not subjects of the republic under its juris-

---

[1] *Ibid.*, pp. lxxxix, cxxvij.

[2] Miltitz, *op. cit.*, vol. i, pp. 401-408.

[3] Pardessus, *op. cit.*, vol. v, p. 230.

[4] *Ibid.*, vol. i, p. 144. The text of the Diploma of 1190 is reproduced in Miltitz, *op. cit.*, vol. ii, pt. i, p. 502.

[5] *Rubrique* xlviii, Pardessus, *op. cit.*, vol. v, pp. 160-161.

diction, the Florentines were forbidden, under severe penalty, to trade with any foreigner who did not engage to submit to the consul's jurisdiction and to appear before him.[1]

IV. PERSONALITY OF LAWS AND DIPLOMATIC ASYLUM

That the principle of the personality of laws bears a causal relationship to the development of extraterritoriality is further manifested by a very interesting bit of evidence. In his study of diplomatic asylum, Professor John Bassett Moore has traced this extraordinary privilege of ambassadors to the time when territorial sovereignty was unknown to the intercourse of nations.[2] He shows further that the decline of diplomatic asylum has been a slow process and that in the history of modern Europe survivals of the decaying institution have not been uncommon, the practice being especially enduring in Spain, where, as late as 1873, a political refugee was sheltered by the British Minister at Madrid.[3] Practically the same thing may be said of extraterritoriality. Its origin is attributable to the absence of absolute territorial sovereignty and the accompanying tradition of the personality of laws, while its survivals in Europe, as will be shown later in this chapter, are equally reminiscent of the tardiness of its decline. But what is most interesting of all is the fact that just as diplomatic asylum lingered longest in Spain, so were extraterritorial rights maintained there at a very late date. By the Capitulations of 1782[4] and 1799,[5] Spain granted reciprocal extraterri-

---

[1] Miltitz, *op. cit.*, vol. ii, pt. i, p. 152. *Cf.* Bonfils, *Manuel de droit international* (7th ed., Paris, 1914), § 737n.

[2] Moore, *op. cit.*, vol. ii, p. 761.

[3] *Ibid.*, pp. 766 *et seq.*, esp. p. 770.

[4] Art. 5: "....it shall be the same with regard to the subjects and merchants of the Ottoman Empire in the dominions of Spain." Noradounghian, *Recueil d'actes internationaux de l'Empire Ottoman* (Paris, 1897-1903), vol. i, p. 346.

[5] Art. 6, Martens, *Recueil des principaux traités* (Gottingue, 1791-1801), vol. vi, p. 585. *Cf. infra*, p. 64, n. 2.

torial jurisdiction respectively to the Ottoman Empire and
Morocco, both of which, be it remembered, were Mohammedan Powers.   These Capitulations thus throw overboard
the theory that extraterritoriality was in any way intended
to derogate from the sovereignty of the State granting it,
inasmuch as the notion of territorial sovereignty was as
yet unknown when extraterritoriality took its root.

V. THE OFFICE OF THE JUDGE-CONSUL

The development of commerce made necessary special
organs to take charge of foreign interests.   Before the advent of the foreign consul, the various States created offices
which exercised administrative and judicial supervision over
foreign residents within their confines.   The office of the
prætor peregrinus in Rome has been mentioned above.[1]
During the reigns of Theodosius the Great (379-395) and
of Honorius (395-423), magistrates were created and invested with the right to decide cases of accidents of the
sea and of salvage.[2]   But the period during which the development of these judge-consuls, as they were sometimes
called, assumed real importance was in the Middle Ages.
Between the tenth and thirteenth centuries, the French,
Italian, and Spanish cities set up courts with authority to
decide commercial disputes and with jurisdiction over resident foreign merchants.[3]   The members of these courts
were given the generic name " consuls " and were variously
designated as *consules mercatorum, consuls des marchands,
consuls de commerce, juge-consuls,* and *juges-conserva-
teurs.*[4]   At about the same time, the Hanseatic cities, though
they did not have consular courts like those in the French,

[1] *Supra,* p. 25.

[2] Miltitz, *op. cit.,* vol. i, p. 160.

[3] *Ibid.,* pp. 162-175.

[4] *Ibid.,* p. 6.

Italian and Spanish cities, conferred upon their deputies
in the diet the authority to decide all commercial and maritime questions.   In 1447, the Hanseatic cities instituted a
tribunal of commerce sitting at Lübeck, of which the President was known as the Alderman, his functions being similar
to those of the judge-consul in the other countries.[1]   The
fact to be noted is that, of the functions of these magistrates, judicial competence was invariably a part.   It is
more than probable that the extraterritorial jurisdiction
granted to the European consuls in the Levant was but an
extension of the functions assumed by the judge-consuls
at home.[2]

VI. THE FOREIGN CONSULATE IN MEDIAEVAL EUROPE

The Crusades, it will be seen later, afforded an effective
medium for the transplantation of the system of judge-consuls.   But in Europe itself, during the same period, the
office of the foreign consul was generally invested with
judicial functions.

The merchants of the Italian cities who traded in France
were subject to the jurisdiction of special judges of their
own nationality, called *Captains of the University of Lombard and Tuscan Merchants,* who decided all cases between
them.[3]   In 1277, a treaty concluded with the French established the Genoese at Nimes and granted to them the right
to be judged by their *recteur* according to their own laws.[4]

---

[1] *Ibid.,* pp. 175-176.

[2] *Cf.* Martens, *Das Consularwesen und die Consularjurisdiction im
Orient* (Berlin, 1874), p. 100; also Depping, *Histoire du Commerce
entre le Levant et l'Europe* (Paris, 1830), vol. ii, p. 52, where the
author says: " It is from a remote antiquity that there were, in all the
States on the shores of the Mediterranean, courts of commerce, where
nearly the same rules were followed.   The consulates were nothing
but courts of this nature transported to foreign countries."

[3] Miltitz, *op. cit.,* vol. ii, pt. i, p. 77.

[4] Vincens, *Histoire de la République de Gênes* (Paris, 1842), vol. i,
p. 389.

In the act of privilege which Ferdinand III of Castile accorded in 1251 to the Genoese at Seville, it is stipulated that the latter should have consuls of their own nationality, with the right to decide without appeal, disputes between themselves.[1]   In the history of Pisa, the consulate is known to have been maintained from the twelfth century onward under the name *consules maris,* with jurisdictional rights.[2]

An interesting treaty between Frederick II, Emperor and King of Sicily and Abbuissac, Prince of the Saracens of Africa, dated 1230, provided that in the island of Corsica there should be a Mohammedan consul or prefect to administer justice to the Mohammedan merchants residing there, although the consul should be established by the Emperor and administer justice in his name.[3]

The French cities likewise enjoyed rights of jurisdiction in Italy and in Spain.[4]   The Aragonians in Seville were granted by King Alfonso I in 1282 the same rights as had been accorded previously to the Genoese in the same city.[5]

As has been seen, the Hanseatic League was particularly jealous of the right of its own members to be exempt from any foreign jurisdiction.[6]   In actual practice, many efforts were made to secure the safeguard of this right.   In Scania, which now belongs to Sweden, privileges were granted to the Hanseatic merchants in 1361 and 1368, including the right to choose from among themselves judges to decide their disputes according to the law of Lübeck.[7]   By the peace of 1285, it was stipulated that disputes between Ger-

---

[1] Depping, *op. cit.,* vol. ii, p. 47.

[2] Pardessus, *op. cit.,* vol. iv, p. 557.

[3] Dumont, *Corps universel diplomatique* (Amsterdam, 1726-31), vol. i, pt. i, p. 168.

[4] Miltitz, *op. cit.,* vol. ii, pt. i, p. 203.

[5] *Ibid.,* p. 294.

[6] *Supra,* p. 29.

[7] Miltitz, *op. cit.,* vol. ii, pt. i, pp. 343-344.

mans in Norway were to be decided by their own judges.[1]
Even in England, King Edward IV granted to the merchants of Hansa the right to be judged by their own magistrates according to their own laws. The treaty of 1474
permitted the Hanseatic merchants in London to hold in
perpetuity their special community known as the Steelyard.
Cases of contract in which Englishmen proceeded against
Germans were to be heard before two specially appointed
English judges, and the same practice was to be observed
in Germany. Within the Steelyard, the merchants were to
have exclusive administration, and, what is more important,
they were completely freed from any judicial process em-
anating from the local authorities (*"Dampnis, Injuris,
Spoliationibus, Rapinis, Incarcerationibus, Arrestationibus
Personarum, Bonorum, & Mercandisarum . . . per viam
Facti, per viam Judici & Sententiae, seu Executionis . . .
absolvunt firmitir per praesentes"*). The special nature of
the privileges granted is indicated by the promise of King
Edward IV not to concede them to other foreigners.[2]

In England, the office of the foreign consul did not make
its appearance until the beginning of the fifteenth century.
But long before England sent consuls abroad to protect the
interests of her nationals, she had made efforts to safeguard
the security of foreign life and property within her own
borders. Even before the Hanseatic treaty of 1474, King
Edward I had issued his great Charter, in 1303, commonly
known as the *Carta Mercatoria,* which contained a provision
that in all cases, except those entailing the death penalty,
in which a foreign merchant was implicated, the jury to be
charged with the trial of the cause should be composed of
an equal number of foreign merchants and natives.[3] Al-

---

[1] *Ibid.,* p. 344.

[2] Rymer, *Foedera* (2nd ed., London, 1726-35), vol. ix, pp. 795, 796, 797.

[3] "6. Item, that in all maner of pleas, sauing in case where punish-

though the nature of the grant differed considerably from a concession of consular jurisdiction, it nevertheless throws some light on the general privileges enjoyed by the foreigner in the Middle Ages. Indeed, the institution of the mixed jury is so important that some writers have regarded it as the origin of the modern mixed court.[1]

In 1404, King Henry IV accorded to the merchants of England in the Hanseatic towns the power to choose a certain number of individuals to be known as " *Gubernatores mercatorum* " and to exercise, in the name of the King, judicial authority over their compatriots. The same power was conferred on English merchants in the Netherlands in 1406, and in Norway, Sweden and Denmark in 1408. In 1485, King Richard III bestowed upon one Lorenzo Strozzi the office of the consul in Italy, with power to decide disputes between the Englishmen resident there.[2] In the letters-patent issued to the consul, it was stated that in creating the office, the King had consulted the experience of other nations,[3] thereby showing the trend of international practice at the time. There is little doubt, therefore, that one of the most important and common functions of the consul during this period was his judicial competence.

ment of death is to be inflicted, where a marchant is impleaded, or sueth another, of what condition soeuer hee bee which is sued, whether stranger or home borne, in fayres, cities, or boroughs, where sufficient numbers of marchants of the foresayd countreis are, and where the triall ought to bee made, let the one halfe of the Iurie be of the sayd marchants, and the other halfe of good and lawfull men of the place where the suite shall fall out to bee: and if sufficient number of marchants of the sayd countries cannot bee found, those which shall be found fit in that place shall be put vpon the iurie, and the rest shall be chosen of good and fit men of the places where such suit shall chance to be." Hakluyt, *The Principal Navigations, Voyages, Traffiques, and Discoveries of the English Nation* (ed. by E. Goldsmid, Edinburgh, 1885-90), vol. i, p. 121.

[1] Lippmann, *Die Konsularjurisdiktion im Orient* (Leipzig, 1898), p. 10.

[2] Miltitz, *op. cit.*, vol. ii, pt. i, pp. 385-386.

[3] *Ibid.*, p. 385.

VII. MODERN SURVIVALS

During the sixteenth and seventeenth centuries, an era of dynastic and colonial rivalry set in. The discovery of America initiated among the more powerful maritime Powers of Europe the struggle for colonial possessions. The ascendancy of these Powers aided their assertion of an exclusive territorial sovereignty, until in 1648 the treaties making up the Peace of Westphalia accepted the latter as a fundamental principle of international intercourse. This development of territorial sovereignty was distinctly fatal to the existence of the system of consular jurisdiction, and facilitated considerably its decadence in Europe, because it was founded on the opposite theory of the personality of laws.

But even from this period some documents have been handed down, which show the persistence of consular jurisdiction in Europe. In the *Principal Navigations of the English Nation,* Hakluyt gives the text of " a copie of the first priuileges graunted by the Emperour of Russia to the English Marchants in the yeere 1555." Among the provisions of this document is the following remarkable article :

4. Item, we giue and graunt vnto the saide Marchants and their successours, that such person as is, or shalbe commended vnto vs, our heires or successours by the Gouernour, Consuls and assistants of the said fellowship residant within the citie of London within the realme of England, to be their chiefe Factor within this our empire and dominions, may and shal haue ful power and authoritie to gouerne and rule all Englishmen that haue had, or shall haue accesse, or repaire in or to this said Empire and iurisdictions, or any part thereof, and shal and may minister vnto them, and euery of them good iustice in all their causes, plaints, quarrels, and disorders betweene them moued, and to be moued, and assemble, deliberate, consult, conclude, define, determine, and make such actes, and ordinances, as he so commended with his associates shall thinke good and meete for the good order, gouernment and rule of the said

Marchants, and all other Englishmen repairing to this our
saide empire or dominions, or any part thereof, and to set
and leuie vpon all, and euery Englishman, offender or offenders,
of such their acts and ordinances made, and to be made, penalties
and mulcts by fine and imprisonment.[1]

The letters-patent granted by Francis II, King of France,
in 1559, to the Swedish subjects trading within his territory
recognized the right of the latter to be judged by their own
magistrates in all differences that might arise among them,
although in mixed cases of any sort they were placed under
the jurisdiction of the local authorities.[2]

By the treaty of February 24, 1606, between Henry IV
of France and James I of England, it was arranged that all
commercial disputes involving nationals of one party in certain portions of the other should be heard and decided by a
mixed tribunal, composed of four merchants, two French
and two English.   In case they could not agree, they should
choose a French merchant if it was in France, or an English
merchant if it was in England, " so that the Judgment
pass'd by the Plurality of Voices shall be follow'd and put
in execution."   These merchant judges were to be known
as " Conservators of Commerce," and in each country the
two foreign Conservators were to be appointed by their
Ambassador.[3]   Later, the system was altered in such a way
that no foreign merchants were to have jurisdictional rights
in either country, the ambassador or his deputy only being
permitted to " assist at any Judgment and Trials whatsoever
which concern the Goods and Life of a Subject of his Prince,
and especially when a Definitive Judgment is to be made or
pass'd." [4]

[1] Hakluyt, *op. cit.*, vol. iii, p. 99.

[2] Dumont, *op. cit.*, vol. v, pt. i, p. 61.

[3] Arts. 7, 8, 9, *A General Collection of Treatys* (London, 1732), vol.
ii, pp. 150-151.

[4] Art. 43, *ibid.*, p. 175.

What is most remarkable, perhaps, is the treaty of September 24, 1631, between Louis XIII, Emperor of France, and Molei Elqualid, Emperor of Morocco, which contains terms of absolute reciprocity, so far as extraterritorial jurisdiction was concerned.[1] The most interesting provision of this document is article 9, which stipulates that the ambassador of the Emperor of Morocco in France and the ambassador or consul of France in Morocco should determine all disputes respectively between Moroccans in France and Frenchmen in Morocco.[2] In cases between Frenchmen and Moors, the local authorities on either side were alone competent,[3] and to make mutual intervention in territorial jurisdiction impossible, article 12 contains the admonition that all judgments and sentences given by the local authorities should be " validly executed " without interference on the part of the other contracting party.[4] Here, then, is a treaty of perfect equality and reciprocity between a Christian and a Mohammedan Power, bearing a strikingly modern date, which assures to the parties thereto reciprocal extraterritorial jurisdiction of a limited sort. The arrangement is all the more significant when it is remembered that France, of all the continental European Powers, was the first in which national sovereignty was most completely established and a systematic jurisprudence most fully developed.[5] It

[1] Dumont, *op. cit.,* vol. vi, pt. i, p. 20.

[2] " That if any difference should arise between the Moorish merchants who are in France, the Ambassador of the Emperor of Morocco residing in France shall terminate them, and the same shall be done by the Ambassador or Consul of France in Africa."

[3] Art. 10.

[4] " That all the judgments and sentences given by the Judges and Officers of the Emperor of Morocco [in disputes] between the subjects of His Christian Majesty and the subjects of the said Emperor, shall be validly executed, without any complaint to the Kingdom of France, and the same shall be practised between the subjects of Morocco and the Frenchmen in France."

[5] Moore, *op. cit.,* vol. ii, p. 762.

ought to go far to prove that the institution of extraterritoriality was not contrived, at the beginning at any rate, and for a long time in the modern period, to meet the special situation of a defective legal system in non-Christian Powers. The explanation must be sought, if anywhere, in the tradition of the personality of laws long prevalent in Europe.[1]

As late as the eighteenth century, a number of interesting survivals of the decadent jurisdiction of the consul invite our attention. It is noteworthy that in the treaty of January 23, 1721, between Great Britain and Morocco, a measure of extraterritorial jurisdiction was granted to the Moors in England.[2] This privilege was repeatedly renewed and confirmed by later treaties.[3]

In the treaty of 1740 between the Ottoman Empire and the Kingdom of the Two Sicilies, there is a reciprocal provision regarding the adjudication of cases arising between Sicilians in Turkey and between Turks in Sicily. According to article 5, these cases should be disposed of by their respective consuls according to their own laws and customs.[4]

[1] In some of the peace treaties of the seventeenth century, provision was made for the remission of prize cases to the home courts of the defendant's nationality. See art. 32, Anglo-French treaty of 1604, *A General Collection of Treatys*, vol. ii, p. 145; art. 30, Anglo-Spanish treaty of Nov. 15, 1630, *ibid.*, p. 289; art. 23, Peace of the Pyrenees, Nov. 7, 1659, *ibid.*, vol. i, p. 49. In later treaties any provision of such a nature was conspicuously absent. See art. 27, Treaty of Nymeguen, Aug. 10, 1678, Dumont, *op. cit.*, vol. vii, pt. i, p. 360; art. 32, Treaty of Ryswik, Sep. 20, 1697, ibid., pt. ii, p. 289.

[2] Art. IX. ".... and if any quarrel or dispute shall happen between Musselmen in England, or in any of the English Dominions, by which hurt may ensue, the same to be heard before 1 Christian and 1 Musselman, and to be determined according to the Laws of Great Britain." *British and Foreign State Papers* (hereafter referred to as *State Papers*), vol. i, p. 430.

[3] Art. 4, treaty of May 10, 1729; art. 4, Feb. 1, 1751; art. 9, July 28, 1760; art. 8, April 8, 1791; and art. 8, June 14, 1801. *Ibid.*, pp. 431, 435, 439, 447, 457.

[4] Noradounghian, *Recueil d'actes internationaux de l'empire ottoman* (Paris, 1897-1903), vol. i, p. 272.

The treaty of 1787 between France and Russia stipulated that the consul of one or the other party might decide disputes between his nationals when they submitted to his jurisdiction by mutual consent.[1]

Still more interesting is the treaty of 1788 between France and the United States, article 12 of which provides:

All differences and suits between the subjects of the Most Christian King in the United States, or between the citizens of the United States within the dominions of the Most Christian King . . . shall be determined by the respective Consuls and Vice-Consuls, either by a reference to arbitrators, or by a summary judgment, and without costs. No officer of the country, civil or military, shall interfere therein, or take any part whatever in the matter; and the appeals from the said consular sentences shall be carried before the tribunals of France or of the United States, to whom it may appertain to take cognizance thereof.[2]

In 1825, Sardinia and Morocco mutually engaged to permit consular intervention in cases which involved the subjects of either country in the other. The pertinent provision is quoted below:

XXII. If, in the States of Morocco, disturbances should arise between our subjects and subjects of Morocco, the difficulties shall be settled in equity and justice, for which purposes our subjects may present themselves before the Court, assisted by our Consul or other Consular official, or may be represented

---

[1] Art. 7, Martens, *Recueil de traités* (2nd ed., Gottingen, 1817-35), vol. iv, p. 199.

[2] U. S. *Treaties, Conventions,* etc. (hereafter referred to as Malloy), Washington, 1910, vol. i, p. 495. In *Villeneuve v. Barron,* it was held that the consular jurisdiction of France did "not extend generally to all differences and suits between Frenchmen." Moore, *op. cit.,* vol. ii, p. 84. The convention of 1788 was abrogated by Act of Congress, July 7, 1798, Malloy, vol. i, p. 490 n.

by an attorney. Appeal from the decision, whether favorable or otherwise, may be made to the Emperor.

On the other hand, should a question arise in our States, it shall be determined by the competent authority in the presence of the Consul of Morocco, or his agent or attorney, and if justice is not accorded, appeal shall be made to a Supreme Judge, to whom shall appertain the jurisdiction in such a case.[1]

The system of judges conservators enjoyed by the English in Portugal is a close approximation to the present-day régime of consular jurisdiction. According to Shillington and Chapman, the system goes as far back as the fifteenth century.[2] A specific provision for the office and functions of the judges conservators is contained in the treaty of July 10, 1654, Article VII of which lays down:

Also, for judging all causes which shall relate to the people of this Republic [England], a judge conservator shall be deputed, from whom no appeal shall be granted, unless to a committee of senators where the disputes shall be determined within the space of four months, at most, after the appeals.[3]

By the treaty of February 19, 1810, it was arranged to give the English merchants " the privilege of nominating and having special magistrates to act for them as Judges Conservator," with jurisdiction over " all causes brought before them by British subjects." It must be pointed out, however, that the selection of these judges conservators, though they were chosen by the British subjects in the locality, had to be approved by the Prince Regent of Portugal.[4] The privi-

[1] *State Papers,* vol. xcviii, p. 979.

[2] Shillington and Chapman, *Commercial Relations of England and Portugal* (New York, 1907), p. 182.

[3] Chalmers, *A Collection of Treaties between Great Britain and Other Powers* (London, 1790), vol. ii, p. 271.

[4] Martens, *Nouveau supplémens au recueil de traités* (Gottingue, 1839-42), vol. ii, p. 158.

lege of maintaining judges conservators was enjoyed by the
English in Brazil until 1827, when a treaty between the
Emperor of Brazil and the King of England abolished it.[1]
In Portugal proper, it is interesting to note, the system of
judge conservators was not formally abolished until 1842.[2]

That the system of judges conservators existed in the
seventeenth and eighteenth centuries in Spanish America is
evidenced by a number of " assiento " treaties or contracts.
The Portuguese, French and English agreements, dated respectively July 12, 1696,[3] August 27, 1701,[4] and March 26,
1713,[5] all provide for these officers.[6] They were to be
chosen by the merchants concerned, with the approval of the
King of Spain, and were " to have cognizance, exclusive of
all others, of all causes, affairs and suits, relating to the
Assiento, with full authority and jurisdiction," but from
their decisions an appeal lay to the supreme council of the
Indies.[7] The author has attempted in vain to ascertain the
actual operation of the system, to which all the available
material gives no clue.

[1] Art. 6, *Annuaire historique universel*, 1827, p. 159.

[2] Art. 17, Martens, *Nouveau recueil général de traités* (Gottingue,
1843-75), vol. iii, p. 338.

[3] Art. 8, Castro, *Colleção de tradados* (Lisbon, 1856-58), vol. i, p. 53.

[4] Art. 13, Dumont, *op. cit.*, vol. viii, pt. i, p. 85.

[5] Art. 13, Jenkinson, *A Collection of All the Treaties* (London, 1785),
vol. i, p. 382.

[6] The treaty of peace signed at Utrecht on June 26, 1714, between
Spain and the United Provinces contained a similar provision (art. 29),
Dumont, *op. cit.*, vol. viii, pt. i, p. 430.

[7] *Cf.* Ortega, *Questiones del derecho publico* (Madrid, 1747), pp. 314
et seq. In this connection, a nineteenth century survival of consular
jurisdiction in Europe may be mentioned. The treaty of May 2, 1889,
between Italy and Ethiopia, provided for the reciprocal exercise of consular jurisdiction in regard to criminal matters. After setting forth
the rights of the Italians in Ethiopia, the agreement goes on to say:
" Similarly, the Ethiopians accused of a crime committed in Italian
territory shall be tried by the Ethiopian authorities." Art. 12, *State
Papers*, vol. lxxxi, p. 735.

In the municipal legislation and orders of some European States, similar survivals were for a time equally evident. The Patent of John Chandler, as English consul to Spain, dated 1631, gave him the power " by way of interposition to compound . . . all contentions . . . that may arise amongst them [English merchants] and may be conveniently ordered without further proceeding to Lawe." [1]

The instructions of Peter the Great to one Jewreinoff, Russian consul at Cadiz, dated 1723, mentioned specifically among his functions the decision of differences between the subjects of the Czar in Spain.[2] Likewise, the consular instructions issued by the King of Denmark and Norway, February 10, 1749, contained a provision ordering the consul to assume jurisdiction not only over the masters and crews of the Danish vessels, but also over the Danish merchants trading abroad.[3] According to the French edict of June, 1778, regulating the judicial and police functions of French consuls abroad, the latter were empowered to take cognizance of all disputes between their compatriots, and all French merchants were prohibited from bringing their fellow-citizens before any other tribunal.[4] In his History of Genoa, M. Vincens confirms the actual enforcement of this edict by relating that, in 1797, the French consul was the magistrate of first instance in Genoa for all civil disputes in which one of his nationals was defendant.[5]

These late survivals of extraterritoriality in Europe are to be explained partly by the as yet deficient judicial systems

[1] Shillington and Chapman, *op. cit.,* app. ii, p. 327.

[2] Borel, *De l'Origine et des fonctions des consuls* (St. Petersburg, 1807), p. 90.

[3] Moser, *Versuch des neuesten europäischen Völkerrechts* (Frankfurt a. M., 1777-80), vol. vii, p. 833.

[4] Arts. 1, 2, Martens, *Recueil de traités,* vol. ii, pp. 632-633.

[5] Vincens, *Hist. de la République de Gênes,* vol. i, p. 86.

of some of the European Powers and partly by the abiding
influence of the theory of the personality of laws. An example of the former is the situation in Portugal. In this
country, according to Shillington and Chapman, " the general desire of the English, in fact, was to escape from the
ordinary Portuguese courts. The administration in Portugal seems to have been both corrupt and arbitrary, and
strangers, ill-acquainted with the customs and language of
the country, suffered considerably." [1] Consequently, the
system of judges conservators was maintained in Portugal
to protect the English against the injustices of the native
courts. That this statement is well-founded is shown by
the treaty which abolished the system in Portugal. This
instrument, dated 1842, gives as the reason for the abolition
" the state of progress in which the system of legislation and
administration of justice in Portugal was found." [2] This
is significant, because in the decline of extraterritoriality,
the improvement of the native judicial system has always
been an important factor. In the discussion to follow, we
shall have repeated occasion to take note of this fact.

In other instances, however, the persistence of extraterritoriality could not be ascribed to judicial deficiency. As we
have pointed out above,[3] to France belonged the honor of
being the continental European Power in which law and
sovereignty received their earliest development. Yet France
made a treaty with Morocco in 1631, in which reciprocal
extraterritorial privileges were provided for. This must
have been due, if anything, to the existence of deep-seated
custom having its basis in the time-honored theory of the
personality of laws.

[1] *Op. cit.*, p. 182.

[2] Art. 17, Martens, *N. R. G.*, vol. iii, p. 338.

[3] *Supra*, p. 39.

VIII. TESTIMONY OF PUBLICISTS

The works of the early writers on international law seem to betray the influence of the once prevalent practice. Wicquefort, whose treatise on *l'Embassadeur* was published in 1681, denied to the consul any public character, but made special mention of his judicial function.[1] Bynkershoek, in his *De Foro Legatorum*, 1721, speaks of the consuls as protectors and sometimes judges of the merchants of their nation.[2] Wolff, whose work was published in 1754, defines the consul as one who is sent abroad to safeguard the privileges and rights of his compatriots and to decide their disputes.[3] In his *Droit des Gens*, published in 1758, Vattel follows closely the definition of Wolff.[4] Of these early writers Moser was the latest to describe the judicial compe-

[1] "Consuls are only merchants, who notwithstanding their Office of *Judge in the Controversies* that may arise among those of their own Nation... are liable to the Justice of the Place where they reside...." *The Ambassador and His Functions*, trans. by Digby (London, 1716), p. 40.

[2] "Et à dire le vrai, ces Consuls ne sont autrechose que des Protecteurs, quelquefois Juges des Marchands de leur Nations:.. d'ordinaire même ce ne sont que des Marchands, que l'on envoie non pour représenter leur Prince auprès d'une autre Puissance Souveraine, mais pour protéger les Sujets de leur Prince, en ce qui regarde le Négoce, souvent aussi pour connoître & décider des differens qu'il pourra y avoir entr'eux au sujet de ces fortes d'affaires." Bynkershoek, *Traité du juge compétent*, trans. by Barbeyrac (The Hague, 1723), ch. x, § vi, p. 112.

[3] "Consul sind solche Personen, welchen in den See-Handelsstäpten oder den Haafen aufgetragen ist, die Privilegien und Rechte der Nation, oder ihres Volkes zu bewahren, und die Streitigkeiten der Kaufleute zu schlichten." Wolff, *Grundsätze des Natur- und Völkerrechts* (Halle, 1754), § 1118, p. 815.

[4] "L'une des institutions modernes les plus utiles au commerce est celle des consuls. Ce sont des gens qui dans les grandes places de commerce, & surtout dans les ports de mer, en pays étrangers, ont la commission de veiller à la conservation des droits et des privileges de leur nation, & de terminer les difficultés qui peuvent naître entre ses marchands." Vattel, *Le Droit des Gens*, (London, 1758), vol. i, bk. ii, ch. ii, § 34.

tence of the consul, and he was also the most specific of them
all. He says that consuls are judges of first instance in
cases involving their compatriots, but that in mixed cases
in which natives of the country where the consuls reside or
foreigners of a third country are concerned, the local
authorities have jurisdiction.[1]   It is not altogether easy to
ascertain the exact limits of consular jurisdiction in mediaeval Europe.[2]   But while Moser's conclusions might reasonably be established as a general proposition, instances are
not lacking, as we have seen, in which it was arranged to
settle even mixed cases according to the principle *actor sequitur forum rei,* one of the basic formulae of modern extraterritoriality.

That the judicial competence of the foreign consul was
treated by these writers as of equal importance to his commercial powers is at once indicative of two things, which
must have been responsible for their views on the subject
as cited above.   First, it is suggestive of the fact that the
principle of territorial sovereignty is only a recent conception, reaching its full development after a painfully slow
process of transformation.   Secondly—and this is but a
corollary of the first consideration—the widely prevalent
theory of the personality of laws held its sway in Europe
long after the inception of the countervailing principle of
territorial sovereignty, and in its decadence left many survivals which have existed in Europe well into the end of the
last century.

[1] " Seynd sie [consuln] die Richtere in erster Instanz, wann zwischen
ihren Landesleuten in Handlungssachen in dem jedem Consul ange-
wisenen Districkt Streitigkeiten entstehen. Wann aber die Streitigkeiten sich zwischen ihren Landesleuten einer-und denen Eingesessenen
oder dritten Fremden, anderer Seits enthalten; so gehören sie für den
Souverain des Orts, und dessen Gerichte." Moser, *Versuch des neuesten
europäischen Völkerrechts,* 1777-80, vol. vii, pp. 840-841.

[2] Un Ancien Diplomate, *Le Régime des capitulations* (Paris, 1898),
p. 27.

CHAPTER II

IN THE LEVANT PRIOR TO 1453

I. EARLY USAGE

IN the preceding chapter the judicial powers of the consul in Europe were briefly considered. The present chapter will deal with the rise of the consulate with its jurisdictional rights in the Levant and in the Mohammedan states prior to 1453.

In Sir Paul Rycaut's *The Present State of the Ottoman Empire* there was published for the first time a document known as the Testament of Mohammed, dated 625, which gave the Christians certain privileges and concessions, one of which was the protection accorded to Christian judges in the Mohammedan provinces.[1] The authenticity of the document is questioned by some writers,[2] but the fact that the Capitulation of Omar, which is referred to below, mentions an act of the Prophet giving security to Christians may be regarded as confirmation of its existence.[3]

---

[1] "By this Covenant...I promise to defend their judges in my Provinces, with my Horse and Foot, Auxiliaries, and other my faithful Followers..." Rycaut, *op. cit.*, p. 100; Van Dyck, "Report on the Capitulations of the Ottoman Empire," U. S. *Sen. Ex. Doc. 3, 46th Cong., Sp. Sess.,* (Appendix I).

[2] Ravndal, *The Origin of the Capitulations* (Washington, 1921), p. 12

[3] "Ils [the Christians] méritent tous les égards, parce qu'ils furent déjà autrefois honorés par le Prophète d'un Document muni de son Sceau, par lequel il nous exhorte à les ménager et à leur accorder la sureté." Text in Miltitz, *op. cit.*, vol. ii, pt. i, p. 500. *Cf.* Féraud-Giraud, *De la Juridiction française dans les Échelles du Levant* (Paris, 1866), vol. i, p. 36, n. 1.

48

The same apochryphal character is ascribed to the Capitulation granted by Caliph Omar Ibn-Khattâb to the Christians in Syria in 636.[1] But although the document may have been fictitious, it is of great historical importance, because in the later disputes between Christians and Turks it was constantly referred to, and it contained many of the stipulations of the later Turkish Capitulations.[2] The Capitulation of Omar granted equal security to the Christian churches, companies and places of pilgrimage. It ordained the Christians to be respected on account of the honor that had been bestowed upon them by the Prophet. Moreover, they were exempted from the capitation tax and all other tolls in the Moslem states, and on their entry into the Holy Sepulchre no one should receive anything from them. But the Christians who visited the Holy Sepulchre should deposit with the Patriarch one and a half drams (*drachme*) of white silver. Finally, it was ordered that the true followers of both sexes, whether rich or poor, should observe this law.

In the ninth century, Charlemagne is said to have obtained from Caliph Haroun-el-Raschid privileges for the Frankish merchants at Jerusalem, but unfortunately the text of the agreement is not in existence.[3]

That the Mohammedans stood for exemption from territorial jurisdiction was confirmed not only by their own concessions to the Christians, but also by their status in some of the foreign countries. An Arab merchant by the name of Soleyman relates that in the city of Canfu,[4] which is the

---

[1] See a French translation of the text in Miltitz, *op. cit.*, vol. ii, pt. i, p 500.

[2] Charrière, *Négociations de la France dans le Levant*, vol. i, pp. lxvi-lxix.

[3] Miltitz, *op. cit.*, vol. ii, pt. i, p. 7; Pardessus, *Collection de lois maritimes*, vol. i, p. lxv.

[4] Klaproth, "*Renseignemens sur les ports de Gampou et de Zaithoum,*

present Haiyen, Chekiang, a Mussulman was charged by the Emperor of China with power to decide the disputes which arose among the men of the Mohammedan religion in the ninth century.[1] This shows that the Mohammedans of that age were just as jealous of their own rights abroad as they were willing to let foreigners in their realm heed their own affairs. The reason for this state of affairs lies in the fundamental religious beliefs which mark off the Mohammedan from the " infidel " and which will be treated of when we come to the later Christian consulates in the Mohammedan Levant.[2]

In the tenth century, Capitulations were entered into between the Byzantine Emperor and the Varangians or Russians. The agreement of 912 provided, *inter alia,* that " He who strikes any one with a sword or any other instrument shall pay for the act a fine of five pounds of silver according to Russian law." [3]   In the treaty of 945, we find the following significant provision:

déscrits par Marco Polo," Journal Asiatique, vol. v, pp. 35 *et seq.* Many writers have erroneously taken Canfu for Canton. Even such a learned scholar as Sir Travers Twiss has fallen into this mistake. Twiss, *Law of Nations,* vol. i, p. 447.

[1] Reinaud, *Relation des voyages* (Paris,, 1845), vol. i, p. 13. *Cf.* Pardessus, *op. cit.,* vol. ii, p. xxviij. Of the authority for the existence of a Mohammedan judge in China in the ninth century, Sir Travers Twiss says: " This interesting fact was first made generally known by a narrative purporting to be the work of two ancient Arab travelers which was translated into French by Eusebius Renaudot in 1718, and subsequently translated into English in 1733. The MS., however, of which there is preserved in the Bibliothèque Nationale in Paris a perfect example, has been subsequently ascertained to be an extract from a larger work by a most famous Arab historian, Ali Abou'l Hassan Mas'oudy, who died in Egypt A.D. 956, and who was a contemporary of the Arab travelers, whose voyage he has handed down to us." *On Consular Jurisdiction in the Levant* (London, 1880), p. 6.

[2] *Infra,* p. 55.

[3] *La Chronique de Nestor,* trans. by L. Paris (Paris, 1834-35), vol. i, p. 40.

If a Russian should attempt to steal from any one in our Empire, he shall be severely punished for that act; and if he shall have accomplished the theft, he shall pay double the value of the object stolen. It shall be the same for the Greek in respect of the Russians; the guilty person, moreover, shall be punished according to the laws of his country.[1]

The reciprocal nature of this treaty inevitably points to the degree of tolerance with which the exemption was regarded on both sides and shows that there was a time when even in the relations of one Christian Power with another the practice of extraterritoriality was by no means such an anomaly as it is now.

II. THE CRUSADES AND THE RISE OF EXTRATERRITORIALITY

The influence of the Crusades upon the development of international commerce is well-known. While the transcendent motive of this great armed movement, which pervaded all classes of men who participated in it, was religious, there were also other considerations which lured them on to their final goal. These latter differed according as the social status of the participants differed: with the princes, it was the love of conquest and adventure; with the lower classes, it was the desire to elevate their social status; and with the bourgeois, it was the thirst for gain.[2] As a result of the notable rôle played by the bourgeois, a great increase in the volume and scope of overseas trade was brought about.

The reasons for this unusual development of international commerce are not far to seek. In a large part the progress is to be ascribed to the favorable situation of Constantinople and of its environs. For a long time, due to their advantageous position, the Byzantines had held in the Mediterranean

---

[1] *Ibid.*, p. 61.

[2] Heyd, *Histoire de commerce du Levant* (Leipzig, 1885-86), vol. i, p. 131.

a supremacy undisputed by the Occidentals. In the south, there was Egypt, where the Red Sea commanded the merchandise of the Levant; in Asia Minor, Syria, where caravan parties from the Arabian Sea, the Persian Gulf or the center of Asia came to discharge their burdens; and on the Black Sea, there were many places of commercial interest.[1]

Brought into contact by the Crusades with this land of opportunity, the Italian and other maritime peoples of the West sought to fortify themselves still further by obtaining numerous privileges and concessions from the Christian princes who planted themselves in the Levant during this period. To the ambitions of the merchants the circumstances of the time were peculiarly favorable, for in the conquests made by the crusading princes, the Italian fleets were constantly called upon to render invaluable services, without which all the bravery and military tactics of the knights would have been in vain. Moreover, even after the taking of the well fortified ports of Syria, the assistance of the Italian fleets was needed for their retention. Evidently, the possession of these ports was a matter of life and death to the Crusaders, as through them unobstructed communication was maintained with the Occident, whence only resources of man power and money could come. The sovereigns of the conquered States could, therefore, hardly be oblivious of the assistance rendered by the Italians, and it was in recognition of this that many concessions were granted to them in their respective establishments. On their side, it was also not uncommon, nor was it unnatural, that the Italians felt at times conscious of the importance of their aid, and in many an instance, made their help conditional on promises of extravagant remuneration. Thus, a large number of *colonies* were founded, which, in the course of time, became commercial centers of greater or less impor-

[1] Heyd, *op. cit.*, p. 24; Nys, *Les Origines du droit international* (Brussels, 1894), p. 281.

tance in the Levant.[1] In the grants made by the Prince of
Tyre to the Pisans in 1188[2] and 1189,[3] for instance, it was
expressly stated that the privileges were conceded on account
of military services rendered by the Pisans.

In the States of the Levant under Christian sovereignty
during the Crusades, special privileges of consular jurisdiction existed in the Byzantine Empire,[4] Syria,[5] and
Cyprus.[6] As it is to be expected, the provisions of the early

[1] Heyd, *op. cit.*, vol. i, pp. 131-132, 135-136. *Cf.* Martens, *Das Consularwesen* (Berlin, 1874), p. 61; Nys. *Les Origines,* p. 283.

[2] Lünig, *Codex Ital. Dip.* (Francfort, 1725-34), vol. i, c. 1060.

[3] Muratori, *Antiq. Ital.* (Avetti, 1773-80), vol. vi, c. 279.

[4] Venice, Nov., 1199, Tafel und Thomas, *Urkunden zur älteren Han-
dels- und Staatsgeschichte der Republik Venedig* (Vienna, 1856-57),
vol. i, pp. 273-276; Genoa, Venice and Pisa, 1265, Pachymeres, *Michael
Palaologus* (Rome, 1666), p. 105; Turkey, 1391, Ducas, *Historia Byzan-
tina* (Paris, 1649), p. 30. According to the last-mentioned grant, the
Turks were to have a *cadi* in Constantinople to decide their own cases.
This is important, as it constitutes a significant basis for the later Turkish
Capitulations, especially as it was granted by a Christian to a Moham-
medan Power. *Cf. infra,* p. 64.

[5] Venice: Jerusalem, 1123, Tafel und Thomas, *op. cit.*, vol. i, p. 87;
May, 1125, *ibid.*, p. 92; 1130, Muratori, *op. cit.*, vol. vi, c. 288; Beirut,
Dec., 1221, Tafel und Thomas, *op. cit.*, vol. ii, p. 231; Tyre, 1275,
Muratori, *Rerum italicarum scriptores* (Mediolani, 1723-51), vol. xii,
c. 382-383.

Pisa: Antioch, 1154, Lünig, *op. cit.*, vol. i, c. 1046; Jerusalem, 1157,
ibid., c. 1047; Antioch, 1170, Muratori, *Antiquitates Italicae,* vol. vi, c.
268; Tripoli, 1187, *ibid.*, c. 271; Tyre, Oct. 6, 1187, Ughelli, *Italia Sacra*
(Venice, 1717-22), vol. iii, c. 415-416; 1188, Lünig, *op. cit.*, vol. i, 1060;
1189, Muratori, *op. cit.*, vol. vi, c. 278; 1191, *ibid.*, c. 281; Antioch, 1216,
ibid., c. 284.

Genoa: Antioch, Sep. 1, 1190, Dumont, *Corps universel diplomatique,*
vol. i, pt. i, p. 115.

Marseilles: Syria, Nov. 8, 1226, *ibid.*, p. 164.

[6] Genoa: July 12, 1218, Mas-Latrie, *Histoire de l'île de Chypre* (Paris,
1852-61), vol. ii, Doc., p. 39; June 10, 1232, *ibid.*, pp. 51-52; Dec. 25,
1233, *ibid.*, p. 58; Feb. 16, 1329 (art. 2), *ibid.*, p. 153; April 18, 1365,
(art. 3), *ibid.*, pp. 258-9.

Venice: June 3, 1306 (art. 7), *ibid.*, pp. 105-6; Sep. 4, 1328, *ibid.*, pp.
142-3; Aug. 16, 1360, *ibid.*, p. 232.

grants were not always specific or comprehensive, but in a
general way the rights conceded were in strict accord with
the principle *actor sequitur forum rei.* With few exceptions,[1] the Italians in the Levant, who were commonly allowed to dwell in special quarters provided for them, were
placed under the exclusive jurisdiction of their own consular courts in cases affecting themselves alone.[2] Mixed
cases were assigned by some of the earlier grants to the
competence of the local courts,[3] but later practice differed in
no wise from the modern rule that the plaintiff should follow
the defendant into his court. Cases of natives against
Christians were under the jurisdiction of the consular court
concerned, and cases of Christians against natives, under
that of the local courts.[4]

It should be pointed out in passing that independently of
these acts of privilege, there existed in Jerusalem a régime
in the nature of a mixed court system. When the Christians
of the First Crusade conquered Palestine and formed the
kingdom of Jerusalem in 1099, they established the military
and feudal constitution known as the "*Assises de Jérusalem.*" The "*Assises*" set up a Commercial Court and a
Cour des Bourgeois. The Commercial Court was composed
of a bailiff and six jurors, two of whom were Christians
and four Syrians. All civil and commercial disputes were
brought before this court; but criminal matters were within

[1] The excepted cases were those of murder, rape, assault, treason and
robbery. See Venice-Beirut, 1221; Pisa-Tripoli, 1187; Genoa-Cyprus,
1218, 1365 (art. 3); Venice-Cyprus, 1306 (art. 7).

[2] See all the acts listed in notes 1-3 on the preceding page.

[3] Pisa-Antioch, 1154, 1170. The Byzantine grant of 1199 to Venice
stated that only the more important cases between Venetians and
Greeks were to be tried by the local court.

[4] Venice-Byzantium, 1199; Venice-Jerusalem, 1123, 1125, 1130; Venice-
Tyre, 1275; Pisa, 1187, 1189; Genoa-Cyprus, 1365 (art. 3); Venice-
Cyprus, 1306 (art. 7).

the sole competence of the *Cour des Bourgeois,* which was composed of the Viscount and jurors.[1]

III. EXTRATERRITORIALITY IN THE MOHAMMEDAN STATES PRIOR TO 1453

The Testament of Mohammed and the Capitulation of Omar furnish the customary basis of Mussulman practice with regard to jurisdiction over foreigners. The explanation for the position held by the Mussulman on this subject, as has been intimated above, has to be sought in his religious beliefs. According to the *Koran,* which is at once a gospel, a code and a constitution, all those who were not followers of the Mohammedan religion were to be treated as enemies and to be slaughtered without mercy.[2] But the exigencies of commerce demanded and effected a mitigation of this rule. "The innate and invincible aversion of the Mohammedans," says Pradier-Fodéré,[3] "to do business outside their country; their inexperience in navigation, which forced them to recruit their crews only from among foreign seamen; the need, which the political chiefs of Islamism felt, of utilizing their extended coast, their fine harbors, the rich products of their fertile soil, and of reaping the numerous advantages of maritime commerce, were early destined to inspire the Sultans with a favorable disposition towards the

[1] Miltitz, *Manuel des consuls,* vol. i, pp. 42-48, 168, n. 6; vol. ii, pt. i, p. 16; Ancien Diplomate, *Le Régime des Capitulations,* pp. 38-39; Depping, *Histoire du commerce* (Paris, 1830), vol. ii, p. 210. *Cf.* Foucher, *Assises de Royaume de Jérusalem,* 1 vol. in 2 (Rennes, 1839-41) ; Beugnot, *Assises de Jérusalem,* 2 vols. (Paris, 1841-43).

[2] *Koran,* sura xlvii, verse 4. "When ye encounter the infidels, strike off their heads till ye have made a great slaughter among them, and of the rest make fast and fetters."

[3] "*La Question des Capitulations,*" *Révue de droit international et de législation comparée* (hereafter referred to as *R. D. I.*), vol. i, p. 119. *Cf.* Féraud-Giraud, *De la Jurisdiction française dans les Echelles du Levant,* vol. i, pp. 33-35.

foreigners. It was necessary to invite the Christians to the exploitation of so many resources and, in the interest of the State, to encourage them to make settlements in the Levant." The writer is here discussing the origin of the Turkish Capitulations, but what he says is, in a general way, applicable to all the Mohammedan States prior to the conquest of Constantinople. The Mussulman's desire to develop commerce and navigation, therefore, saved the unbeliever from the Damoclean sword of Islam.

Indeed, the commercial motive, before which even religious bigotry gave way, was so overwhelming that it has left its imprint in the very Capitulations granted by the Mussulman rulers. It is a remarkable fact that all these Capitulations are unilateral or one-sided, dispensing favors without exacting any consideration. The explanation is again to be sought in the exuberant zeal for commercial development or nowhere. The object of the Capitulations was to regulate the conditions under which Europeans were to do business in the Levant; the interests of the Mussulman, whether at sea or abroad in a Christian country, were ignored in the scramble for the benefit of European commerce at home.[1] Thus, the element of reciprocity was conspicuously absent, but its absence, though conspicuous, ought not to betray any derogation from sovereignty on the part of the proud Saracens. The fact is that during the period under examination,

---

[1] Mas-Latrie, *Traités de paix et de commerce* (Paris, 1865), Introduction Historique, pp. 114, 115. According to M. Mas-Latrie, who has made an exhaustive study of the documents bearing on the commercial relations between the Christian States of Europe and the Mohammedans of North Africa, a condition of reciprocity in all but one respect, could have come about. "Save this case [of religion] and this case alone, perhaps, the Mussulmans would probably have obtained in Europe complete equality of treatment, if the Arab plenipotentiaries, nearly always charged with the first draft of the treaties, of which the Latin text was only an interpretative version, had felt it opportune to stipulate for it." *Ibid.*, p. 115.

the notion of exclusive sovereignty was still unborn, and
it is highly improbable that much attention could have been
paid to it by the negotiators on either side. Be this as it
may, the consul, who was usually invested with the judicial
authority, occupied a not at all exalted position in the Levant
at the time.[1]

Saved as the foreigner was from the fate of the infidel,
by the Mohammedan quest after the boon of European commerce, he was nevertheless outside the pale of the Mohammedan religion. In the *Koran,* we find a passage to the
following effect:

> Say: O ye Unbelievers!
> I worship not what ye worship,
> And ye are not worshippers of what I worship;
> And I am not a worshipper of what ye have worshipped,
> And ye are not worshippers of what I worship.
> To you your religion; and to me my religion.[2]

Inasmuch as the *Koran* was a judicial as well as a moral
or religious code, one who was not a follower of the religion was naturally not amenable to the law. Hence, it
was necessary to submit the foreigner to a special jurisdiction, the most reasonable being that of his own country.[3]

[1] In the writings of Khalil ben-Schahin Dhahéri occurs a passage,
which is translated by M. Silvestre de Sacy into French as follows:
"Dans cette ville [Alexandria] sont otages des consuls, c'est-à-dire, de
grands seigneurs d'entre les Francs des diverses nations: toutes les fois
que la nation de l'un d'eux fait quelque chose de nuisible a l'islamisme,
on en demande compte à son consul, qu'on en rend responsable." Silvestre de Sacy, *Christomathie arabe* (Paris, 1806), vol. ii, p. 318.

[2] Sura cix.

[3] *Cf.* Pelissié du Rausas, *Le Régime des Capitulations dans l'Empire
Ottoman* (2nd ed., Paris, 1910-11), vol. i, p. 21, where it is said: "The
Mussulman law was not made for the foreigner, since he is a non-
Mussulman; it is necessary that he remain subject to his own law. The
Mussulman law can neither protect him nor judge him nor punish him,
since it protects, judges and punishes only Mussulmans; it is necessary

Amalfi is said to have been the first Christian Power to enter into commercial relations with Egypt. According to Sir Travers Twiss, the merchants of that city obtained from the Caliphs of Egypt towards the end of the ninth century the privilege of trading at Alexandria under a consul of their own nationality, though the text of such a grant does not exist.[1]

The earliest grant made by Egypt to a Christian Power, which has been preserved is a letter of 1154 addressed by an Egyptian official to Pisa, which guaranteed to the Pisans their own jurisdiction.[2] In this letter, allusion was made to the maintenance of old rights,[3] which indicates the existence of consular jurisdiction in Egypt prior to 1154. Other Italian republics which enjoyed extraterritorial privileges in Egypt at this time were Venice,[4] Genoa [5] and Florence.[6]

Outside of Egypt, rights of consular jurisdiction existed also in the Barbary States in favor of the Italian and Spanish States.[7]

that he be protected, judged and punished by his own law. The Mussulman law is the *Jus Quiritium;* it is the exclusive right, the privilege of the Mussulmans; and it it is the *Jus Gentium* that rules the foreigner."

[1] Twiss, *Law of Nations* (2nd ed., Oxford, 1884), vol. i, p. 446.

[2] Amari, *I Diplomi Arabi* (Firenze, 1863), p. 247. This letter was confirmed by another letter from Saladin dated Sep. 25, 1173, *ibid.*, p. 257, and a treaty of 1215-16 (art. 33), *ibid.*, p. 287.

[3] *Ibid.*, p. 248.

[4] Nov. 14, 1238, Tafel und Thomas, *op. cit.*, vol. ii, p. 338.

[5] 1290, *Notices et extraits des manuscrits de la Bibliothèque Nationale et autres bibliothèques,* vol. xi, p. 35.

[6] June 14, 1422, Amari, *op. cit.*, p. 333; 1488 (arts. 11, 12, 14), *ibid.*, p. 384; 1496, *ibid.*, p. 212; 1509, *ibid.*, p. 223.

[7] Tunis: Venice, 1251 (arts. 4, 23), Mas-Latrie, *Traités de paix et de commerce,* Doc., pp. 200, 202; 1271 (art. 3), *ibid.*, p. 204; 1305 (art. 3), *ibid.*, p. 212; 1317 (art. 3), *ibid.*, p. 217; 1392 (art. 3), *ibid.*, p. 233; 1438 (art. 3), *ibid.*, p. 251; 1456, *ibid.*, p. 255; Genoa, June 10, 1236 (art. 15), *ibid.*, p. 117; Oct. 18, 1250 (art. 15), *ibid.*, p. 120; Oct. 17, 1391, *ibid.*, p. 132; Oct. 19, 1433 (arts. 3, 15), *ibid.*, p. 135; 1445, *ibid.*,

According to these Capitulations, the Christians were
allowed to dwell in specially provided quarters under their
own administration. Cases, whether civil or criminal, involving Christians of the same nationality were within the
exclusive competence of their consul administering their own
laws.[1] In mixed cases, the principle *actor sequitur forum
rei* was generally adopted, but not without vagueness and
confusion at times. Thus, while the Pisans were completely
exempted from local interference in any cases involving
them[2] and were required to proceed against criminals in
the court of the admiral of Alexandria,[3] and while the
Venetian consul was to take cognizance of cases between
Venetians and other Christians in Egypt,[4] the Florentines,
when they succeeded to the rights of the Pisans, were subjected to the jurisdiction of the sultan in their litigations
with other Christians in Egypt.[5] This deviation from the
general principle was removed by the treaty of 1496, which
granted to the Pisans the same rights as had been enjoyed
by the Venetians.[6] In general, cases involving foreigners
of different nationalities were to be disposed of by their
consuls, and cases between natives and Christians were likewise placed under the jurisdiction of the defendant's court.[7]

p. 142; Pisa, May 16, 1353 (arts. 9, 35), *ibid.*, pp. 58, 62; Dec. 14, 1397
(art. 5), *ibid.*, p. 74; Florence, 1421 (arts. 2, 3, 5), *ibid.*, p. 347; Aragon,
1271 (arts. 9, 28), *ibid.*, p. 283; 1285 (art. 28), *ibid.*, p. 289; 1314 (art.
15), *ibid.*, p. 309; 1323 (arts. 16, 17, 18), *ibid.*, p. 322.
  Morocco: Pisa, 1358 (art. 11), *ibid.*, p. 68.

  [1] See all the Captulations listed in notes 4-7 on the preceding page.

  [2] Letter of Saladin, Sep. 25, 1173.

  [3] 1215-16, art. 33.

  [4] 1238.

  [5] 1488, art. 24.

  [6] Amari, *op. cit.*, p. 212.

  [7] Venice-Egypt, 1238; Genoa-Egypt, 1290; Venice-Tunis, 1251, art. 23;
1305, art. 3; 1317, art. 3; 1392, art. 3; 1438, art. 3; Genoa-Tunis and

In some of the treaties, a right of appeal was allowed to the local courts in cases where natives proceeded against Christians in their consular courts.[1]

Tripoli, 1236, art. 15; Genoa-Tunis, 1250, art. 15; 1433, art. 3; Pisa-Tunis, 1353, art. 9; 1397, art. 5; Florence-Tunis, 1421, arts. 2, 3, 5; Aragon-Tunis, 1271, art. 9; 1323, art. 16; Pisa-Morocco, 1358, art. 11. The treaty of 1356 between Venice and Tripoli contained the peculiar provision that cases between Saracens and Christians should be tried by special local judges, according to the laws of each party (art. 4).

[1] Venice-Tunis, 1305, art. 3; 1317, art. 3; 1392, art. 3; 1438, art. 3; Pisa-Tunis, 1397, art. 5; Florence-Tunis, 1421, art. 5; Aragon-Tunis, 1323, art. 16.

CHAPTER III

IN THE LEVANT AND AFRICA AFTER 1453

I. ORIGIN OF EXTRATERRITORIALITY IN THE OTTOMAN EMPIRE AND THE LEVANT

IN explaining the development of consular jurisdiction in the Ottoman Empire and the Levant, writers have attached an almost undue amount of importance to the differences between the Christian and Mohamemdan religions. They have sought to ascribe the special status of the foreigner in Turkey principally, if not wholly, to the fundamental discrepancies between the two faiths. A typical pronouncement to this effect is that made by M. Féraud-Giraud:

> When there exists between two peoples a very great difference in respect of religion, manners, laws, and customs, lasting and proper [*suivis*] relations are possible only when one of these peoples, drawn to the territory of the other by their activity, finds there exceptional guarantees, without which security of person and property cannot exist.[1]

In the footsteps of this eminent jurist has followed many a subsequent writer.[2]

It is true that the Mohammedan religion makes certain discriminations against the infidel, but to say that this was the principal ground on which the right of extraterritoriality

---

[1] *De la Juridiction française dans les Échelles du Levant et de Barbarie*, vol. i., p. 29.

[2] See, e. g., Pradier-Fodéré, *Traité de droit international* (Paris, 1885-1906), vol. iv, p. 713; Bonfils, *Manuel de droit international public* (Paris, 1914), p. 514.

was imposed upon or wrested from the sultans would be inconsistent with the facts of the case. The first Capitulations granted to France, on which all later claims of Europe to extraterritorial jurisdiction in the Ottoman Empire are chiefly based, bear the date of 1535. In the instructions which Francis I issued to his envoy in Constantinople, M. Jean de la Forêt,[1] one would look in vain for the slightest intimation of a demand for special judicial status. As a matter of fact, had any demand of the sort been made, it would have been categorically rejected, for it must be remembered that when it granted the Capitulations of 1535, Turkey was at the zenith of its power. True, the idea of exclusive sovereignty had not yet emerged, but had it been suggested that the rights accorded were to be a derogation from Ottoman sovereignty, they could scarcely have been acceded to. No such suggestion was ventured, however, no exorbitant demand was made upon the Porte, which gratuitously conferred upon the Christians their judicial rights. And it is of great interest to note in this connection that seven years before France obtained her first Capitulations in the Ottoman Empire, Sultan Suleyman II confirmed the treaty between the Mameluke Sultans and the French and Catalonian consuls,[2] at a time when Francis I was in captivity at Madrid and was in no position to ride rough-shod over the Turks.

That the Capitulations were not imposed upon the sultans at the beginning and were but gratuitous concessions on their part may further be corroborated by the exemption of the sultan's non-Moslem subjects from Ottoman justice. Immediately after the conquest of Constantinople, Sultan Mohammed II granted to the Armenians, Greeks and Jews

[1] Charrière, *Négociations de la France dans le Levant,* vol. i, pp. 255 *et seq.*

[2] *Cf. infra,* p. 66.

their special rights of jurisdiction. At Constantinople, a
Greek patriarch was chosen as chief of the nation, president
of the synod, and supreme judge of all the civil and religious
affairs of the Greeks. The Armenians had at Constantinople, Caesarea, and Jerusalem three patriarchs invested with
the right of deciding civil disputes. The Jews likewise had
their courts, and a triumvirate composed of three rabbis
served as their supreme court at Constantinople.[1] This was
in accord with the Mohammedan theory that those who were
outside the pale of religion were also outside the pale of
law.[2]

The influence of religious differences on the development
of extraterritoriality in the Ottoman Empire can, of course,
hardly be denied. But what these differences did was not
to furnish the Franks with a ground for demanding special
concessions, but rather to give the sultans an additional impetus to make these concessions.[3]

The aversion of the Mohammedans to overseas commerce
has been referred to above.[4] Its effect on the attitude of
the Sultans towards foreigners was, to say the least, considerable, but its importance as a factor in bringing about
their special status is assuredly second to yet other considerations.

Of all the explanations which have been given for the
existence of the capitulatory régime in the Ottoman Empire, none is as near an approximation to the truth as the
one based on the force of custom. Whatever may have
been the intention of the Sultans in doling out privileges to
their foreign residents without exacting any consideration,
the motivating force of long-established custom must have

[1] Féraud-Giraud, *op. cit.,* vol. i, pp. 31-32.

[2] *Supra,* p. 57.

[3] *Cf.* Twiss, *On Consular Jurisdiction in the Levant,* p. 4.

[4] *Supra,* p. 55.

been the strongest and the most persuasive. Here was an institution of several centuries of standing. It had been in vogue in Christian as well as in non-Christian countries and prominent in the relations between non-Christians and Christians and even between Christians and Christians. Furthermore, it was a system in perfect accord with Mohammedan theories of law and religion. Was the Ottoman Empire to throw overboard this long prevalent usage? The answer to this question was self-evident, and the sultans chose the line of least resistance.

In discussing the same question, M. Renault makes the following observation:

Suleyman the Magnificent, with whom Francis I sought an alliance in 1535, did not make a concession which could have been regarded as humiliating. It must be considered that in the early days, territorial sovereignty had a less exclusive character than it does to-day and was not repugnant to the exercise of jurisdiction by foreign authorities. Thus, the curious fact has been noted that sixty years before Constantinople passed under the domination of the Turks, a Mussulman community had resided there under the administration of the *Cadi* who rendered justice according to Mohammedan laws.[1] It is then not surprising that Mohammed II, after the conquest, accorded to the merchants of Genoa and of Venice the continuation of the privileges which they had enjoyed under the Christian emperors.[2]

Another writer goes even farther than M. Renault and dismisses all the other explanations, expressing himself in favor of the customary origin of the Capitulations in the Levant. He says:

I repeat that there has existed no period in the history of

[1] *Supra*, p. 53, n. 4.
[2] L. Renault, Article on " Capitulations," *Grand Encyclopédie*, vol. ix, p. 213.

Constantinople in which foreigners have not enjoyed the advantages, and been subject to the disabilities, of exterritoriality. The existing system of Capitulations is a survival rather than, as it is generally represented, a new invention specially adapted to Turkey. Still less is it a system, as it is often said to be, of magnanimous concessions made by far-sighted sultans of Turkey in order to encourage foreigners to trade with and reside in the empire. The Capitulations were neither badges of inferiority imposed on foreigners, as they have been described, nor proofs of exceptional wisdom peculiar to the sultans. As a fact, foreigners have never held so important a position in the capital under Ottoman rule as under that of the Christian emperors, and especially at the close of the twelfth century.[1]

II. CAPITULATIONS AND TREATIES WITH THE LEVANT AND AFRICA

Having dealt with the circumstances which have conduced to the maintenance of the capitulatory régime in the Ottoman Empire, we may now proceed to examine the individual acts which have established the rights of the various European Powers in Turkey and in the Levant and Africa.

The first document which conferred extraterritorial rights on Christians in the Ottoman Empire was the firman of 1453 respecting the Genoese in Galata. On May 29, a few days after the conquest of Constantinople, the firman was issued, which granted to the Genoese the right of retaining their own laws and customs and of choosing from among themselves an *ancien* to decide their own disputes.[2] This act was renewed in 1612.[3]

In 1454, a treaty was concluded with Venice, giving the latter the right to send to Constantinople a consul or *bailo*, with his customary suite, who should exercise civil jurisdic-

---

[1] Pears, *Fall of Constantinople* (New York, 1886), p. 152.

[2] The text, with a French translation, is given in Hammer, *Histoire de l'Empire Ottoman* (Paris, 1835-43), vol. ii, pp. 523 *et seq.*

[3] Noradhounghian, *Recueil,* vol. i, p. 111.

tion over Venetians of every description, the *Grand Seigneur* engaging to accord to him protection and assistance whenever necessary.[1] The privileges were renewed in 1479, 1482, 1502, 1517, 1539, 1575, and 1595.[2]

On September 20, 1528, Sultan Suleyman II entered into a treaty with France, which confirmed the jurisdictional rights of the French and Catalonian consuls in Egypt granted to them by the Mameluke Sultans.[3]

So far as the Ottoman Empire as a whole was concerned, however, the first instrument which established the French régime in Turkey was the Capitulations of February, 1535.[4] It was the earliest treaty defining in detail the rights to which the foreigners were entitled in Turkey.

As it was the Turkish theory that treaties should not last longer than the lifetime of a single sultan, this document was renewed by each sultan in succession,[5] with occasional modifications, until, in 1740,[6] the treaties were given their final form, to constitute the principal basis of the European claim to extraterritorial privileges in Turkey.

The Capitulations of 1740 were also renewed repeatedly in 1802, 1838, and 1861.[7] The document of 1802 was the first engagement between France and Turkey in modern treaty form. Article 2 provided that " The treaties or capitulations which, before the War, determined respectively

---

[1] Daru, *Histoire de Venise* (2nd ed., Paris, 1821), vol. ii, p. 514; Miltitz, *op. cit.*, vol. ii, pt. i, pp. 217-218.

[2] *Ibid.*, pp. 76-77.

[3] Testa, *Recueil des traités de la Porte Ottomane* (Paris, 1864-1901), vol. i, p. 24; Charrière, *op. cit.*, vol. i, p. 116.

[4] Noradounghian, *Recueil*, vol. i, p. 83.

[5] Prior to 1740, renewals were made in 1569, 1581, 1597, 1604, 1607, 1609, 1618, 1624, 1640, 1673, and 1684. See Noradounghian, *Recueil*, vol. i, pp. 88, 35, 37, 93, 108, 40, 43, 45, 47, 49, 136, 54.

[6] Arts. 15, 26, 52, 65, *ibid.*, pp. 282, 285, 290, 294.

[7] *Ibid.*, vol. ii, pp. 52, 257, vol. iii, p. 131.

relations of every kind existing between the two Powers, are hereby renewed in their entirety."

For a long time after France obtained her first Capitulations, she was the protector of European merchants, who were required to trade under her flag.[1] In the sixteenth and seventeenth centuries, the English sought to dispute the right of the French to protect non-treaty interests and to arrogate to themselves the same authority.[2] But these attempts were for a time fruitless, and as late as the Capitulations of 1740, France was allowed to retain the right.[3] It was only in 1607 that England herself was exempted from the obligation of trading under the French flag.[4] In 1675, however, Great Britain was given the authority to exercise protection over the merchants of Spain, Portugal, Ancona, Sicily, Florence, Catalonia and the Netherlands.[5]

Following the example of France, other Powers obtained capitulatory rights from the Ottoman Empire in rapid succession. These included Great Britain,[6] the Netherlands,[7]

[1] See article 1 of the Capitulations of 1581: " That henceforth Venetian, Genoese, English, Portuguese, Catalonian, Sicilian, Anconian, Ragusian merchants, and all those who have traded [*cheminé*] under the name and flag of France, from antiquity to to-day, shall trade in the same manner." Hauterive et Cussy, *Recueil des traités de commerce et de navigation* (Paris, 1834-44), vol. ii, pt. i, p. 446.

[2] On the controversy between France and England regarding the privilege of protection, see *Mémoires de St. Priest* (Paris, 1877), p. 287; *Ambassade en Turquie de Jean de Contaut Biron, Baron de Salignac, 1605 à 1610* (Paris, 1888-89), pp. 136, 143, 146, 155, 156, 160, 184, 415, 419, 422; Additional Act of 1607, Noradounghian, *op. cit.*, vol. i, p. 108.

[3] Arts. 32, 38, *ibid.*, pp. 286, 288.

[4] *Ibid.*, p. 110.

[5] Art. 33, *ibid.*, p. 154.

[6] Treaty of June, 1580, Hakluyt, *op. cit.*, vol. v, p. 264; Oct. 28, 1641, Noradounghian, *op. cit.*, vol. i, p. 48; Sep., 1675 (arts. 15, 16, 24, 42), *ibid.*, pp. 149, 151, 156. The last was renewed in 1838 and 1861, *ibid.*, vol. ii, p. 249; vol. iii, p. 136.

[7] 1612 (arts. 3, 11, 38), Dumont, *Corps univ. dip.*, vol. v, pt. ii, pp. 207, 208, 211; renewals in 1680, 1840, and 1862, Noradounghian, *op. cit.*, vol. i, p. 169; vol. ii, p. 298; vol. iii, p. 180.

Austria-Hungary,[1] Sweden,[2] Italy,[3] Denmark,[4] Prussia and
later Germany,[5] Russia,[6] Spain,[7] Persia,[8] Belgium,[9] Portugal,[10] Greece,[11] the United States,[12] Brazil,[13] and Mexico.[14]

[1] July 27, 1718 (art. 5), *ibid.*, vol. i, p. 224; renewals in 1784, 1862,
ibid., p. 379; vol. iii, p. 194.

[2] Jan. 10, 1737 (arts. 6, 8), *ibid.*, vol. i, p. 240; renewals in 1840 and
1862, *ibid.*, vol. ii, p. 298; vol. iii, p. 182.

[3] Treaty with the Two Sicilies, April 7, 1740 (art. 5), *ibid.*, vol. i, p
272, which was renewed in 1851, *ibid.*, vol. ii, p. 395; treaty with
Tuscany, May 25, 1747 (art. 4), Martens, *Supplément au Recueil,* vol.
i, p. 293, which was renewed in 1833 and 1841, Noradounghian, *op. cit.*,
vol. ii, pp. 219, 338; treaty with Sardinia, Oct. 25, 1823 (art. 8), *ibid.*,
p. 101, which was renewed in 1839 and 1854, *ibid.*, pp. 283, 425.
The Kingdom of Italy succeeded to all these treaties by virtue of
article 1 of the treaty of July 10, 1861, *ibid.*, vol. iii, p. 152.

[4] Oct. 14, 1746 (art. 10), *ibid.*, vol. i, p. 311; renewals in 1841 and 1862,
ibid., vol. ii, p. 330; vol. iii, p. 183.

[5] Treaty with Prussia, Mar. 23, 1761 (art. 5), *ibid.*, vol. i, p. 317, which
was renewed in 1840 and 1862, *ibid.*, vol. ii, p. 314; vol. iii, p. 185; treaty
with the Hanseatic League, 1839 (art. 8), *State Papers,* vol. xxviii, p.
450, which was renewed in 1841 and 1862, Noradounghian, *op. cit.*, vol.
ii, p. 345; vol. iii, p. 206. The German Empire succeeded to these
treaties by virtue of article 24 of the treaty of Aug. 26, 1890, *ibid.*,
vol. iv, p. 493.

[6] July 10/21, 1774 (art. 11), *ibid.*, vol. i, p. 325; June 10/21, 1783 (art.
63), p. 369; renewals in 1792, 1812, 1829, 1846, and 1862, *ibid.*, vol. ii,
pp. 16, 86, 166, 371; vol. iii, p. 171.

[7] Sept. 14, 1782 (art. 5), *ibid.*, vol. i, p. 345, which was renewed in
1840 and 1862, *ibid.*, vol. ii, p. 298; vol. iii, p. 184.

[8] July 28, 1823 (art. 2), *State Papers,* vol. xi, p. 838; May 20, 1847
(art. 7), Noradounghian, *op. cit.*, vol. ii, p. 384; Dec. 20, 1875 (arts. 1,
7, 10), *ibid.*, vol. iii, pp. 391, 393, 394.

[9] Aug. 3, 1838 (art. 8), *ibid.*, vol. ii, p. 245; renewals 1839, 1840, 1861,
ibid., pp. 276, 302; vol. iii, p. 160.

[10] March 20, 1843 (art. 8), *ibid.*, vol. ii, p, 356; renewal in 1868, *ibid.*,
vol. iii, p. 263.

[11] May 23, 1855 (arts. 24, 25), *ibid.*, vol. ii, p. 443.

[12] May 7, 1830 (art. 4), Malloy, vol. ii, p. 1319; renewal in 1862, *ibid.*,
p. 1321.

[13] Feb. 5, 1858 (art. 7), Noradounghian, *op. cit.*, vol. iii, p. 107.

[14] May 6, 1866 (arts. 10, 13), *ibid.*, p. 249.

The extraterritorial rights conferred by these treaties were formally abolished in 1923.[1]

Outside of the Ottoman Empire, extraterritoriality has also existed in the following States of the Levant and Africa: Algiers,[2] Morocco,[3] Tripoli,[4] Tunis,[5] Persia,[6] Mus-

[1] *Cf. infra*, pp. 185 *et seq.*

[2] Great Britain, April 10, 1682 (arts. 15, 16), *State Papers*, vol. i, p. 358; April 5, 1686 (arts. 15, 16), *ibid.*, p. 364; France, May 17, 1666 (art. 11), Rouard de Card, *Les Traités de la France avec les pays d'Afrique du Nord* (Paris, 1906), p. 36; April 25, 1684 (arts. 17, 19, 22), *ibid.*, p. 49; Sep. 24, 1689 (arts. 18, 21, 24), *ibid.*, p. 58; Dec. 28, 1801 (arts. 2, 12), *ibid.*, pp. 83, 84; U. S., Sep. 5, 1795 (arts. 15, 16), Malloy, vol. i, p. 4; June 30/July 6, 1815 (arts. 19, 20), *ibid.*, p. 10; Portugal, June 14, 1813 (art. 10), *State Papers*, vol. i, p. 187; Sicily, April 3, 1816 (art. 9), *ibid.*, vol. iii, p. 525. When France occupied Algiers in 1830, these treaties came to an end. *Cf. infra*, p. 104.

[3] France, Sep. 17, 1631 (art. 9), Dumont, *op. cit.*, vol. vi, pt. i, p. 20; Sep. 24, 1631 (arts. 9, 10, 12), *ibid.;* Jan. 29, 1682 (arts. 12, 13, 16), Rouard de Card, *op. cit.*, p. 318; May 28, 1767 (arts. 12, 13), *ibid.*, p. 324; Great Britain, Jan. 23, 1721 (art. 9), *State Papers*, vol. i, p. 430; Add. Articles, July 10, 1729 (art. 3), *ibid.*, p. 431; Jan. 15, 1750 (art. 3), *ibid.*, p. 433; Feb. 1, 1751 (art. 3), *ibid.*, p. 435; July 28, 1760 (art. 9), *ibid.*, p. 439; April 8, 1791 (arts. 7, 8), *ibid.*, pp. 447, 448; June 14, 1801 (arts. 7, 8), *ibid.*, pp. 456, 457; Jan. 19, 1824, *ibid.* vol. xiv, p. 641; Dec. 9, 1856 (arts. 8, 9, 14), *ibid.*, vol. xlvi, pp. 179-181; U. S., Jan., 1787 (arts. 20, 21), Malloy, vol. i, p. 1210; Sep. 16, 1836 (arts. 20, 21), *ibid.*, p. 1215; The Netherlands, May 26, 1683 (arts. 15, 16), Dumont, *op. cit.*, vol. vii, pt. ii, p. 68; Denmark, July 25, 1767 (art. 14), *State Papers*, vol. ci, p. 285; Spain, March 1, 1799 (art. 6), Martens, *Recueil des principaux traités*, vol. vi, p. 585; Nov. 20, 1861 (arts. 9, 10, 11), *State Papers*, vol. liii, p. 1093; Sardinia, June 30, 1825 (art. 22), *ibid.*, vol. xcviii, p. 979. The majority of these States, except Great Britain and the United States, have suspended their extraterritorial rights in Morocco. *Cf. infra*, pp. 161 *et seq.*

[4] Great Britain, Oct. 18, 1662 (arts, 8, 10), *State Papers*, vol. i, p. 712; March 5, 1675 (arts. 14, 15), *ibid.*, p. 716; July 19, 1716 (arts. 11, 12), *ibid.*, p. 722; Sep. 19, 1751 (arts. 11, 12), *ibid.*, p. 727; France, Jan. 29, 1685 (arts. 18, 20, 23), Rouard de Card, *op. cit.*, pp. 249, 250; July 4, 1720 (arts. 15, 17, 20), *ibid.*, pp. 259, 260; June 9, 1729 (arts. 23, 25, 29), *ibid.*, pp. 268, 269; June 18, 1801 (arts. 18, 19, 23), *ibid.*, pp. 281, 282, 283; Aug. 11, 1830 (art. 8), *ibid.*, p. 292; Spain, Sep. 10, 1784 (arts. 31, 32, 34), Martens, *Recueil de traités*, vol. iii, pp. 773, 775; U. S., Nov.

cat,[7] Zanzibar,[8] Senna (in Arabia),[9] Egypt,[10] Congo,[11] Ethiopia,[12] and Madagascar.[13]

4, 1796 (art. 9), Malloy, vol. ii, p. 1786; June 4, 1805 (arts. 18, 19), *ibid.*, p. 1792. When Tripoli was annexed by Italy in 1912, the extraterritorial régime in that country came to an end. *Cf. infra*, p. 113.

[5] France, Nov. 25, 1665 (arts. 21, 22, 23), Rouard de Card, *op. cit.*, pp. 121, 122; June 28, 1672 (arts. 21, 22, 23), *ibid.*, p. 135; Aug. 30, 1685 (arts. 18, 21, 24), *ibid.*, pp. 146, 147; Dec. 16, 1710 (arts. 13, 16, 19), *ibid.*, p. 159; Feb. 20, 1720 (arts. 14, 16, 19), *ibid.*, pp. 166, 167; Nov. 9, 1742 (arts. 13, 16, 19), *ibid.*, pp. 177, 178; renewals in 1743 (art. 1), 1802 (art. 2), 1824 (art. 2), and 1830 (art. 7), *ibid.*, pp. 182, 204, 208, 215; Great Britain, Oct. 5, 1662 (art. 8), *State Papers,* vol. i, p. 734; Aug. 30, 1716 (art. 8), *ibid.*, p. 736; Oct. 19, 1751 (art. 8), *ibid.*, p. 740; July 19, 1875 (arts. 24-26), *ibid.*, vol. lxvi, p. 101; U. S., Aug., 1797 (arts. 20, 21, 22), Malloy, vol. ii, p. 1799. The texts or extracts of all the principal treaties between Tunis and the European Powers prior to the year 1881 are given in *Documents diplomatiques, revision des traités tunisiens, 1881-1897,* pp. 7-41. Since that date, the majority of the Powers have suspended their rights of jurisdiction in Tunis. Great Britain claims, however, that these rights are subject to resumption. *Cf. infra*, pp. 142 *et seq.*

[6] France, Sep., 1708 (arts. 16, 18, 24), Hauterive et Cussy, *Recueil des traités* (Paris, 1834-44), pt. i, vol. ii, pp. 385, 386, 388, confirmed in 1715 and 1808, *ibid.*, pp. 402, 410; July 12, 1855 (art. 5), Martens et Cussy, *Recueil manuel et pratique,* (Leipzig, 1885-88), vol. vii, p. 578; Russia, Feb. 10/22, 1828 (arts. 7, 8), *State Papers,* vol. xlv, pp. 867, 868; Great Britain, July 2, 1763 (art. 4), Martens, *N. R. G.,* vol. xvi, pt. ii, p. 94; Spain, March 4, 1842 (art. 5), *State Papers,* vol. lviii, p. 594; U. S., Dec. 13, 1856 (art. 5), Malloy, vol. ii, p. 1372; Sardinia, April 26, 1857 (art. 5), *State Papers,* vol. xlix, p. 1343; Austria, May 17, 1857 (art. 9), *ibid.*, vol. xlvii, p. 1162; Prussia, June 25, 1857 (art. 5), *ibid.*, vol. lix, p. 910; Belgium, July 31, 1857 (art. 5), *ibid.*, vol. xlvii, p. 624; Greece, Oct. 16/28, 1861 (art. 9), *ibid.*, vol. li, p. 537; Italy, Sept. 24/29, 1862 (art. 5), *ibid.*, vol. lvii, p. 319; Germany, June 11, 1873 (art. 13), *ibid.*, vol. lxiii, p. 49; Switzerland, July 23, 1873 (art. 5), *ibid.*, p. 626; Turkey, Dec. 16, 1873 (arts. 7, 10), *Archives diplomatiques,* 1875, vol. iv, p. 142. The extraterritorial privileges of the following States in Persia rest on most-favored-nation clauses: Great Britain, March 4, 1857 (art. 9), *State Papers,* vol. xlvii, p. 44; Sweden & Norway, Nov. 17, 1857 (art. 3), *ibid.*, vol. lxxv, p. 907; Denmark, Nov. 30, 1857 (art. 3), *ibid.*, vol. xlvii, p. 1157; Argentina, July 27, 1902 (art. 3), *ibid.*, vol. xcvi, p. 1240; Mexico, May 14, 1902 (art. 3), *ibid.*, p. 174; Chile, Mar. 30, 1903 (art. 3), *ibid.*, vol. c, p. 827.

[7] U. S., Sep. 21, 1833 (art. 9), Malloy, vol. i, p. 1230; Great Britain,

The rights of jurisdiction granted by the above Capitula-

May 31, 1839 (art. 5), *State Papers,* vol. xxviii, p. 1082; March 19, 1891 (arts. 13, 14), *ibid.,* vol. lxxxiii, pp. 15-16; France, Nov. 17, 1844 (art. 6), *ibid.,* vol. xxxv, p. 1012.

[8] Hanseatic Republics, June 13, 1859 (art. 12), *ibid.,* vol. l, p. 1121; Portugal, Oct. 25, 1879 (art. 12), *ibid.,* vol. lxx, p. 1249; Italy, May 28, 1885 (art. 5), *ibid.,* vol. lxxvi, p. 270; Belgium, May 30, 1885 (art. 1), *ibid.,* p. 291; Germany, Dec. 20, 1885 (art. 16), *ibid.,* p. 253; Great Britain, April 30, 1886 (arts. 16, 17), *ibid.,* vol. lxxvii, p. 60; U. S., July 3, 1886, (art. 2), Malloy, vol. ii, p. 1900; Austria-Hungary, Aug. 11, 1887 (art. 1), *State Papers,* vol. lxxviii, p. 943. Extraterritoriality ended in Zanzibar soon after the British protectorate over that country took effect in 1890. *Cf. infra,* pp. 140 *et seq.*

[9] Great Britain, Jan. 15, 1821 (art. 6), *State Papers,* vol. xii, p. 503; France, Firman of the Iman, Dec. 26, 1824, Martens et Cussy, *Recueil manuel et pratique,* vol. iii, p. 616.

[10] Sec. 5 of the Separate Act annexed to the Convention of London, 1840, stipulated for the application of all the treaties and laws of the Ottoman Empire in Egypt. *State Papers,* vol. xxviii, p. 346. Since Egypt was placed under British protection in 1914, some of the Powers have abandoned their capitulatory rights in Egypt. *Cf. infra,* pp. 173-174.

[11] Great Britain, Dec. 16, 1884 (arts. 5-8), *State Papers,* vol. lxxv, p. 32; Sweden & Norway, Feb. 10, 1885 (arts. 7-9), *ibid.,* vol. lxxvi, p. 581; Turkey, June 25, 1885 (art. 6), *ibid.,* vol. ci, p. 632. Most-favored-nation treatment was extended to Germany, Nov. 8, 1884 (art. 2); Italy, Dec. 19, 1884 (art. 2); the Netherlands, Dec. 27, 1884 (art. 2); Austria-Hungary, Dec. 24, 1884 (art. 2); Spain, Jan. 7, 1885 (art. 2); Russia, Feb. 5, 1885 (art. 2); France, Feb. 5, 1885 (art. 1); Portugal, Feb. 14, 1885 (art. 1); Denmark, Feb. 23, 1885 (art. 3); and the United States, Jan. 24, 1891 (art. 1). For these treaties see *State Papers,* vol. lxxv, pp. 355, 634, 323, 991; vol. lxxvi, pp. 576, 1010, 578, 583, 587; Malloy, vol. i, p. 329. The régime of extraterritoriality in Congo came to an end when the country was placed under the sovereignty of Belgium in 1908. *Cf. infra,* p. 111.

[12] Great Britain, Nov. 2, 1849 (art. 17), *State Papers,* vol. xxxvii, p. 6; Italy, May 2, 1889 (arts. 10, 12), *ibid.,* vol. lxxxi, pp. 734, 735; U. S., Dec. 27, 1903 (art. 3), Malloy, vol. i, p. 466; June 27, 1914 (art. 3), *ibid.,* vol. iii (Washington, 1923), p. 2578. The American treaties contain most-favored-nation clauses " in respect to customs duties, imposts and jurisdiction."

[13] France, Sep. 12, 1862 (art. 9), *State Papers,* vol. liii, p. 155; Aug. 8,

tions and treaties may be summarized in three categories:
(1) in cases between foreigners of the same nationality;
(2) in cases between natives and foreigners; and (3) in
cases between foreigners of different nationalities. In none
of these agreements was there any provision made for the
jurisdiction over cases between natives exclusively, the implication being, however, that it was reserved to the local
authorities.

(1) In cases between foreigners of the same nationality,
all the treaties conferred the jurisdiction upon the diplomatic or consular representative of their own country, to
be exercised according to its laws, all interference and molestation on the part of the local magistrates being disallowed.[1]

1868 (arts. 6, 7), *ibid.,* vol. lviii, p. 192; Great Britain, June 27, 1865
(art. 11), *ibid.,* vol. lv, p. 23; U. S., Feb. 14, 1867 (art. 5), Malloy, vol.
i, p. 1060; May 13, 1881 (art. 6), *ibid.,* p. 1067. The following treaties
contained most-favored-nation clauses: Germany, May 15, 1883 (art. 2),
State Papers, vol. lxxiv, p. 717; Italy, July 6, 1883 (art. 2), *ibid.* vol.
lxxvi, p. 301. The system of consular jurisdiction ceased to operate in
Madagascar soon after the island was occupied by France in 1896. *Cf.
infra,* pp. 105 *et seq.*

[1] Turkey: France, 1535; 1604 (arts. 24, 43); 1673 (arts. 16, 37); 1740
(art. 15); Great Britain, 1675 (art. 16); the Netherlands, 1612 (art. 11),
1680 (art. 5); Austria, 1718 (art. 5); Sweden, 1737 (art. 6); Sicily,
1740 (art. 5); Sardinia, 1823 (art. 8); Tuscany, 1833 (art. 6); Denmark, 1746 (art. 10). Prussia, 1761 (art. 5); Hanseatic League, 1839
(art. 8); Russia, 1783 (art. 63); Persia, 1823 (art. 2); 1875 (art. 7);
Greece, 1855 (art. 24); Mexico, 1866 (art. 10).

Algiers: Great Britain, 1682 (art. 15); 1686 (art. 15); France, 1684
art. 17); 1689 (art. 18); U. S., 1795 (art. 15); 1815 (art 19); Portugal,
1813 (art. 10); Sicily, 1816 (art. 9).

Morocco: France, Sep. 17, 1631 (art. 9); Sep. 24, 1631 (art. 9);
1682 (art. 12); Great Britain, 1721 (art. 9); 1760 (art. 9); 1791 (art.
7); 1856 (art. 8), U. S., 1787 (art. 20); 1836 (art. 20); the Netherlands, 1683 (art. 15); Spain, 1861 (art. 10).

Tripoli: Great Britain, 1662 (art. 8); 1675 (art. 14); 1716 (art. 11);
1751 (art. 11); France, 1685 (art. 18); 1720 (art. 15); 1729 (art. 23);
1801 (art. 18); Spain, 1784 (art. 34); U. S., 1805 (art. 18).

Tunis: France, 1665 (art. 23); 1672 (art. 23); 1685 (art. 18); 1710

(2) Mixed cases between natives and foreigners were assigned by the earlier treaties, as by the Turkish, to the competence of the local authorities, who should, however, try them in the presence of the foreign diplomatic or consular officer concerned; but it was expressly provided that the pretext of the absence of the foreign representative should not be abused.[1]   In general, the principle *actor sequi-*

(art. 13); 1720 (art. 14); 1742 (art. 13); Great Britain, 1716 (art. 8); 1751 (art. 8); 1875 (art. 24); U. S., 1797 (art. 20).

Persia: France, 1708 (art. 16); 1855 (art. 5); Russia, 1828 (arts. 7, 8); U. S., 1856 (art. 5); Sardinia, 1857 (art. 5); Austria, 1857 (art. 9); Prussia, 1857 (art. 5); Belgium, 1857 (art. 5); Italy, 1862 (art. 5); Germany, 1873 (art. 13); Switzerland, 1873 (art. 5); Turkey, 1873 (art. 7).

Muscat: U. S., 1833 (art. 9); Great Britain, 1839 (art. 5); 1891 (art. 13); France, 1844 (art. 6).

Zanzibar: Hanseatic Republics, 1859 (art. 12); Portugal, 1879 (art. 12); Italy, 1885 (art. 5); Germany, 1885 (art. 16); Great Britain, 1886 (art. 16).

Congo: Great Britain, 1884 (art. 5); Sweden and Norway, 1885 (art. 6); Turkey, 1885 (art. 6).

Ethiopia: Great Britain, 1849 (art. 17); Italy, 1889 (art. 10).

Madagascar: France, 1862 (art. 9); 1868 (art. 6); Great Britain, 1865 (art. 11); U. S., 1867 (art. 5); 1881 (art. 6, §2).

[1] Turkey: France, 1535; 1604 (art. 42); 1673 (art. 36); 1740 (arts. 26, 65); Great Britain, 1675 (arts. 24, 42); the Netherlands, 1612 (art. 38); 1680 (art. 36); Sweden, 1737 (art. 8); Sicily, 1740 (art. 5); Sardinia, 1823 (art. 8); Denmark, 1746 (art. 10); Prussia, 1761 (art. 5); the Hanseatic League, 1839 (art. 8); Russia, 1783 (art. 63); Spain, 1782 (art. 5); Belgium, 1838 (art. 8); Portugal, 1843 (art. 8); U. S., 1830 (art. 4); Mexico, 1866 (arts. 10, 13).

Algiers: France, 1666 (art. 11); 1684 (art. 22); 1689 (art. 24); 1801 (art. 12); U. S., 1815 (art. 20); Portugal, 1813 (art. 10); Sicily, 1816 (art. 9).

Morocco: France, 1682 (art. 16); 1767 (art. 13); Great Britain, 1750 (art. 3); 1791 (art. 7); 1801 (art. 7); 1824 (art. 7). U. S., 1787 (art. 21); 1836 (art. 21); Denmark, 1767 (art. 14); Sardinia, 1825 (art. 22).

Tripoli: France, 1685 (arts. 20, 23): 1720 (arts. 18, 20); 1729 (arts. 25, 29); 1801 (arts. 19, 23); Spain, 1784 (arts. 31, 32); U. S., 1805 (art. 19).

Tunis: France, 1685 (arts. 21, 24); 1710 (arts. 16, 19); 1720 (art. 19);

tur forum rei was adhered to, and in a number of the treaties mentioned, it was laid down that in all mixed cases, civil or criminal, the plaintiff should be brought under the jurisdiction and laws of the defendant's courts, an officer of the plaintiff's nationality being deputed to attend the proceedings in the interests of justice.[1]

(3) Finally, mixed cases involving foreigners of different nationalities were left to be disposed of by their respective diplomatic or consular officers, all local interference being disallowed.[2]

1742 (arts. 16, 19); Great Britain, 1875 (arts. 25, 26); U. S., 1797 (arts. 21, 22).

Persia: France, 1708 (art. 18); 1855 (art. 5); Russia, 1828 (arts. 7, 8); Spain, 1842 (art. 5); U. S., 1856 (art. 5); Sardinia, 1857 (art. 5); Belgium, 1857 (art. 5); Greece, 1861 (art. 9); Italy, 1862 (art. 5); Germany, 1873 (art. 13); Switzerland, 1873 (art. 5).

Ethiopia: Italy, 1889 (art. 11).

Madagascar: France, 1862 (art. 9); 1868 (art. 6); Great Britain, 1865 (art. 11); U. S., 1867 (art. 5).

In many cases, it was specified that only the higher authorities of the native administration could have cognizance of mixed cases between foreigners and natives. See the following treaties:

Algiers: Great Britain, 1682 (arts. 15, 16); 1686 (art. 11); France, 1666 (art. 11); 1684 (art. 19); 1689 (arts. 21, 24); 1801 (art. 12); U. S., 1795 (arts. 15, 16).

Morocco: France, 1682 (art. 13); 1767 (art. 12); Great Britain, 1721 (art. 9); 1760 (art. 9); 1791 (art. 8); 1801 (art. 8); 1824 (art. 8).

Tripoli: Great Britain, 1675 (art. 14); 1716 (art. 11); 1751 (art. 11).

Tunis: France, 1665 (art. 22); 1672 (art. 22); 1685 (art. 21); 1710 (art. 16); 1720 (art. 16).

[1] Morocco: Great Britain, 1856 (art. 9); Spain, 1861 (art. 11).

Muscat: Great Britain, 1839 (art. 5); 1891 (art. 13); France, 1844 (art. 6).

Zanzibar: Hanseatic League, 1859 (art. 12); Portugal, 1879 (art. 12); Italy, 1885 (art. 5); Germany, 1885 (art. 16); Great Britain, 1886 (art. 16).

Madagascar: U. S., 1881 (art. 6, §§ 7-14).

[2] Turkey: France, 1740 (art. 52).

Algiers: U. S., 1815 (art. 19).

Morocco: Great Britain, 1856 (art. 14).

Tunis: France, 1665 (art. 23); 1672 (art. 23); Great Britain, 1875 (art. 24).

Persia: France, 1855 (art. 5); Sardinia, 1857 (art. 5); Austria, 1857 (art. 9). Prussia, 1857 (art. 5); Belgium, 1857 (art. 5); Italy, 1862 (art. 5); Germany, 1873 (art. 13); Switzerland, 1873 (art. 5).

Muscat: Great Britain, 1839 (art. 5); 1891 (art. 13); France, 1844 (art. 6).

Zanzibar: Hanseatic League, 1859 (art. 12); Portugal, 1879 (art. 12); Italy, 1885 (art. 5); Germany, 1885 (art. 16); Great Britain, 1886 (art. 16).

Ethiopia: Great Britain, 1849 (art. 17).

Madagascar: France, 1862 (art. 9); 1868 (art. 6); Great Britain, 1865 (art. 11); U. S., 1881 (art. 6, § 3).

CHAPTER IV

IN THE FAR EAST

I. ORIGIN OF EXTRATERRITORIALITY IN THE FAR EAST

IN Turkey and the Levant, as has been seen above, the concession of capitulatory rights to foreigners may be ascribed to various factors. The union of Mohammedan law and religion, the desire of Islam to invite foreign commerce, and, above all, the existence of long-established custom and usage have all contributed to perpetuate the system of consular jurisdiction in the Mohammedan world.

A different story, however, must be told of the establishment of extraterritoriality in the Far East. There, religious differences did not necessitate a special jurisdiction, the motive of foreign intercourse was by no means persistent, and the force of custom was distinctly averse to the assertion of judicial competence by foreign magistrates.

As is well known, Confucianism and Buddhism, the dominant systems of philosophy and religion in the Far East, make no discriminating distinctions between the native and the alien. They teach tolerance and indulgence to all alike. For this reason, the peculiar situation to which the Mohammedan religion gave rise in regard to the unbeliever did not exist in Eastern Asia.

In the matter of world intercourse, the Far East is noted for its excessive indifference. Vast empires lived in a state of splendid isolation for countless ages, and had it not been for the insistence of the foreign merchant—an insistence often amounting to open violence—it is difficult to speculate how soon the East would have waked up to the need of

76

contact with the Occident. Thus, it is not within the realm of possibility that the countries of the East could have been disposed to induce Western nations to trade with them by extending such special privileges as those of consular jurisdiction.

When we come to the consideration of custom as a motivating force in bringing about the establishment of extraterritoriality in the Far East, a preponderance of the evidence leads us to a conclusion different from that reached in connection with the Capitulations of the Ottoman Empire and the Levant. With the possible exception of Japan,[1] the assertion of territorial jurisdiction was quite general in the more important countries of Asia prior to the introduction of extraterritoriality in the nineteenth century. Let us examine the prevailing practice of the pre-conventional period in Siam and in China.

Siam had exercised complete jurisdiction over foreigners prior to the year 1664, when a treaty with the Dutch United East India Company, dated August 22, provided that cases of grave crime committed by Dutch merchants were to be disposed of by the Company's chief according to Dutch law.[2]

---

[1] "The Shogun's government, in the beginning of the seventeenth century, left the Portuguese, Spanish, English, and Dutch traders to their own law. This privilege, which was granted to them by letters-patent, was held at the pleasure of the Shogun, and was liable to be annulled. The Japanese, however, were more familiar with the idea of personal than of territorial law; and when, in a later age, they formed treaty relations with the West, they seem not to have insisted upon the principle of territoriality. Harris states that, when he proposed that Americans should be subject to the jurisdiction of their consuls, 'to my great and agreeable surprise this was agreed to without demur.'" Hishida, *The International Position of Japan as a Great Power* (New York, 1905), p. 133. The entry from Harris's diary is quoted from Griffis, *Townsend Harris* (Boston and New York, 1895), p. 124.

[2] *Records of the Relations between Siam and Foreign Countries in the 17th Century*, vol. ii, p. 66.

In 1685, M. de Chaumont, heading an embassy from France, negotiated two treaties with Siam, one on religious and the other on commercial matters. The first, dated December 10, granted the French request for a special "mandarin" empowered to hear and judge all cases involving Christian converts, with the proviso that the mandarin must refer such matters to one of the judges of the king of Siam before passing sentence.[1] The second treaty, dated December 11, 1685, is as yet unpublished, but is referred to by a writer on foreign jurisdiction in Siam, according to whom "the second treaty of M. de Chaumont provided for the adjudication by the captain of the *Compagnie des Indes Orientales* of cases between French alone and of cases of theft or any other offense committed by them, and for the joint competence of the captain and the Siamese judges in cases, civil or criminal, between the merchants and others not French."[2] Mr. James also mentions another treaty between France and Siam, dated December 11, 1687, which contained stipulations on extraterritorial jurisdiction. The principal officer of the company was to have complete civil and criminal jurisdiction over those in the employ of the company, regardless of their nationality. If one of the parties was not in the service of the company, the case was within the competence of the king of Siam, but the principal officer of the company was to sit in the court and to have a definite voice in the determination of the case, after taking an oath to judge according to right and justice.[3]

Later practice, however, was directly contrary to the spirit of these treaties. In the treaty of June 20, 1826, be-

[1] Art. 5, Dumont, *op. cit.,* vol. vii, pt. ii, p. 120.

[2] James, "Jurisdiction over Foreigners in Siam," *American Journal of International Law* (hereafter referred to as *A. J. I. L.*), vol. xvi, p. 588.

[3] Art. 5, *Journal of the Siam Society,* vol. xiv, pt. ii, p. 32.

tween England and Siam, it was expressly provided that
" Should a Siamese or English merchant have any complaint or suit, he must complain to the Officers and Governors, on either side; and they will examine and settle the
same according to the established Laws of the place or
Country, on either side." [1]   In the first American treaty
with Siam, dated March 20, 1833, it was likewise provided
that " Merchants of the United States trading in the Kingdom of Siam shall respect and follow the laws and customs
of the country in all respects." [2]

Prior to the definitive establishment of the extraterritorial system in Siam in the middle of the nineteenth century, therefore, the most recent practice was on the side of
subjecting the foreigner to the local laws and jurisdiction.
Thus, after a careful study of the early period, a competent
writer comes to this conclusion: " While the treaties of the
seventeenth century undoubtedly contained the germs of an
exterritorial system, they had long since become obsolete
and inoperative, and it is not, therefore, too much to say
that in 1855 exterritoriality was unknown in Siam." [3]

Before China entered into formal treaty relations with
the European nations, it had been customary for her to
assume over all foreigners resident within her territory a
measure of protection and control commensurate with her
own sovereignty and independence. The idea of personal
law was never conceded by the Chinese Government, until
it was forced upon it by treaty. " The Chinese notion of
territorial sovereignty and jurisdiction," observed Dr. Wellington Koo, " as entertained, though at times vaguely, by
the officials of the Empire in the early days, was not essentially different from that which is maintained by modern

[1] Art. 6, *State Papers,* vol. xxiii, p. 1156.
[2] Art. 9, Malloy, vol. ii, p. 1628
[3] James, *A. J. I. L., loc. cit.,* p. 589.

international jurists." [1] Up to the middle of the nineteenth century, this principle was tenaciously adhered to, so that even on the eve of the Opium War, when Captain Elliott, British Superintendent of Trade at Canton, questioned the subjection of opium smugglers to penalties laid down by Chinese law, Commissioner Lin asked him this pertinent question: " How can you bring the laws of your nation with you to the Celestial Empire? " [2]

To be sure, there were exceptions to the claim on China's part to territorial jurisdiction over the foreign residents. Mention has already been made of the grant of an exemption from the local laws to the Arabians at Canfu in the ninth century. [3] But from all later evidence, this tradition seems to have been forgotten and fallen into disuse long before the formal introduction of extraterritoriality into China. It could not have constituted an authoritative precedent, inasmuch as it was a mere unilateral grant, and could have been revoked at the pleasure of the grantor. As a matter of fact, no claim to special jurisdiction appears to have ever been entertained by any Power on the basis of this early grant.

Another important exception to the Chinese rule of territorial jurisdiction was the series of treaties entered into with Russia. Article 4 of the Treaty of Nipchu or Nerchinsk, 1689, provides: " If hereafter any of the subjects of either nation pass the frontier and commit crimes of violence against property or life, they are at once to be arrested and sent to the frontier of their country and handed over to the chief local authority for punishment." [4]

[1] The Status of Aliens in China (New York, 1912), p. 47.

[2] Sargent, Anglo-Chinese Commerce and Diplomacy (Oxford, 1907), pp. 75-76.

[3] Supra, p. 49.

[4] China. The Maritime Customs. Treaties, Conventions, etc., between China and Foreign States (hereafter referred to as China, Maritime Treaties) 2nd ed., Shanghai, 1917, vol. i, p. 6.

The " Treaty of the Frontier," signed at Kiakhta in 1727,[1] and the Supplementary Treaty of Kiakhta, signed in 1768,[2] contained similar provisions relative to the suppression of brigandage and other disturbances along the coterminous frontiers. These treaties are regarded by some writers as constituting a recognition of the principle of extraterritoriality in China.[3] As a matter of fact, however, nothing of the kind was intended. Being reciprocal in nature, the whole arrangement was merely a temporary expedient to facilitate the administration of the frontiers on the part of the two Governments, which, as Dr. Koo points out, " far from establishing the principle of extraterritoriality, seems to have involved nothing more than an application, in exceptional circumstances, of the principle of personal law, which is found in the criminal jurisprudence of substantially all civilized nations to a greater or less extent." [4]

Quite in keeping with her territorial sovereignty, China had always asserted a complete control over the foreign residents. This is illustrated unequivocally by the insistence on the exercise of criminal jurisdiction.[5] Section 34 of the Penal Code, in force before the introduction of extraterritoriality, provided: " In general, all foreigners who come to submit themselves to the government of the Empire, shall,

---

[1] Art. 10, *ibid.*, p. 36.

[2] Art. 10, *ibid.*, p. 62.

[3] See, e. g., Morse, *International Relations of the Chinese Empire* (London, New York, etc., 1910-18), vol. i, p. 60; *Trade and Administration of the Chinese Empire* (London, New York & Calcutta, 1908), p. 181. In the latter place, the author declares, " Here, then, for one to two centuries before the first of the treaties with any of the maritime powers, we have the principle of extraterritoriality accepted..."

[4] Koo, *op. cit.*, p. 53.

[5] In civil matters, the Chinese courts had little occasion to exercise jurisdiction over disputes between Chinese and foreigners, these being usually settled by direct negotiations between the parties concerned and by arbitration. *Cf.* Morse, *International Relations*, vol. i, p. 96.

when guilty of offences, be tried and sentenced according
to the established laws." [1] Instances abound in which the
rule was applied with an uncompromising uniformity and
strictness. Space does not allow a detailed examination of
them all, and for this the reader is referred to other
authoritative accounts.[2]

One interesting fact, however, must be pointed out at this
juncture. In the assertion of territorial jurisdiction, the
Chinese Government received the unconditional submission
of some Powers, such as the United States. When the well-
known case of Terranova was being tried in 1821, the
American merchants made this remark to the Chinese
authorities: " We are bound to submit to your laws while
we are in your waters, be they ever so unjust. We will not
resist them." [3]

In another instance, not only was open confession made
of the customary American obedience to Chinese law and
jurisdiction, but the responsibility was laid on the Chinese
Government for prosecuting violations of her territorial
sovereignty. During the first quarter of the nineteenth
century, British naval authorities were in the habit of
searching American vessels for deserters. After a fruitless
demand for the surrender of certain seamen taken on one
of these occasions, a meeting was held by the Americans in
1805, as a result of which a formal representation was
drawn up and signed by the consul and twenty-seven other
Americans and addressed to the governor of Canton. After
reciting the facts of the controversy, the letter continued:

The undersigned further respectfully represent to Your
Excellency that the citizens of the United States have for many

---

[1] Geo. Staunton, *Penal Code of China* (London, 1810), p. 36.

[2] Morse, *op. cit.*, vol. i, pp. 100-107; Koo, *op. cit.*, pp. 50-55.

[3] *North American Review*, vol. xl, p. 66.

years visited the city of Canton in the pursuit of honest commerce, that their conduct during the whole period of intercourse
has been regulated by a strict regard and respect for the laws
and usages of this Empire, as well as the general law of nations,
and that by their fidelity in trade, and their peaceable demeanor,
the most perfect harmony, confidence, and good understanding
has ever been maintained between the subjects of this country
and the citizens of the United States, from which has flowed a
very extensive and rapidly increasing commerce, mutually advantageous and honorable to both parties.

That by the ancient and well-established laws and usages of
all civilized nations, the persons and property of friendly foreigners within the territory and jurisdiction of a sovereign and
independent Empire, are under the special protection of the
Government thereof, and any violence or indignity offered to
such persons or to the flag of the nation to which they belong,
is justly considered as done to the government within whose
territory the outrage is committed.

That by the same law of nations, the civil and military agents
of the government are strictly prohibited from assuming any
authority whatever within the territory of the other, nor can
they seize the person of the highest state criminal, who may
have eluded the justice of their own.[1]

Nothing can be more explicit than these voluntary admis-
sions, and as one reads them to-day, one is struck by the
radical departure from them when, a generation later, far-
reaching limitations were imposed on the operation of territorial jurisdiction in China. The reason for the change will
be dealt with shortly; for the present, it is sufficient to note
that it is not to be sought in the force of custom. With
the exception of Japan, the Powers of Eastern Asia, prior
to the middle of the nineteenth century, assumed their territorial jurisdiction and were not in the habit of granting to
foreigners extraterritorial privileges.

[1] Dennett, *Americans in Eastern Asia* (New York, 1922), pp. 81-84.
Passage quoted is on p. 84.

Just as the above considerations cannot explain the rise of extraterritoriality in the Far East, so the differences of civilization between the Orient and the Occident give no clue to the explanation. It is recognized by all that the countries of the Far East had attained a high degree of civilization long before the system of extraterritoriality was established there. Claims to special treatment could hardly have been advanced by the Westerners on this ground, and they were not advanced. Even Caleb Cushing, who regarded the extension of extraterritoriality to non-Christian peoples as a rule of international law, refuted the argument of civilization. "Europeans and Americans," he said, "had a vague idea that they ought not to be subject to the local jurisdiction of barbarian Governments, and that the question of jurisdiction depended on the question, whether the country was a civilized one or not; and this erroneous idea confused all their reasonings in opposition to the claims of the Chinese; for it is impossible to deny to China a high degree of civilization, though the civilization is, in many respects, different from ours." [1]

Failing to find the original justification of the extraterritorial régime in the Far East in any of the circumstances enumerated above, we have but one alternative left, i. e., to seek an explanation in the alleged deficiency of the Oriental legal systems. Rightly or wrongly, there lurked in the hidden nooks of every Western mind a vague notion that Oriental jurisprudence could not possibly be in keeping with Western ideas of justice, and that an Occidental would certainly do violence to his dignity and pride by rendering obeisance to a deficient judicial régime. That this was the dominant state of mind, of which the Europeans in the Far East were possessed, is evidenced by a number of facts.

[1] Mr. Cushing to Mr. Calhoun, Sep. 29, 1844, U. S. *Sen. Doc. no. 58, 28th Cong., 2d Sess.*

In spite of the vigorous attempts made by the Chinese Government to assert its territorial sovereignty, there was an equally strong tendency on the part of the nationals of some foreign Powers, especially of Great Britain, to set Chinese law and jurisdiction at defiance.[1] The reasons given for their resistance center around the imperfections of the Chinese legal system.[2] The justice or injustice of these contentions is of no concern to our present study;[3] what we aim to ascertain is whether the foreign governments were conscious of the same reluctance to enjoin compliance with the laws of China.

Writing in 1836, Sir George Staunton, although he deprecated the proposals then made for aggressive hostilities with China in order to force on her certain concessions,[4] and although he advocated the treatment of China on a footing of equality with the other Powers,[5] admitting the defectiveness of her judicial system. "The Chinese laws," he declared, "as specially applied, and endeavored to be enforced, in cases of homicide, committed by foreigners, are not only *unjust*, but absolutely *intolerable*. The demand of blood for blood, in all cases, without reference to circumstances, whether palliative or even justifying, is undoubtedly an intolerable grievance."[6]

The remarks of Sir George are of greater interest and importance when we recall that it was he who was instrumental in framing and introducing to the House of Com-

---

[1] For specific cases see Koo, *op. cit.*, pp. 68-79.

[2] *Ibid.*, pp. 79-95; Morse, *op. cit.*, vol. i, pp. 109 *et seq.*

[3] Dr. Koo gives an excellent critical account of these reasons in the section of his work just referred to.

[4] *Remarks on the British Relations with China and the Proposed Plans for Improving Them* (2nd ed., London, 1836).

[5] *Ibid.*, p. 20.

[6] *Ibid.*, p. 18. It must be pointed out that the last assertion is grossly inaccurate. See Koo, *op. cit.*, pp. 80-84.

mons, in 1833, a set of resolutions, looking, *inter alia,* to the glaringly illegal measure of establishing a British court of justice on Chinese soil without the consent of the territorial sovereign. In the body of the resolutions, complaint was again made against the unsatisfactory state of Chinese laws. The pertinent section reads:

That, lastly, the state of the trade under the operation of the Chinese laws in respect to homicides committed by foreigners in that country, calls for the early interposition of the Legislature, those laws being practically so unjust and intolerable that they have in no instance for the last forty-nine years been submitted to by British subjects; great loss and injury to their commercial interests accruing from the suspension of trade in consequence of such resistance, and the guilty as well as the innocent escape with impunity; and that, it is, therefore, expedient to put an end to this anomalous state of law by the creation of a British naval tribunal upon the spot, with competent authority for the trial and punishment of such offences.[1]

The resolutions failed of adoption, but in their stead a bill was introduced on July 1, 1833, under the title of "an act to regulate the trade to China and India," which was adopted by both Houses and became an act of Parliament on August 28, 1833. Article 6 authorized the creation of a British court of justice with criminal and admiralty jurisdiction for the trial of offenses committed by British subjects in China.[2] In pursuance of this act, a number of Orders in Council were issued on December 9, 1833, bringing the legislation into effect.[3] But although the machinery was thus set up for the administration of justice by Great

[1] Hansard, *Parliamentary Debates,* 3rd ser., vol. xviii, p. 700.

[2] 3 & 4 Will. IV, c. 93. The act does not state where the court was to sit, but from the context the general intention was to set it up on Chinese soil.

[3] *State Papers,* vol. xx, pp. 260, 262.

Britain in China—a machinery that had no legal sanction at all, inasmuch as it was not consented to by China—yet as a matter of fact, the powers assumed were never actually exercised, due partly to the vigorous resistance of the Chinese and partly to the hesitancy on the part of the British authorities themselves.[1]

In 1838, a new bill was introduced by Lord Palmerston, suggesting the establishment of a court in China, with even larger powers than those authorized by the act of 1833, for the new bill contemplated a court with civil as well as criminal and admiralty jurisdiction.[2] On this bill a long debate ensued in the House of Commons, with Lord Palmerston defending it and Sir James Graham taking the opposite side. The arguments advanced by the former were again in accord with the indictments made by the British merchants against the legal system of China.[3] Due to the lack of support and the general opposition to the bill, Lord Palmerston stated that he had " no objection to postponing it until the next session," whereupon the bill was withdrawn.[4]

The record of the British attempts to introduce extraterritorial jurisdiction into China by means of legislative enactment prior to the Opium War was, therefore, one of failure and disappointment to their sponsors. In the midst of an obstinate resistance to the assertion and exercise, on China's part, of her rightful territorial sovereignty, there was not lacking an enlightened public opinion, which, while crying against certain imperfections in the operation of Chinese laws, insisted upon a strict regard for the rules of international law.[5] It was only after the termination of the

---

[1] See Koo, *op. cit.,* p. 109.

[2] *Journal of the House of Commons,* vol. xciii, p. 476.

[3] Dr. Koo gives a critical review of the arguments on both sides, *op. cit.,* pp. 114-30.

[4] Hansard, *op. cit.,* 3rd ser., vol. xliv, p. 751.

[5] In the debate of the House of Commons on July 28, 1838, on the

Opium War in 1842 that extraterritoriality was formally introduced into China by a treaty premised upon her independence and sovereignty. For this treaty the bitter controversy of the previous decade between the Chinese and British authorities on the question of jurisdiction undoubtedly prepared the ground, and it is only in this light that we have dealt briefly with the events of this period. No matter what is to be said of the accusations of the foreign merchants and governments against Chinese jurisprudence, the important fact for us to note in this connection is that such accusations were made and were influential in contributing to the establishment of extraterritoriality in China.[1]

Later developments in the history of extraterritoriality in China throw still more light on the relation between a defective judicial system and the establishment of foreign jurisdiction in the Orient. Ever since the opening of the present century, treaties have been concluded by China with

---

bill looking toward the establishment of a British court in China, Mr. Hawes said that "he had carefully looked over the papers, the noble Lord [Palmerston] had laid before the House, and he could not discover in them the smallest trace of the smallest consent on the part of the authorities of China to the jurisdiction proposed to be given by the noble Lord. He wished to ask the noble Lord, whether the authorities of China recognized this interference with their laws?" *Ibid.*, p. 744. Another speaker, Sir James Graham, while approving a part of the bill felt that consistently with the whole course of British policy, with international law and past experience, it would be unadvisable to pass the remainder of the bill, including the part on the creation of a British court in China. *Ibid.*, p. 751. When the House went into committee on the bill, Mr. Hawes again rose to move its omission, saying that there could be no objection to the establishment of a court for the trial of offenses committed by British subjects, but protesting against the court's interfering with an independent power like China. *Ibid.*, p. 752. On account of this opposition, the bill was withdrawn on Lord Palmerston's own motion. *Cf. supra*, p. 87.

[1] It is to be admitted that there were some irregularities in the administration of justice in China at the time; but, to say the least, they were unduly exaggerated. *Cf.* Koo, *op. cit.*, pp. 79-95.

foreign Powers, which, while granting them extraterritorial rights, embody at the same time promises for their abandonment on condition that certain reforms were carried out.[1] From these stipulations one can hardly resist the logical inference that judicial deficiency has been at the very foundation of the installation of the extraterritorial system in the Far East.

In Siam, as in China, the principal ground on which the European claim to extraterritorial jurisdiction was originally based seems to have been the discrepancy between European and Siamese laws. This statement finds its corroboration in official pronouncements as well as in treaty provisions. In the Memorandum prepared by the British Minister in Siam, in 1909, explanatory of the origin and modification of British jurisdiction in Siam, it is said:

By the Anglo-Siamese Treaty of 1855 full extra-territorial privileges were guaranteed to British subjects in Siam. Comparatively little being then known concerning Siamese laws and customs, it was considered necessary by the British negotiators that British subjects for their security should be placed under the sole jurisdiction and control of their consular authorities.[2]

Again, when Japan first obtained her extraterritorial rights in Siam, by virtue of the treaty of February 25, 1898, the protocol granting the said rights provides:

1. The Siamese Government consent that Japanese officers shall exercise jurisdiction over Japanese subjects in Siam, until the judicial reforms of Siam shall have been completed, that is, until a Criminal Code, a Code of Criminal Procedure, a Civil

---

[1] Treaty with Sweden, July 2, 1908, art. 10, MacMurray, *Treaties and Agreements with and concerning China, 1894-1919* (New York, 1921), vol. i, 1908/11, p. 745; treaty with Switzerland, July 13, 1918, Declaration, *ibid.*, vol. ii, 1918/8, p. 1430.

[2] *Parliamentary Papers,* 1909 [cd. 4646], Siam, no. 1 (1909), p. 7.

Code, . . . a Code of Civil Procedure, and a Law of Constitution of the Courts of Justice will come into force.[1]

The necessary implication of this provision is, of course, that at the time of the conclusion of the treaty, Siamese laws were imperfect, because of which extraterritorial jurisdiction was conferred on Japan over her own nationals.

The treaties which Corea[2] had with the Western Powers granting extraterritoriality to them all embodied provisions for its abandonment upon the completion of Corea's legal reform. A representative provision to this effect is that contained in the protocol attached to the British treaty of November 26, 1883:

1. With reference to Article III of this Treaty, it is hereby declared that the right of extraterritorial jurisdiction over British subjects in Corea granted by this Treaty shall be relinquished when, in the judgment of the British Government, the laws and legal procedure of Corea shall have been so far modified and reformed as to remove the objections which exist to British subjects being placed under Corean jurisdiction, and Corean Judges shall have attained similar legal qualifications and a similar independent position to those of British Judges.[3]

[1] *State Papers,* vol. xc, p. 70.

[2] Although Corea was at first a vassal state to China, she was fully independent in her relations with the foreign Powers, and the latter were regulated by Corea's own treaties. In 1870, the American Minister at Peking wrote to his government: "Corea is substantially an independent nation. To be sure, it sends tribute to China annually, but from the information I am able to obtain, the tribute is sent rather as a *quid pro quo* for the privilege of trading with the Chinese than as a governmental tribute." Mr. F. F. Low to Mr. Fish, July 16, 1870, U. S. *For. Rel.,* 1870, p. 362. This opinion was later confirmed by a statement of the Chinese Foreign Office, dated March 28, 1871, to the effect "that although Corea is regarded as a country subordinate to China, yet she is wholly independent in everything that relates to her government, her religion, her prohibitions, and her laws; in none of these things has China hitherto interfered." *Ibid.,* 1871, p. 112.

[3] *State Papers,* vol. lxxiv, p. 105. *Cf.* U. S., May 22, 1882, art. 4.

II. Rights of Extraterritoriality Conferred by the Treaties with the Far Eastern Countries

In the Far East, extraterritorial rights have been enjoyed by foreign Powers in China, Japan, Corea, Siam, Borneo, Tonga and Samoa. The earliest grant of such rights made by China to Great Britain was contained in the supplemental treaty of July, 1843.[1] The first treaty entered into by Japan

Malloy, vol. i, p. 336; Germany, Nov. 22, 1883, Protocol, *State Papers,* vol. lxxiv, p. 649; Russia, June 25/July 5, 1884, Protocol, *ibid.,* vol. lxxv, p. 527; China, Sep. 11, 1899, art. 5, *ibid.,* vol. xcii, p. 1049; Belgium, March 23, 1901, art. 3, § 11, *ibid.,* voi. xciv, p. 541; and Denmark, July 15, 1902, art. 3, § 11, *ibid.,* vol. xcv, p. 172.

[1] Art. 13 of General Regulations, China, *Maritime Treaties,* vol. i, p. 388. Other Powers which had extraterritorial treaties with China are the United States (July 3, 1844, arts. 21, 25, Malloy, vol. i, pp. 202, 203; June 8, 1858, arts. 11, 27, *ibid.,* pp. 215, 220; Nov. 17, 1880, art. 4, *ibid.,* p. 240), France (Oct. 24, 1844, arts. 25, 27, 28, China, *Maritime Treaties,* vol. i, pp. 785, 786; June 28, 1858, arts. 35, 38, 39, *ibid.,* pp. 831, 833), Norway and Sweden (March 20, 1847, arts. 21, 25, *ibid.* pp. 56, 58), Russia (June 1/13, 1858, art. 7, *ibid.,* p. 88), Germany (Sep. 2, 1861, arts. 35, 38, 39, *ibid.,* vol. ii, pp. 132, 133, 134), Denmark (July 13, 1863, arts. 15, 16, 17, *ibid.,* pp. 318-319), the Netherlands (Oct. 6, 1863, art. 6, *ibid.,* p. 343), Spain (Oct. 10, 1864, arts. 12-13, *ibid.,* p. 364), Belgium (Nov. 2, 1865, arts. 16, 19, *ibid.,* pp. 11, 12), Italy (Oct. 26, 1866, arts. 15-17, *ibid.,* pp. 408-9), Austria-Hungary (Sep. 2, 1869, arts. 38-40, *ibid.,* p. 473), Peru (June 26, 1874, arts. 12-14, *ibid.,* 804-5), Brazil (Oct. 3, 1881, arts. 9-11, *ibid.,* pp. 818-9), Portugal (Dec. 1, 1887, arts. 47, 48, 51, *ibid.,* pp. 291, 292), Japan (July 21, 1896, arts. 20-22, *ibid.,* pp. 611-2), Mexico (Dec. 14, 1899, arts. 13-15, *ibid.,* pp. 840-1), Sweden (May 24, 1908, art. 10, MacMurray, *Treaties,* vol. i, 1908/11, p. 744), and Switzerland (July 13, 1918, Declaration annexed, *ibid.,* vol. ii, 1918/8, p. 1430). The provisions of these treaties will be summarized presently. The German treaty was abolished by a Presidential Proclamation of Aug. 14, 1917, making a declaration of war against Germany and Austria-Hungary, *ibid.,* 1917/7, p. 1363, and by the treaty of May 20, 1921, art. 3, *China Year Book,* 1921-22, p. 739. The same Presidential Proclamation also abrogated China's treaty with Austria-Hungary. The Treaty of St. Germain, Sep. 10, 1919, which concluded peace between China and Austria, does not mention extraterritorial rights. The Mexican treaty was denounced by the Mexican Government on Nov. 11, 1920, *State Papers,* vol. cxiv, p. 878.

In this connection, the doubtful case of Chile may be mentioned.

was that of March 31, 1854, with the United States,[1] but
it included no provision regarding extraterritorial jurisdiction. Of all the European treaties the Russian, dated Jan-

According to article 2 of the treaty of Feb. 18, 1915, the Diplomatic
and Consular Agents of Chile and China "shall enjoy the same rights,
privileges, favors, immunities, and exemptions as are or may be conceded to the Diplomatic and Consular Agents of the most favored
Powers." MacMurray, *op. cit.*, vol. ii, p. 1190. No specific mention is
made of the grant of extraterritorial rights. Whether this is implied
in article 2 or not is not certain. But inasmuch as the same article appears in the British treaty of 1858 (art. 7), which makes express provision for extraterritorial jurisdiction in other parts of the same agreement, it is reasonable to infer that the article comprehends only the
ordinary privileges and immunities of diplomatic and consular agents
which are sanctioned by international law, and does not *ipso facto*
carry with it an exceptional right such as that of extraterritoriality. In
order to lay claim to the latter in China, it is, in the author's opinion,
essential that the claimant should be able to invoke an express treaty
provision to that effect, the omission of which in the agreement of
1915 would seem to imply the denial of the right to Chile. "Even if
there were commercial treaties with other countries," says Hinckley,
"containing most-favored-nation clauses, such clauses would probably
not extend the extraterritorial exemption... The substantial fact is that
China has continuously maintained her jurisdiction sovereignty, excepting as specifically abrogated by treaty." Hinckley, "Extraterritoriality in China," *American Academy of Political and Social Science,
Annals*, vol. xxxix, p. 97. Recently, an attempt was made by the
Chilean consul at Shanghai to exercise jurisdiction over a Chinese
claiming Chilean nationality. The claim was made on the basis of the
most-favored-nation clause referred to. The Chinese Government having refused to entertain the Chilean point of view, the Chilean consul
appealed to the Diplomatic Corps at Peking, which seems to have
espoused the cause of Chile. The Chinese Government, however, still
regards it as an open question. The diplomatic correspondence on this
subject has not yet been made available, but whatever may have been
the facts involved, the assertion by Chile of extraterritoriality in China
on the basis of a most-favored-nation clause would be contrary to
established usage in that country. That this is so is further shown by
the notes exchanged between China and Bolivia, also a South American
Republic, in 1919, to the effect that the most-favored-nation clause
embodied in the new treaty between the two countries should not affect
the question of extraterritoriality. *Cf. infra*, p. 221.

[1] Malloy, vol. i, p. 996.

uary 26/February 7, 1855, appears to have contained the earliest germs of extraterritorial jurisdiction in Japan.[1] In Corea, Japan was the first foreign Power to secure extraterritorial rights.[2] The formal establishment of extraterritoriality in Siam dates from the treaty of April 18, 1855, with Great Britain.[3] The United States and Great Britain

[1] Art. 8 of this treaty provides that criminals should be judged according to the laws of their own country. *State Papers*, vol. lvii, p. 1055. Other Powers which had extraterritoriality treaties with Japan were the United States (June 17, 1857, art. 4, Malloy, vol. i, p. 999; July 29, 1858, art. 6, *ibid.*, p. 1033), Great Britain (Aug. 26, 1858, arts. 4-6, *State Papers*, vol. xlviii, p. 30), France (Oct. 9, 1858, arts. 5-7, *ibid.*, vol. l, p. 402), Portugal (Aug. 3, 1860, arts. 4-6, *ibid.*, vol. lix, p. 510), Prussia (Jan. 24, 1861, arts. 5-6, *ibid.*, pp. 520-1), the Netherlands (Nov. 9, 1855, arts. 2-3, *ibid.*, vol. xlvii, p. 1087), Switzerland (Feb. 6, 1864, arts. 5-6, *ibid.*, vol. liv, pp. 513-4), Belgium (Aug. 1, 1866, arts. 5-6, *ibid.*, vol. lix, p. 557), Italy (Aug. 25, 1866, arts. 5-6, *ibid.*, p. 866), Denmark (Jan. 12, 1867, arts. 5-6, *ibid.*, vol. lxii, p. 292), Sweden and Norway (Nov. 11, 1868, arts. 5-6, *ibid.*, vol. lxi, p. 561), Spain (Nov. 12, 1868, arts. 5-7, *ibid.*, vol. lviii, p. 197), Austria-Hungary (Oct. 18, 1869, arts. 5-6, *ibid.*, vol. lix, p. 531), Hawaii (Aug. 19, 1871, art. 4, *ibid.*, vol. lxii, p. 1013), China (Sep. 13, 1871, arts. 8-9, China, *Maritime Treaties*, vol. ii, p. 510), and Peru (Aug. 21, 1873, art. 6, *State Papers*, vol. lxiii, p. 54). These treaties were superseded by the treaties concluded by Japan with the various Powers between 1894 and 1899. *Cf. infra*, pp. 208 *et seq.*

[2] Treaty of Feb. 26, 1876, art. 10, *State Papers*, vol. lxvii, p. 533. Other Powers which enjoyed extraterritorial rights in Corea prior to 1910 were China (Sep. 11, 1899, art. 5, China, *Maritime Treaties*, vol. ii, p. 867), the United States (May 22, 1882, art. 4, Malloy, vol. i, p. 336), Great Britain (Nov. 26, 1883, art. 3, *State Papers*, vol. lxxiv, p. 87), Germany (Nov. 26, 1886, art. 3, *ibid.*, p. 634), Russia (June 25/July 7, 1884, art. 3, *ibid.*, vol. lxxv, p. 511), Italy (June 26, 1884, art. 3, *ibid.*, p. 310), Austria-Hungary (June 23, 1892, art. 3, *ibid.*, vol. lxxxiv, p. 121), Belgium (March 23, 1901, art. 3, *ibid.*, vol. xciv, p. 540), and Denmark (July 15, 1902, art. 3, *ibid.*, vol. xcv, p. 171). These treaties came to an end when Corea was annexed by Japan in 1910. *Cf. infra*, pp. 112-113.

[3] Art. 2, *State Papers*, vol. xlvi, p. 139. Other Powers which had similar treaties with Siam were the United States (May 29, 1856, art. 2, Malloy, vol. ii, p. 1630), France (Aug. 15, 1856, arts. 8-9, *State Papers*, vol. xlvii, p. 997), Denmark (May 21, 1858, arts. 9-10, *ibid.*,

have enjoyed extraterritorial rights in Borneo since the middle of the last century.[1] Before the Tongo Islands fell under the protection of Great Britain, various Powers obtained title to rights of jurisdiction in that country. The first treaty containing a specific grant of this nature was that with Great Britain, dated November 29, 1879.[2] Finally, in Samoa, the United States, Germany and Great Britain enjoyed extraterritorial rights [3] before the islands were divided up between Germany and the United States in 1899.[4]

The provisions of the above-mentioned treaties respecting extraterritorial jurisdiction may be divided into four categories: (1) jurisdiction in cases between natives exclusively; (2) jurisdiction in cases between foreigners of the same

vol. i, p. 1077), Portugal (Feb. 10, 1859, art. 6, *ibid.* vol. lxxii, p. 111), the Netherlands (Dec. 17, 1860, art. 9, *ibid.,* vol. lviii, p. 266), Prussia, etc. (Feb. 7, 1862, arts. 9-10, *ibid.,* vol liii, p. 745), Sweden and Norway (May 18, 1868, arts. 9-10, *ibid.,* vol. lxix, p. 1139), Belgium (Aug. 29, 1868, arts. 9-10, *ibid.,* vol. lix, p. 409), Italy (Oct. 3, 1868, art. 9, *ibid.,* vol. lx, p. 775), Austria-Hungary (May 17, 1869, arts 9-10, *ibid.,* vol. lxi, p. 1312), Spain (Feb. 23, 1870, arts. 6-7, *ibid.,* p. 484), and Japan (Feb. 25, 1898, Protocol, art. 1, *ibid.,* vol. xc, p. 70). The United States abolished her extraterritoriality in Siam conditionally by the treaty of Dec. 16, 1920, while Great Britain, France, and Denmark subsequently agreed to a substantial curtailment of their judicial rights in Siam. *Cf. infra,* pp. 213 *et seq.*

[1] U. S., June 23, 1850, art. 9, Malloy, vol. i, p. 132; Great Britain, Nov. 26, 1856, *State Papers,* vol. lxv, p. 1170.

[2] Art. 3, *ibid.,* vol. lxx, p. 10. Other Powers which enjoyed extraterritorial rights in Tonga were the United States (Oct. 2, 1886, art. 12, Malloy, vol. ii, p. 1784) and Germany (Nov. 1, 1876, art. 9, *Reichsgesetzblatt,* 1877, p. 521). After Tonga became a protectorate of Great Britain, the German and American Governments were deprived of their extraterritorial privileges there. *Cf. infra,* p. 142.

[3] U. S., Jan. 17, 1878, art. 4, Malloy, vol. ii, p. 1575; Germany, Jan. 24, 1879, art. 7, *State Papers,* vol. lxx, p. 244; Great Britain, Aug. 28, 1879, arts. 4, 5, *ibid.,* p. 134.

[4] *Infra,* p. 111.

nationality; (3) jurisdiction in cases between natives and foreigners; and (4) jurisdiction in cases between foreigners of different nationalities.

(1) In civil and criminal cases between natives exclusively, it is generally implied and, in some instances expressly provided, that the native authorities should administer justice according to their own laws and usages without interference on the part of the foreign representatives.[1]

(2) Cases, civil or criminal, between foreigners of the same nationality were placed under the exclusive jurisdiction of their own officials, to be decided according to their laws and usages, without interference on the part of the native authorities.[2]   In Borneo, the procedure laid down by the British treaty of November 26, 1856, differs somewhat from the general practice observed in the countries of the Far East.   According to this treaty, crimes committed by

[1] Siam: Great Britain, 1855, art. 2; U. S., 1856, art. 2; France, 1856, art. 8; Portugal, 1859, art, 6; the Netherlands, 1860, art. 9; Italy, 1868, art. 9.

[2] China: U. S., 1844, art. 25; 1858, art. 27; Great Britain, 1858, art. 15; France, 1844, art. 27; 1858, art. 39; Sweden and Norway, 1847, art. 25; Germany, 1861, art. 39; Denmark, 1863, art. 15; the Netherlands, 1863, art. 6; Spain, 1864, art. 12; Italy, 1866, art. 15; Austria-Hungary, 1869, art. 40; Peru, 1874, art. 14; Brazil, 1881, art. 11; Portugal, 1887, art. 47; Japan, 1896, art. 20; Mexico, 1899, art. 15; Sweden, 1908, art. 10.

Japan: Great Britain, 1858, art. 4; France, 1858, art. 5; Portugal, 1860, art. 4; Prussia, 1861, art. 5; Switzerland, 1864, art. 5; Belgium, 1866, art. 5; Italy, 1866, art. 5; Denmark, 1867, art. 5; Spain, 1868, art. 5; Germany, 1869, art. 5; Austria-Hungary, 1869, art. 5; China, 1871, art. 8.

Corea: Great Britain, 1883, art. 3; Germany, 1883, art. 3; Russia, 1884, art. 3; Italy, 1884, art. 3; Austria-Hungary, 1892, art. 3; Belgium, 1901, art. 3; Denmark, 1902, art. 3.

Siam: Great Britain, 1855, art. 2; U. S., 1856, art. 2; France, 1856, art. 8; Portugal, 1859, art. 6; the Netherlands, 1860, art. 9; Italy, 1868, art. 9.

Borneo: U. S., 1850, art. 9.

Tonga: U. S., 1886, art. 17.

Samoa: U. S., 1878, art. 4; Great Britain, 1879, art. 4.

British subjects—the treaty does not specify the nationality
of the victims, nor does it state whether this makes any
difference—should be tried and adjudicated jointly by the
British consular representative and " an officer chosen by
His Highness." In civil disputes between British subjects,
the same authorities should have jurisdiction, but " according to the customs of Borneo." [1]

(3) In mixed cases, the principle *actor sequitur forum rei*
was generally adopted,[2] that is to say, that the plaintiff
should follow the defendant into his court. Crimes committed by the natives against the nationals of a Treaty
Power should be tried and punished by the native authorities
according to their own laws, and crimes committed by the
nationals of a Treaty Power against the natives, by the
consular representatives of the defendant's nationality according to the latter's laws and customs.[3] In civil matters

[1] *State Papers,* vol. lxv, p. 1170.

[2] See, e. g., China-Mexico, 1899, art. 14, which provides: "As a general
rule, every civil or criminal suit instituted in China between the subjects or citizens of the two Contracting Parties shall be tried according
to the laws and by the authorities of the country to which the defendant or accused belongs."

[3] China: Great Britain, 1843, Gen. Reg., art. 13; 1858, art. 16; U. S.,
1844, art. 21; 1858, art. 11; France, 1844, art. 27; 1858; art. 38; Sweden
and Norway, 1847, art. 21; Germany, 1861, art. 38; Denmark, 1863,
art. 16; the Netherlands, 1863, art. 6; Spain, 1864, art. 13; Belgium,
1865, art. 19; Italy, 1866, art. 16; Austria-Hungary, 1869, art. 39; Peru,
1874, art. 13; Brazil, 1881, art. 10; Portugal, 1887, art. 48; Japan, 1896,
art. 22; Mexico, 1899, art. 14; Sweden, 1908, art. 10.

Japan: the Netherlands, 1858, art. 5; U. S., 1857, art. 4; 1858, art.
6; Russia, 1858, art. 14; Great Britain, 1858, art. 5; France, 1858, art.
6; Portugal, 1860, art. 6; Prussia, 1861, art. 6; Switzerland, 1864, art.
6; Belgium, 1866, art. 6; Italy, 1866, art. 6; Denmark, 1867, art. 6;
Sweden and Norway, 1868, art. 6; Spain, 1868, art. 7; Germany, 1869,
art. 6; Austria-Hungary, 1869, art. 6.

Corea: U. S., 1882, art. 4; Germany, 1883, art. 3; Russia, 1884, art.
3; Italy, 1884, art. 3; Austria-Hungary, 1892, art. 3; Belgium, 1901,
art. 3; Denmark, 1902, art. 3.

Siam: Great Britain, 1855, art. 2; U. S., 1856, art. 2; France, 1856.

of this nature, the self-same rule was applied.[1] The procedure laid down by the treaties was briefly as follows: In
all civil cases between natives and foreigners, the consul was
charged with the duty of hearing the complaint on either
side and of settling it amicably without causing litigation.
In case of failure to placate the parties, the consul should
have recourse to the assistance of the local authorities, that
they might together examine into the merits of the case and
decide it equitably.[2]   Subsequently, the joint competence of

art. 9; Denmark, 1858, art. 10; Portugal, 1859, art. 6; the Netherlands,
1860, art. 9; Prussia, 1862, art. 10; Sweden and Norway, 1868, art. 10;
Belgium, 1868, art. 6; Italy, 1868, art. 9; Austria-Hungary, 1869, art.
10; Spain, 1870, art. 7.

  Borneo: Great Britain, 1856.

  Tonga: Great Britain, 1879, art. 3; U. S., 1866, art. 12.

  Samoa: U. S., 1878, art. 4; Great Britain, 1879, art. 4. In Samoa,
the Germans had a special system, whereby the German authorities in
Samoa and the Samoan judges exercised a joint jurisdiction over penal
matters. See the German treaty, 1884, art. 4, *State Papers*, vol. lxxv,
p. 508.

  [1] China: Japan, 1896, art. 21; Sweden, 1908, art. 10.

  Japan: Austria-Hungary, 1869, art. 5.

  Corea: All the treaties referred to in the preceding note.

  Siam: Portugal, 1859, art. 6; the Netherlands, 1860, art. 9.

  Borneo: U. S., 1850, art. 9.

  Tonga: Great Britain, 1879, art. 3 (d); U. S., 1886, art. 12.

  Samoa: Great Britain, 1879, art. 5.

  [2] China: Great Britain, 1843, Gen. Reg., art. 13; 1858, art. 17;
France, 1844, art. 25; 1858, art. 35; Russia, 1858, art. 7; Germany, 1861,
art. 35; Denmark, 1863, art. 17; Spain, 1864, art. 14; Belgium, 1865,
art. 16; Italy, 1866, art. 17; Austria-Hungary, 1869, art. 38; Peru, 1874,
art. 12; Brazil, 1881, art. 9; Portugal, 1887, art. 51; Mexico, 1899,
art. 13.

  Japan: Great Britain, 1858, art. 6; France, 1858, art. 7; Portugal,
1860, art. 5; Belgium, 1866, art. 5; Italy, 1866, art. 5; Denmark, 1867,
art. 5; Sweden and Norway, 1868, art. 5.

  Siam: Great Britain, 1855, art. 2; U. S., 1856, art. 2; France, 1856,
art. 8; Denmark, 1858, art. 9; Prussia, 1862, art. 9; Sweden and Norway,
1868, art. 9; Belgium, 1868, art. 9; Italy, 1868, art. 9; Austria-Hungary,
1869, art. 9; Spain, 1870, art. 6.

the consul and the local authorities was brought into accord with the rule embodied in the principle *actor sequitur forum rei* by an interpretative provision to the effect that " the case is tried by the official of the defendant's nationality, the official of the plaintiff's nationality merely attending to watch the proceedings in the interest of justice," and that " the law administered will be the law of the nationality of the officer trying the case." ¹   The privileges of the " assessor ", i. e., the officer of the plaintiff's nationality watching the proceedings of a mixed civil case, were described in the Sino-American treaty of November 17, 1880, as follows:

The properly authorized official of the plaintiff's nationality shall be freely permitted to attend the trial, and shall be treated with the courtesy due to his position.   He shall be granted all proper facilities for watching the proceedings in the interests of justice.   If he so desires, he shall have the right to present, to examine, and to cross-examine witnesses.   If he is dissatisfied with the proceedings, he shall be permitted to protest against them in detail.²

It is a lamentable fact that in the case of some countries, as in that of China, the foreign assessor, instead of stopping with the treaty right of attending to watch the proceedings

Samoa: U. S., 1878, art. 4.

Art. 8 of the Sino-Japanese treaty, Sep. 13, 1871, provided that in questions where subjects of both parties were concerned, the complainant should address a petition to the consul of the accused, who should acquaint the local authorities, the latter being charged with the duty of investigating the case, arresting offenders, and recovering debts. *State Papers,* vol. lxii, p. 322.

¹ China: Great Britain, 1876, sec. ii (3).

Corea: U. S., 1882, art. 4; Great Britain, 1883, art. 3; Germany, 1883, art. 3; Russia, 1884, art. 3; Italy, 1884, art. 3; Austria-Hungary, 1892, art. 3; Belgium, 1901, art. 3; Denmark, 1902, art. 3.

Siam: Portugal, 1859, art. 6.

² Art. 4, Malloy, vol. i, p. 240. *Cf.* China-Britain, 1876, sec. ii (3) and all the Corean treaties referred to in the preceding note.

in the interests of justice, has gradually arrogated to himself
the rôle of the principal magistrate.[1] What is equally an
unjustifiable violation of treaty is the usurpation by the
foreign Powers in 1911 of the Shanghai International
Mixed Court, which will be treated of later.[2]

(4) In civil and criminal cases between foreigners of
different nationalities, the jurisdiction is said to be regulated by the treaties between the foreign Powers concerned,
and no interference on the part of the territorial sovereign
is allowed.[3] In actual practice, no such treaties have ever
been entered into, but the settled rule is again that embodied
in the principle *actor sequitur forum rei.*

[1] Hinckley, "Extraterritoriality in China," *Am. Acad. of Poli. and Soc. Science, Annals,* vol. xxxix, p. 97.

[2] *Infra,* pp. 225 *et seq.*

[3] China: U. S., 1844, art. 25; 1858, art. 27; France, 1844, art. 28; 1858, art. 39; Sweden and Norway, 1847, art. 25; Germany, 1861, art. 39; Denmark, 1863, art. 15; Spain, 1864, art. 12; Italy, 1866, art. 15; Austria-Hungary, 1869, art. 40; Peru, 1874, art. 14; Brazil, 1881, art. 11; Japan, 1896, art. 20; Mexico, 1899, art. 15; Sweden, 1908, art. 10.

PART II
THE DECLINE OF EXTRATERRITORIALITY

CHAPTER V

ANNEXATION

WITH the growth of the territorial theory of law, States fettered with the anomaly of extraterritoriality have labored again and again to throw it off. Little by little, the statesmen of these countries have awakened to the fact that what had once been a normal practice had become a distinct limitation and derogation of their sovereignty. They have come to realize that the system is regarded as a humiliating sign of backwardness, which the Christian States had seen fit to put an end to, and which the non-Christian States should also claim a right to depart from. But the attempts of the latter have not been greeted with uniform success, and it is only by fulfilling many conditions that some States have been able to rid themselves of the increasingly distasteful anomaly.

The methods by means of which the abolition of extraterritoriality has been accomplished or attempted are varied. Broadly speaking, they may be classified under the following six categories:—(1) by passing under the sovereignty of States which do not recognize or grant the right of exemption from local jurisdiction; (2) by passing under the temporary jurisdiction of such a State; (3) by breaking off from a State in which the extraterritorial system exists; (4) by becoming a protectorate of a State which does not concede rights of extraterritoriality; (5) by unilateral cancellation; and (6) by diplomatic negotiation leading to a mutual agreement on the abolition or the preliminaries to it.

Extraterritoriality ceases when part or all of a country with such a system passes under the permanent sovereignty of a country without it.

I. ALGIERS

In 1830, Algiers was captured by France, and consular jurisdiction forthwith came to an end.   The Algerians were clothed with French citizenship and came under French jurisdiction in the Ottoman Empire.   On August 10, 1834, an ordinance was issued, concerning the organization of the judicial system in the French possessions of North Africa. Article 4 of this ordinance sets forth that " the jurisdiction of the tribunals of Algiers, Bone, and Oran extends over all the territory occupied by each of these Provinces up to the limits which shall be determined by a special order of the Governor." [1]

II. MADAGASCAR

On December 17, 1885, the island of Madagascar was by treaty placed under the protection of France.[2]   It was understood, however, that this treaty " changes nothing in the Treaties already existing between the Hova Government and other States." [3]

Shortly after the establishment of the French protectorate over Madagascar, the French Government contemplated the inauguration of a French tribunal in the island and was desirous of receiving an assurance from the British Government that the latter would be prepared to accept for British subjects the jurisdiction of such a tribunal and to forego in its favor the extraterritorial privileges which they enjoyed

[1] *State Papers*, vol. xxii, p. 351.

[2] *Parliamentary Papers,* 1886 [C. 4652], Africa, no. 2 (1886), p. 4; *State Papers*, vol. lxxvi, p. 477.

[3] M. de Freycinet to the French Ambassadors abroad, Dec. 27, 1885, *ibid.,* p. 7.

under existing treaties with Madagascar.[1] To this proposition, the Marquess of Salisbury showed himself to be favorably inclined. He stated that his government was willing
to give the assurance and to consent to the establishment in
Madagascar of a jurisdiction similar to that which was introduced in Tunis in 1883,[2] and that the procedure adopted
in that year regarding the waiver of British jurisdiction in
Tunis would be followed closely.[3]

On February 11, 1896, the British Government was informed of a military occupation of Madagascar by France.[4]
In taking cognizance of this information, the British Government reserved all its rights in the island pending the
communication of the terms of the treaty understood to have
been concluded between France and Madagascar.[5] It was
later brought to the knowledge of the British Government
that no treaty had been concluded between France and the
Malagasy Government, but that " in consequence of the military operations rendered necessary by the resistance of the
Malagasy authorities to the exercise of the French Protectorate, the French Government have simply taken possession of the island. The Queen of Madagascar," it was
added, " to whom the annexation was notified, has submitted
to this decision, and accepted conditions which it was thought
needful to impose in order to secure the proper administration of the country." [6] Under these circumstances, the
French Government proposed to exercise jurisdiction over
foreigners in Madagascar, and to that end had organized

---

[1] The following summary is made from *Parliamentary Papers*, 1898
[C. 8700], Africa, no. 8 (1897).

[2] *Infra*, p. 145.

[3] The Marquess of Salisbury to M. Waddington, May 6, 1892.

[4] Baron de Courcel to the Marquess of Salisbury, Feb. 11, 1896.

[5] The Marquess of Salisbury to Baron de Courcel, Feb. 20, 1896.

[6] See the Declaration of the Queen, Jan. 18, 1896, *ibid.*, p. 14.

French courts in that country, by a decree of December 28, 1895.[1] Consequently, the British consent to surrender consular jurisdiction was requested.[2]

In his instructions to the British Ambassador at Paris relative to the above French note, Lord Salisbury alluded to the treaty of 1865 between Great Britain and Madagascar giving the British subjects their extraterritorial rights in the island; to the assurance made by the French Government in 1885 that the protectorate did not affect the treaty rights of foreign Powers; to the declaration exchanged between the British and French Governments on August 5, 1890, in which the former agreed to recognize the protectorate of France over Madagascar " with its consequences," and the latter engaged that the establishment of the protectorate should not " affect any rights or immunities enjoyed by British subjects in that island; " [3] and to later declarations to the same effect. It was contended by Great Britain that the Act signed by the Queen of Madagascar on January 18, 1896, did not confer sovereignty on France, and that " the position of the Queen remains in every respect the same as it was under the October treaty, in which it was expressly recorded that the status of her kingdom was that of a protectorate." [4] To the argument that there was a similarity between the status of Madagascar and that of the protected States of India, the British note replied:

The States of India are not annexed to, nor incorporated in, the possessions of the Crown. The rulers have the right of internal administration subject to the control of the Protecting Power for the maintenance of peace and order and the suppression of abuses. The latter conducts all external relations. The

[1] *Parliamentary Papers*, 1898 [C. 8700], Africa, no. 8 (1897), p. 17.

[2] M. Geoffray to the Marquess of Salisbury, Apr. 10, 1896.

[3] See *Parliamentary Papers*, 1890 [C. 6130], Africa, no. 9 (1890).

[4] Art. 1, *State Papers*, vol. lxxxviii, p. 447.

position has been defined as that of subordinate alliance. It has, however, never been contended that if those States had had pre-existing treaties with foreign Powers the assumption of Protectorate by Great Britain would have abrogated these treaties.

In conclusion, it was reiterated that "the treaty between Great Britain and Madagascar is still in full and undimin-ished force," but France was given to understand that the British Government would give its consent to the cessation of British extraterritoriality in Madagascar, on condition that a similar cessation of French extraterritoriality in Zan-zibar, over which Great Britain exercised a protectorate, should take place.[1]

On August 18, 1896, the British Government was ap-prised of the final organization of the French courts in Madagascar by the Decree of June 9, 1896. "The French courts constituted by this Decree," it was pointed out by the note transmitting it, "take cognizance of all civil and criminal suits between Europeans or those in a similar position [*assimilés*], and between Europeans or those in a similar position [*assimilés*] and natives; likewise of all crimes, misdemeanors, and offences committed within the area of jurisdiction, whatever the nationality of the persons accused or inculpated." These courts were formally estab-lished, and necessary instructions had been sent for them to exercise their jurisdiction over all the inhabitants of the island of Madagascar. The British Government was, there-fore, requested to notify the British Consul in Madagascar to that effect.[2]

In reply, the British Government stated that it would comply with the request on learning from the French Gov-

[1] The Marquess of Salisbury to the Marquess of Dufferin, Apr. 25, 1896.
[2] Baron de Courcel to the Marquess of Salisbury, Aug. 18, 1896.

ernment that instructions would also be given to the French
consular officers in Zanzibar to terminate their exercise of
extraterritorial jurisdiction in that country.[1]   In the later
negotiations between the British and French Governments,
the former took the position that it would renounce the
British rights in Madagascar on " receiving from the French
Government a note undertaking to renounce their exterritorial rights in Zanzibar, as soon as they should be satisfied
that adequate provision had been made for the administration of justice by the Tribunals, in cases where French subjects were concerned."   The French Government contended
that there was no analogy in this matter between Madagascar
and Zanzibar, since Great Britain had not as yet established
courts in the latter, and that when she had done so, France
would make no difficulty about admitting their jurisdiction
over French citizens.   She would not, however, give an
assurance as to a future contingency, of which there was
then no prospect.[2]

Contrary to the apparent firmness of the above statement,
the French Government shortly afterwards gave the assurance desired by the British Government, that " the Government of the Republic are prepared to abandon the exercise
of their rights of jurisdiction over their nationals at Zanzibar, as soon as the administration of justice there, by regularly constituted British tribunals, shall be assured." [3]
Consequently, the British Government gave instructions to
the British consular officers in Madagascar to recognize the
jurisdiction of the French courts over the British subjects
in that island.[4]   Thus, the British rights of extraterritoriality in Madagascar were formally renounced.

[1] The Marquess of Salisbury to Baron de Courcel, Aug. 24, 1896.

[2] The Marquess of Salisbury to the Marquess of Dufferin, Sept. 14, 1896.

[3] M. Hanotaux to Mr. Gosselin, Apr. 5, 1897.

[4] Sir E. Monson to M. Hanotaux, Apr. 12, 1897.

On February 12, 1896, the United States Government was informed of the French occupation of Madagascar.[1] In his reply, Secretary Olney observed that " the Department has noted the contents of your note with due reserve as to the effect of the action of the Government of France upon the treaty rights of the United States." [2] The American Ambassador at Paris was instructed to obtain from the French Government an " explicit statement " on the effect of the occupation upon American treaty rights.[3]

In the meantime, the French Resident at Tamatave had informed the United States Consul there of the raising of the siege of Madagascar and of the fact that " Madagascar having become a French possession, justice will be henceforth rendered to your nationality and those under its jurisdiction, by the French tribunals." [4] In reply, Mr. Wetter, United States Consul at Tamatave, stated that as Consul of the United States he had received no formal notification of Madagascar having become a French possession, and that pending instructions from his government he could not " accept or acquiesce in any abridgment or change of American interests and of the powers of this consulate under the treaty of 1881-1883." [5]

In the subsequent negotiations, the French Government indicated " that in the opinion of the Government of the Republic, the maintenance of the treaty of May 13, 1881, is inconsistent with the new order of things created by the taking possession of Madagascar," and " that, on the other

[1] M. Patenôtre to Mr. Olney, Feb. 12, 1896, U. S. *Foreign Relations,* 1896, p. 118.

[2] Mr. Olney to M. Patenôtre, Feb. 26, 1896, *ibid.,* p. 119.

[3] Mr. Olney to Mr. Eustis, Mar. 30, 1896, *ibid.*

[4] M. Ferraud to Mr. Wetter, Feb. 18, 1896, *ibid.,* p. 120.

[5] Mr. Wetter to M. Ferraud, Feb. 18, 1896, *ibid.,* p. 120; *cf.* Same to Same, Feb. 20, 1896, *ibid.,* p. 121.

hand, the Government of the Republic is disposed to extend
to the great African island the whole (*ensemble*) of the conventions applicable to the Government or citizens of the
United States in France and in French possessions, and
which have enabled them to entertain their relations of all
kinds so profitable to both countries." [1] But the Government
of the United States desired a " categorical statement " that
the American treaty with Madagascar had been superseded
by those with France " in virtue of complete absorption of
Madagascar and the substitution of a wholly French government for that of the Hovas," with which the United
States had theretofore maintained relations.[2] Pending the
receipt of such a " categorical statement," Secretary Olney
instructed the American Consul at Tamatave by telegraph
to suspend, until further instruction, the exercise of his
judicial functions in all cases where the operation of an established French court was ascertained to be available for
the disposition of judicial cases affecting American citizens
or interests.[3]

On July 22, 1896, M. Patenôtre, French Ambassador at
Washington, informed the American Government of the
passing by the Chamber of Deputies and the ratification by
the Senate of a bill to the effect that " the island of Madagascar, with its dependent islands, is declared a French
colony." [4] The bill was promulgated by the President as
law on August 6.[5] Thereupon, the French Ambassador inquired at the State Department whether further instructions

[1] M. Bourgeois to Mr. Eustis, Apr. 16, 1896, U. S. *Foreign Relations,*
1896, p. 123; *cf.* M. Patenôtre to Mr. Olney, Apr. 18, 1896, *ibid.*, p. 124.

[2] Mr. Olney to Mr. Eustis, Apr. 27, 1896, *ibid.*, p. 125; *cf.* Mr. Olney
to M. Patenôtre, May 2, 1896, *ibid.*, p. 126.

[3] Mr. Olney to M. Patenôtre, May 2, 1896, *ibid.*, p. 127.

[4] M. Patenôtre to Mr. Olney, July 22, 1896, *ibid.*, p. 133.

[5] *Ibid.*, p. 135.

were necessary to insure the transfer of the jurisdiction exercised by the American Consul at Tamatave to the French tribunals.[1] In reply, Mr. Rockhill, Acting Secretary of State, stated that the instructions already given to the United States consulate at Tamatave on the subject in question were deemed sufficient by the Department.[2]

III. SAMOA

By the General Act of Berlin, June 14, 1889, Samoa was recognized by Great Britain, Germany, and the United States as an independent power, and a supreme court was established, the chief justice of which was to be nominated by the three governments in common accord and appointed by the Samoan Government. With a few exceptions, the court had jurisdiction over all the residents of Samoa.[3]

The régime established by the Berlin Act lasted only ten years. In 1899, the Samoan Islands were divided between Germany and the United States, and each renounced its extraterritorial rights in the part falling under the sovereignty of the other.[4]

IV. CONGO

On April 28-30, 1885, resolutions were passed by the Belgian Chamber of Representatives and Senate, authorizing King Leopold II to be the Chief of the Congo Free State, and declaring the union between Belgium and the Congo Free State to be exclusively personal.[5] In 1908, the per-

---

[1] M. Patenôtre to Mr. Olney, Aug. 8, 1896, *ibid.*, p. 134.

[2] Mr. Rockhill to M. Patenôtre, Aug. 12, 1896, *ibid.*, p. 135.

[3] Malloy, vol. ii, pp. 1577-1579.

[4] Treaty of Dec. 2, 1899, between Great Britain, Germany and the United States, art. 2, *State Papers,* vol. xci, p. 77; *cf.* arts. 1 and 3 of the treaty between Great Britain and Germany, Nov. 14, 1899, *ibid.*, p. 71.

[5] *Ibid.*, vol. lxxvi, p. 327.

sonal union was dissolved, and the Congo Free State was placed under the sovereignty of Belgium as one of her colonies.[1] This put an end to the system of extraterritoriality in that country.

V. COREA

In 1910, Corea was annexed by Japan. Article 1 of the treaty of annexation, dated August 22, 1910, provided that the annexation covered " all rights of sovereignty over the whole of Corea." [2] On August 29, 1910, a Declaration was published by the Japanese Government, announcing that " The Imperial Government of Japan undertake the entire government and administration of Corea." A number of rules were drawn up relating to the status of foreigners in Corea, one of which abolished all the treaties of Corea with foreign Powers.[3] On the same day a statement was issued by the Japanese Foreign Office to the following effect:

At the same time, the right of extraterritoriality which foreigners have hitherto enjoyed in Corea comes definitely to an end from today. The Japanese Government believe that they are entirely justified in regarding such right of extraterritoriality as ended upon the termination of Corea's treaties in consequence of the annexation, considering that the continuance of that system would inevitably prove a serious obstacle and interfere with the unification of the administration of Corea. Moreover, it seems only natural that foreigners, being allowed to enjoy in Corea the same rights and privileges as in Japan proper, should be called upon to surrender the right of extraterritoriality which is not granted to them in Japan proper.[4]

All the Powers but the United States acquiesced in the

[1] Decree of Mar. 5, 1908, *State Papers,* vol. ci, p. 731.

[2] *Ibid.,* vol. ciii, p. 993.

[3] *Ibid.,* vol. cv, p. 687.

[4] *Ibid.,* p. 691.

Japanese announcement. The United States maintained that consular jurisdiction should be continued until the old Corean system was completely replaced, under Japanese supervision, by actually operating laws and courts, in substantial conformity to those of Japan itself; or that the trial of American citizens under Japanese laws should be limited to such courts in Corea as were maintained at a high standard of efficiency.[1] The Japanese reply was that the judicial system in Corea was substantially the same as in Japan, and that the system of consular jurisdiction being wholly unsuited to the new condition of things, its revival would be " both unnecessary and inadvisable." [2] The United States persisted for a while in its original attitude,[3] but although no agreement has been reached on the subject between the American and Japanese Governments, the former appears no longer to enjoy extraterritorial rights in Corea.[4]

VI. TRIPOLI

After the Turco-Italian War of 1911-1912, the Italian Government took possession of Tripoli. By a Decree of October 17, 1912, it was declared that in accordance with a Law of February 25, 1912, " Tripoli and Cyrenaica were

[1] The Acting Secretary of State to the American Ambassador, Sep. 18, 1910, U. S. *Foreign Relations*, 1911, p. 321.

[2] The Minister for Foreign Affairs to the American Ambassador, Oct. 6, 1910, *ibid.*, p. 324.

[3] " In all my conversations with Mr. Ishii [acting Japanese Minister for Foreign Affairs] and others since the Treaty of annexation was published, I have consistently made the point that American consular jurisdiction was not abolished and could not be so until some definite action to that end had been taken by the Government of the United States." The American Chargé d'Affaires to the Secretary of State, Nov. 29, 1910, *ibid.*, p. 327.

[4] In reply to an inquiry addressed by the author, the United States Department of State " regrets that it has no information on this subject available for dissemination."

placed under the full and entire sovereignty of the Kingdom of Italy." [1]   A year later, on February 28, 1913, the American Secretary of State informed the Italian Chargé d'Affaires that instructions had been issued to the diplomatic and consular representatives of the United States to conform to the judicial régime established by Italy in Libya and to discontinue their extraterritorial jurisdiction. [2]

[1] *State Papers*, vol. cvi, p. 1079.
[2] U. S. *Foreign Relations*, 1913, p. 609.

CHAPTER VI

TRANSFER OF JURISDICTION

THE second method by means of which the abolition of extraterritoriality has been brought about consists in the subjection of portions of the territory of a country in which the system exists to the temporary occupation, administration or jurisdiction of a country in which it does not. In some cases, the temporary transfer of jurisdiction has ended in outright annexation, while in others, as in those of the leaseholds in China, the legal ownership of the territory has been retained to this day by the lessor sovereign. But in either case, the rights of jurisdiction have been exercised by the temporary occupant or usufructuary of the territory concerned, and the extraterritorial system has been suspended during the term of the temporary occupation, administration, or leasing.

I. PROVISIONAL OCCUPATION AND ADMINISTRATION

In 1878, the island of Cyprus was assigned by Turkey "to be occupied and administered by England." [1] Shortly afterwards, an additional article was agreed upon, declaring that for the term of the occupation, the Queen of England should have " full powers for making Laws and Conventions for the government of the Island in Her Majesty's name, and for the regulation of its commercial and consular relations and affairs free from the Porte's control." [2]

---

[1] Art. 1, Treaty of Constantinople, June 4, 1878, *State Papers*, vol. lxix, p. 745.

[2] Agreement of Aug. 14, 1878, *ibid.*, p. 769.

In accordance with these agreements, a British Order in Council, dated September 14, 1878, made provision for a High Commissioner for the administration of the island. Article 21 of the Order gave the High Commissioner power " to constitute and appoint " judges and other officials in the island.[1] Subsequently, the High Commissioner issued an Ordinance, establishing a High Court of Justice with " all jurisdiction, criminal and civil, over all persons and in all cases other than such as would have been under the sole jurisdiction and authority of the Ottoman Courts if the said Convention of June 4, 1878, had not been made." [2]

The British régime in Cyprus was recognized by Austria-Hungary by a declaration of the latter, dated September 14, 1880.[3] The other Powers have taken no action on this matter, but have apparently tacitly acquiesced in it as a *fait accompli*.[4]

In the same year that Cyprus was transferred to British occupation and administration, the provinces of Bosnia and Herzegovina were subjected to Austrian occupation and administration.[5] By an Ordinance of March 5, 1880, Austria-

---

[1] *State Papers*, vol. lxix, p. 724.

[2] *Ibid.*, vol. lxx, p. 661.

[3] *Ibid.*, vol. xciv, p. 838.

[4] The measure taken by the British Government to assume jurisdiction over all foreigners in Cyprus was adversely criticized by some writers at the time. An article in *The Law Magazine and Review*, 4th ser., vol. iv, declared that "wheresoever throughout the Ottoman Empire the Capitulations have not been ' totidem verbis,' suspended or abrogated, there they are still in force. And for Great Britain to assume the opposite would be, apart from the grave questions of Law and Fact, a very ungracious return towards at least one of her nearest neighbors on the Continent" (p. 139). M. Esperson, in an article in the *Révue de droit international*, vol. x, pp. 587-593, also maintained that the island of Cyprus was still an integral part of the Ottoman Empire even after the British occupation and that as such the Capitulations continued to be in force there.

[5] Art. 25, Treaty of Berlin, July 13, 1878, *State Papers*, vol. lxix, p. 758.

Hungary put an end to her consulates in both provinces and to the extraterritorial régime there.[1] England acquiesced in the Austro-Hungarian action on October 15, 1880, when she made a declaration to the following effect:

Whereas Her Majesty's Government recognize that the powers of the Government of His Imperial, Royal and Apostolic Majesty with regard to the administration of Bosnia and of the Herzegovina should not be restricted in matters of jurisdiction by the anterior engagements of the Sublime Porte known as the " Capitulations "; and whereas a judicial administration founded on the principles of European law has been introduced by the said Imperial and Royal Government in Bosnia and in the Herzegovina, it is hereby declared that from the 1st November next Her Majesty's Consuls in Bosnia and in the Herzegovina shall be bound to respect in its full extent, and without regard to the " Capitulations," the jurisdiction of the Tribunals established in Bosnia and in the Herzegovina by His Imperial and Royal Majesty's Government, and that they shall not exercise any rights and functions, nor claim any privileges, other than those which appertain to other Consuls of Her Britannic Majesty residing in the Austro-Hungarian Monarchy.[2]

Russia, France, and Italy followed the example of England in 1881,[3]

II. LEASEHOLDS IN CHINA

The leaseholds possessed by the various Powers in China illustrate further the effect of the temporary transfer of jurisdiction on the existence of extraterritoriality. With the leasing of Kiaochow to Germany, of Port Arthur to

[1] J. Trigant-Geneste, " *Le Droit international privé en Bosnie et Herzégovine," Journal du droit international privé* (hereafter referred to as *J. D. I. P.*), vol. xviii, p. 783.

[2] *State Papers*, vol. xciv, p. 838.

[3] *Ibid.*, vol. lxxiii, pp. 643, 644.

Russia, and of Weihaiwei to Great Britain in 1898, a question was raised as to the status of consular jurisdiction in these territories. With the exception of Japan, all the Powers recognized that the transfer of jurisdiction over them by China to the respective Powers, though coupled with the retention of sovereignty, meant the abolition of the extraterritorial rights formerly enjoyed by foreigners therein.[1]

The question having been referred by the United States Secretary of State to the Solicitor of the Department of State, the latter rendered his opinion as follows:

As it is expressly stipulated in the leases that China retains sovereignty over the territory leased, it could doubtless be asserted that such territory is still *Chinese territory* and that the provisions of our treaties with China granting consular jurisdiction are still applicable. But in view of the express relinquishment of jurisdiction by China, I infer that the reservation of sovereignty is merely intended to cut off possible future claims of the lessees that the sovereignty of the territory is *permanently* vested in them. The intention and effect of these leases appear to me to have been the relinquishment by China, *during the term of the leases,* and the conferring upon the foreign power in each case of *all jurisdiction over the territory*. Such relinquishment would seem, also, to involve the loss by the United States of its right to exercise consular jurisdiction in the territories leased.[2]

In a recent case, decided by United States Commissioner Lurton, it was held that the United States Court for China had jurisdiction over Americans in the leasehold of Port Arthur and Dairen. The facts of this case were briefly as follows: When the S. S. *Patrick Henry,* an American vessel, was docked at Dairen, two of the crew were assaulted by

[1] See United States *Foreign Relations,* 1900, pp. 382, 390.
[2] *Ibid.,* p. 389.

the captain of the ship in a Japanese saloon on shore. Upon complaint to the American Consul at Dairen, the plaintiffs were advised to take the matter up in the United States Court for China when their steamer reached Shanghai. This was done, and at the preliminary hearing the question of jurisdiction was raised by defendant's counsel.[1]

The opinion of the Commissioner was based on the theory that sovereign rights were expressly retained by China in the territory leased to Japan, and that as long as China exercised such rights in Port Arthur and Dairen, her treaties with the United States, including those granting extraterritorial jurisdiction, should have force there until the rights conferred were waived by the United States. At first sight, the premises of the Commissioner's reasoning seem scarcely to differ from those of the Solicitor of the State Department, and one is at a loss to see why a difference of opinion should have existed with regard to the exercise of jurisdiction in the leased territories. Upon closer examination, however, one discovers that whereas what the Solicitor calls sovereignty *excludes* the right of jurisdiction (which is held to have been ceded, for the term of the lease, to the lessee), what the Commissioner calls sovereignty *includes* the right of jurisdiction (which is held not to have ceded to the lessee, in this case, Japan). An analysis of the arguments of the Commissioner will clarify the whole situation.

The opinion of Commissioner Lurton begins with an examination of the provisions of treaties between China and the United States bearing on the exercise of extraterritorial jurisdiction in the former. Then it proceeds to describe and explain the origin of the Japanese leasehold in Port Arthur and Dairen. A provision of the treaty of May 25, 1915, which extended the term of the lease, and constructions placed on the same are cited to show the retention of

[1] *China Weekly Review*, vol. xxvii, p. 384.

sovereign rights by China in the territory leased. The American note of May 13, 1915, making reservations regarding American treaty rights, etc., in China, is produced to prove that "the United States has not been a party to or has in any way waived her extraterritorial rights given to her by the various treaties with China, and took occasion to so notify both China and Japan before this treaty [of May 25, 1915] was actually signed." Moreover, at the Washington Conference of 1921-22, it was argued, Japan expressly announced her intention to respect China's sovereign rights and the principle of equal opportunity in South Manchuria, and the United States reasserted its right to most-favored-nation treatment, "showing conclusively that it never has relinquished its extraterritorial rights in this particular territory in question." The precedent of 1900 embodied in the instructions of Mr. John Hay and in the Memorandum of the Solicitor of the State Department is alluded to, and the position held that "before the United States relinquished extraterritoriality in any portion of China as existed in 1844, there must be definite action taken by it." After citing the principles of international law bearing on the validity of treaties, the Commissioner comes to the following conclusion:

Having taken into consideration the various phases of this novel case, I fail to find that the United States Court for China has lost its jurisdiction over this defendant who is charged with committing a crime within the Leased Territory of China, and more particularly described as being in the City of Dairen. The defendant's demurrer is accordingly overruled, and as there appears to be sufficient evidence adduced to make out a *prima facie* case of assault against him, he is required to answer the information filed herein.[1]

The theory that sovereignty is expressly retained by

[1] *China Weekly Review*, vol. xxvii, pp. 384-385.

China in the leaseholds is indisputable, and it was so recognized by the Solicitor of the State Department in his opinion of 1900. So long as China retains her sovereign rights in the territory leased, the treaties between her and foreign States are in force there as they are everywhere else in China, and the rights conferred by these treaties can be waived only by the government to which they are granted. Such is the law, and the Commissioner adds nothing to it when he propounds the self-same principle. But the crucial point of the Commissioner's decision, as the author has suggested, seems to be in the inclusion of the right of jurisdiction in what he terms sovereignty. After dealing with the transfer of the Russian leasehold to Japan in 1905 and the extension of its term in 1915, Commissioner Lurton quotes the language of article 5 of the treaty of May 25, 1915, as follows:

Civil and criminal cases in which the defendants are Japanese shall be tried and adjudicated by the Japanese Consul; those in which the defendants are Chinese shall be tried and adjudicated by Chinese authorities. In either case, an officer may be deputed to the Court to attend the proceedings; but amongst [mixed] civil cause [cases] between Chinese and Japanese relating to land shall be tried and adjudicated by delegates of both nations conjointly in accordance with Chinese laws [law] and local usage.[1]

Commenting on this provision, the Commissioner says:

In construing this part of the treaty, it shows conclusively that Japan recognized the Sovereignty of China, and reiterated in specific terms her extraterritorial rights for her subjects and does not claim supreme powers to herself to the exclusion of Chinese Sovereignty in this particular territory.[2]

[1] The words in brackets are from the correct version of the provision cited. *Cf.* MacMurray, *Treaties*, vol. ii, 1915/8, p. 1220; also China, *Maritime Treaties*, vol. ii, p. 791.

[2] *China Weekly Review, loc cit.,* p. 384.

Here is in fact the crux of Commissioner Lurton's argument and here it is that he differs from the Solicitor of the State Department. What he is trying to drive home is not that China retained her sovereignty in the leasehold of Port Arthur and Dairen, stripped of her right of jurisdiction, as she did in the treaties with Great Britain, Germany, France,[1] and, in a qualified sense, also Russia,[2] in

---

[1] The case of France was not treated of by the Solicitor's Memorandum. It may be pointed out that in the treaty of 1898, leasing Kwanchow Wan to France, it was likewise provided: "The territory shall be governed and administered during the 99 years of the lease by France alone." Art. 3, MacMurray, *op. cit.*, vol. i, 1898/10, p. 129.

[2] The treaty of March 27, 1898, leasing Port Arthur and Dairen to Russia provided: "In the event of a Chinese subject committing any crime within the limits of the leased territory, the offender will be handed over to the nearest Chinese authorities for trial and punishment in accordance with Chinese laws, as laid down in Article VIII of the Treaty of Peking of 1860." Art. 4, MacMurray, *op. cit.*, vol. i, p. 120 (1898/5). In his despatch to Mr. Hay, dated Dec. 11, 1898, Mr. Conger, American Minister at Peking, reported: "The Russian legation informs me that that provision [cited above] is not correctly translated, and that construing it in connection with Article VIII of the treaty of 1860 they have the right and do try Chinese for crimes against Russians." U. S. *Foreign Relations*, 1900, p. 385. Reference to the Chinese version fails to reveal where the inaccuracy of translation occurs. See China, *Maritime Treaties*, vol. i, p. 220. The Russian claim to try crimes committed by Chinese against Russians, if it was made, rested on a questionable ground, since it is expressly provided by the article cited that Chinese criminals should be sent to the nearest Chinese authorities for trial and punishment. Even construing it with article 8 of the treaty of 1860, one can hardly reconcile the Russian claim to the actual grant. The reference to article 8 of the treaty of 1860 was directed apparently to that particular portion of the article which stipulated for the rendition of Russians guilty of grave crimes in China to Russia for trial and punishment. What was meant was that the procedure to be followed in the sending of Chinese criminals from the Russian leasehold to the nearest Chinese authorities should be the same as in the sending of Russian criminals to Russia, hence the phrase "as laid down in Article VIII of the Treaty of Peking of 1860." See China, *Maritime Treaties*, vol. i, p. 106. Leaving aside this point, we find further that this article 8 of the Treaty of Peking made express provision against the trial, punishment and imprisonment by either party

1898; but that she retained this sovereignty, together with the right of jurisdiction, as modified, of course, by her treaties of extraterritoriality. In 1898, China allowed the lessee Powers to exercise complete jurisdiction in the territories leased to them; in 1915, she failed to make the same concession to Japan in the case of Port Arthur and Dairen. The provision quoted by Commissioner Lurton from the treaty in question shows this; and that it admits of no question is further attested by what follows in the same article, a portion which the Commissioner omits to cite but which is of great importance in the present connection:

When, in future, the judicial system in the said region is completely reformed, all civil and criminal cases concerning Japanese subjects shall be tried and adjudicated entirely by Chinese law courts.[1]

of persons not its subjects in any criminal case whatever. "*En cas de crime, quelle qu'en soit la gravité, le Consul et le chef local ne peuvent prendre les mesures nécessaires que relativement au coupable appartenant à leur pays, et ni l'un ni l'autre n'a le droit d'incarcérer ni de juger séparément, et encore moins de châtier un individu non-sujet de son Gouvernement.*" *Ibid.* It appears, therefore, to be difficult, if not impossible, to justify the assumption by Russia of jurisdiction over Chinese criminals in Port Arthur and Dairen on any legal ground. Outside of such jurisdiction over Chinese criminals, however, the Russian Government was given complete administrative authority in the leased territory. To quote from another part of the same article of the treaty of May 27, 1898, cited above, "During the above-specified period, on the territory leased by the Russian Government and its adjacent water area, the entire military command of the land and naval forces and equally the supreme civil administration will be entirely given over to the Russian authorities." MacMurray, vol. i, p. 120. From this, it is clear that complete jurisdiction was ceded to Russia in the leased territory, except over Chinese criminals. Even in their case, as the treaty provided, they should simply be withdrawn from the Russian jurisdiction there, and sent to the nearest Chinese authorities for trial and punishment, the Chinese Government asserting no jurisdiction in Port Arthur and Dairen.

[1] MacMurray, *op. cit.*, vol. ii, 1915/8, p. 1220.

This is, of course, unequivocal language, and it is conclusive evidence that the leasing of the territory to Japan did not carry with it the transfer of jurisdiction, except in so far as it was conceded to her under the régime of extraterritoriality, applicable alike to this and to other portions of Chinese territory.   As the cessation of extraterritoriality in a leasehold, according to the Memorandum of the Solicitor of the State Department, was ascribed to the transfer of jurisdiction from China to the lessee Powers, it could not take place unless such a transfer was made.   Therefore, while the Solicitor decided in favor of the termination of American extraterritorial jurisdiction in the British, German and Russian leaseholds, Commissioner Lurton went counter to it in the case of the Japanese leasehold of Port Arthur and Dairen.   In one case, a transfer of jurisdiction took place; in the other, it did not.

But although the two are widely different in effect, in fact diametrically opposed, the later opinion, it must be pointed out, does not necessarily overrule the earlier, because in principle either is strictly complementary to the other.   Both of them recognize the explicit retention of China's sovereignty in the leaseholds, and both of them uphold the treaty rights of the United States.   The only respect in which the Commissioner goes a step beyond the opinion of the Solicitor of the State Department is in declaring that where complete jurisdiction is not ceded to a lessee Power, extraterritoriality does not cease.   This is clearly a logical deduction from the Solicitor's opinion, for if the cessation of extraterritoriality in a leasehold depends on the transfer of jurisdiction, there is hardly any room for doubt that no right need be waived by a third Power if no such transfer of jurisdiction is made.

Perhaps it may be added that due to the fact that the Solicitor and the Commissioner were concerned with the interpretation of two different groups of treaties, it is not necessary to reconcile their opinions. But in comparing the latter, it should not be overlooked that they were based on essentially identical reasoning and that neither was inconsistent with the other.

III. THE A MANDATES

In this connection, the suspension of the capitulatory régime in the A Mandates may be discussed. The legal status of these areas is still undecided,[1] but without entering into the juristic niceties involved in the determination of the sovereignty of Palestine, Iraq, and Syria and the Lebanon, we may well consider them as instances at least of a temporary transfer of jurisdiction by the Principal Allied Powers [2] to the Mandatories concerned, after Turkey had lost control over the several areas.[3]

In the case of Palestine, the intention of the Principal Allied Powers to transfer the administration of the mandated area to Great Britain was explicit. In the articles of the mandate it was expressly laid down that " the Manda-

[1] See Wright, " Sovereignty of the Mandates," *A.J.I.L.*, vol. xvii, pp. 691-703; Rougier, " *La Première Assemblée de la Société des Nations,*" (ch. x, *Les Mandats*), *Révue générale de droit international public* (hereafter referred to as *R. G. D. I. P.*), vol. xxviii, p. 333; Pic, " *Le Régime du Mandat d'après le Traité de Versailles,*" (ii, *Charactères Juridiques du Mandat*), ibid., vol. xxx, p. 330.

[2] See the preambles to the articles of the mandates, League of Nations, *Official Journal*, 1922, no. 8, pt. ii, pp. 1007, 1013; 1924, no. 10, p. 1346.

[3] Before the conclusion of the unratified Treaty of Sèvres, Aug. 10, 1920, these areas were conquered territories under the *de facto* control of Great Britain and France. The Treaty of Sèvres recognized the provisional independence of Syria and Mesopotamia, but entrusted the selection of the Mandatories over them as well as over Palestine to the Principal Allied Powers. Arts. 94 and 95, Great Britain, *Treaty Series,* no. 11 (1920), p. 26. By the Treaty of Lausanne, July 24, 1923, Turkey renounced " all rights and title whatsoever over or respecting the territories" situated outside her frontiers. Art. 16, *ibid.*, no. 16 (1923), p. 21.

tory shall have full powers of legislation and of administration save as they may be limited by the terms of this mandate." [1]   Moreover, in connection with the judicial system of Palestine, Great Britain was entrusted with the responsibility for its establishment in such a way as might assure complete security to foreigners and natives alike.[2]

As to Syria and the Lebanon, the Mandatory, France, was charged with the framing of an organic law in agreement with the native authorities, but " pending the coming into effect of the organic law, the Government of Syria and the Lebanon shall be conducted in accordance with the spirit of this mandate," [3] one of whose provisions was that the Mandatory should establish in the mandated areas a judicial régime compatible with the guarantee of the rights of natives and foreigners.[4]   Thus, like Palestine, Syria and the Lebanon were placed under the temporary administration of France, at least as far as the judicial department was concerned.

Finally, in regard to Iraq, although it was recognized as an independent country by Great Britain in virtue of the Treaty of Alliance dated October 10, 1922,[5] it was agreed in this same treaty that "His Majesty the King of Iraq undertakes that he will accept and give effect to such reasonable provisions as His Britannic Majesty may consider necessary in judicial matters to safeguard the interests of foreigners." [6]   This shows that Great Britain exercises in Iraq a considerable share of the judicial power of the so-called independent government.

[1] Art. 1, League of Nations, *Official Journal,* 1922, no. 8, pt. ii, p. 1007.

[2] Art. 9, *ibid.,* p. 1008.

[3] Art. 1, *ibid.,* p. 1013.

[4] Art. 6, *ibid.,* p. 1014.

[5] Great Britain, *Parliamentary Papers,* 1922 [Cmd. 1757], Iraq, Treaty with King Feisal.

[6] Art. 9, *ibid.,* p. 4.

All in all, we may say that the A Mandates constitute instances at least of a temporary transfer of jurisdiction to the Mandatories by the principal Allied Powers. The temporary nature of the mandatory system is indicated by the principle set forth in article 22 of the Covenant of the League of Nations with respect to the A Mandates, that " certain communities formerly belonging to the Turkish Empire have reached a stage of development where their existence as independent nations can be provisionally recognized subject to the rendering of administrative advice and assistance by a Mandatory until such time as they are able to stand alone."

The articles of the mandates for Palestine and Syria and the Lebanon were approved by the Council of the League of Nations on July 24, 1922,[1] and came into effect on September 29, 1923.[2] The articles of the mandate for Iraq were not approved until September 27, 1924.[3] By these articles, the capitulatory system was suspended, and foreigners were subjected, during the continuance of the mandates, to the judicial régimes established by the respective Mandatories.[4]

[1] League of Nations, *Official Journal,* 1922, no. 8, pt. ii, p. 825.

[2] *Ibid.,* 1923, no. 10, p. 1217.

[3] *Ibid.,* 1924, no. 10, pp. 1346-1347.

[4] Palestine, art. 8, " The privileges and immunities of foreigners, including the benefit of consular jurisdiction and protection as formerly enjoyed by Capitulation or usage in the Ottoman Empire, shall not be applicable in Palestine. Unless the Powers whose nationals enjoyed the aforementioned privileges and immunities on August first, 1914, shall have previously renounced the right to their re-establishment, or shall have agreed to their non-application for a specific period, these privileges and immunities shall, at the expiration of the mandate, be immediately reestablished in their entirety or with such modifications as may have been agreed upon between the Powers concerned." *Ibid.,* 1922, no. 8, pt. ii, p. 1008. Art. 5 of the mandate for Syria and the Lebanon was to the same effect, *ibid.,* p. 1014. The Council of the League, in approving the articles of the mandate for Iraq, decided upon the non-application of the Capitulations in that country " as long as the Treaty of Alliance [between Great Britain and Iraq] is in force." *Ibid.,* 1924, no. 10, p. 1347.

In Palestine, after the articles of the mandate were approved, Great Britain issued an Order in Council, dated August 10, 1922, providing for the judicial régime to be established in the mandated territory. It gave the Civil Courts jurisdicton over foreigners, subject to the following provisos. In offenses punishable with imprisonment for a term exceeding fifteen days or a fine exceeding £E.5, foreigners might claim to be tried by a British magistrate; in offenses not triable by a magistrate, foreigners might claim that their interrogation during the preliminary investigation should be undertaken by a British magistrate; and foreigners committed for trial before the District Court or the Court of Criminal Assize might claim that the Court sholud contain a majority of British judges. In civil cases, they might claim that at least one member of the Court should be a British judge. In civil and criminal cases heard by the Supreme Court in its appellate capacity, a foreigner might claim that the Court should contain a majority of British judges. Matters of personal status affecting foreigners other than Moslems should be decided by the District Court according to the personal law of the parties concerned. The District Court, in trying matters of this nature, should be constituted by the British president sitting alone. Where persons other than British subjects were involved, the president might invite the consul or a representative of the consulate of the foreigner concerned to sit as an assessor for the purpose of advising upon the personal law in question. In case of appeals, the consul or his representative should sit in the same capacity in the Court of Appeal.[1] Up to 1923, all the Powers, except the United States, had ceased to exercise their consular jurisdiction in Palestine.[2]

[1] Great Britain, *Statutory Rules and Orders,* 1922, no. 1282, art. 58, 60, 61, 62, 63, 64.

[2] See *Report on Palestine Administration,* 1923, p. 19.

Following the conclusion of the Treaty of Alliance between Great Britain and Iraq, a number of subsidiary agreements were entered into, one of which, dated March 25, 1924, dealt with jurisdiction over foreigners. In this agreement, substantially the same provisions were made as in the Palestine Order in Council of 1922, with a view to the guarantee of the rights of foreigners in Iraq.[1]

By way of summary, it may be said that in all these cases, according to the terms of the mandates, the Capitulations were merely suspended and that as a condition of this suspension, the Mandatories were charged with the duty of establishing in the respective areas a judicial system calculated to protect the rights of foreigners as well as of natives.

[1] Arts. 2 & 4, Great Britain, *Parl. Pap.*, 1924 [Cmd. 2120], Iraq.

CHAPTER VII

SEPARATION

THE third way in which extraterritorial rights are brought or tend to be brought to an end is by the separation from the parent State of a part of an Oriental country in which the system exists. Here the abolition of consular jurisdiction has not always followed immediately upon the separation, but the tendency has been in the direction of abolition whenever a portion of a Power whose jurisdiction is impaired by treaty is able to assert its independence.

I. GREECE

The independence of Greece in 1830 ended the régime of extraterritoriality in that country, although there was no express provision to that effect in the main acts relating to the establishment of the independent government in Greece. The régime was discontinued, " for the reason, apparently, that the new kingdom was placed under the protection of Great Britain, France, and Russia." [1]

II. ROUMANIA

In Roumania, the foreign Powers began to enjoy the privileges accorded to them by the Turkish Capitulations in the eighteenth century. Russia was the first Power to secure the right to establish a consulate in Moldavia and Wallachia. The treaty of Kutschuk Kaïnardji, July 10/21, 1774, recognized the special interest of Russia in the Danubian Principalities by allowing her to address representa-

---

[1] Hinckley, *American Consular Jurisdiction in the Orient* (Washington, 1906), p. 183.

tions to the Porte on their behalf.[1] This treaty paved the
way for the assumption by Russia of consular jurisdiction
in Roumania, which dated from the unpublished treaty of
1781.[2] The other Powers, including Austria, Prussia,
France and England, established their consulates in the
Danubian Principalities toward the end of the eighteenth
century and at the beginning of the nineteenth.[3]

In the nineteenth century, before the independence of
Roumania was recognized, she made several endeavors to
secure the abrogation of foreign jurisdiction within her
confines. In September, 1857, the Divan of Moldavia discussed the question, and, in the *projet* which was drawn up,
after demonstrating the illegality of applying the Turkish
Capitulations in the Principalities, the Divan contended for
the discontinuance of the foreign rights of extraterritoriality, inasmuch as they had been granted by Turkey under
conditions peculiar to herself and as the laws and judicial
system of Roumania gave sufficient security to the life and
property of her foreign residents. Upon these considerations it was concluded that " the Christian States can have
no interest in maintaining in the Principalities the Capitulations which are not applicable at all and which are the cause
of confusion and of innumerable conflicts," and the wish
(*voeu*) was expressed " that the foreigners who inhabit the
Principalities submit to the jurisdiction of the country." [4]
No action was taken by the Powers.

After the Paris Conference, the treaty of March 30,

[1] Art. 16, Noradounghian, *Recueil,* vol. i, p. 327.

[2] Schoell, *Histoire abrégée des traités de paix* (Paris, 1817-18), vol.
xiv, p. 444. *Cf.* Boéresco, " *La Situation politique des anciennes Prin-
cipautés du Danube avant 1878,*" R. G. D. I .P., vol. iv, pp. 349-350.

[3] *Ibid.,* pp. 351, 352, 354, 356.

[4] *Ibid.,* pp. 369-370.

1856, provided for the meeting of a Special Commission at Bucharest " to inquire into the actual state of the Principalities and to propose the bases for their future organization." [1]   The Commission met at Bucharest the following year and rendered a report, which declared: " Consular jurisdiction having been established originally in the Orient only to protect the Christian foreigners against the Mussulman legislation, its application appears to be an anomaly in a State where there are no Mussulmans and where the legislation is Christian." The Russian Consul added, besides, that this jurisdiction had undergone such an extension that, on the one hand, it assimilated to the status of foreigners and extraterritorialized thousands of working families in the Principalities, and that, on the other, it arrogated to itself the right of deciding cases which, according to the treaties, were within the exclusive competence of the local courts.[2] It was, perhaps, in response to this report that the Russian Government entered into a treaty with the Principalities on November 22, 1869, giving up her extraterritorial rights there.[3]

In 1869, B. Boéresco, then Minister of Justice, published his *Mémoire* on consular jurisdiction in Roumania.   He advanced the theory, as had been done before, that the Capitulations did not apply to the Principalities and that the privileges guaranteed by them should not be maintained by the European Powers.   The arguments on which this theory was based were, briefly, that the sole intention of the negotiators of the Capitulations was to apply them to Mussulman countries; that Roumania, being a Christian country, was not within their purview; that in spite of the suzerainty of Turkey over the Principalities, Roumania had always re-

---

[1] Art. 23, *State Papers*, vol. xlvi, p. 15.

[2] Boéresco, *loc. cit.*, pp. 372-373.

[1] Art. 18, *Archives diplomatiques*, 1874, vol. iv, p. 105.

tained its sovereign rights; that the Sublime Porte having
no judicial power in Roumania, could not confer it upon
foreign Powers; that Roumania having retained its treaty-
making power, the Ottoman Empire could not exercise it
on Roumania's behalf; that the Capitulations had never
been promulgated or published in Roumania, and therefore
were not in force there; that the stipulations of the Capitulations were in conflict with the laws of the Principalities, which
measured up to the standard of those of the other Christian
Powers and which, therefore, excluded the operation of
consular jurisdiction in Roumania; that there were in force
in Roumania a Civil Code, a Penal Code, a Code of Criminal Procedure, a Code of Civil Procedure, and a Commercial Code, all of which were modeled on the best systems
of European jurisprudence; and that although the judicial
officers of Roumania were by no means perfect, measures
were adopted to ensure a stable, independent and efficient
judiciary.[1]

At the end of the Congress of Berlin, in 1878, the privileges of extraterritoriality enjoyed by the Powers in Roumania were retained,[2] although the independence of the
latter was formally recognized.[3] As a matter of fact, however, the system of extraterritoriality in Roumania has long
since fallen into desuetude. Thus, it is said by a German
authority:

Ever since the beginning of their national regeneration, the
Roumanian authorities have refused to enforce the judgments of
the foreign consuls and to lend assistance to the execution of the
judicial acts of the same [consuls], and since the declaration
of independence of March 14/26, 1877, the jurisdiction of the

[1] B. Boéresco, *Mémoire sur la jurisdiction consulaire en Roumanie*
(Bucharest, 1869).

[2] Art. 49, *State Papers*, vol. lxix, p. 764.

[3] Art. 43, *ibid.*, p. 763.

foreign consuls has actually been put an end to, for the idea of
national judicial sovereignty [*Justizhoheit*], which was guaranteed to the Roumanians by article 7 of the Treaty of Paris of
March 18/30, 1856, does not permit a foreign jurisdiction in
their own country.[1]

To-day, a number of treaties are in existence, which
pledge the Roumanian Government to accord "the most
complete protection" to the person and property of their
foreign residents, who, in turn, are held to the same "conditions and formalities" as are prescribed for the natives.[2]
The British treaty of October 31, 1905, is even more explicit. It provides: "They [subjects of either country in
the other] shall, on compliance with the laws of the country, have free access to the Courts of Justice, either for the
prosecution or for the defence of their rights, and in this
respect they shall enjoy all privileges and immunities of
native subjects." [3] No special privileges are given to the
foreigners by these treaties, and during their sojourn in
Roumania they are simply placed on the same footing as the
natives.

III. SERBIA

Before Serbia attained her independence in 1878, attempts
had been made by her to throw off the yoke of extraterritoriality. In 1862, from January 25 to February 5, a conference was held in Belgrade by the foreign Consular Body
to discuss the maintenance of consular jurisdiction in Serbia. At the conference the British, French, Italian, Russian, Prussian and Austrian consuls were present. Although

[1] Leske und Loewenfeld, *Die Rechtsverfolgung im internationalen
Verkehr* (Berlin, 1895-1904), vol. ii, p. 192.

[2] Art. 5, Italian treaty of Aug. 5/17, 1880, *State Papers*, vol. lxxi,
p. 165.

[3] Art. 3, *State Papers,* vol. xcviii, p. 88. *Cf.* art. 2 of French treaty of
March 6, 1907, *ibid.,* vol. ci, p. 319.

some of the members referred to the improved system of law in Serbia, others stressed the insufficiency of a mere improvement of the letter of the law and the necessity of having an impartial judiciary, of whose existence in Serbia they were uncertain.

On the other hand, the Serbian Government contended that legislation in Serbia had reached a high stage of development, that a criminal procedure had long been in force, which afforded the necessary guarantees to the accused, and that the project of a formal code of criminal procedure had been drawn up and was being submitted to the deliberation of the Senate. In view of the development of the Serbian State, the hope was entertained that " the Powers would cease to assert in a Christian country, provided with a European legislation and organization, the privileges adapted to non-Christian countries, in order that in this manner the letter of the Capitulations may hereafter cease to be in opposition to their spirit." [1]

The conference adjourned without doing anything in the interest of the Serbian aspirations. Even after the Berlin Congress of 1878, when the Powers recognized the independence of Serbia,[2] their rights of extraterritoriality remained intact. " The immunities and privileges of the foreign subjects," article 37 of the treaty of July 13, 1878, provided, " as well as the rights of Consular jurisdiction and protection, such as they exist to-day, shall remain in full force so long as they are not modified by common accord between the Principality and the interested Powers." [3]

Soon after the conclusion of the Treaty of Berlin, however, the Powers vied with each other in giving up their

[1] Archives diplomatiques, 1863, vol. ii, pp. 94-114.

[2] Art. 34, Treaty of Berlin, July 13, 1878, State Papers, vol. lxix, p. 761.

[3] Ibid., p. 762.

extraterritorial rights in Serbia. On October 20/November 9, 1879, Italy entered into a convention with Serbia, which recognized the principle that subjects of either party should enjoy " the most constant and complete protection for their person and property " and that, in this regard, they should simply enjoy the same privileges as the natives.[1] In 1880, Great Britain consented " to surrender the privileges and immunities hitherto enjoyed by her subjects in Serbia, in virtue of the Capitulations between Great Britain and the Ottoman Empire." The surrender was made on the specific proviso, " that the said Capitulations shall, as regards all judicial matters, except those affecting real estate in Servia, remain in full force as far as they concern the mutual relations between British subjects and the subjects of those other Powers, which, having a right to the privileges and immunities accorded by the aforesaid Capitulations, shall not have surrendered them." [2] This condition was fulfilled when all the important Powers later made treaties with Serbia, abandoning their jurisdiction in that country. The list includes Austria-Hungary,[3] the United States,[4] Germany [5] and France.[6]

IV. MONTENEGRO

Montenegro was the third of the Balkan triumvirate which gained complete independence after the Congress of Berlin.[7] No disposition was made of the status of the Capitulations in Montenegro, but the Powers had ceased to

---

[1] Art. 2, *State Papers*, vol. lxx, p. 574.

[2] Art. 13, treaty of Jan. 26/Feb. 7, 1880, *ibid.*, vol. lxxi, p. 19.

[3] April 24/May 6, 1881, art. 13, *ibid.*, vol. lxxii, p. 940.

[4] Oct. 14, 1881, art. 12, Malloy, vol. ii, p. 1621.

[5] Jan. 6, 1883, art. 25, *State Papers*, vol. lxxix, p. 541.

[6] Jan. 18, 1883, art. 66, *ibid.*, vol. lxiv, p. 138.

[7] Art. 26, *ibid.*, Treaty of Berlin, July 13, 1878, vol. lxix, p. 758.

exercise their consular jurisdiction there long before Montenegro was merged in the newly established Serb-Croat-Slovene State.[1]

V. BULGARIA

Up to 1878, Bulgaria had been a province of the Ottoman Empire, to which all the Capitulations applied. By the Treaty of Berlin, July 13, 1878, she was constituted into an autonomous tributary principality of the Sultan.[2] The change of the status of Bulgaria, however, did not affect the existence and operation of the Capitulations in that country.[3]

Since the proclamation of her independence in 1908, Bulgaria has entered into consular treaties with Italy,[4] Austria-Hungary[5] and Russia,[6] and also extradition treaties with Austria-Hungary[7] and Russia,[8] all of which omit mention of the status of the Capitulations. Whether it was intended thus to do away permanently with the right of extraterritoriality enjoyed by these powers in Bulgaria may be a moot question. At the Paris Peace Conference of 1919, when the Bulgarian delegation was apprised of the terms of the peace, it raised the point that the above-mentioned treaties actually had the effect of excluding the system of the Capitu-

[1] Leske und Loewenfeld, *op. cit.*, p. 343.

[2] Art. 1, *State Papers*, vol. lxix, p. 751.

[3] Art. 8 of the Treaty of Berlin provides: " The immunities and privileges of the foreign subjects, as well as the rights of consular jurisdiction and protection, such as have been established by the Capitulations and usages, shall remain in full force as long as they are not modified by consent of the interested parties." *Ibid.*, p. 754.

[4] March 10, 1910, *ibid.*, vol. ciii, p. 389.

[5] May 18, 1911, *ibid.*, vol. civ, p. 695.

[6] Oct. 29, 1911, *ibid.*, vol. cvii, p. 693.

[7] May 18, 1911, *ibid.*, vol. civ, p. 720.

Oct. 29, 1911, *ibid.*, vol. cvii, p. 700.

lations and lodged a strong protest against article 175 of the draft treaty,[1] which, as signed at Neuilly on November 27, 1919, provided: " The immunities and privileges of foreigners as well as the rights of jurisdiction and of consular protection enjoyed by the Allied and Associated Powers in Bulgaria by virtue of the Capitulations, usages, and treaties, may form the subject of special conventions between the Powers concerned and Bulgaria." [2]   At the time of writing, no conventions of this sort appear to have been made.

The latest published expression of American policy on the status of the Capitulations in Bulgaria is contained in a note of the Department of State to its representative at Sofia, dated February 12, 1913, which declared:

You are authorized to bring to the knowledge of the Foreign Office, in whatever manner you may deem expedient, the fact that this Government, recognizing that it has no intrinsic right to the benefit of the Capitulations as established by the Treaty of Berlin, stands ready to facilitate the negotiations in which the Bulgarian Government is engaged, by assenting in advance to the relinquishment of such rights as it now enjoys in this respect, at such time as the signatory Powers shall all have consented to the discontinuance of the Capitulatory régime.[3]

The United States Government, however, did not ratify the Treaty of Neuilly of November 27, 1919, and, according to a letter from the Department of State, in answer to the author's inquiry, " no convention of the character contemplated in Article 175 of that treaty has been concluded between the United States and Bulgaria."

[1] *Observations of the Bulgarian Delegation on the Conditions of Peace with Bulgaria* (Paris, 1919), pp. 123-124.

[2] Great Britain, *Treaty Series*, 1920, no. 5, p. [127].

[3] U. S. *Foreign Relations*, 1913, p. 77.

CHAPTER VIII

PROTECTION

THE fourth method whereby extraterritoriality is sometimes abrogated is by the passing of a Power in which such a system exists under the protection of another in which it does not. The form of protection varies according as the treaties which bring it about vary in providing for it. It never involves any change of sovereignty and does not always entail a transfer of jurisdiction. We shall find further on that protection in itself does not *ipso facto* abrogate extraterritoriality. As a rule, the abandonment of foreign jurisdiction in a protectorate is conditioned upon an improvement of the judicial system there consistent with the principles of modern jurisprudence.

I. MADAGASCAR

In Madagascar, as we have seen, extraterritoriality was abolished only after France annexed the island in 1896. While it was under the protection of France, the latter's attempts to seek the consent of Great Britain to the discontinuance of her consular jurisdiction in Madagascar were unfruitful. One of the reasons for the British refusal to comply with the request of France was that the status of the island was not changed by the forcible annexation on the part of France and remained to be that of a protectorate, which should not involve the abrogation of all treaties between Madagascar and other Powers. The United States, likewise, insisted upon a " categorical statement " regarding the effect of the annexation, before she would give up her extraterritorial rights in the island. All this goes to show that the establishment of a protectorate does not necessarily put an end to extraterritoriality in the protected State.[1]

II. ZANZIBAR

Zanzibar became a British protectorate by the treaty of June 14, 1890,[2] and notification was sent out by the British Foreign Office to this effect on November 4.[3] On May 11, 1906, an Order in Council was made public, which established the British judicial system in Zanzibar. According to this Order, the jurisdiction of the British Court " extends to British subjects, to British protected persons, to foreigners with respect to whom the Sultan of Zanzibar has decreed, or the Sovereign or Government whose subjects or citizens they are or are claimed as being, has, by Treaty or otherwise, agreed with His Majesty for, or consented to the exercise of jurisdiction by His Majesty, and to Zanzibar subjects in the regular service of such foreigners." [4] This Order took effect on November 4, 1908,[5] on which date the sultan issued a decree to the same effect.[6]

After the establishment of the British protectorate over Zanzibar, France by a declaration exchanged with the British Government on August 5, 1890, engaged to recognize it as soon as she should receive notification of the same. But it was understood on either side that the establishment of the protectorate would not affect the rights and immunities enjoyed by French citizens in the territory in question.[7] In

---

[1] *Cf. supra*, pp. 104 *et seq.*

[2] *State Papers,* vol lxxxii, p. 653.

[3] *Ibid.,* p. 654; U. S. *Foreign Relations,* 1890, p. 476.

[4] *State Papers,* vol. xcix, p. 461.

[5] *Ibid.,* vol. ci, p. 78.

[6] *Ibid.,* p. 649.

[7] *Parliamentary Papers,* 1890 [C. 6130], Africa, no. 9 (1890), p. 2.

1897, in compliance with a British request in connection with the British rights in Madagascar, France gave the British Government the assurance that she would abandon her extraterritorial jurisdiction in Zanzibar, as soon as regularly constituted judicial authorities should be set up there.[1] This promise was fulfilled in 1904, when France formally gave up her rights of jurisdiction in Zanzibar.[2]

On November 14, 1899, a convention was concluded between Germany and Great Britain, by which the former renounced her rights of extraterritoriality in Zanzibar, the renunciation being understood, however, to take effect only when the other nations had also given up their rights.[3] The condition was deemed by the German Government to have been fulfilled in 1907, when Portugal abandoned her jurisdiction in Zanzibar. Consequently, an exchange of notes was effected on February 25/March 15, 1907, between Germany and Great Britain, giving effect to the renunciation of 1899, and on June 1, 1907, the German emperor issued a decree announcing the abolition of German jurisdiction in Zanzibar.[4]

The United States made a treaty with Great Britain on February 25, 1905, which contained a conditional renunciation of her extraterritorial rights in Zanzibar, similar to that embodied in the German treaty of 1899.[5] After Portugal and Germany definitely gave up their rights, the United States followed suit in 1907.[6]

[1] *Supra*, p. 107.

[2] Exchange of Notes, March 13/18, 1904, *State Papers*, vol. xcix, pp. 357 *et seq.*

[3] *Ibid.*, vol. ci, p. 234.

[4] *Ibid.*, p. 235.

[5] Malloy, vol. i, p. 795.

U. S. *Foreign Relations*, 1907, pt. i, p. 574.

Similar renunciations were made by Italy in 1905,[1] and by Portugal,[2] Belgium,[3] Austria-Hungary[4] and Russia[5] in 1907.

III. TONGA

The German Empire concluded a treaty with Great Britain on November 14, 1899, by which the former renounced in favor of the latter all her rights in Tonga, including those of extraterritoriality.[6]   In 1900, Tonga was placed under British protection. The treaty which established the protectorate provided also that " Her Majesty shall have and exercise jurisdiction . . . in the case of the subjects or citizens of all foreign Powers in Tonga." [7]   The German renunciation took effect on September 1, 1902, by the Imperial Order of June 26, 1902.[8]   The United States was deprived of her jurisdictional rights in Tonga on July 28, 1919, when Lord Curzon, British Foreign Secretary, notified the American Government of the denunciation by Great Britain on behalf of the Queen of Tonga of the treaty of October 2, 1886.[9]

IV. TUNIS

In 1881, Tunis was placed under the protection of France.[10]   On March 27, 1883, the French president promulgated a law, passed by Parliament, establishing a French tribunal and six magistrates' courts in Tunis, to take cog-

---

[1] *State Papers,* vol. xcix, p. 375.

[2] *Ibid.,* vol. ci, p. 237.

[3] *Ibid.,* p. 233.

[4] *Ibid.* p. 232.

[5] *Ibid.,* p. 237.

[6] *Ibid.,* vol. xci, p. 71.

[7] Treaty of May 18, 1900, *State Papers,* vol. cvi, pp. 521, 522.

[8] *Ibid.,* vol. ci, p. 656.

[9] *Ibid.,* vol. cxii, p. 580.

[10] Treaty of May 12, 1881, Rouard de Card, *op. cit.,* p. 232.

nizance of all civil and commercial questions between
Frenchmen and French-protected subjects and of all criminal
cases in which Frenchmen and French-protected subjects are
defendants, and authorizing His Highness the Bey to extend
the jurisdiction of these courts by edicts or decrees with the
assent of the French Government.[1] By virtue of this
authority, the Bey of Tunis issued a decree on May 5, 1883,
to the effect that " the subjects of the friendly Powers whose
Consular Tribunals shall be suppressed shall become amenable to the jurisdiction of the French Tribunals under the
same conditions as the French themselves." [2]

On September 13, 1882, the French Ambassador at London, M. Tissot, spoke informally to Earl Granville, British
Foreign Secretary, on the subject of a proposed judicial reform in Tunis, saying that the French Government intended
to establish in Tunis on January 1, 1883, tribunals which
would render useless the exercise of the rights then existing
under the Capitulations. " There would be no inconvenience," he said, " in the change to foreigners, because the
object of the Capitulations was to defend foreigners from
the injustice to which they would have been exposed by recourse to the Native Courts." The French Government
proposed to do in Tunis, he added, what England had done
in Cyprus. Earl Granville thanked him for the information, but said that the matter required his careful consideration before he could express an opinion.[3]

In his conversation with Sir Julian Pauncefote, British
Under Secretary for Foreign Affairs, on October 4, 1882,
M. Tissot again alluded to the subject of consular jurisdic-
tion in Tunis. In the course of discussion, Sir Julian

[1] *Parliamentary Papers*, 1884 [C. 3843)], Tunis. no. 1 (1884), p. 15.

[2] *Ibid.*, p. 18.

[3] Earl Granville to Mr. Plunkett, Sep. 13, 1882, *Parliamentary Papers*,
1884 [C. 3843], Tunis, no. 1 (1884).

stressed the importance of British interests in Tunis and expressed the desire to know what guarantees the French Government was prepared to offer to these interests. In reply, M. Tissot assured Sir Julian that the judicial institutions which the French Government proposed to establish in Tunis would leave nothing to be desired and that the foreigners in Tunis would find the same security as was afforded to them by the judiciary in France.[1]

The British attitude toward the question of extraterritoriality in Tunis was from the outset favorable to the French point of view. Early in the negotiations, Lord Granville said:

Her Majesty's Government are willing to recognize the justice of the contention that there would be no sufficient reason for maintaining Consular jurisdiction in Tunis when the Native Courts are superseded by French Tribunals. The institutions which have grown up under the Capitulations with Turkey have been found essential for the protection of foreigners under the peculiar circumstances of the Ottoman Empire, and the necessity for them disappears when Tribunals organized and controlled by an European Government take the place of the Mussulman Courts.

Concluding this correspondence, Lord Granville evinced on behalf of his government the readiness to entertain any proposals on the subject the French Government might make, with the proviso that Great Britain would reserve all other rights and privileges, commercial or otherwise, guaranteed to her subjects by treaties.[2]

[1] M. Tissot to M. le Président du Conseil, Ministre des Affaires Étrangères, Oct. 5, 1882, *Publications of the Permanent Court of International Justice* (hereafter referred to as *P. P. C. I. J.*), series c, no. 2, add. vol., p. 287.

[2] Earl Granville to Mr. Plunkett, Oct. 16, 1882, *Parliamentary Paper* cited.

On May 10, 1883, Count d'Aunay left with the British
Foreign Office a *note verbale,* together with copies of the
laws providing for the organization of French jurisdiction
in Tunis. The note adverted once more to the precedent
of England's assumption of jurisdiction over foreigners in
Cyprus, and to the belief on the part of France that England would accord to the French proposal the same reception as France had accorded to the British régime in Cyprus.
It took occasion also to reiterate the judicial guarantees
offered by the laws establishing the French régime in Tunis,
with a view of convincing the British Government of the
acceptability of the French request.[1]

Having taken cognizance of the French note and laws,
Earl Granville expressed his willingness to accede to the
French proposal in the following terms:

As I have had occasion to inform Your Excellency in the
course of conversation on this subject, Her Majesty's Government are quite disposed to waive the rights of this country,
under the Capitulations and Treaties, to the extent which may
be required to give full scope to the exercise of civil and criminal
jurisdiction over British subjects by the new French tribunals.

In a separate Memorandum, inquiries were made as to certain technical details, which do not need to detain us here.[2]
To this Memorandum a reply was made also in the form
of a Memorandum.[3] While this communication was regarded by the British Government as on the whole satisfactory, there still remained some points as to which the British
Government considered that it was called upon to make

[1] *Ibid. Cf.* Le Ministre des Affaires Étrangères à M. Tissot, May 8,
1883, *P. P. C. I. J., loc. cit.,* p. 289.

[2] Earl Granville to M. Tissot, June 20, 1883, *Parliamentary Paper*
cited.

[3] Reply to Memorandum annexed to the Letter from the Foreign
Office of June 20, 1883, *ibid.*

reservations before surrendering British consular jurisdiction in Tunis.   These reservations were:

1. The right of British subjects to challenge assessors in the new Courts.

2. The admission of duly qualified British advocates to practice before the Courts, without this privilege being limited, as at present proposed, to those only who are now established in Tunis.

3. The extension to Great Britain of all privileges reserved to any other Power in connection with the new system of jurisdiction in Tunis.

4. The immediate settlement by arbitration, or otherwise, of outstanding claims of British subjects in Tunis.

5. The cesser of military jurisdiction over British subjects in cases cognizable by the Civil Tribunals.[1]

These reservations were agreed to by the French Government without difficulty.[2]

In the meantime, the British consular authorities in Tunis were informed of the passing of an Order in Council, regarding the cessation of British extraterritoriality there, and they were instructed to take cognizance of no new cases after December 31, 1883.[3]   The Order in Council referred to was issued on December 31, 1883, providing for the cessation of British jurisdiction on January 1, 1884.[4]

On September 18, 1897, an arrangement was entered into between Great Britain and France to the following effect:

Art. 1. The treaties and conventions of every kind in force between the United Kingdom of Great Britain and Ireland and France are extended to the Regency of Tunis.

The Government of Her Britannic Majesty will abstain from

[1] Earl Granville to M. Waddington, Nov. 16, 1883, *Parliamentary Paper* cited.

[2] M. Waddington to Earl Granville, Dec. 29, 1883, *ibid*.

[3] Earl Granville to Dr. Arpa, Dec. 28, 1883, *ibid*.

[4] *State Papers*, vol. lxxiv, p. 695.

claiming for its consuls, its subjects and its establishments in the Regency of Tunis other rights and privileges than those secured for it in France.[1]

Cognizance was taken of this arrangement by the Bey of Tunis, who, on October 16, 1897, decreed the abrogation of all earlier treaties with foreign Powers relative to Tunis.[2]

In a recent case, the British Government took occasion to remind the French Government that what the former had engaged to do in 1883 and 1897 was simply to delegate the exercise of British jurisdiction in Tunis to French tribunals, and not to abolish it irrevocably. The arguments advanced on both sides in connection with this case, so far as they relate to the question of extraterritoriality in Tunis, are essentially a part of our study. Let us first examine briefly the facts of the case.

On November 8, 1921, the French Government published in Tunis and Morocco (French zone) under the sovereignty of the Bey of Tunis and the Sultan of Morocco respectively, certain national decrees, the effect of which was shortly to confer French nationality on persons born in those countries of parents also born there and justiciable before French tribunals.[3] In virtue of these decrees, the French Government claimed to impose the obligations of French nationality on British subjects in Tunis and Morocco (French zone) in such a manner as to override their status as British subjects and render them liable to French military service.

Upon being informed by Consul-General Sarell that the French authorities in Tunis had ordered the enlistment of all British subjects born there in 1902 of parents also born

[1] *Documents diplomatiques, revision des traités tunisiens, 1881-1897*, p. 87.

[2] *Documents diplomatiques, Afrique, 1881-1898*, p. 88.

[3] See *P. P. C. I. J.*, series c, no. 2, add. vol., pp. 120, 121, 158, 159

in Tunis,[1] Lord Hardinge, British Ambassador at Paris, lodged a protest with the French Foreign Office, on January 3, 1922, which contained, among other things, the following statement:

English law provides that persons born of British parents of whatever generation in countries where His Majesty's Government possesses extraterritorial rights, are deemed to have been born within British allegiance and so placed on the same footing as persons who derive British nationality in virtue of birth within the British dominions. In foreign countries where His Majesty's Government do not possess extraterritorial rights, children of British parents of the first generation are British subjects in contemplation of British law. It was not till September 18th, 1897, that His Majesty's Government finally gave up British capitulatory rights in the Regency. It follows, therefore, that in contemplation of English law, all persons born of British parents in Tunis before the 18th September, 1897, and all children of such parents, are British subjects.[2]

In his reply, dated January 10, 1922, M. Poincaré wrote to Lord Hardinge, in answer to the British argument based on the capitulatory rights of Great Britain, that the provision of the English law under which the children of British subjects born in countries where His Majesty has capitulatory rights of jurisdiction are deemed to be born within His Majesty's allegiance dates only from the passing of the British Nationality and Status of Aliens Act of 1914, and cannot, therefore, apply to Tunis, where British capitulatory rights had already ceased; that the capitulatory rights of jurisdiction possessed by Great Britain in Tunis came to a definite end in 1884; that in so far as the Anglo-French arrangement of September 18, 1897, relative to Tunis,

[1] *P. P. C. I. J., loc. cit.*, p. 160.
[2] *Ibid.*, p. 164.

might be held to apply to the question at issue, there was
entire similarity in the treatment of British subjects in that
protectorate and those born in France, inasmuch as the children born in France of foreign parents also born there were
in French law deemed to be French citizens.[1]

On February 6, 1922, Lord Hardinge replied to M. Poincaré on the above points as follows: That the principle of
English law embodied in section (i) of the British Nationality and Status of Aliens Act of 1914 was not of recent
origin but was declaratory of a long-established usage; that
the British extraterritorial rights did not come to an end
in 1884, but that the change effected between Lord Granville and M. Tissot on June 20, 1883, amounted to no more
than the consent of His Majesty's Government to the exercise by the French Government in their behalf of the capitulatory rights of jurisdiction which the British Government
still maintained *vis-à-vis* his Highness the Bey of Tunis;
and that the treatment accorded to British subjects in Tunis
and that accorded to those in France were not similar, since
the latter were given the right to opt against French nationality.   In conclusion, the British Government offered to
submit the dispute to the Permanent Court of International
Justice at the Hague.[2]

M. Poincaré, on the contrary, contended that the principle of the English law referred to above was unknown to
common law, which recognized only the principle of *jus soli,*
whereas the principle of *jus sanguinis* was introduced by
statute law, which made its first appearance in 1914.   Regarding the cessation of the British capitulatory rights in
Tunis in 1884, it was pointed out once more that such was
the case and that, furthermore, in the correspondence between Lord Granville and M. Tissot, in 1883, no mention

[1] *Ibid.,* pp. 167-168.

[2] *Ibid.,* pp. 170-173.

was made of the delegation to France of the rights enjoyed by Great Britain, which had been suggested in Lord Hardinge's note of February 6. Moreover, the British Order in Council of December 31, 1883, had expressly provided for the termination of these rights in Tunis. As to the similarity of treatment accorded to British subjects in Tunis and in France, the French Government admitted that the British observation relative to the right of option was true of the law of 1874, but added that the right was taken away in 1889 from foreigners born in France of parents also born there and that if it was restored by the law of July 22, 1893, it was only in the case where one of the parents who was born in France would not give his or her nationality to the child. Finally, M. Poincaré insisted on treating the question as one of domestic jurisdiction and not subject to arbitration.[1]

On July 14, 1922, a Memorandum prepared by the British Government was communicated by Sir Milne Cheetham, British Chargé d'Affaires at Paris, to the French Government. The arguments stated above were summarized and re-emphasized in the Memorandum, which closed with the wish that the French Government might consent to the submission of the dispute to arbitration and the determined announcement that " should they nevertheless persist in their decision to refuse arbitration, His Majesty's Government will, in this event, have no alternative but to place the whole question before the Council of the League of Nations in accordance with the terms of the Covenant of the League.[2]

In the midst of these negotiations, a report was received at the British Foreign Office that ten British subjects had been arrested by the *gendarmerie* in Tunis and forcibly put

[1] *P. P. C. I. J., loc. cit.*, pp. 178-184.
[2] *Ibid.*, p. 189.

into military uniform.[1]   Protests were lodged by Mr. Andrews with the French Resident-General, and the immediate
release of the British subjects arrested was demanded.[2]   At
the same time, Sir Milne Cheetham protested to M. Poincaré against the proceedings of the French authorities at
Tunis and repeated the declaration that " His Majesty's
Government must hold the French Government responsible
for any losses or damage consequent upon the action taken
by their officials." [3]

In the meantime, the French Government refused its
consent to the submission of the case either to the Permanent Court of International Justice or to the Council of the
League of Nations.[4]   On August 14, Sir Milne Cheetham
informed M. Poincaré of the fact " that, in view of the
attitude displayed by the French Government, His Majesty's
Government have now no alternative but to submit the dispute which has arisen to the Council of the League of Nations; and that they are taking steps with a view to this
question being placed upon the agenda for the Council of the
League at its forthcoming meeting." [5]

Accordingly, the question was submitted by the British
Government to the Council of the League.[6]   On October 4,
1922, the Council adopted a resolution, referring to the Permanent Court of International Justice the question as to
whether the dispute between Great Britain and France " is
or is not by international law solely a matter of domestic

[1] Acting Consul-General Andrews to the Earl of Balfour, July 22,
1922, *ibid.*, p. 192.

[2] *Ibid.*, pp. 198, 199.

[3] Sir Milne Cheetham to M. Poincaré, Aug. 1, 1922, *ibid.*, pp. 200-201.

[4] M. Poincaré to Sir Milne Cheetham, Aug. 5, 1922, *ibid.*, p. 204.

[5] *Ibid.*, p. 205.

[6] League of Nations, *Official Journal,* 3rd. yr., no. ii (pt. ii), p. 1206.

jurisdiction." [1]   After seven sittings, one private and six public, the Court answered the question in the negative.[2]

During the preliminary hearings at the Hague, the French Government submitted its Case, which argued, as in the previous correspondence, that British jurisdiction in Tunis had been terminated since 1884.[3] The British Case, after referring to the treaty of May 12, 1881, which established the French protectorate over Tunis and to the treaty of July 19, 1875, which regulated the relations of Great Britain to Tunis, reviewed the negotiations between France and Great Britain between 1882 and 1883 regarding the cessation of British extraterritoriality in Tunis. The note of Lord Granville to M. Tissot, June 20, 1883, was cited to show " that it merely amounts to a consent on the part of Great Britain to allow French tribunals to exercise on its behalf capitulatory rights of jurisdiction, which it still maintained *vis-à-vis* the Bey of Tunis."   Then, the Order in Council of December 31, 1883, was quoted, and commenting on this Order, the British Case said:

It will be observed that by the terms of this Order in Council, the jurisdiction which Her Majesty abandoned was expressly limited to " such matters and cases as come within the jurisdiction of the said French tribunals," and further, that it is only " the operation of the Orders in Council regulating Her Majesty's Consular Jurisdiction in Tunis," which is determined and not the convention with the Bey of Tunis whereby capitulatory rights of jurisdiction were conferred upon Her Majesty.

The arrangement of September 18, 1897, was likewise referred to and quoted, and certain modifications of it agreed upon in 1919 between the British and French Governments were taken note of. In conclusion, the British Case declared:

[1] *P. P. C. I. J.*, series b, no. 4, p. 8.
[2] *Ibid.*, p. 32.
[3] *Ibid.*, ser. c, no. 2, add. vol., p. 30.

It is desired to be pointed out that (in the submission of His Majesty's Government) neither by the Convention of 1897, nor by the modifications introduced by the aforesaid notes were the rights of Great Britain as against the Bey of Tunis under the Convention of 1875 between Great Britain and Tunis affected.[1]

In reply to the British Case, the French Government submitted its Counter-Case, wherein they reviewed the diplomatic correspondence had with England on the subject and reasserted that the renunciation of British jurisdiction in Tunis took place in 1883 with the issuance of the Order in Council of December 31, and not in 1897. The Counter-Case further stated:

Even if the Note of June 20, 1883, and the Order in Council of December 31 of the same year, were not to be considered as a complete abandonment of the Capitulations, it seems difficult [to maintain] that after the Arrangement of September 18, 1897, Great Britain could still affirm that her relations with Tunis continue to be regulated by the general Anglo-Tunisian Treaty of July 19, 1875.

Referring to the British argument that the British rights of extraterritoriality in Tunis were simply delegated to the French tribunals there and were not definitively abandoned, the French Counter-Case observed:

This allegation is materially inexact. France, the protector of Tunis, renders justice in Tunis, not in the name of the foreign Powers, but in her own name. The suppression of foreign consular jurisdiction has been effected, not by delegation to France of the exercise of rights whose enjoyment belonged to the Powers and which they might still revive, but by extinction, to the benefit of the Bey of Tunis, of rights retransferred by the latter to France. This is so true that the Bey of Tunis himself,

[1] *Ibid.*, pp. 41-44.

by a decree of May 5, 1883, declared that in case of the renunciation by the Powers of their privileges of jurisdiction, he would
renounce the exercise of the right of jurisdiction which he
would then recover, normally, in full. From the legal analysis
of the extinction of the Capitulations in Tunis, it follows that
it is not each of the Treaty Powers that transmits to France
its rights of consular jurisdiction, but it is Tunis that transmits
to France the exercise of a right of jurisdiction, the enjoyment of which she [Tunis] has, under the condition of the
exercise, recovered.

Finally, the French advanced the argument that all the
treaties and conventions between Tunis and foreign Powers
had been definitely abrogated by decrees of the Bey of Tunis
at one time or other,[1] and that they had been superseded by
arrangements of a different nature, entitling the Powers to
no greater privileges in Tunis than were granted to them in
France, so that the rights of consular jurisdiction were abolished once and for all and could not be revived.[2]

To the French Case the British Government submitted a
reply in the form of a Counter-Case, which asserted:

It is the contention of His Majesty's Government, as explained in the British Case, that the convention of 1875 between
Great Britain and Tunis, under which capitulatory rights were
conferred upon Great Britain, was, on November 8th, 1921, and
still is, in force as between Great Britain and Tunis. . . . By
the delegation to France in 1883 of the exercise of British rights
and the Convention of 1897, both of which were a consequence
of the recognition of the French régime of Protection, Great
Britain did not forego its capitulatory rights as against the Bey.
There is no basis either in Lord Granville's note of June 20th,
1883, or the Convention for such a result, which would be

---

[1] See the Decrees of Feb. 1, Aug. 30 and Oct. 16, 1897, *ibid.*, pp. 333,
337, 338.

[2] *Ibid.*, pp. 234-250.

clearly contrary to the intention of the parties concerned, having regard to the safeguards consistently demanded and obtained by European States in Mussulman countries.[1]

To sum up the arguments of both sides before the Permanent Court of International Justice at the Hague, in so far as they related to the status of British extraterritoriality in Tunis: The British Government contended that the note of Lord Granville of June 20, 1883, merely signified the consent of the British Government to the exercise by the French tribunals on behalf of the British Government of rights which were maintained *vis-à-vis* the Bey of Tunis; that the Order in Council of December 31, 1883, instead of abrogating the British treaty of 1875 with Tunis, terminated only the operation of the Orders in Council regulating British jurisdiction in Tunis and limited the British renunciation to " such matters and cases as come within the jurisdiction of the said French tribunals "; that neither by the convention of September 18, 1897, nor by the modifications introduced by the notes of 1919, did the British Government forego its rights as against the Bey of Tunis; and that, therefore, the convention of July 19, 1875, between Great Britain and Tunis " was, on November 8th, 1921, and still is, in force as between Great Britain and Tunis." On the other hand, the French Government took the position that the note of June 20, 1883, and the Order in Council of December 31 of the same year, amounted to a complete abandonment of British jurisdiction in Tunis; that even if these documents could not be so regarded, the arrangement of September 18, 1897, must be construed to mean such a renunciation; that the rights of jurisdiction exercised by France in Tunis were not delegated by the Powers but expressly by the Bey of Tunis himself by virtue of his Decree of May 5, 1883; that successive Decrees of the Bey in 1897

[1] *Ibid.*, p. 459.

had announced the definite abrogation of all the treaties with foreign Powers which contained extraterritorial provisions; and that, therefore, the treaty of July 19, 1875, between Great Britain and Tunis had become null and void.

In the question referred to the Permanent Court of International Justice, the latter was not called upon to pass on the merits of the case; what it was requested to do was only to decide whether the question at issue between France and Great Britain " is or is not by international law solely a matter of domestic jurisdiction." Consequently, in the opinion rendered by the Court, it merely took note of the " different views " taken by the two Governments " with regard to the scope of the declarations made by Great Britain in this respect and also with regard to the construction to be placed upon the Arrangement of 1897," [1] without taking upon itself to pass upon these views; and with respect to the main question submitted to it, the Court ruled that it should be answered in the negative, that is to say, that the dispute " is not by international law solely a matter of domestic jurisdiction." [2]

By an exchange of notes effected between the Marquess Curzon of Kedleston and Count de Saint-Aulaire on May 24, 1923, at London, it was agreed, on certain conditions, to discontinue the proceedings relative to the French Nationality Decrees, but " it is of course understood that in agreeing to discontinue the proceedings at the Hague, neither His Majesty's Government nor the French Government abandon the point of view which they have maintained in the diplomatic correspondence and in the preliminary hearings at the Hague." [3]

Thus, the question is still an open one, for definite settle-

[1] *P. P. C. I. J.*, series b, no. 4, p. 29.

[2] *Ibid.*, p. 32.

[3] Great Britain, *Treaty Series*, no. 11 (1923).

ment has been avoided. Leaving aside the technical bearings of the rights of extraterritoriality on the question of nationality, one may well conjecture that so long as France maintains regularly constituted judicial authorities in Tunis, it is quite unlikely that Great Britain will ever reassert its extraterritorial jurisdiction in the Regency on the basis of the treaty of July 19, 1875, which is claimed by the British Government still to be in force. However, the mere fact that Great Britain takes issue with the view that she abandoned her capitulary rights as against the bey of Tunis and maintains that she delegated the rights to be exercised by France in her behalf leads to two inevitable conclusions: (1) That the establishment of a protectorate does not *ipso facto* terminate existing treaty rights enjoyed by third parties in the protectorate, including those of extraterritoriality; and (2) that wherever these rights of jurisdiction are given up, they are abandoned because of a general improvement of the native judicial system brought about by the protecting State. This is assuming that the British view is the correct one.

The negotiations between France and Italy for the suspension of the latter's capitulatory rights in Tunis are equally suggestive of these views. It was on February 8, 1883, that the formal opening of the conversations on the subject in question took place between France and Italy. In discussing the question, the Italian Minister, Mancini, emphasized the guarantees to be offered by the new French judicial system, and inquired as to what was precisely proposed to be done in this respect.[1] After a number of conditions were laid down by the one party and fulfilled by the other,[2] the Italian Government finally agreed to the suspen-

---

[1] Minister of Foreign Affairs to the Italian Ambassador at Paris, Feb. 9, 1883, *Archives diplomatiques*, 1884, vol. iv, pp. 263, 264.

[2] *Ibid.*, p. 282; 1885, vol. i, pp. 65, 69, 72-74, 74-77, 80, 84-88.

sion of Italy's consular jurisdiction in Tunis. The protocol
of suspension was signed on January 25, 1884, and by it
the Italian Government agreed to "suspend in Tunis the
exercise of the jurisdiction of the Italian Consular Courts,"
this jurisdiction to be "transferred to the Courts recently
instituted in Tunis, whose competence His Highness the
Bey, by a Decree of May 5, 1883, extended to the nationals
of the States which should consent to cause their own Consular Courts to cease functioning." [1]

Before this agreement was reached, however, it had been
expressly declared by the Italian Government (1) that what
was abandoned by the latter was merely its judicial competence in Tunis, all other immunities and guarantees flowing
from the Capitulations, usages and treaties, remaining in
full force; (2) that the Italian Government, in view of the
substitution of the Tunisian Courts by a French régime,
agreed merely to a suspension of their extraterritorial
rights; and (3) that this suspension was conditioned on the
equal adhesion of all the other Powers, and that whatever
privileges and immunities were extended to them should
equally be extended to Italy.[2]

Other Powers have followed in the footsteps of England
and Italy in suspending or abandoning their extraterritorial
rights. According to the language of the declarations made
by these Powers, these documents may be divided into two
categories. Some of them provide for the renunciation of
the right of invoking the Capitulations, while others merely
express the intention to abstain from claiming any more
privileges in Tunis than are accorded to them in France.

[1] *State Papers,* vol. lxxv, p. 469.

[2] *Aide-Mémoire* of the Minister of Foreign Aaffairs to the Ambassador
of France, July 13, 1883, *Archives diplomatiques,* 1884, vol. iv, p. 281;
also The Minister of Foreign Affairs to the Italian Consul-General at
Tunis, *ibid.,* 1885, vol. i, pp. 83-84.

An example of the first group is the declaration between Austria-Hungary and France, dated July 20, 1896, which stipulated:

Austria-Hungary declares that it renounces the right of invoking in Tunis the régime of the Capitulations and that it will refrain from claiming there for its Consuls and its Nationals other rights than those acquired for them in France in virtue of the treaties existing between Austria-Hungary and France.[1]

Declarations similar to this were made by Germany, November 18, 1896,[2] Belgium, January 2, 1897,[3] and the United States, March 15, 1904.[4]

Examples of the second group are more numerous than of the first. Their language is similar, save in the former the engagement to " renounce the right of invoking the régime of the Capitulations " is conspicuously absent. To this group belong the declarations of Russia, October 2/14, 1896,[5] Switzerland, October 14, 1896,[6] Spain, January 12, 1897,[7] Denmark, January 26, 1897,[8] the Netherlands, April 3, 1897,[9] Sweden and Norway, May 5, 1897,[10] and the arrangement between France and Great Britain, September 18, 1897.[11]

---

[1] *Documents diplomatiques, revision des traités tunisiens, 1881-1897*, p. 47.

[2] *Ibid.*, p. 74.

[3] *Ibid.*

[4] Malloy, vol. i, p. 545.

[5] *Doc. dip. cited*, p. 73.

[6] *Ibid.*

[7] *Ibid.*, p. 75.

[8] *Ibid.*, p. 76.

[9] *Ibid.*

[10] *Ibid.*, p. 77.

[11] *Ibid.*, p. 78.

In all these cases, some difficulty may be encountered in ascertaining the precise extent of the abstention. If we take the British view as a standard, which is, at least as far as France is concerned, open to question, the second group of declarations must be construed to mean that the Capitulations were not abrogated, although the exercise of the rights conferred by them was suspended by these declarations. Whether any difference of interpretation was intended by the insertion, in the first group of declarations, of the engagement " to renounce the right of invoking the régime of the Capitulations," and whether an abstention greater in extent than was embodied in the second group of arrangements was intended, are disputable questions. But it appears from the absence, in either group, of any specific renunciation of the Capitulations that both may be regarded as connoting the same thing. Although it is not expressly so stated in the declarations of the second group, what is terminated by them is, as by those of the first group, the right of invoking the Capitulations and not the Capitulations themselves. This is again taking it for granted that the British view is the correct one.

As has been mentioned above, all the treaties and conventions between Tunis and the foreign Powers were declared to be and to remain " definitely abrogated " by decrees of the bey, dated respectively February 1, August 30 and October 16, 1897.[1] Whether the action of the bey is tantamount to the intended nullification is a question still unanswered.

V. MOROCCO

On March 30, 1912, Morocco was by treaty placed under the protection of France.[2] Eight months later, on Novem-

[1] *Documents diplomatiques, Afrique, 1881-1898*, pp. 85, 87, 88.
[2] *State Papers*, vol. cvi, p. 1023.

ber 27, by a treaty concluded with Spain, France recognized
the latter's interests in the Spanish "zone of influence" in
the Shereefian Empire.[1]

In both the French and Spanish zones, steps have been
taken by the majority of the Powers to renounce their extraterritorial rights, but there are some exceptions to the rule.

One of the Powers which has not yet given up its extraterritorial jurisdiction in Morocco (French zone) is Great
Britain. Although the secret articles annexed to the Anglo-
French declaration of April 8, 1904, expressed the willingness of the British Government to entertain any suggestions
that the French Government might make with regard to
judicial reforms in Morocco,[2] Great Britain has shown no
sign of transferring her rights of jurisdiction in the Shereefian Empire to the established French courts. On the
contrary, she has insisted on their maintenance by the British
authorities. An occasion for the unmistakable reaffirmation
of the British policy relating to this question in Morocco,
as in Tunis, was furnished by the case of the French Nationality Decrees.

The facts of the case have been related above.[3] After
the French Government sought to apply to the British subjects in Morocco the decrees in question, Lord Hardinge,

[1] Art. 1, *ibid.*, p. 1025.

[2] "Article 2. His Britannic Majesty's Government have no present
intention of proposing to the Powers any changes in the system of the
Capitulations, or in the judicial organization of Egypt. In the event
of their considering it desirable to introduce in Egypt reforms tending
to assimilate the Egyptian legislative system to that in force in other
civilized countries, the Government of the French Republic will not
refuse to entertain any such proposals, on the understanding that His
Britannic Majesty's Government will agree to entertain the suggestions
that the Government of the French Republic may have to make to
them with a view of introducing similar reforms in Morocco." *P. P.
C. I. J.,* ser. c, no. 2, add. vol., p. 501.

[3] *Supra,* pp. 147 *et seq.*

British Ambassador at Paris, protested that such a position was untenable on account of the capitulatory rights still enjoyed by the British subjects in Morocco.[1] In a later despatch, the British Government further contended that the Nationality Act of 1914, which regarded as British subjects those who were born of British parents in countries where Great Britain enjoyed extraterritorial rights, was merely declaratory of existing practice, and that France could not establish the principle of *jus soli* in a country over which it had no sovereign rights, but exercised only the powers of a protectorate. The note suggested that unless the French Government withdrew the decrees from application to British subjects, His Majesty's Government could only reiterate the demand that the question be referred to arbitration.[2]

In reply, M. Poincaré, in addition to denying the existence in English law of the principle of the Act of 1914, claimed that " responsible for the order and reforms in the French zone of the Shereefian Empire, the French Government has, conjointly with the Sultan, the sovereign right to legislate on the nationality of the descendants of foreigners, in virtue of their birth on the territory, from the moment the foreign Powers which claim them have, in accepting the protectorate, abdicated all title to the maintenance of the prolongation of their jurisdictional privileges." The exercise of this sovereign right, it was argued, was not a subject for arbitration.[3]

The British Memorandum of July 14, 1922, referring to Morocco, merely stated that " the question does not indeed, at present, arise so far as concerns British subjects, seeing that British capitulatory rights exist, and the British com-

---

[1] Lord Hardinge to M. Poincaré, Jan. 10, 1922. *P. P. C. I. J.*, series c, no. 2, add vol. p. 165.

[2] Same to Same, Feb. 28, 1922, *ibid.*, pp. 176-178.

[3] M. Poincaré to Lord Hardinge, April 7, 1922, *ibid.*, pp. 185, 186.

munity in Morocco are therefore [subject?] neither to native
nor to French legislation." [1]

Finally, as has been seen, the question was submitted by
the British Government to the Council of the League of
Nations, and by the latter it was referred to the Permanent
Court of International Justice, which was requested to decide whether the dispute between France and Great Britain
was or was not by international law solely a matter of domestic jurisdiction.

Before the Permanent Court of International Justice, the
French Government admitted in their Case that the British
Government still exercised capitulatory rights in Morocco,
but contended that the refusal of Great Britain to close her
consular courts in Morocco was illegitimate and in contra-
vention of the engagement which she had made in adhering
to the Franco-German convention of November 4, 1911,[2]
to recognize the French tribunals when they should be constituted and then to renounce, in concert with the other
Powers, her judicial régime in Morocco.[3]

After referring to the French treaty of 1912 establishing
the protectorate over Morocco, and the British treaty of
1856 regulating the relations between Great Britain and
Morocco, the British Case went on to say:

[1] *Ibid.*, p. 191.

[2] " Art. 9. In order to avoid, as far as possible, diplomatic representations, the French Government will urge the Moorish Government to
refer to an arbitrator, nominated *ad hoc* in each case by agreement
between the French consul and the consul of the Power interested, or,
failing them, by the two Governments, such complaints brought by
foreign subjects against the Moorish authorities or agents acting in the
capacity of Moorish authorities as shall not have been found capable of
adjustment through the intermediary of the French consul and the
consul of the Power interested. This mode of procedure shall remain
in force until such time as a judicial system, founded on the general
principles embodied in the legislation of the Powers interested, shall
have been introduced, which shall ultimately, by agreement between
those Powers, replace the consular courts." *Ibid.*, p. 508.

[3] *Ibid.*, p. 30.

The capitulatory rights of jurisdiction conferred upon His Britannic Majesty by the above treaty are still being exercised by His Majesty's Consular Courts in Morocco, there has been no delegation of those rights to the French tribunals, as in the case of Tunis, nor have those rights been waived, abandoned, or modified in any way.[1]

The Counter-Case of the French Government again relied upon the British adhesion to the Franco-German convention of 1911 as a ground for holding that " Great Britain is not free to delay indefinitely the recognition of the French courts " in Morocco, and added that " the same effects which are deduced in Tunis from the creation of the French courts of the Protectorate, should be deduced in Morocco from the same creation." [2]

In the British Counter-Case, it was reiterated that " in Morocco His Majesty's capitulatory rights were, on November 8th, 1921, and still are, indisputably, in full vigour, and in direct exercise by the British Authorities." [3]

To the French argument that the British Government should put an end to their extraterritorial rights in Morocco on account of their adhesion to the Franco-German convention of 1911, the British Counter-Case devoted an extended refutation. In the first place, it was declared, the Franco-German convention of 1911 was not an agreement for the suppression of the Capitulations; what it did was to provide a means of dealing with the claims by foreigners against the Moorish authorities prior to the establishment of the new French judicial system. The wording of article 9 clearly contemplated that the replacement of the consular courts by the new régime could only be effected by agreement between the Powers concerned. Moreover, as between

[1] *P. P. C. I. J., loc. cit.*, p. 54.
[2] *Ibid.*, p. 252.
[3] *Ibid.*, p. 464.

France and Great Britain, the question of the Capitulations
in Egypt and Morocco was already regulated by article 2 of
the Anglo-French declaration of 1904, in which the British
Government agreed to " entertain proposals " for the abolition of the Capitulations in Morocco on condition that the
French Government would do the same in Egypt, and the
British Government, by acceding to the Franco-German convention of 1911, had no intention of substituting " the introduction of the new judicial system in Morocco for the
abolition of Capitulations in Egypt as the date on which
His Majesty's Government were pledged to abandon their
rights." Article 2 of the Anglo-French declaration of 1904
still held good, and article 9 of the 1911 convention could
only be regarded as subordinate thereto. Furthermore, the
French assumption that the British accession to the convention of 1911 was unconditional was shown to be incompatible with the facts, as the accession was explicitly declared
to be conditional on the internationalization of Tangier, " a
condition which has not yet been fulfilled." Finally, it was
asserted by the British Counter-Case that after the British
accession to the convention of 1911, negotiations were
opened between Great Britain and France for the reciprocal
abrogation of the Capitulations in Egypt and Morocco, but
that it was due to the refusal of the French Government to
sign the draft convention that the British consular tribunals
still remained in existence in Morocco.[1]

To sum up, the position taken respectively by the British
and French Governments is perfectly simple and intelligible.
The French Government held Great Britain to the engagement of 1911, which, according to the latter, could not be
brought into effect, so long as the French Government failed
and refused to live up to the conditions on which the adhesion of Great Britain had been made. It was contended

[1] *Ibid.*, pp. 471-473. Draft convention referred to given on p. 518.

by the British, and admitted by the French Government, that the capitulatory rights enjoyed by Great Britain in Morocco had never been given up and were still in force.

By a convention signed at Paris, on December 18, 1923,[1] by Great Britain, France and Spain, regarding the organization of the statute of the Tangier Zone, it was agreed that the Capitulations should be abolished in the Zone and that a Mixed Court should be established to replace the existing consular jurisdictions.[2]   The details of the new Mixed Court of Tangier were regulated by a special *dahir* annexed to the convention.   According to the *dahir*, the Mixed Court should be composed of four titular members, including one French, one Spanish, and two British magistrates, and of a number of deputy members (*membres adjoints*), including subjects or citizens of each of the Powers signatory to the Act of Algeciras, except Germany, Austria and Hungary.[3]

In 1913, the French Government requested the United States Secretary of State to recognize the French protectorate over Morocco and to renounce American consular jurisdiction in the Shereefian Empire.[4]   In his reply, dated February 13, 1914, Mr. John Bassett Moore, Acting Secretary of State, conditioned the recognition of the reforms adopted by the French Government in Morocco on the settlement of certain pending issues regarding American interests in Morocco.[5]   The negotiations went on until the War intervened.   In 1915, the attention of the United States Government was called to the decision of the French Resident-General that pending the duration of a state of siege which

[1] Great Britain, *Treaty Series*, no. 23 (1924). Ratifications were deposited May 14, 1924, *ibid.*, p. 3.

[2] Arts. 13, 48, *ibid.*, pp. 9, 41.

[3] Art. 1, *ibid.*, p. 64.

[4] U. S. *Foreign Relations*, 1914, pp. 905, 906.

[5] *Ibid.*, pp. 907-914.

had been declared, certain cases hitherto tried before the
civil courts should be transferred to the French military
courts, even if the offenders were citizens of a country enjoying capitulatory rights.[1] Thereupon, Mr. F. L. Polk,
Acting Secretary of State, took occasion to reassert the
rights of the United States and instructed the American
Ambassador at Paris to bring to the notice of the French
Government the action of the French Resident-General in
Morocco and " to protest against it in so far as it affects
citizens of the United States." [2] Since that date, nothing
further has been published as to the progress of the negotiations for the abrogation of American extraterritorial
rights in Morocco.[3]

The majority of the Powers have, however, relinquished
their extraterritoriality in Morocco (French zone). These
include Russia, January 15 (18), 1914;[4] Spain, March 7,
1914;[5] Norway, May 5, 1914;[6] Greece, May 8 (21),
1914;[7] Sweden, June 4, 1914;[8] Switzerland, June 11,

[1] Chargé Blake to the Secretary of State, Dec. 8, 1915, U. S. *Foreign
Relations*, 1915, p. 1097.

[2] The Acting Secretary of State to Ambassador Sharp, Dec. 29, 1915,
ibid., p. 1098.

[3] In reply to an inquiry addressed by the author, the Department of
State informs him that the judicial status of American citizens in
Morocco has not changed since 1913. "The recognition of the French
protectorate," says the Department's letter, "by a note of January 15,
1917, from the Secretary of State to the French Ambassador at Washington was given upon the understanding that the question of the recognition of the protectorate was distinct from that of the modification of extraterritorial rights." The American Government, moreover,
has not adhered to the Tangier Convention of Dec. 18, 1923.

[4] *State Papers*, vol. cvii, p. 821.

[5] *Ibid.*, vol. cix, p. 939.

[6] *Ibid.*, vol. cvii, p. 818.

[7] *Ibid.*, vol. cviii, p. 876.

[8] *Ibid.*, p. 877.

1914;[1] Denmark, May 12, 1915;[2] Bolivia, June 21, 1915;[3] Japan, July 14, 1915;[4] Belgium, September 22, 1915;[5] Italy, March 9, 1916;[6] Portugal, April 6, 1916;[7] the Netherlands, May 26, 1916;[8] and Costa Rica, May 31, 1916.[9] All the declarations made by these Powers with France give as the ground for relinquishing their extraterritorial jurisdiction in Morocco (French zone) the improved judicial system in the Shereefian Empire under French protection; they all begin with the statement, "Taking into consideration the guarantees of judicial equality offered to foreigners by the French Tribunals of the protectorate, etc."

By the Treaty of Versailles, June 28, 1919, Germany, having recognized the French protectorate in Morocco, agreed to accept all the consequences of its establishment, and thereby renounced the régime of Capitulations therein, such renunciation taking effect from August 3, 1914.[10] A similar renunciation was made by Austria in the Treaty of St. Germain, September 10, 1919,[11] and by Hungary in the Treaty of Trianon, June 4, 1920.[12]

In the Spanish, as in the French zone of Morocco, Great

---

[1] *State Papers*, vol. cxiii, p. 1042.

[2] *Ibid.*, vol. cix, p. 913.

[3] *Ibid.*, p. 872.

[4] *Ibid.*, p. 939.

[5] *Ibid.*, p. 871.

[6] *Ibid.*, vol. cxiv, p. 767.

[7] *Ibid.*, vol. cx, p. 878.

[8] *Ibid.*, p. 875.

[9] *Ibid.*, p. 835.

[10] Art. 142, *Treaty of Peace between the Allied and Associated Powers and Germany* (London, 1919), p. 73.

[11] Art. 97, *Treaty of Peace between the Allied and Associated Powers and Austria* (London, 1921), p. 41.

[12] Art. 81, Great Britain, *Treaty Series*, no. 10 (1920), p. 23.

Britain and the United States do not seem to have made any express renunciation of their extraterritorial rights. All the other Powers, however, have definitely given up their privileges of jurisdiction there. These include France, November 17, 1914;[1] Norway, March 9, 1915;[2] Russia, May 4 (17), 1915;[3] Sweden, May 5, 1915;[4] Belgium, December 29, 1915;[5] Denmark, January 29, 1916;[6] Italy, November 28, 1916;[7] Greece, May 17 (30), 1917;[8] and Portugal, July 20, 1918.[9] The declarations made by these Powers with Spain, as in the case of the French zone, all mention the fact of the guarantees of judicial equality offered to foreigners by the Spanish tribunals in Morocco as justifying the abandonment of consular jurisdiction.

VI. EGYPT

In Egypt, under Mehemet Ali and his successors, the privileges of the Capitulations received such an extension that they constituted a total departure from the terms of the Capitulations themselves, and, in effect, a gross violation of these treaties. The foreign consuls usurped power which was not conferred upon them, and altogether the situation presented a spectacle of an unfounded invasion of the sovereignty of the territorial power.[10]

[1] *State Papers*, vol. cviii, p. 470.

[2] *Ibid.*, vol. civ, p. 986.

[3] *Ibid.*, p. 1011.

[4] *Ibid.*, vol. cxii, p. 1165.

[5] *Ibid.*, vol. cix, p. 871.

[6] *Ibid.*, vol. cx, p. 842.

[7] *Ibid.*, p. 915.

[8] *Ibid.*, vol. cxii, p. 1108.

[9] *Ibid.*, vol. cxiv, p. 950.

[10] Scott, *The Law Affecting Foreigners in Egypt* (rev. ed., Edinburgh, 1908), pp. 196-200.

The abuses indulged in by the foreign consuls called forth
the report of Nubar Pasha, Minister of Foreign Affairs, to
the Khedive Ismail, appealing for the speedy amelioration
of the situation.[1] This report was transmitted to the
Powers, and after eight years of protracted negotiation, the
régime of the Mixed Courts was established in 1875 and
went into operation on February 1, 1876. "The privilege
of jurisdiction," says Scott, "was very considerably modified by the institution of the Egyptian Mixed Tribunals in
1876. The principal result of the reform was to reduce the
competence of the Consular Courts; but, although greatly
restricted, the jurisdiction of the consuls was not abolished.
They still retained their competence in questions of personal
status, in actions where both parties were their nationals,
and in cases of crime and delict where the accused was their
fellow-subject." [2]

The régime set up in 1876 consists of three courts of first
instance, which have their seats respectively in Alexandria,
Cairo and Mansourah, and a court of appeal at Alexandria.[3]
"The Court of First Instance at Alexandria has a Bench of
eighteen judges, twelve of whom are foreigners and six
natives; the court of Cairo has thirteen foreign and six
native judges; the Mansourah court has six foreign and
three native judges; while the Court of Appeal has a Bench
of fifteen judges, ten of whom are foreign and five native." [4]
All these judges are appointed by the Egyptian Government,
but to assure the competence of the foreign judges, the
latter must be nominated by their own governments.[5] These

[1] *Documents diplomatiques,* no. xiii, Nov. 1869, p. 77.

[2] Scott, *op cit.,* p. 209.

[3] *Réglement d'Organisation Judiciaire pour les Procès Mixtes en Égypte,* tit. i, ch. i, arts. 1, 3, *State Papers,* vol. lxvi, p. 593.

[4] Scott, *op. cit.,* p. 210.

[5] *Réglement,* tit. i, ch. 1, art. 5, *State Papers,* vol. lxvi, p. 593.

judges, whether native or foreign, are all declared to be irremovable, thus guaranteeing their absolute independence.[1]

The civil jurisdiction of the Mixed Courts extends to all cases, except those of personal status, between foreigners and natives and between foreigners of different nationalities; to all cases of immovable property between natives and foreigners or between foreigners of the same nationality or of different nationalities.[2] Owing to the incompetence of the native courts during the early days of the Mixed Court régime, the jurisdiction of the Mixed Tribunals has been considerably extended by judicial interpretation, so as to cover cases which would not come under their competence, if strict regard were had to the original articles of the *Réglement.* Thus, by applying the theory of "mixed interest," it has been held that cases involving the interest of a third party, even if they may be between persons of the same nationality, are cognizable by the Mixed Courts.[3] The penal jurisdiction of the Mixed Courts embraces police contraventions committed by one foreigner against another or a native, and certain delicts and crimes committed by or against the judges and officials of the Mixed Courts.[4]

In civil matters, the First Instance Courts are divided into (1) the Summary Court, (2) the Civil Court, (3) the Commercial Court, and (4) the *Tribunal des Référés.* The Summary Court consists of one judge, whose duty is first to conciliate parties in dispute, and, in case this is impossible, to decide some civil cases of a certain value in first instance and others in last resort. The Civil Court is composed of five judges, three of whom are foreign and two native, and

---

[1] *Réglement,* tit. i, ch. i, art. 19, *ibid.,* p. 595.

[2] *Réglement,* tit. i, ch. i, art. 19, as modified by Decree (1) of March 26, 1900, art. 1, *ibid.,* p. 594; vol. xciv, p. 882.

[3] Scott, *op. cit.,* pp. 219 *et seq.*

[4] *Réglement,* tit. ii, ch. i, arts. 6-9, *State Papers,* vol. lxiv, pp. 598-9.

takes cognizance, in first instance, of all civil cases not deferred to the Summary Court, and, on appeal, of all judgments rendered by the last court in all matters other than possessory actions and actions of restoration (*reintégrande*) and actions respecting leases of wakf lands, which are taken before the Court of Appeal. The Commercial Court is made up of five judges, three foreign and two native, and decides, in first instance, all cases which are considered as commercial by the rules of the Commercial Code, other than those which are deferred to the Summary Court. The *Tribunal des Référés* is held by one judge, who shall decide after hearing both parties, in civil as well as commercial matters, what summary measures are to be taken without prejudice to the question at issue, and on the execution of judgments without prejudice to questions of interpretation.[1]

Penal matters are of three kinds, police contraventions, delicts and crimes. The court for the contraventions consists of a single foreign judge. For the delicts, a Correctional Court is created, of which two judges are foreign and one native, assisted by four assessors. The latter should all be of foreign nationality, if the defendant is a foreigner. If the defendant is native, half of the assessors should be native. Finally, the Court of Assizes, which is competent to try crimes, consists of three judges of the Court of Appeal, of whom two are foreign and one native. The Court of Assizes is assisted by twelve jurymen, half of whom should be of the nationality of the defendant.[2]

---

[1] *Code de Procédure Civile et Commerciale Mixte,* tit. i, ch. i, arts. 26, 29, 32, 33, 34, Wathelet et Brunton, *Codes Egyptiens* (Brussels, 1919-20), vol. i, pp. 338-340; *Réglement,* tit. i, ch. i, art. 14, *State Papers,* vol. lxvi, p. 594; Decree (11) of March 26, 1900, art. 33, *ibid.,* vol. xcii, p. 898. *Cf.* Scott, *op. cit.,* pp. 213-214.

[2] *Réglement,* tit. ii, ch. i, § 1, *State Papers,* vol. lxvi, pp. 597-8; Decree (3) of March 26, 1900, art. 3, *ibid.,* vol. xcii, p. 884. *Cf.* Scott, *op. cit., p.* 215.

By a notification of the British Foreign Office, December 18, 1914, Egypt was placed under British protection, and it was declared that " His Majesty's Government will adopt all measures necessary for the defense of Egypt and the protection of its inhabitants and interests." [1]   Since that date, a number of Powers have relinquished their consular jurisdiction in Egypt. These include Greece,[2] Portugal,[3] Norway,[4] Sweden [5] and Denmark.[6]   According to the Treaty of Versailles, June 28, 1919, Germany recognized the British protectorate over Egypt and renounced her extra-territorial rights therein, the renunciation taking effect from August 4, 1914.[7]   A similar renunciation was made by Austria in the Treaty of St. Germain, September 10, 1919.[8]

At the beginning of 1922, the British Government declared the termination of the British protectorate over Egypt and granted its independence.[9] By taking this action, the British Government did not intend to alter the *status quo* with regard to the protection of foreign interests in Egypt pending the conclusion of a formal agreement between the British and Egyptian Governments.[10]   Under these circum-

[1] *State Papers*, vol. xviii, p. 185.

[2] Sep. 4, 1920, *ibid.*, vol. cxiii, p. 367.

[3] Dec. 9, 1920, *ibid.*, p. 424.

[4] April 22, 1921, *ibid.*, vol. cxiv, p. 350.

[5] July 28, 1921, *ibid.*, p. 390.

[6] July 14, 1921, *ibid.*, p. 199.

[7] Art. 147, *The Treaty of Peace between the Allied and Associated Powers and Germany* (London, 1919), p. 74.

[8] Art. 102, *The Treaty of Peace between the Allied and Associated Powers and Austria* (London, 1921), p. 42.

[9] See Declaration to Egypt, Feb. 21, 1922, *Parl. Pap.*, 1922 [Cmd. 1592], Egypt, no. 1 (1922), p. 29; Circular Despatch to His Majesty's Representatives Abroad, March 15, 1922, *ibid.* [Cmd. 1617], Egypt, no. 2 (1922).

[10] In the Declaration to Egypt, it was stated that "the protection of foreign interests in Egypt and the protection of minorities" was one

stances, the régime of extraterritoriality in its modified form is retained by those Powers which have not expressly renounced it.[1]

of the matters absolutely reserved to the discretion of the British Government pending the conclusion of an agreement with Egypt, but that until then the *status quo* should remain intact. The Circular Despatch of March 15 announced that "the termination of the British protectorate over Egypt involves, however, no change in the *status quo* as regards the position of other Powers in Egypt itself." See *Parl. Pap.* cited.

[1] So far as the United States Government is concerned, it still maintains its extraterritorial rights in Egypt. In reply to a letter of inquiry addressed by the author, the Department of State informs him that "in recognizing the British protectorate over Egypt in April, 1919, this Government reserved for further discussion the question of the modification of any rights belonging to the United States which might be deemed to be affected by the recognition," and that "this Government's recognition of the independence of Egypt in April, 1922, was made subject to the maintenance of the rights which had theretofore existed."

CHAPTER IX

UNILATERAL CANCELLATION

THE fifth method of procedure in discontinuing the system of extraterritoriality is by unilateral cancellation. This method was resorted to by Turkey more than once, always eliciting loud protests from the Powers. On October 11, 1881, a circular was sent out to the effect that certain rights accorded to the consuls by virtue of a long established usage was thenceforth to be abolished. In reply, the Powers declared by their joint notes of December 25, 1881, and February 25, 1882, that the sultan had no authority to annul the existing usages without previous consultation and agreement with the Powers concerned.[1]

At the beginning of the World War, Turkey endeavored once more to abrogate the extraterritorial system by unilateral action. On September 10, 1914, the foreign embassies at Constantinople received a note from the Turkish Ministry for Foreign Affairs, to the effect that on and after the first of October, the Ottoman Empire would abolish the Capitulations which restricted the sovereignty of Turkey in her relations with certain Powers. It was stated that owing to the improved state of Ottoman jurisprudence and to the interference entailed by the Capitulations with the legislative and administrative autonomy of the Ottoman Empire, the decision had been taken to abrogate, from the above-stated date, the Capitulations, " as well as all privileges and toleration accessory to these Capitulations or resulting from

---

[1] Rivier, *Principes du droit des gens* (Paris, 1896), vol. i, p. 544.

them, and to adopt as the basis of relations with all States
the general principles of international law." [1]

The United States Government lodged its protest by sending, on September 16, 1914, the following telegram to the
American Ambassador at Constantinople:

You are instructed to notify the Ottoman Government that
this Government does not acquiesce in the attempt of the Ottoman Government to abrogate the Capitulations, and does not
recognize that it has a right to do so or that its action, being
unilateral, has any effect upon the rights and privileges enjoyed
under those conventions. You will further state that this
Government reserves for the present the consideration of the
grounds for its refusal to acquiesce in the action of the Ottoman
Government and the right to make further representations later.[2]

A copy of this telegram was also sent to the Turkish Ambassador at Washington on the same day.[3]   On September
10, all the other embassies at Constantinople, including the
German and Austrian, sent identic notes to the Sublime
Porte, stating that while communicating to their respective
governments the note respecting the abolition of the Capitulations, they must point out that the capitulatory régime was
not an autonomous institution of the Empire but the resul-
tant of international treaties, which could not be abolished
either wholly or in part without the consent of the contracting parties.   It was, therefore, declared that in the absence
of an understandng arrived at before the first of October
between the Ottoman Porte and the foreign governments
concerned, the ambassadors could not recognize the executory
force after that date of a unilateral decision of the Turkish
Government.[4]

[1] U. S. *Foreign Relations*, 1914, p. 1092.

[2] *Ibid.*, p. 1093.

[3] *Ibid.*, p. 1094.

[4] Sir L. Mallet to Sir Edward Grey, Sept. 10, 1914, *Parl. Pap.*, 1914-
16 [Cd. 7628], Miscellaneous, no. 13 (1914), p. 23.

Later, the protest of the British Ambassador was confirmed by his Government, which instructed him to reiterate to the Ottoman Government the binding nature of the Capitulations and the invalidity of the unilateral action of the Porte in abrogating them. He was also authorized to say to the Turkish Government that the British Government would reserve their liberty of action in regard to any Turkish violation of the Capitulations and would demand due reparation for any prejudice to the British subjects resulting therefrom.[1]

To the American contention that the Capitulations were bilateral agreements and could not be abrogated by unilateral action, the Turkish Ministry for Foreign Affairs answered that " the Sublime Porte had, like every State, the right to denounce, at any time, international acts concluded without stipulations of duration." It was maintained that the change of conditions justified the action of the Turkish Government, " since the régime of the Capitulations, obsolete and no longer responding to modern needs, even when it is confined within its true contractual limits, threatens its own existence, and renders very difficult the conduct of Ottoman public affairs." [2] As we shall see presently, this point of view is open to serious question.

On September 4, 1915, the Turkish Foreign Office communicated to the American Ambassador a *note verbale,* which insisted that the Capitulations had been definitively abrogated and that " since October 1, 1914, the European international public law must govern the relations of the states and foreign subjects with the Imperial authorities and Ottoman subjects." It was added that if the Imperial Ministry re-

[1] *Note Verbale* communicated to the Sublime Porte, Oct. 1, 1914, *ibid.,* p. 53.

[2] The Minister for Foreign Affairs to Ambassador Morgenthau, Dec. 5, 1914, U. S. *Foreign Relations,* 1915, p. 1302.

ceived any further communication on the subject, it would, to its regret, " find itself in the painful necessity not to give it any effect and to pay no attention to the matter to which it refers." ¹ The United States Government, however, was in total disagreement with the Porte as to the effect of this declaration. It insisted on the continued validity of the Capitulations, although it indicated its willingness to consider the abandonment of its extraterritorial rights in Turkey whenever the state of Turkish justice warranted such a measure. Ambassador Morgenthau was instructed to notify the Ottoman Government that the United States would hold it responsible for any injury which might be occasioned to the United States or to its citizens by a failure to observe the Capitulations.²

At the First Lausanne Conference on Near Eastern Affairs, held November 22, 1922–February 4, 1923, the Turkish delegation defended the cancellation of the Capitulations by their government in 1914. One of the arguments advanced was that the Capitulations were unilateral in nature and could be revoked at the will of the Sublime Porte. " It is an undoubted fact," said the Memorandum of the Turkish delegation, " that in taking such a decision Turkey merely exercised a legitimate right. As a matter of fact, the Capitulations are essentially unilateral acts. In order that an act may be regarded as reciprocal, it must above all contain reciprocal engagements. From an examination of the texts, the evidence shows that in granting the privileges in question to foreigners in Turkey, the Ottoman emperors had no thought of obtaining similar privileges in favor of their subjects traveling or trading in Europe." It was further contended that the Capitulations were voidable on the prin-

¹ U. S. *Foreign Relations*, 1915, p. 1304.
² The Secretary of State to Ambassador Morgenthau, Nov. 4, 1915, *ibid.*, p. 1305.

ciple of *rebus sic stantibus.* " Even supposing that the
Capitulations were bilateral conventions," the Turkish statement asserted, " it would be unjust to infer from that that
they are unchangeable and must remain everlastingly irre-
vocable. Treaties whose duration is not fixed imply the
clause *rebus sic stantibus,* in virtue of which a change in
the circumstances which have given rise to the conclusion
of a treaty may bring about its cancellation by one of the
contracting parties, if it is not possible to cancel it by mutual
agreement." [1]

That the Capitulations were at first unilateral in form
there can be no question. This is admitted by the authorities who have examined the matter.[2] But to say that they
have remained unilateral acts would be incorrect. In every
case, as we know, the Capitulations were at one time or
other converted into treaties consistent with the forms laid
down by international law and binding on each contracting
party. Indeed, the Sublime Porte itself admitted, on one occasion, the validity of these agreements as mutually binding
treaties. In a *Mémoire* addressed by the Porte to the representatives of the foreign Powers, in May, 1869, it was declared in unequivocal terms:

The Capitulations having been consecrated by treaties subse-

[1] Great Britain, *Parl. Pap.,* 1923 [Cmd. 1814], Turkey, no. 1 (1923),
p. 478; France, *Documents diplomatiques, Conférence de Lausanne,* vol.
i, pp. 450-451.

[2] " The Capitulations were, in principle, gracious concessions (*concessions gracieuses*)." Pradier-Fodéré, " *La Question des Capitulations,*"
R. D. I., vol. i, p. 119. According to another writer, it is a mistake to
give to the Capitulations the name of treaties, which presuppose two
contracting parties stipulating for their interests. " Here [in the Capi-
tulations] one finds only concessions and privileges and exemptions of pure
liberality given by the Porte to France." Lawrence, *Commentaire sur les
éléments du droit international et sur l'histoire des progrès du droit des
gens de Henry Wheaton* (Leipzig, 1868-80), vol. iv, p. 123; *cf.* Ancien
Diplomate, *Le Régime des Capitulations,* p. 9.

quently concluded between the Sublime Porte and the foreign Powers, should, so long as they are in force, be scrupulously respected in the same manner as these treaties.[1]

It is certainly unthinkable that the Turkish delegation to the Lausanne Conference should have taken upon themselves to contradict a solemn engagement of their own government made over half a century before.

As to the statement that treaties, in order to be reciprocal, must contain reciprocal engagements, one would look in vain for a sound basis of this contention. To give one instance, treaties of peace concluded at the end of a war have never been reciprocal in nature. Does this mean that all such treaties are of no effect and can be annulled at the will of the vanquished? Nothing of the sort is sanctioned by international law.

In regard to the second contention of the Turkish delegation, it is admitted that the principle *rebus sic stantibus* is recognized by the majority of publicists to be an implied clause of all unnotifiable treaties.[2] But, taking it for granted that the change of the circumstances which had led to the conclusion of the Capitulations had, in 1914, reached such a stage as to justify the demand for their abrogation, we cannot absolve the Sublime Porte from the responsibility for a breach of good faith. For while the rule *rebus sic stantibus* is recognized by a vast number of writers, it is also their opinion that the clause " ought not to give a State

[1] *Archives diplomatiques*, 1870, vol. i, p. 249.

[2] " For it is an almost universally recognized fact that vital changes of circumstances may be of such a kind as to justify a party in demanding to be released from the obligations of an unnotifiable treaty. The vast majority of publicists, as well as the Governments of the Civilized States, defend the principle *conventio omnis intelligitur rebus sic stantibus*, and they agree, therefore, that all treaties are concluded under the tacit condition *rebus sic stantibus*." Oppenheim, *International Law* (3rd ed., London, 1920), vol. i, pp. 688-9.

the right, immediately upon the happening of a vital change
of circumstances, to declare itself free from the obligations
of a treaty, but should only entitle it to claim to be released
from them by the other party or parties to the treaty." [1]
In other words, before a State can release itself from the
obligations of a treaty on the principle *rebus sic stantibus,* it
must first enter into negotiations with the other contracting
party or parties to that effect,[2] with a view of examining
the reasons for the proposed cancellation or modification of
the obligations in question and reaching a common accord on
the subject.[3]

In the case of Turkey, there is all the more reason for
such a common accord.   Ever since the admission of the
Ottoman Empire in 1856 " to participate in the advantages
of the European public law and concert," [4] every important
question of Turkish foreign relations has been a concern
of the general European polity.   Far more than ordinary
synallagmatic agreements, therefore, the Capitulations had
a binding force which should not be lightly brushed aside.

Contrary to established principle, the Sublime Porte, without making any earnest attempt to reach a satisfactory
agreement with the Powers, announced by unilateral action
the end of all the Capitulations, and when the United
States Government protested against it, the Turkish Foreign
Office categorically replied that the abrogation had become
a *fait accompli* and that no further discussion of the ques-
ion would be engaged in.   This shows that while the Turkish
Government intended to make use of the clause *rebus sic*

[1] *Ibid.*, p. 692.

[2] *Ibid., cf.* Phillimore, *Three Centuries of Treaties of Peace* (London,
1919), p. 138.

[3] Pouritch, *De la clause " rebus sic stantibus " en droit international
public* (Paris, 1918), p. 81.

[4] Art. 7, Treaty of Paris, Mar. 30, 1856, *State Papers*, vol. xlvi, p. 12.

stantibus, it refused to enter into negotiations the which are recognized to be a necessary part of the procedure laid down by international law for the application of that principle.

In fine, it may be reiterated that the measure taken by the Turkish Government in 1914 to abrogate its treaty obligations by unilateral action is wholly unfounded in law and has been vigorously opposed by the Powers. The policy has failed of its desired end, and, as will be seen,[1] the Ottoman Empire was finally compelled to seek the restoration of its judicial autonomy by means of bilateral or rather multilateral negotiations instead of unilateral cancellation.[2]

[1] *Cf. infra,* pp. 185 *et seq.*

[2] It is interesting to note that even before the Lausanne Conference of 1922-1923, the Turkish Government had consented in the suspension of the unilateral cancellation of the Capitulations. Russian Ambassador at Constantinople to Russian Minister of For. Aff., Sep. 18 (Oct. 1), 1914, Scott, *Dip. Doc. relating to the Outbreak of the European War* (New York, 1916), pt. ii, pp. 1422-3.

CHAPTER X

DIPLOMATIC NEGOTIATION

THE last method of procedure in attempting to secure the modification or abrogation of extraterritoriality is by diplomatic negotiation, which usually results in an agreement of one sort or another. In classifying this method as distinct from the above-mentioned, the fact is not lost sight of that in all the other methods described, a larger or smaller measure of diplomatic negotiation is also involved. But in all of them, except in the case of unilateral cancellation, which is an illegal method, the negotiation is carried on between the foreign Powers on the one side and, on the other, Powers other than those which originally granted the extraterritorial rights. In this chapter, we shall deal with the negotiations in which the States granting these rights have engaged with the foreign Powers to get rid of the same.

I. TURKEY

Turkey availed herself of this method at the Congress of Paris in 1856. During the session of March 25, the question of abolition was brought up for discussion. Ali Pasha argued that the Capitulations were disadvantageous alike to the foreigner and to the Ottoman Government; that they created " a multiplicity of governments in the Government;" and that they were an insuperable obstacle to all reform. Count Clarendon, Count Walewski and Count Cavour expressed themselves very sympathetically and were favorably inclined to the Turkish point of view. On the

other hand, Count de Buol and Baron de Burquency hesi-
tated to grant to Turkey her judicial autonomy at once.
While agreeing that the Capitulations needed modification,
Baron de Burquency deemed it important that the modification should be proportionate to the judicial reforms inaugurated by the Ottoman Empire. A protocol was drawn up
and signed, embodying the wish (*voeu*) that a conference
should be assembled at Constantinople, after the conclusion
of peace, to deliberate upon the matter.[1] The promised
conference was, however, never held.

After the failure of 1856, Turkey was for a long time
unable to shake off completely the restrictions on her judicial autonomy. It was only recently that some Powers
evinced a readiness to assist Turkey in recovering her independence in the realm of justice. By the treaty of February 26, 1909, Austria-Hungary engaged to give " her full
and sincere support " to the Turkish negotiations for the
abolition of the capitulatory régime.[2] In 1912, Italy made
an identical promise.[3]

More recently, the Ottoman Empire has succeeded in concluding treaties with certain Powers, recognizing the cessation of the capitulatory régime in Turkey. At the beginning
of the European War, Germany and Austria-Hungary
offered as the price of Turkish assistance in the conflict their
consent to abrogate the Capitulations. This was later confirmed by Germany in a treaty of January 11, 1917, which
provided that Germans in Turkey and Turks in Germany
should enjoy the same treatment as the natives in respect
of the legal and judicial protection of their persons and
property and that to this end they should have free access
to the courts and be subjected to the same conditions as the

[1] *State Papers*, vol. xlvi, pp. 100-101.
[2] Art. 8, *ibid.*, vol. cii, p. 182.
[3] Treaty of Lausanne, Oct. 18, 1912, art. 8, *ibid.*, vol. cvi, p. 1102.

natives.[1] On August 6, 1917, a law was promulgated by
the German Emperor for the execution of the treaties of
January 11, 1917. It laid down that by imperial order it
could be determined (*bestimmt*) to abolish the rights of
jurisdiction enjoyed by the German consuls in Turkey.[2]
Austria abolished her extraterritorial rights in Turkey by
the treaty of March 12, 1918.[3]

On January 6, 1921, a treaty was concluded with the
Soviet Government in Russia, which declared:

> The Government of the R. S. F. S. R. considers the Capitu-
> latory régime to be incompatible with the free national develop-
> ment and with the sovereignty of any country; and it regards
> all the rights and acts relating in any way to this régime as
> annulled and abrogated.[4]

At the Conference of Lausanne, November 22, 1922–
February 4, 1923, a Commission headed by Marquis Garroni
of Italy was charged with the examination of questions relating to the régime of foreigners in Turkey. The Commission held its first meeting on December 2, 1922, at the
opening of which Marquis Garroni recognized " that according to present-day ideas of law the capitulatory régime
is regarded as liable to diminish the sovereign powers of an
independent State; and it is intelligible," he added, " that
Turkey should demand the abolition of this régime, which
has had its day." He desired, however, that the Turkish
Government would " substitute for it such guarantees as
regards legislation and administration of justice as will inspire confidence in all those who will be obliged to have re-

[1] Art. 1, Martens, *N. R. G.*, 3rd ser., vol. ix, p. 709.

[2] *Reichsgesetzblatt*, 1918, p. 355.

[3] The text of this treaty is not available; it is referred to by Hamid,
Das Fremdenrecht in der Türkei (Berlin, 1919), p. 22.

[4] Art. 7, *Current History*, vol. xvii, p. 278.

course thereto." Three Sub-Commissions were created, the first of which was to deal with the legal position of foreign persons in Turkey.[1]

At this same meeting a memorandum was read by the Turkish delegation. It began by explaining the origin of the Capitulations and after reviewing what was promised by the Powers in 1856, continued thus:

This shows that as long as sixty-six years ago the representatives of England, France and Italy recognized in so solemn a Congress as the one described, the necessity of terminating the Capitulations because of their incompatibility with modern conceptions of law, and because of the manner in which they infringed the sovereignty of the State.

During the period subsequent to the conclusion of the Treaty of Paris, Turkey has worked feverishly at the perfection of her judicial system, which she had already taken in hand.

The commercial code, the penal code, the codes of civil and penal procedure, as well as the laws regarding the " Tribunaux de Paix," and also all the administrative laws and regulations, have been established on the model of codes and laws in force in European countries.

Above all, it has quite recently been possible to carry out a very important reform in the civil law, by which our judicial institutions have been completely secularized; the free will of the parties in the matter of contracts and agreements has been recognized as paramount, and the principle of the freedom of the will has been accorded the same place as in Europe; further, while these laws were being elaborated and promulgated, a faculty of law was instituted at Constantinople, whose programme is more or less identical with that of the corresponding faculties in Europe. This situation has produced during forty years a body of distinguished judges and advocates who possess all the necessary qualifications, and it is to them that at the

[1] *Parliamentary Papers*, 1923 [*Cmd.* 1814], Turkey, no. 1 (1923), p. 467; *Documents diplomatiques, Conférence de Lausanne*, vol. i, p. 443.

present time the important task of administering justice is assigned.

A considerable number of young men have since the change of régime in 1908 studied in the various faculties of law of the Empire, and are now appointed to various posts in the magistracy.

After mentioning the treaties which the Turkish Government concluded with Austria-Hungary, Italy, Germany and Russia in the present century,[1] the Turkish statement went on to enumerate the defects of the capitulatory régime.

With regard to civil matters, the Turkish statement alluded to the unsavory effects of the existence of a multiplicity of laws and jurisdictions. The parties to a contract had to be familiar with the laws of each foreign country, in order to live up to their requirements, and in case of an appeal, application had to be made to a court of appeal of the country whose nationals the foreigners concerned were. Even in the mixed tribunals, difficulties of procedure were not wanting. The judges were not men of legal training; they were as a rule partial to their compatriots; and they had so many other duties to perform that interminable delays were caused in the administration of justice.

The attitude of the foreign members (who supported the foreigner with great partiality as though they were his advocates), and especially that of the dragomans, caused regrettable misunderstandings which caused the matter to be transferred from the judicial domain to that of diplomacy. This state of affairs caused the suits to drag on for a very long time and made it impossible for the Commercial Court to bring them to an end.

Even after the judgment had been pronounced, there were numerous obstacles to its execution. " Indeed, it was no rare thing to see judgments given against foreigners remain unexecuted."

[1] *Supra*, p. 185.

On the penal side, the hands of the Turkish authorities were tied by the treaty restrictions, of which the consular officers made the widest use, " in order to withhold deliberately from justice offenders who had infringed the public order and security of the country." When a criminal took refuge in the abode of a foreigner, the police could not lay its hands upon him in the absence of the dragoman, and in the meantime the criminal found a means of escaping. Besides, owing to the requirement of hearing a foreign witness in the presence of the dragoman, either or both could exercise an influence on the progress of the prosecution " by answering the summons or by refusing to appear." The statement ended the enumeration of the defects of the capitulatory régime with the assertion that " similarly, difficulties arose in connection with the execution of sentences in criminal cases," and that " the sovereignty of the state and the prestige of the judicial authority were as gravely prejudiced." Then the statement went on to cite authorities in substantiation of the defects and disadvantages mentioned, and sought to justify the cancellation of the Capitulations by the Porte in 1914, on the ground that they were originally unilateral acts subject to revocation, and that a treaty is voidable on the principle of *rebus sic stantibus*.[1] Finally, after summing up the arguments advanced, the Turkish delegation concluded their memorandum by saying:

In view of the foregoing, the Government of the Grand National Assembly of Turkey can in no wise agree to the reestablishment of the Capitulations, which are in direct conflict with the modern conception of a State and with the principles of public law.[2]

[1] For a criticism of this view, *vide supra*, pp. 180 *et seq.*

[2] *Parliamentary Papers*, 1923 [*Cmd.* 1814], Turkey, no. 1 (1923), pp. 471-479; *Documents diplomatiques, Conférence de Lausanne*, vol. i, pp. 446-451.

At the second meeting of the Commission on the Régime of Foreigners in Turkey, held on December 28, 1922, Marquis Garroni told the delegates that the sub-commission dealing with the judicial régime of foreigners in Turkey, under the presidency of Sir Horace Rumbold, had found it impossible to continue its labors in consequence of differences of view between the Allies and Turkey.[1] A report rendered by Sir Horace was read, telling of what had transpired at the meetings of the sub-commission. According to this report, the Allied and Turkish delegates exchanged questionnaires and answers, proposals and counter-proposals, on the various questions discussed. From the very beginning, the discussion revealed a considerable, though not fundamental divergence of view—a divergence which was fortunately narrowed by concessions made on either side. One of the concessions made by the Turkish delegation was that all questions of personal status affecting foreigners were to be subject to the exclusive jurisdiction of the national tribunals or other competent national authorities in the country to which the foreigners belonged. As the discussion proceeded further, the divergence of view increased, especially when it was proposed that Turkey should admit foreign judges to its magistracy and permit them to participate in its legal reform. Regarding these two questions

the Turkish delegation strongly maintained that any introduction into the Turkish judicature of a special element, even in the conditions suggested in the questionnaire, would constitute an encroachment on the sovereignty and independence of Turkey. The Turkish delegation maintained with no less insistence that existing Turkish legislation amply met the requirements of modern life; that one could without any apprehension leave to the Grand National Assembly the duty of applying to this legislation such modifications as might seem

[1] *Parliamentary Paper* cited, p. 481.

necessary from time to time; that the Turkish judicature, which had been recruited for over forty years from among the graduates of the faculty of law [in Constantinople], was fully qualified for its task, and that foreigners no less than Turkish nationals would find in the legislative and judicial system of Turkey all the guarantees required for the safety of their persons and their interests.

At the end of this dscussion of the sub-commission, a draft containing the detailed proposals of the Allies was handed by the president to the Turkish delegation, inviting the latter to entrust its legal adviser with the examination of this draft, in consultation with the Allied legal advisers, with a view to the satisfactory settlement of the question. Finally, the Allied legal advisers had to inform the sub-commission of their failure to reach an agreement with the Turkish adviser, and after a fruitless attempt to secure from the Turkish delegation any counter-proposals which they might desire to make, the sub-commission had to report to Marquis Garroni that it was unable to continue its work.[1]

At the second meeting of the Commission on the Régime of Foreigners, Ismet Pasha once more objected strenuously to the imposition of foreign judges on the Turkish magistracy. "The Turkish delegation were greatly astonished," he declared, " to find themselves confronted with such a proposal, the purpose of which is to institute a régime clearly incompatible with the independence and sovereignty of Turkey." He emphasized and re-emphasized the progress which Turkey had made in her judicial reform and the sufficiency of the guarantees offered by it in place of the Capitulations. As evidence of this fact, he testified that

the régime of general international law which has been operative in Turkey since 1914, without the conclusion of any con-

[1] *Parliamentary Paper* cited, pp. 500-508.

vention whatever, has never given rise to any complaint on the part of the very numerous nationals of neutral States, or on that of the Allied nationals who remained in Turkey. The experience acquired during this long period of eight years has proved that Turkish institutions are entirely adequate and contain all the guarantees necessary for safeguarding the interests in question.

On the other hand, it was asserted that of the new countries no such guarantee as it was sought to impose on Turkey were required. The address of the Turkish delegate ended with the challenge that

the Turkish Government have no fear in calling upon the public opinion of the world to judge and compare the treatment accorded to foreigners in Turkey by the Turks, both in the past and at present, and the cruel and arbitrary treatment to which the Turks have been subjected by foreigners at Constantinople and elsewhere at the same time and under the same conditions.

In the discussion that followed, the Allied delegations showed their dissatisfaction with the position taken by Turkey. M. Barrère was the first to speak, and he found it impossible for the French delegation to accept the blank refusal meted out by the Turkish delegation to the Allied proposals. It would be impossible, he said, for the French delegation to consent to the suppression of the Capitulations, were sufficient guarantees not offered by the Turkish Government. Baron Hayashi dwelt upon the experience of Japan with regard to the abolition of extraterritoriality, and urged the Turkish delegation to adopt a conciliatory attitude. Mr. Child, the American unofficial " observer," discoursed on the sanctity of international obligations and the fundamental equity which foreigners might expect from the Turkish Government, pointing out " that treaties which give foreigners a status of security in Turkey can deprive Turkey of nothing, and indeed would be the very foundation of her economic future." Lord Curzon, after alluding to the remarks that had been made by his colleagues, openly declared himself to be in accord with what the French delegate had said. He then reviewed the arguments of Ismet Pasha, showing their invalidity, and ended with the plea that the Turkish Government consider very carefully what had been said and perhaps at a later date give the Allies an opportunity of hearing their revised views on the subject.[1]

The third meeting of the Commission on the Régime of Foreigners was held on January 6, 1923. In reply to the speeches made by the Allied representatives at the previous meeting, Ismet Pasha read a long statement, adhering to the decision that the Turkish Government had already come to. Comments were made by the various delegations on the substance of the speech, the general hope being that the Turkish delegation would formulate counter-proposals, which would make it possible to find some common ground of agreement. But Ismet Pasha insisted that he was not in a position to make further concessions.[2]

At the fourth meeting of the Second Commission, held on January 27, 1923, Marquis Garroni reported on the suggestions that had been made to the Turkish delegation regarding the judicial guarantees to be offered to the foreigners. What had been suggested was the attachment of certain European legal advisers to the Turkish Ministry of Justice and judicial régime.[3]

In the draft terms of the treaty of peace presented to the Turkish delegation on January 31, 1923, it was provided that "the High Contracting Parties agree to abrogate the Capitulations relating to the régime of foreigners in Turkey

---

[1] *Parl. Pap.* cited, pp. 488-498; *Doc. dip.* cited, pp. 459-467.

[2] *Parl. Pap.* cited, pp. 509-519; *Doc. dip.* cited, pp. 469-476.

[3] *Parl. Pap.* cited, p. 523; *Doc. dip.* cited, p. 479.

both as regards conditions of entry and residence and as regards fiscal and judicial questions." [1]   Together with the draft treaty was sent a draft convention, in pursuance of which the foreigners were to have free access to the Turkish courts; actions in real property, as well as in civil, commercial and criminal matters, were placed under the jurisdiction of the Turkish courts; questions of personal status, under that of the national tribunals or other national authorities established in the country of which the parties were nationals; and the Turkish Government was obliged to ensure to foreigners in Turkey, both as regards person and property, protection in accordance with international law. [2] To this draft convention a draft declaration was attached, whereby Turkey was to engage that foreign legal counsellors would be chosen to assist in the administration of justice in Turkey in accordance with the latest proposals of the Allied delegations. [3]

Subsequent to the meetings of the Commission on January 31 and February 1, informal conversations between Ismet Pasha and the plenipotentiaries of the three inviting Powers took place, as a result of which further concessions were offered to Ismet Pasha on February 3 and 4.   Regarding the draft declaration relative to the administration of justice in Turkey, the inviting Powers offered to replace it by another, under which the legal advisers were to possess no judicial functions and were to have merely general powers of observing the working of the Turkish courts, ensuring appeals against improper decisions and bringing complaints to the notice of the proper Turkish authorities. [4]

[1] Art. 26, *Parl. Pap.* cited, p. 695.

[2] Ch. iii, Draft Convention respecting the Régime Applicable to Foreigners in Turkey, *ibid.*, pp. 798-780.

[3] *Ibid.*, pp. 801-803.

[4] *Ibid.*, pp. 834-836; *Doc. dip.* cited, vol. ii, Feb. 1, 1923-Feb. 4, 1923, pp. 11-12.

In his reply to the Allied offers, dated February 4, 1923, Ismet Pasha, expressing the hope that there would be no longer any difficulty in settling the small differences which had arisen regarding the judicial guarantees to be offered by Turkey, attached a revised draft of the declaration, which tended to curtail the powers of the legal counsellors.[1]

On this same day, a last-minute effort was made by Lord Curzon and his French and Italian colleagues, in an informal meeting in the British delegate's room, to arrive at a final settlement, but owing to the Turkish delegation's insistence on their point of view with regard to the economic and judicial issues, the conference was broken up without accomplishing its desired end.[2]

The Lausanne Conference was resumed on April 23, 1923,[3] when three committees were created, the first of which was designated as the General Committee, to deal with the outstanding political questions and the judicial part of the draft convention respecting the régime of foreigners in Turkey.[4] At a meeting of this Committee, on May 1, the Turkish delegation took exception to any specific provision for the abrogation of the Capitulations in Turkey, as, in their view, the latter had become a *fait accompli* since 1914. The Allies, supported by the Americans, held that bilateral treaties could not be abolished by a unilateral act, but they accepted the Turkish point of view in principle, subject to the discovery of a satisfactory formula for article 26 of the draft treaty. This article, as has been seen, provided

[1] *Parl. Pap.* cited, pp. 840, 852-853; *Doc. dip.* cited, vol. ii, pp. 19, 21.

[2] *Parl. Pap.* cited, pp. 842-851. See also M. Bompard's report to M. Poincaré, *Doc. dip.* cited, vol. ii, pp. 126-9.

[3] The official proceedings of the conference have not yet been made public. What is given below is gathered from the despatches to the London *Times*, which are necessarily incomplete.

[4] London *Times*, Apr. 24, 1923, 14c.

that the High Contracting Parties " agree to abrogate " the
Capitulations, while the Turkish delegation desired it to
read " declare completely abrogated." [1]

The discussion with regard to the judicial status of foreigners in Turkey came to a head at the meeting of the first
committee on May 4. The point at issue was a provision
in the draft declaration to the effect that domiciliary visits,
searches or arrests of persons other than those taken in
flagrante delicto could be carried out in the judicial areas
of Constantinople, Smyrna, Samsoun and Adana only with
the previous consent of one of the foreign legal counsellors.[2]
The Turks claimed that the Allies had accepted a counter-
draft presented by the Turkish delegation on February 4,
which omitted this provision,[3] while the Allies denied it.
After a prolonged debate, Sir Horace Rumbold proposed
that the Allies' counter-draft and the old draft would be
examined by the drafting committee. Ismet Pasha still persisted, and finally Sir Horace said that the Allies would
circulate their counter-draft and, waiving its proposed examination by the drafting committee, reserved the right to
discuss it again in committee.[4]

On June 4, the Allied and Turkish delegations smoothed
over their difficulty by reaching a compromise on the disputed point. Instead of requiring the previous consent of
the legal counsellors to the domiciliary visits, searches and
arrests in the four judicial areas, all such measures taken
in Constantinople and Smyrna should be brought without
delay to the notice of the legal counsellors.[5]

The Treaty of Peace, together with the subsidiary agree-

[1] *Ibid.*, May 2, 1923, 13c.
[2] *Cf. Parl. Pap.* cited, p. 835.
[3] *Ibid.*, p. 852.
[4] London *Times*, May 5, 1923, 12e.
[5] *Ibid.*, June 5, 1923, 13a.

ments, was signed on July 24, 1923. Article 28 of the Treaty of Peace provided: " Each of the High Contracting Parties accepts, in so far as it is concerned, the complete abolition of the Capitulations in Turkey in every respect." [1] The Convention (IV) respecting Conditions of Residence and Business and Jurisdiction recognized the application of the principles of international law in all questions of jurisdiction.[2] The much-debated declaration was also signed in the form accepted on June 4 by the Turkish delegation. By this declaration, the Turkish Government proposed to engage for a period of not less than five years a number of European legal counsellors, to be selected from a list prepared by the Permanent Court of International Justice from among jurists nationals of countries which did not take part in the World War. These legal counsellors were to serve as Turkish officials under the Minister of Justice, some of them being posted in Constantinople and others in Smyrna. Their duties were specified as follows: to take part in the work of the legislative commissions; to observe the working of the Turkish courts and to forward such reports to the Minister of Justice as were deemed by them necessary; to receive all complaints regarding the administration of justice, with a view of bringing them to the notice of the Minister of Justice in order to ensure the strict observance of law; and to receive all complaints caused by domiciliary visits, perquisitions or arrests, which should, in Constantinople and Smyrna, be brought immediately after their execution to the notice of the legal counsellor by the local representative of the Minister of Justice.[3]

[1] Great Britain, *Treaty Series*, 1923, no. 16, p. 25.

[2] "Art. 15. Subject to the provisions of Article 16, all questions of jurisdiction shall, as between Turkey and the other Contracting Powers, be decided in accordance with the principles of international law." Art. 16 provides for the adjudication of questions of personal status involving non-Moslem foreigners by their home authorities. *Ibid.*, p. 201.

[3] *Ibid.*, pp. 201-203.

Article ii of the as yet unratified Turco-American treaty of August 6, 1923, also provides for the termination of the extraterritorial rights of the United States in Turkey.[1]

II. PERSIA

At the Paris Peace Conference, the Persian delegation presented three groups of claims, the first group containing their case for the abolition of extraterritoriality. After reciting briefly the facts involved, the statement of the Persian delegation went on to say:

Meanwhile, for a number of years, the Persian Government have entered resolutely in the path of judicial reforms, with the aid of foreign advisers, taking France as a model. The work of codification is being actively pursued and Persian justice will shortly offer all the guarantees of justice as in the European States. Consequently, there is no reason to continue indefinitely the peculiar situation created in favor of foreigners in Persia and the time has come to terminate it.[2]

Therefore, the Persian Government claimed "that the treaties made between Persia and foreign countries be subjected to a revision, to the end that all clauses contravening the political, judicial, and economic independence of Persia be eliminated."[3] But due to the inability of the Persian Government to "organize, administer, or control the Kingdom of Persia within the pre-war boundaries," the Persian delegation did not get a chance to state their case.[4]

The only European Power which has abandoned its rights of jurisdiction in Persia is Russia. By the treaty of Feb-

---

[1] *Current History*, vol. xix, p. 100.

[2] *Claims of Persia before the Conference of the Preliminaries of Peace at Paris*, p. 4.

[3] *Ibid.*, p. 6.

[4] Temperley, *A History of the Paris Peace Conference* (London, 1920-24), vol. vi, p. 211.

ruary 26, 1921, it was agreed by Persia and Russia " that Russian subjects in Persia and Persian subjects in Russia shall, as from the date of the present Treaty, be placed upon the same footing as the inhabitants of the towns in which they reside; they shall be subject to the laws of their country of residence, and shall submit their complaints to the local courts." [1] The reason for the action of the Soviet Government is plainly stated in the opening article of the treaty:

In order to confirm its declarations regarding Russian policy towards the Persian nation, . . . the R. S. F. S. R. formally affirms once again that it definitely renounces the tyrannical policy carried out by the colonizing governments of Russia which has been overthrown by the will of the workers and peasants of Russia.

Inspired by this principle and desiring that the Persian people should be happy and independent and should be able to dispose freely of its patrimony, the Russian Republic declares the whole body of treaties and conventions concluded with Persia by the Tsarist Government, which crushed the rights of the Persian people, to be null and void.[2]

Thus, the relinquishment by Russia of extraterritoriality in Persia represents partly an attempt to atone for the injustices inflicted by Czarist Russia on Persia, and partly an endeavor to restore the administrative autonomy of the latter country.[3]

---

[1] Art. 16, *State Papers,* vol. cxiv, p. 905. *Cf.* League of Nations, *Treaty Series,* no. 268.

[2] Art. 1, *State Papers,* vol. cxiv, p. 901.

[3] The Soviet Civil Code, moreover, contains some extraordinary provisions, so that the Soviet Government may be regarded as having been so generous with malice prepense. See *Columbia Law Review,* vol. xxiv, p. 689.

III. JAPAN

After the disturbances incident to the overthrow of the Shogunate and the restoration of the Mikado, Japanese statesmen addressed themselves seriously to a movement for reform, which was destined to startle the world. They saw that two of the sovereign rights of their country—tariff and jurisdiction—had been sadly impaired, and that in order to take her place among the Great Powers of the world, it was imperative for Japan to regain her autonomy in these particulars. They took advantage of the provision made in various treaties for their general revision in 1872, and a commission headed by Prince Iwakura, and including Kido, Okuba, Ito, Yamagutsi, was sent out in 1871, to negotiate for the revision and to study institutions abroad. The Commissioners were heartily received by the people and government of the United States. The American Government promised to treat with Japan most liberally, but it was found that the Commissioners were not clothed with the authority to conclude and sign a treaty. Their mission to Europe proved to be a complete failure. The Powers were unwilling to relinquish their extraterritorial rights before Japan could show an improved system of law and judicial administration.[1]

In the meantime, the Minister of Italy at Yedo proposed, in 1873, a special convention with Japan relative to the travel of foreigners in the interior. The draft convention contained a provision which required the foreigners traveling beyond the limits of the jurisdiction of their consuls to submit to the protection and jurisdiction of the territorial authorities, "according to the usages which prevail in the countries of Europe and America."[2]

---

[1] Foster, *American Diplomacy in the Orient* (Boston & New York, 1903), pp. 345-348.

[2] U. S. *Foreign Relations*, 1873, pt. i, p. 270.

Taking cognizance of this draft treaty, the French Government instructed its representative at Washington to sound the American Government on its opinion regarding the Italian proposal.[1]　On June 21, 1873, Mr. Hamilton Fish, American Secretary of State, wrote to Mr. Schenck, American Minister at London, to seek an interview with Earl Granville and to communicate to him the views of the American Government.　Mr. Fish declared:

Japan has no firmer friend than the United States; no one more ready than we to recognize her rightful autonomy.　But on a candid review of the situation, the President is forced to the conclusion that it is not yet safe to surrender to the local authorities the guaranteed rights of ex-territoriality.　We have not such knowledge of the administration of justice in that kingdom, and of the means for the protection of the liberty and rights of foreigners, as would justify such surrender at this time.[2]

Similar instructions were sent out to the American Ministers at Paris, Berlin and the Hague.[3]　Due to the disapproval of the Powers,[4] the Italian Government was obliged to "refuse to accept the conditions proposed by the projected convention as a basis of free travel in the interior of Japan."[5]

The importance of this episode lies in the fact that from the very outset, the Powers have conditioned their consent to the modification of extraterritoriality in Japan on a commensurate amelioration of the judicial system in that country.　As the following account of the Japanese negotiations

[1] U. S. *Foreign Relations*, 1873, pt. i, p. 169.

[2] *Ibid.*, p. 383.

[3] *Ibid.*, p. 383.

[4] For the French and German attitude, see *ibid.*, pp. 261, 296.

[5] *Ibid.*, p. 272.

with the Powers will show, this fact was ever present in the minds of the negotiators on both sides.

Impressed with the failure of the mission of 1871, and with the need of speedy reform in her judicial system as well as in other matters, Japan plunged into a vigorous attempt to improve her internal conditions. Students were sent abroad to imbibe the spirit of Western civilization, at the same time that foreigners of distinction were called to Japan to help and advise in this general reform movement.[1] In 1875, an imperial decree was issued, convoking the provincial assemblies, in order that the emperor might " govern in harmony with public opinion." In the same year, British and French troops stationed in Yokohama for the protection of their respective nationals were withdrawn, the first manifestation on the part of the European nations of a disposition to respect the sovereignty of Japan. Edicts followed in rapid succession, which provided for the compilation of a constitution after Western models, enacted and put into force a penal code and a code of procedure, and announced the convocation of a national parliament.[2]

With this program of reform under way, the Japanese Government, in 1878, approached the Diplomatic Corps at Tokio for a revision of the treaties. The Foreign Minister of Japan pointed out to the foreign Powers concerned the abuses of the extraterritorial system [3] and asked for its modification. To this, the Powers, except the United States, again turned a deaf ear, Great Britain being the leading

[1] Notably M. Boissonade, of the University of Paris, whose assistance in compiling the Japanese codes has made his name immortal in the annals of Japan's legal reform.

[2] U. S. *Foreign Relations,* 1875, pt. ii, pp. 787, 794; 1876, p. 381; 1881, pp. 658, 692, 728.

[3] For a contemporary account of these abuses see D. C. Greene, *Extraterritoriality in Japan* (an essay read before the Kobe and Osaka Missionary Conference in April, 1884), pp. 2-11.

obstructionist. The United States dissented from the general attitude of the Powers by concluding with Japan a treaty giving the latter full right over her tariff.[1] This treaty was of no significance except as a specimen of American sympathy with the Japanese aspirations, as its validity was conditioned on the conclusion of similar treaties with other Powers, which was not done.[2]

On February 25, 1882, a conference was opened at Tokio, to consider the question of treaty revision. Count Inouye, representing Japan, told the foreign representatives of the efforts made by his country to reform her internal administration in every respect. " I may call your attention," he said, " especially to the reforms brought into our laws and our judicial procedure, which assure the security of person and property by the introduction of codes of law and of criminal procedure in conformity with modern ideas." He believed that the moment had come when all the obstacles to the free intercourse between Japan and the Powers should be removed. The Japanese Government, he declared, " proposes now to open the whole country to foreigners and to accord to them access to all parts of the Empire, on condition that they submit to Japanese law." [3] Due to a disagreement on the permanency of treaties, however, Japan was unable to reap anything out of the conference.[4]

A more formal effort was made in 1886, when a diplomatic conference was called at Tokio. At this conference, Count Inouye, the Foreign Minister, again took an active part. The deliberations were extended to the following year, when Japan agreed that in addition to the native

[1] Art. 1, Malloy, vol. i, p. 1022.

[2] Art. 10, *ibid.*, p. 1024.

[3] *Archives diplomatiques*, 1897, vol, iv, pp. 213-214.

[4] Japan was willing to sign only temporary treaties, while the Powers insisted on permanent agreements. *Ibid.*, p. 345.

judges there should be a body of European and American
experts, who should constitute a majority in every court
before which aliens might be required to appear. When
this important concession was obtained, the Europeans went
further and insisted that the judges should be nominated
by the Diplomatic Corps and that the latter should control
the laws, rules of procedure, and details of the administration of justice. Upon receiving news of these exorbitant
demands, the Japanese public was greatly excited, and a
wave of indignation swept over the whole country. Count
Inouye was forced to give up his portfolio, and in July, 1887,
the Foreign Office notified the foreign representatives that
the treaty negotiations were to be adjourned till the completion of the new codes under preparation.[1] During the
conference, the United States showed a friendly attitude to
the Japanese point of view and concluded with Japan a
treaty of extradition on April 29, 1886.[2] In submitting
the treaty to the Senate, President Cleveland declared that
it had been made partly because of the support which its
conclusion would give to Japan in her efforts towards judicial autonomy and complete sovereignty.[3]

Count Inouye was succeeded by Count Okuma in the
Foreign Office. The new Minister changed his tactics, and
instead of seeking for the collective support of all the
Powers, he endeavored to enter into separate agreements
with each one of them. On November 30, 1888, a treaty
was concluded with Mexico, which fully recognized Japan's
judicial control over Mexican citizens and vessels within
the territorial limits of Japan.[4] Meanwhile, negotiations

[1] *Archives diplomatiques,* 1897, vol. iv, p. 346. *Cf.* Foster, *op. cit.,*
pp. 357-358.

[2] Malloy, vol. i, p. 1025.

[3] U. S. *Sen. Ex. Journal,* vol. xxv, p. 495.

[4] Art. 8, *State Papers,* vol. lxxix, p. 131.

were resumed with Great Britain. On January 19, 1889, a draft treaty and two draft notes were transmitted to the British Government by the Japanese Minister at London. The terms contained in these drafts pertaining to extraterritoriality were briefly: that for five years after the coming into force of the proposed treaty, British consular jurisdiction in Japan should be limited to a restricted number of ports; that outside of these limits Japanese courts should have exclusive jurisdiction; that British consular jurisdiction should " wholly cease and determine " at the expiration of the five-year period; that the Government of Japan should strive to complete the elaboration of Japan's law codes within the following year; that in case such elaboration should be delayed beyond two years after the proposed treaty was concluded, the Japanese Government should then ask for the postponement of the date of totally abolishing British consular jurisdiction until at least three years after the codes in question should have been promulgated; and that the Japanese Government should engage a number of foreign judges in the Supreme Court, to constitute a majority in cases involving foreigners as defendants.[1]   In their counterdrafts, the British Government accepted the Japanese terms with slight modifications.[2]   But the offers made by Japan were again resented by the Japanese public, and the party in opposition to Count Okuma declared his treaty measure to be unconstitutional.   The popular indignation became so intense that on October 19, 1889, a fanatic threw a bomb at Count Okuma, and the work of treaty revision was again suspended.[3]

After these failures, the Japanese Government abandoned

---

[1] *Parliamentahy Papers,* 1894 [C. 7548], *Japan,* no. 1 (1894), pp. 7, 10, 11.

[2] *Ibid.,* pp. 19, 20, 23.

[3] Hishida, *International Position of Japan,* pp. 142-143.

the hope of success in diplomatic negotiations. Efforts were exerted to push on the reform movement, with a view of winning over foreign sentiment by means of visible signs of progress. In this, the Japanese were much more successful than in their previous resort to diplomacy. The reforms culminated in the promulgation of the imperial constitution in 1889.[1] In 1891, the Civil Code, the Code of Civil Procedure, the Commercial Code, and the Code of the Constitution of Courts were promulgated, thus completing the entire Japanese legal system.[2]

Viscount Aoki, who succeeded Count Okuma as Foreign Minister, again took up the negotiations for treaty revision. He insisted on the judicial autonomy of Japan. His correspondence with the British Government on the employment of foreign judges and the completion of Japan's legal codes, gives additional evidence of the importance of the legal argument in every attempt at the modification of the extraterritorial régime.

With reference to the improvement of the Japanese judiciary, Viscount Aoki enumerated the specific reforms brought about since 1872, viz.: the creation of a separate and independent system of courts; the promulgation of various codes of law and the imperial constitution; the introduction of a system of competitive examinations for appointments to the judgeships; and the promulgation of a new law providing for a comprehensive and complete reorganization of the imperial courts of justice. Having dwelt upon the above-mentioned reforms, Viscount Aoki declared:

In the light of these important facts, it may be asserted, without fear of contradiction, that when Japanese Tribunals supersede Consular Courts, no case in which a foreigner is

[1] U. S. *Foreign Relations*, 1889, p. 536.

[2] Okamura, " The Progress of the Judicial System in Japan," *Journal of the Society of Comparative Legislation,* new series, vol. i, p. 51.

interested will ever be tried in Last Instance, except by a Court composed, at least, of a majority of Judges, who have submitted to the test of a severe competitive examination, and are, consequently, well grounded in the principles of Western jurisprudence, besides being thoroughly conversant with the laws of Japan.

In addition to the improvement of the Japanese courts, Viscount Aoki attempted also to show the progress which the Japanese Government had made in bringing the work of codification to its completion. He said:

Nearly ten years have elapsed since the Criminal Code and the Code of Criminal Procedure were promulgated, and the time can now only be reckoned by months before the Constitution which was prumulgated a year ago will come into force. The Imperial Government have for years been engaged in the labor of elaborating Civil and Commercial Codes, and it is a matter of public notoriety that these great works are nearly completed, and will ere long be proclaimed. And the fact that they have not already been promulgated, in the presence of so many inducements connected with Treaty revision, betrays the solicitude of the Imperial Government that, when issued, they shall be complete.[1]

The British Government proposed a new draft treaty, which provided that British consular jurisdiction should continue to be exercised for five years and that if at the end of this period the new codes of Japan should have been in actual and satisfactory operation for twelve months, Great Britain would relinquish her extraterritorial jurisdiction.[2] This draft treaty was accepted by Viscount Aoki as a basis for further negotiation.[3]

[1] *Parl. Pap.*, 1894 [C. 7548], Japan, no. 1 (1894), p. 51.
[2] *Ibid.*, p. 63.
[3] Viscount Aoki to Mr. Fraser, Sep. 12, 1890, *ibid.*, p. 65.

Viscount Aoki was succeeded by Viscount Enomotto, who shared the view that before the abolition of extraterritoriality could be expected, there should exist in Japan in actual operation a satisfactory system of jurisprudence. Although the new codes had been promulgated in 1891, the civil and commercial codes were not immediately put into force. When the Upper House was deliberating on the question, on May 26, 1892, Viscount Enomotto appeared on the scene and made a speech, in which he openly disabused the minds of those who dreamed of securing judicial autonomy without offering adequate guarantees to foreign life and property. He said:

In considering the clauses in need of revision as a whole, our motto must be simply the protection of our ancient national rights and national interests, and for the accomplishment of this purpose there is one method, and one only, that of enacting and carrying into effect a Code of Laws fit to be accepted by the civilized nations of the world.

However eagerly all classes of Japanese may desire to possess a Treaty free from all imperfections and defects, it admits of no manner of doubt that until such a Code of Laws shall be in operation friendly countries will withhold their consent to revision. . . . Those persons who descant upon the shortcomings of the present Treaties are in the habit of looking back to the time of their inception, and attributing their defects to the limited knowledge of foreign affairs possessed by the Ministers of the day. But the Ministers of thirty years ago could not possibly be intimately acquainted with the circumstances of foreign countries, and even granting the necessary experience in exceptional instances, the Treaty Powers could not have been induced to subject the precious lives and property of their subjects to the laws of Japan, and that for the very good reason that there were at that time no laws fit to be enforced in a civilized society, to whose protection their lives and property could have been committed.[1]

[1] *Ibid.*, p. 71.

In spite of Viscount Enomotto's eloquent plea, the imperial diet passed a law, which was sanctioned by imperial decree on November 24, 1892, postponing the operation of the Civil and Commercial Codes.[1]

In 1892, the Japanese Government took advantage of the withdrawal of consuls by Portugal, and issued an ordinance putting an end to the consular jurisdiction hitherto enjoyed by Portugal in Japan.[2] Between January 18, 1893, and April 10, 1894, notes were exchanged with the Hawaiian Government, by which the latter abandoned their rights of jurisdiction in Japan.[3]

Meanwhile, negotiations had once more been resumed with Great Britain and other Powers for the revision of their treaties with Japan.   In 1894, the conversations with Great Britain were transferred from Tokio to London.   Viscount Aoki, who was then Japanese Minister at Berlin, was instructed to go over to London to carry on and finish the work of treaty revision.   Finally, after assuring the British Government of the actual reforms introduced by Japan into her judicial system,[4] Viscount Aoki succeeded in obtaining from Great Britain a new treaty, which was signed on July 16, 1894.   Article 20 provides for the abrogation of all existing treaties and of the extraterritorial rights enjoyed by Great Britain under them.   Article 21 stipulates that " the present Treaty shall not take effect until at least five years after its signature." [5]   The intent of the latter provision is clearly explained by the note of Viscount Aoki to Earl Kimberley, July 16, 1894, which announced:

[1] *Parl. Pap.*, cited, p. 74.

[2] Hishida, *op. cit.*, p. 143.   Presumably with Portugal's consent, but no information is available on this point.

[3] *State Papers,* vol. lxxxvi, p. 1185.

[4] *Parl. Pap.*, cited, pp. 94-95.

[5] *State Papers,* vol. lxxxvi, pp. 46, 47.

That the Imperial Japanese Government, recognizing the advantage of having the Codes of the Empire which have already been promulgated in actual operation when the Treaty stipulations at present subsisting between the Government of Japan and that of Great Britain cease to be binding, engage not to give the notice provided for by the first paragraph of Article XXI of the Treaty of Commerce and Navigation, signed this day, until those portions of said Codes which are now in abeyance are brought into actual force.[1]

Treaties were also entered into with the United States, November 22, 1894,[2] Italy, December 1, 1894,[3] Peru, March 20, 1895,[4] Russia, May 27/June 8, 1895,[5] Denmark, October 19, 1895,[6] Brazil, November 5, 1895,[7] Germany, April 4, 1896,[8] Sweden and Norway, May 2, 1896,[9] Belgium, June 22, 1896,[10] France, August 4, 1896,[11] the Netherlands, September 8, 1896,[12] Switzerland, November 10, 1896,[13] Spain, January 2, 1897,[14] Portugal, January 26, 1897,[15] Chile, September 25, 1897,[16] Austria-Hungary, December 5, 1897,[17] Argentina, February 3, 1898,[18] and Greece, May 20/

[1] *Ibid.*, p. 52.

[2] Art. 18, Malloy, vol. i, p. 1035.

[3] Art. 19, *State Papers,* vol. lxxxvi, p. 1194.

[4] Art. 17, *ibid.*, vol. lxxxvii, p. 1223.

[5] Art. 18, *ibid.*, p. 862.

[6] Art. 18, *ibid.*, p. 694.

[7] Art. 10, *ibid.*, p. 1194.

[8] Art. 20, *ibid.*, vol. lxxxviii, p. 588.

[9] Art. 17, *ibid.*, p. 458.

[10] Art. 18, *ibid.*, p. 404.

[11] Art. 23, *ibid.*, p. 536.

[12] Art. 18, *ibid.*, p. 547.

[13] Art. 14, *ibid.*, p. 490.

[14] Art. 19, *ibid.*, vol. lxxxix, p. 965.

[15] Art. 18, *ibid.*, p. 976.

[16] Art. 11, *ibid.*, vol. xcix, p. 936.

[17] Art. 22, *ibid.*, vol. lxxxix, p. 987.

[18] Art. 10, *ibid.*, vol. xcii, p. 226.

June 1, 1899.[1]   These treaties put an end to consular jurisdiction in Japan; they all took effect in July and August,
1899.

The close proximity of the dates of these negotiations and of the Sino-Japanese War has led to the conception or misconception that Japan's success in that conflict
was mainly responsible for the restoration of her judicial
autonomy and her other rights of sovereignty.   To cite a
typically inaccurate statement,

Prior to her victory over China, she [Japan] was subject to
foreign aggression as much as China, but subsequent to the
Chino-Japanese War, when she had demonstrated her prowess
and ability, her sovereignty remained intact and immune from
all external aggressions; what is more, she recovered her lost,
or delegated rights of sovereignty.[2]

For the sake of scientific accuracy, the author deems it
necessary to devote a few words to the refutation of this
widely held belief.

At the very outset, it may be admitted that the victory of
Japan over China in the war of 1894-95 had much to do
with the increase of Japan's prestige in the world.   To the
political ascendancy of the island empire, the Sino-Japanese
War doubtless contributed signally.   But to say that the
recovery of Japan's sovereign rights was due to her defeat
of China and especially to ascribe the abolition of extraterritoriality in Japan to that event would be to ignore many
other important considerations.

In the first place, it must be pointed out that if we compare the dates more carefully than is usually done, we will
find that the most important treaty abolishing extraterri-

[1] Art. 11, *ibid.*, p. 369.

[2] Bau, *Foreign Relations of China* (rev. and enl. ed., New York,
Chicago, etc., 1923), p. 494.

toriality in Japan was concluded prior to the opening of the
Sino-Japanese War; to say nothing of the treaty of November 30, 1888, with Mexico, and the exchange of notes
of January 13, 1893/April 10, 1894, with the Hawaiian
Islands, the British treaty was concluded on July 16, 1894.
Owing to the predominant interest of Great Britain in Japan,
her treaty was by far the most important, and its importance
is indicated by the fact that all the later agreements of the
same nature were largely modeled after it.   Contrary to
the popular belief, this treaty was concluded before instead
of after the outbreak of the Sino-Japanese War.[1]   When
we recall that negotiations for the revision of her treaties
had been embarked upon by Japan since 1871, twenty-three
years before the war with China took place, and that the
main lines of the British treaty had been fairly settled by the
end of 1890, it is impossible to establish any causal relationship between the war and the abolition of extraterritoriality
in Japan.

True, the American and other treaties were concluded
after the opening of hostilities between China and Japan,
and, in fact, the majority of them were signed and ratified
after the Peace of Shimonoseki, which bears the date of
April 17, 1895.   Had the Japanese success in the late war
exerted any influence on the consummation of the protracted
negotiations in these cases, it could not have been an important, much less a controlling, one.   As has been mentioned, the provisions of the later treaties were but verbal
reproductions of the terms of the British treaty, which, it
must have been thought, if they could regulate the rights
and obligations of the nationals of the country with the

[1] Actual hostilities began on July 25, 1894, when two Chinese vessels,
the *Kuang-yi* and the *Tsi-yuen*, opened fire on the Japanese naval forces
off the islands of Phung and Shapain.   A declaration of war was
issued by both governments simultaneously on August first.   See Vladimir, *The China-Japan War* (New York, 1896), pp. 95-96, 113.

greatest commercial interest in Japan, could do the same thing with regard to the nationals of all the other Treaty Powers.

In the case of the United States particularly, little importance need be attached to the outcome of the Sino-Japanese War and its effect on the abolition of extraterritoriality in Japan. It is to be borne in mind that of all the Powers which had treaty relations with Japan, the United States was the earliest to evince a willingness to respond to Japan's appeal for treaty revision. The support of the American Government and people was pledged as early as 1871 to the efforts of Japan, while successively in 1878 and 1886, the United States Government displayed its friendship by concluding extradition and tariff conventions with Japan. This background of sincere support was a natural prelude to the final promise for the abolition of American extraterritoriality in Japan, and even if the Sino-Japanese War had not occurred, it is unlikely that the United States would have delayed its action much longer. Moreover, if the United States Government had chosen to procrastinate, the progress of the war would have furnished the best pretext. On the contrary, however, that government made its treaty for the abolition of extraterritoriality in Japan while the storm was still raging.

As a matter of fact, the most important consideration which prompted the Powers to agree to the restoration of Japan's judicial autonomy was the progress which Japan had achieved in the way of judicial reform. Had the war been the controlling factor and had Japan's military success alone been regarded as sufficient to entitle her to complete judicial rights, the Powers would logically have had to give up their extraterritoriality without imposing any other conditions. But this was not what happened. All the treaties were to take effect in 1899, although some of them had been concluded as early as 1894, the intervening period being intended for the coming into force of the Japanese Codes; and as has been stated above, the Japanese Government agreed to refrain from giving notice of the cessation of the old treaties, " until those portions of said Codes which are now in abeyance are brought into actual operation." It is evident, therefore, that glamorous as it was, Japan's successful emergence from the war with China did not of itself lead to the abolition of extraterritoriality. Any attempt simply to explain the situation on this score and to ignore the more important considerations altogether, is an unfounded conjecture and should be discredited by any student of the history of international relations.

IV. SIAM

Ever since the extraterritorial system was formally introduced into Siam, this State has been undergoing a series of judicial reforms. The fruit of these reforms was the formal renunciation or promise of renunciation on the part of the foreign Powers of their consular jurisdiction in Siam. In 1883, Great Britain entered into a treaty with Siam which granted to the Siamese Government the right to establish an " International Court " composed of Siamese judges and administering Siamese law, to decide disputes between British subjects in Chiengmai, Lakon and Lampoonchi, the right of the British consul to intervene in such cases being reserved.[1] The International Court system was extended in 1884-1885 and 1896 to other Siamese provinces.[2] On February 13, 1904, France made a similar agreement with Siam, the operation of the Siamese International Court being extended to cases arising in Chiengmai, Lakon, Lampoonchi and Nan.[3] Denmark on March 24, 1905, and Italy

[1] *State Papers,* vol. lxxiv, p. 81.
[2] Great Britain, *Treaty Series,* no. 9 (1897), pp. 2, 3.
[3] *State Papers,* vol. xcvii, p. 964.

on April 8, 1905, concluded treaties with Siam to identically
the same effect.[1] By her treaty of March 23, 1907, France
agreed to the extension of the system to all her Asiatic subjects and protégés, and to the abolition of the International
Court régime after the promulgation and putting into effect
of the Siamese codes.[2] On March 10, 1909, Great Britain
agreed by a new treaty to extend the jurisdiction of the
International Courts to " all British subjects in Siam registered at the British consulate after the date of the present
Treaty." The transfer of the jurisdiction of the International Courts to the ordinary Siamese courts was also
promised on the same conditions as were laid down by the
French treaty of 1907. All other British subjects in Siam
not belonging to the class mentioned above were subjected
to the jurisdiction of the ordinary Siamese courts.[3] The
right of evocation was maintained, but it should " cease to
be exercised in all matters coming within the scope of codes
of laws regularly promulgated." [4] Denmark agreed, on
March 15, 1913, to submit all Danish subjects coming to
Siam after the ratification of the treaty of that date to the
jurisdiction of the ordinary Siamese courts.[5] In 1916, the
Russian Government, upon its own initiative, entered into
negotiations for a treaty similar to the British treaty of
1909, but the outbreak of the revolution in Russia cut the
matter short.[6]

In explaining the conclusion of the treaty of 1909, the
British Minister at Bangkok, besides alluding to the admin-

[1] *State Papers*, vol. ci, pp. 290-409.

[2] *Ibid.*, vol. c, p. 1029.

[3] *Ibid.*, vol. cii, p. 127.

[4] Sec. 3 of the protocol annexed to the treaty of March 10, 1909,
ibid., p. 130.

[5] *Ibid.*, vol. cvii, p. 751.

[6] *Siam's Case for Revision of Obsolete Treaty Obligations* (1919), p. 11.

istrative inconveniences occasioned by the partial cessation
of extraterritoriality in one section of Siam and its maintenance in another, mentioned "various additional factors,
such as the desire of British subjects to acquire the right to
hold land . . . , the codification of Siamese law, and the
very creditable and successful efforts made by the Siamese
Government to improve the standard of their judicial administration." [1]   This is cited to show that here, as in every
other case, a preponderating amount of importance is attached to the improvement of the judicial régime as a pre-
requisite for the restoration, partial or complete, of judicial
autonomy.

At the Paris Peace Conference of 1919, Siam prepared a
Case for the revision of her treaty obligations. One of the
latter which Siam sought to get rid of completely was that
of extraterritoriality. After presenting briefly the history
of extraterritoriality in Siam,[2] the *Case* of Siam gave the
following as reasons for requesting its abolition: (1) that
it invaded the sovereignty of Siam, a free nation; (2) that
it made the administration of impartial justice difficult, if
not impossible; (3) that it put obstacles in the way of the
maintenance of order, being a continual affront to Siam's
dignity and a fruitful source of irritation; (4) that it was
expensive—involving, as it did, the maintenance of European judges and advisers; and (5) that it tended to dis-
courage the completion of the Siamese codes of laws then in
progress, since there was nowhere even in the British or
Danish treaty any assurance that once these codes were completed and promulgated, the requirement that European
judges and advisers assist in the Siamese courts would be

[1] Memorandum explanatory of the circumstances which render the
modification of the present system of British extraterritorial jurisdiction in Siam desirable. *Parliamentary Papers,* 1909 [Cd. 4646],
Siam, no. 1 (1909).

[2] *Siam's Case,* pp. 7-13.

yielded and these courts restored to their full measure of authority, as recognized by the treaties previous to 1855.

Under these circumstances, a transfer of jurisdiction from the international to the ordinary Siamese courts would be in name only, even with the obliteration of the privilege of evocation, which was rarely exercised. For these reasons, it was declared " that this oppressive scheme of exterritoriality must be removed in its entirety, both because it works practical and unnecessary hardship to Siam and because it is unjust." [1]

All Siam succeeded in doing at Paris was to secure from the defeated Powers the abrogation of their extraterritorial rights in Siam. By the Treaty of Versailles, June 28, 1919, Germany made such a renunciation as from June 22, 1917.[2] Similar renunciations were made by Austria in the Treaty of St. Germain, September 10, 1919,[3] and by Hungary in the Treaty of Trianon, June 4, 1920.[4]

On December 16, 1920, the United States entered into a treaty with Siam, containing a protocol, article 1 of which announced that the system of extraterritorial jurisdiction established in Siam for citizens of the United States and " the privileges, exemptions, and immunities " now enjoyed by them as a part of or appurtenant to the system " shall absolutely cease and determine on the date of the exchange of ratifications " and that thereafter all citizens of the United States, and persons, corporations, companies and associations entitled to its protection in Siam should be subjected to the jurisdiction of the Siamese courts. However, until

---

[1] *Siam's Case*, pp. 17-20.

[2] Art. 135, *The Treaty of Peace between the Allied and Associated Powers and Germany* (London, 1919), p. 71.

[3] Art. 110, *The Treaty of Peace between the Allied and Associated Powers and Austria* (London, 1921), p. 43.

[4] Art. 94, Great Britain, *Treaty Series*, no. 10 (1920), p. 25.

the promulgation and putting into force of all the Siamese codes, and for a period of five years thereafter, but no longer, the United States, through its diplomatic and consular agents in Siam, whenever in its discretion it deems proper so to do in the interests of justice, may evoke any case pending before any Siamese court, except the Supreme or Dika Court, in which an American citizen, or a person, etc., entitled to its protection, is defendant or accused.[1] This is the most important concession obtained by Siam after the treaties of peace with Germany, Austria and Hungary, so far as extraterritorial jurisdiction in Siam is concerned. The protocol subjects American citizens in Siam to the jurisdiction of the ordinary Siamese courts without the intermediary stage of the "International Courts." The only guarantee the United States has deemed it necessary to impose on Siam is that of evocation, which can take place only in the rarest cases of miscarriage of justice.[2]

V. CHINA

Ever since the opening of the present century, China has made repeated attempts to secure the modification of the extraterritorial régime. Up to the present time, no less than six Powers have promised the ultimate abolition of extraterritoriality in China in addition to a number of others, which have been deprived of their judicial rights. The first treaty embodying a promise for the abolition was that of September 5, 1902, with Great Britain, article 12 of which provides:

China having expressed a strong desire to reform her judicial

[1] Malloy, vol. iii (1923), p. 2835.
[2] See art. 2 of the protocol. According to a recent press despatch, a new commercial treaty was concluded between France and Siam on February 14, 1925, by which the former, subject to certain conditions, engaged to abolish her extraterritorial rights in Siam. London *Times,* February, 16, 1925, 11 c.

system and to bring it into accord with that of Western nations, Great Britain agrees to give every assistance to such reform, and she will also be prepared to relinquish her extra-territorial rights when she is satisfied that the state of Chinese laws, the arrangement for their administration, and other considerations warrant her in so doing.[1]

Similar provisions were contained in the treaties with Japan [2] and the United States,[3] signed separately on October 8, 1903.[4] Article 10 of the treaty with Sweden, dated July 2, 1908, provides that " as soon as all the Treaty Powers have agreed to relinquish their extraterritorial rights, Sweden will also be prepared to do so." [5] By a declaration annexed to the treaty of June 13, 1918, the Swiss Government made the same promise.[6] Finally, by an exchange of notes between China and Mexico, September 26, 1921, embodying an agreement for the provisional modification of the Sino-Mexican treaty of December 14, 1899, which had been denounced by Mexico on November 11, 1920,[7] the Mexican Government engaged to " express on one of the amendments of the above-mentioned Treaty the renouncement that will be made to the consular jurisdiction in China." [8]

With the declaration of war on Germany and Austria-Hungary, on August 14, 1917, China abrogated all her treaties with these countries and put an end to their extra-

[1] MacMurray, *Treaties*, vol. i, 1902/7, p. 351.

[2] *Ibid.*, 1903/4, p. 414.

[3] *Ibid.*, 1903/5, p. 431.

[4] Art. 16 of the unratified treaty with Portugal of November 11, 1904, had an identical provision. *Ibid.*, 1902/9, p. 374.

[5] *Ibid.*, 1908/11, p. 745.

[6] *Ibid.*, vol. ii, 1918/8, p. 1430.

[7] *Cf. supra*, p. 91, n. 1.

[8] League of Nations, *Treaty Series*, vol. xiii, p. 208.

territorial privileges.¹   A circular note was sent on the same
day to the Diplomatic Corps, stating:

Now that China has declared that a state of war exists with
Germany and Austria-Hungary, as regards all civil and criminal
cases involving Germans and Austrians in China, a set of provisional regulations governing the trial of civil and criminal
cases of enemy subjects has been drawn up, which were promulgated and put into effect on the 14th instant.

The first article of these regulations provided: " Civil and
criminal cases of enemy subjects will be tried during the
period of the War by the Chinese courts." ²

At the Paris Peace Conference of 1919, China made another attempt to secure the abolition of extraterritoriality.
A statement was made and presented by the Chinese delegation, which set forth the Chinese claim to territorial jurisdiction.   After reviewing briefly the basis of extraterritorial
rights enjoyed by foreigners in China, and the successive
promises made by the Powers to relinquish them, the statement declares:

While we do not claim that the Chinese laws and their administration have reached such a state as has been attained by the
most advanced nations, we do feel confident to assert that China
has made very considerable progress in the administration of
justice and in all matters pertaining thereto since the signing of
the above-mentioned Commercial Treaties.

The evidences of this progress are given as follows: (1)
adoption of a National Constitution; (2) preparation of
Civil, Criminal, and Commercial Codes, and Codes of Civil
and Criminal Procedure; (3) establishment of new Courts,
viz., District Courts, High Courts or Courts of Appeal, and

---

¹ *Presidential Mandate*, Aug. 14, 1917, *ibid.*, 1917/7, pp. 1361-2.
² *Ibid.*, pp. 1372-3.

the *Taliyuan* or Supreme Court; (4) improvements in legal procedure, such as the separation of civil and criminal cases, publicity of trial and judgments, etc.; (5) careful training of judicial officers; and (6) reform of prison and police systems.

Furthermore, the maintenance of the system of extraterritoriality in China appears to be still less justifiable, if we look at the serious defects in its operation. Among these defects the statement mentions (1) diversity of laws applied; (2) lack of effective control over witnesses or plaintiffs of another nationality; (3) difficulty in obtaining evidence where a foreigner commits a crime in the interior; and (4) conflict of consular and judicial functions. These defects, it is contended, have led to the total abolition of the system in Japan by all the Powers, and to its partial abolition in Siam by certain Powers. "China, therefore, asks that the system will also disappear in China at the expiration of a definite period and upon the fulfilment of the following conditions:" (1) promulgation of a Criminal, a Civil, and a Commercial Code, a Code of Civil Procedure, and a Code of Criminal Procedure; and (2) establishment of new courts in all the localities where foreigners reside. China undertakes to fulfil these conditions by the end of 1924. But before the actual abolition of extraterritoriality, China requests the Powers (1) to submit every mixed case where the defendant is a Chinese to Chinese courts without interference on the part of the foreigners, and (2) to allow the execution of warrants issued or judgments delivered by Chinese courts within the Concessions or within the precincts of any foreign building without any previous examination by any consular or foreign judicial officer.

Finally, the statement asserts that the abolition of extraterritoriality in China would be of benefit to the foreign Powers as well as to China, in that it would tend to remove the many inconveniences involved in cases between foreigners of different nationalities, and to develop international commerce, possibly to open the whole country to the trade and residence of foreigners.[1] No action seems to have been taken by the Conference on the question, and the *status quo* was maintained.

In 1919, China concluded a treaty with Bolivia, article 2 of which contained a most-favored-nation clause. In an exchange of notes between the two governments, Bolivia has agreed to refrain from interpreting the inclusion of this clause in the treaty as an admission of the Bolivians in China to extraterritorial rights.[2]

On June 1, 1920, a treaty was entered into by China with Persia, which provided expressly that " in all civil and criminal cases to which Persian subjects are parties, they shall be subject to Chinese law and jurisdiction." [3]

China severed her treaty relations with Russia in 1920, because of her indisposition to recognize the Soviet régime in that country. At the instance of the Minister of Foreign Affairs, a Presidential Mandate was issued on September 23, 1920, declaring " the suspension of the recognition of the Russian Minister and Consuls in China." Following this, Prince Koudacheff, then Minister of Russia to China, addressed a note to the Doyen of the Dipomatic Corps at Peking, requesting the heads of the missions in China to examine into the status of Russians resident there. In a note, dated October 11, 1920, the Doyen inquired the Chinese Foreign Office on the subject. In reply, the Minister of Foreign Affairs said, in his note of October 22, " Russian citizens in China will continue to enjoy the rights secured

[1] *Questions for Readjustment submitted by China to the Peace Conference* (Paris, 1919), pp. 14-18.

[2] *China Year Book,* 1921-22, p. 371.

[3] Art. 4, *State Papers,* vol. cxiv, p. 677; *cf.* League of Nations, *Treaty Series,* vol. ix, p. 21.

to them by treaties." But "Russian consular jurisdiction must, of course, cease. In the trying of cases in which foreigners are plaintiffs and Russians defendants, the Chinese courts may apply Russian laws, but only those which do not conflict with Chinese legal rights. Possibly persons, well versed in Russian law, may be employed as advisers to the Chinese law courts." Desiring further elucidation, the Diplomatic Corps addressed another note on November 18, which was replied on November 29 to the following effect: " Both civil and criminal cases in which Russians are involved undoubtedly come, by treaty, under the jurisdiction of Consular Courts. But China has at present ceased to recognize the Russian Consuls in their official capacity and, as a result of this measure, there are now no persons capable of exercising this function. China could therefore not do otherwise than assume jurisdiction over the civil and criminal cases in which Russians resident in China are involved. This measure naturally results from the present situation." [1] The abolition of Russian extraterritorial rights was confirmed by the new treaty between China and Russia, signed on May 31, 1924.[2]

By the treaty of May 20, 1921, Germany renounced her extraterritorial privileges in China and consented to the proposition that thereafter her nationals in China should be subjected to Chinese local jurisdiction.[3]

---

[1] *China Year Book,* 1921-22, pp. 626-632. Quotations are from the unofficial translation of the *Year Book.*

[2] Art. 12, *Chinese Social and Political Science Review,* vol. viii, p. 224.

[3] On May 20, 1921, H. von Borch, "authorized representative of the Government of the Republic of Germany," made a written declaration to Dr. W. W. Yen, Chinese Minister of Foreign Affairs, in which he "formally declares to consent to the abrogation of the consular jurisdiction in China." The declaration was embodied in the Sino-German Commercial Treaty of even date, article 3 of which reads: "They [nationals of each country in the other] shall be placed, their persons

The most recent attempt on the part of China to obtain the consent of the Powers to the abolition of extraterritoriality was made at the Conference on the Limitation of Armament opened in Washington on November 12, 1921. On November 25 of that year, Dr. Chung Hui Wang, representing the Chinese delegation, presented to the Committee on Pacific and Far Eastern Affairs a statement, setting forth China's wishes with regard to the modification and ultimate abolition of consular jurisdiction. Dr. Wang pointed out the following as some of the serious objections to the system of extraterritoriality in China:

(a) In the first place, it is in derogation of China's sovereign rights, and is regarded by the Chinese people as a national humiliation.

(b) There is a multiplicity of courts in one and the same locality, and the interrelation of such courts has given rise to a legal situation perplexing both to the trained lawyer and to the layman.

(c) Disadvantages arise from the uncertainty of the law. The general rule is that the law to be applied in a given case is the law of the defendant's nationality, and so, in a commercial transaction between, say, X and Y of different nationalities, the rights and liabilities of the parties vary according as to whether X sued Y first, or Y sued X first.

(d) When causes of action, civil or criminal, arise in which foreigners are defendants, it is necessary for adjudication that they should be carried to the nearest Consular Court, which might be many miles away; and so it often happens that it is practically impossible to obtain the attendance of the necessary witnesses, or to produce other necessary evidence.

(e) Finally, it is a further disadvantage to the Chinese that

as well as their properties, under the jurisdiction of the local courts; they shall conform themselves to the laws of the country where they reside." The treaty was ratified by China on July 1, 1921. *China Year Book,* 1921-22, pp. 738 *et seq.*

foreigners in China, under cover of extraterritoriality, claim immunity from local taxes and excises which the Chinese themselves are required to pay.

Dr. Wang then dwelt upon the progress made by China in her judicial reform. He enumerated (1) the Civil Code, still in course of revision; (2) the Criminal Code, in force since 1912; (3) the Code of Civil Procedure; (4) the Code of Criminal Procedure, both of which had just been promulgated; and (5) the Commercial Code, part of which had been put into force. " Then there is a new system of law courts established in 1910. The judges are all modern, trained lawyers, and no one could be appointed a judge unless he had attained the requisite legal training." Dr. Wang declared that the China of today was not like the China of twenty years ago, when Great Britain encouraged her to reform her judicial system, and that, *a fortiori*, she was not the China of eighty years ago, when the system of extraterritoriality was first imposed on her. This, Dr. Wang continued, warranted the wish of China for the progressive modification and ultimate abolition of the system.[1]

A sub-committee was appointed to consider the proposals submitted by China. At the ninth meeting of the Committee of the Whole, November 29, 1921, the Sub-Committee on Extraterritoriality submitted some draft resolutions, which were unanimously adopted by the Committee without further discussion, and later approved, also without discussion, by the Conference at its fourth Plenary Session, held on December 10, 1921. One of the resolutions adopted was:

That the Governments of the Powers above named shall establish a Commission (to which each of such Governments shall appoint one member) to inquire into the present practice of

[1] *Conference on the Limitation of Armament* (Washington, 1922), pp. 932-936.

extraterritorial jurisdiction in China, and into the laws and
judicial system and methods of judicial administration in China,
and to assist and further the efforts of the Chinese Government
to effect such legislation and judicial reforms as would warrant
the several Powers in relinquishing, either progressively or
otherwise, their respective rights of extraterritoriality.[1]

The resolutions provided that " the Commission herein
contemplated shall be constituted within three months after
the adjournment of the Conference;" but due to the unsettled conditions in China, the Chinese Government requested and the Powers agreed that the investigation by the
Commission be temporarily postponed.[2] Nothing has been
heard of the Commission since then. The Chinese Government, on the other hand, has been hard at work in preparation for the long-promised investigation. In June, 1922,
the Commission on Extraterritoriality, which had been organized in 1920, was entrusted with " the study of all problems relating to the eventual abolition of consular jurisdiction and other extraterritorial rights and privileges, and
the formulation of plans to be laid before the International
Commission of Inquiry." In addition to other work, the
Commission on Extraterritoriality has undertaken the publication in English and French of the principal modern
Chinese legislative enactments, including the Constitutional
Laws, organic and political, the Codes, Commercial and
Criminal and other Civil Laws, Laws and regulations of the
Organization of the Judiciary, the principal Administrative
Laws, a summary of the Cases decided in the Supreme Court
and in other high judicial tribunals, the Codes of Civil and
Criminal Procedure, and the Provisional Criminal Code.

One of the greatest abuses connected with the extraterritorial system in China as well as one of the most unjusti-

[1] *Ibid.*, p. 1010.

[2] New York *Times,* May 4, 1922.

fiable violations of Chinese treaty right is the usurpation by
the foreign Powers of the Shanghai International Mixed
Court. This Court was established in 1864, and though
designated as a mixed court, the latter is a misnomer, for
it was a purely Chinese court having jurisdiction over
Chinese defendants and administering Chinese law.[1] The
judges of the court were, moreover, appointed by the Chinese
Government.

With the outbreak of the Revolution, in 1911, Shanghai
declared its independence of the Manchu dynasty, and the
Taotai was unable to function in the " native city." He
was compelled to ask the permission of the foreign consuls
to exercise his official duties within the International Settlement. The consent of the Diplomatic Corps at Peking was
withheld from this proposition, and the Consular Body was
instructed to exercise such powers of control as might be
necessary to protect foreign life and property and to maintain the status of the International Settlement. Advantage
was taken of this authority to take a highly questionable
step, for which the Powers have not yet atoned. The Consular Body issued, on November 10, 1911, a public proclamation, taking over the International Mixed Court and con-
firming the appointments held by the three Chinese judges.[2]

Thus, the International Mixed Court, which should be,
and up to 1911 was, a purely Chinese court, was peremp-
torily subjected to foreign control by the action of a consular body, who had no diplomatic authority at all and with-

---

[1] According to the revised rules of 1869, " An official having the rank
of Sub-Prefect will be deputed to reside within the foreign Settlements.... He will decide all civil and commercial suits between Chinese
resident within the Settlements, and also between Chinese and foreign
residents, in cases where Chinese are defendants, by Chinese Law."
Hertslet, *China Treaties* (London, 1908), vol. ii, p. 662.

[2] Willoughby, *Foreign Rights and Interests in China* (Baltimore, 1920),
p. 60.

out the slightest legal justification. Though apparently demanded by the circumstances of the time, foreign control had absolutely no right to exist when a recognized government was established in China. And yet the Powers have been slow in restoring the Court to Chinese supervision, and they have repeatedly refused to consider the Chinese demand for its rendition. The Chinese have, however, never ceased to reiterate the demand. Even at this minute, a widespread movement is being sponsored in various centers, looking to the equitable settlement of the question by the Diplomatic Corps at Peking. The details of the correspondence have no place here, both because very little is as yet published [1] and because the Mixed Court issue in China is purely a violation of Chinese treaty right and should not be confused with the question of extraterritoriality, which, though anomalous, has a sound treaty basis.

It may be pointed out that the present policy of the Chinese Government is not to grant extraterritorial rights to any Powers, which have not entered into treaty relations with her and which may desire to do so in future. In October, 1919,

Prime Minister Chin . . . made it quite clear in reply to inquiries that all future treaties between China and the new or old nations would be based absolutely on equality, reciprocity, fairness and justice. This is the new policy of the Chinese Government which is endorsed by all its public servants. This policy was put to a test when the Greek Government in the course of negotiations of a commercial treaty requested that a clause be therein inserted providing for the enjoyment by Greek subjects in Chinese territory of the right of extraterritoriality as

[1] See Hollington K. Tong, " The Shanghai Mixed Court and the Settlement Extension," *Millard's Review*, vol. x, pp. 445-454; also *Lei Kuo Tsai Hua Ling Ssu Tsai Pan Chuan Chih Yao* (a résumé of the extraterritorial rights enjoyed by the Powers in China), published by the Commission on Extraterritoriality, appendix i, pp. 23 *et seq.*

enjoyed by subjects or citizens of the other treaty nations. In reply the Chinese Ministry of Foreign Affairs stated that while permitting Greece to have commercial relations with China, it could never grant to her subjects the privilege of extraterritoriality. The reason given was the adoption of a modern judicial system in China to supersede the ancient Oriental judicial system which prevailed in this country formerly when China first came into contact with the Western Powers. . . . [1]

[1] H. K. T., " Extraterritoriality and the New Nations," *Millard's Review,* vol. x (Oct. 25, 1919), p. 314. See also H. K. Tong's report of an interview with Dr. Philip Tyau, Councillor of the Ministry of Foreign Affairs, *ibid.,* vol. x (Dec. 13, 1919), pp. 56-60.

RECAPITULATION AND CONCLUSION

In the foregoing study the author has attempted to show that in its origin extraterritoriality was by no means a novel device contrived at any particular date to meet the special situation existing in any particular country. It was nothing but a legacy of the undefined or, at best, vaguely defined status of the alien in the ancient world, and a survival of the mediaeval theory of the personality of laws, which was once prevalent everywhere in Europe. The fact that there have existed in modern Europe countless vestiges of the latter principle is conclusive evidence of its abiding influence. Writers on international law in the seventeenth and eighteenth centuries, moreover, have not failed to bear testimony to the judicial competence of the foreign consul.

The Mohammedan religion coincided perfectly with the legal conceptions of ancient and mediaeval Europe. The *Koran* ordained the infidel to be outside the pale of Mussulman jurisdiction, and he was compelled to live under his own national laws. Long before the Europeans carried their crusading spirit into the Levant, Mohammed and his descendants had been in the habit of granting to foreigners the right to submit to their own jurisdiction. When the Crusades began, the conditions were favorable to the transplantation of the European system of " judge-consuls " to alien soil. Unwonted commercial opportunities were opened up, and numerous and important interests awaited protection against untoward mishaps. Furthermore, in order to induce the maritime States to keep up their indispensable assistance, the Christian conquerers were obliged to dole out exceptional privileges. These factors combined to establish in the territory conquered by the Crusaders the system of consular jurisdiction.

At the same time, the Mohammedan world was on the point of a steady expansion. Barred by their inborn disposition from seafaring adventure, the Mussulmans were compelled to invite external assistance. To the foreigners who flocked to their coasts they extended the privilege of judicial extraterritoriality, partly as an inducement to their enterprise, partly in deference to the commands of the *Koran,* and partly in accordance with established usage.

In 1453, the Turks conquered Constantinople. In the midst of transcendent glory, the sultans voluntarily perpetuated what is now regarded as the abnormal régime of the Capitulations. The motives responsible for this action were manifold. Influenced by the religious differences which divided Islam and Christendom, by the prospects of commercial development, and, above all, by the force of custom, the sultans left not only the foreign merchants, but also the non-Moslem subjects of the Porte, to follow their own persuasion and government. The grants to the foreigners were made in a series of public acts known as Capitulations. In essence, these Capitulations were gratuitous concessions on the part of the victorious sultans, who made them without the least intention of derogating from their sovereignty. In other countries of the Levant and of the African continent, privileges of the same nature were extended to foreigners.

In the Far East, the origin of extraterritoriality differed entirely from the rise of the Capitulations in the Levant. Neither differences of civilization, nor religious discrepancies, nor commercial considerations could have influenced the establishment of the extraterritorial régime in Eastern Asia. With the exception of Japan, the force of custom was rather against such a régime than in favor of it. The only plausible explanation is to be sought in the alleged imperfections of the native judicial systems. With the merits of the allegation we are not concerned here, but the fact is that in their intercourse with the Eastern Asiatic Powers, Western nations have not infrequently been led to voice their dissatisfaction with the local jurisdiction.

With the introduction of the territorial basis of sovereignty, to which the feudal system signally contributed, the theory of the personality of laws inevitably gave way to that of absolute territorial jurisdiction. In Europe, the system of " judge-consuls " began gradually to decline, and the incumbent of the consular office was forthwith converted into a mere commercial representative, although even there, as described in Chapter I, numerous survivals of the old régime have existed well into comparatively recent times.

Outside of Europe, the system of consular jurisdiction has likewise undergone a process of decline, the inception of which has, however, been late in coming. In the main, this process may be said to have dated from the middle of the nineteenth century. It was in the nineteenth century, as is well known, that the growth of nationalism reached its very climax in Europe. The contagion of national consciousness soon took hold of the entire world, and was destined sooner or later to exert an influence upon the progress of many an awakening race. Imbued with the spirit of nationalism, the peoples which have been burdened with extraterritoriality have realized its absolute incompatibility with their independence and sovereignty. In Turkey, Japan, China, Siam, and every other country where the system has prevailed, attempts have been made to put an end to it and to restore judicial autonomy.

The methods by means of which the abolition of extraterritoriality has been brought about or attempted are (1) annexation, (2) transfer of jurisdiction, (3) separation, (4) protection, (5) unilateral cancellation, and (6) diplomatic negotiation.

Of the reasons which have been responsible for the decline of extraterritoriality, the growth of national sovereignty has undoubtedly been an influential one. In the case of the territories annexed to countries which cede no rights of jurisdiction, the assertion of the principle of sovereignty as disallowing the continuance of the extraterritorial régime is, of course, implied. On the other hand, the independent Powers which have moaned under the yoke of consular jurisdiction have never failed to contend expressly for their sovereign rights in their fight for the restoration of judicial autonomy.

A second dominating reason for the decadence of extraterritoriality is to be found in the innumerable defects and abuses of the system itself. It is true that many efforts have been made by the Powers to remedy these disadvantages. The Mixed Court régime in Egypt and the International Court system in Siam represent conscientious endeavors to remedy some of the evils incident to the operation of conflicting jurisdictions. But there are many abuses inherent in the system, which are neither removable nor remediable. As an eminent authority says: " The actual organization of [consular] jurisdiction is very unsatisfactory in many respects, and it provokes the just complaints of the peoples and governments of the countries where it exists." [1] In elaboration of this statement, another writer makes this remark:

It is futile to find out . . . if a consul and, notably, if the assessors or judges who live so far from their country, in necessary and daily contact with their nationals, can always restrain

[1] Martens, *Traité de droit international* (Paris, 1883-87), vol. ii, p. 132.

themselves from the sometimes involuntary sentiment of weakness, partiality, and indulgence toward their compatriots. I repeat, all that is not indispensable to my subject. In my opinion, the evil is not with the persons; I even affirm, as a general thesis, their capacity and their conscience. It is the institution of consular jurisdiction which is defective and, from all points of view, inferior to the sole jursdiction of the territorial sovereign, from the moment the territorial sovereign possesses a complete judicial organization which responds to the exigencies of the general community of law.[1]

The third and most important reason is the general improvement of the judicial systems in the various countries concerned. Whatever may have been the original justification of extraterritoriality, in the course of time it has come to be adapted to meet the need of coping with a defective system of jurisprudence. As soon as reforms are introduced into the latter, however, it is evidently unjust and unnecessary to maintain an extraterritorial régime. In their claims for the restoration of judicial autonomy, all the governments concerned have invariably made use of this argument, calling the attention of the foreign governments to the reforms, if any, which have been inaugurated. Likewise, in their pledges for immediate or remote consent to the abolition of their extraterritorial rights, governments have been solicitous about conditioning their promises on the judicial guarantees that are offered to the life and property of their nationals. Indeed, even in the case of protectorates, the mere assumption of the power of protection does not necessarily transfer the rights of jurisdiction, which is usually dependent on the maintenance by the protecting Power of regularly constituted judicial authorities in the country over which it exercises protection.

[1] Paternostro, " *La Revision des traités avec le Japon au point de vue de droit international*," R. D. I., vol. xxiii, p. 176.

Besides these reasons, there have doubtless been others peculiar to the different cases discussed. Sometimes, political as well as commercial considerations have entered into this complex situation. The abandonment of foreign jurisdiction in Japan, for instance, is in a large measure ascribable to the Japanese consent to open the entire country to foreign intercourse. At other times, widely varying conditions have been placed upon the ultimate surrender of extraterritorial jurisdiction. Great Britain gave up her jurisdiction in Madagascar only after France engaged to do likewise in the future in Zanzibar. The United States, in 1914, was unwilling to put an end to her extraterritoriality in Morocco, before certain pending issues regarding American interests in the Shereefian Empire were settled. Still other illustrations might be given, but they are not necessary. For such considerations as have just been pointed out are not essential to the present study, inasmuch as in the first place they are peculiar to each case individually, and in the second place they explain nothing in the continual development of extraterritoriality.

Such, then, is the story of extraterritoriality. It grew up at a time when the principle of territorial sovereignty was unknown. It has steered its course through centuries of legal transformation, and in its journey has kept abreast of the times. Now that the science of international law is developed to a point where territorial sovereignty has become the cornerstone of state existence, extraterritoriality is doomed to decay. For one reason or another, it has not completely disappeared from the structure of international intercourse. It is believed, however, that from an understanding of the salient facts connected with the rise and decline of consular jurisdiction, those countries whose judicial power is still impaired may take fresh impetus in their attempt to get rid of the yoke of extraterritoriality, and those countries which are still beneficiaries of this system may realize that it is a decadent institution and that reasonable demands for its progressive abrogation should at times be countenanced and granted. The interests of justice and fairness will best be served by the conscientious endeavor of the one side to improve the judicial system and of the other to refrain from introducing into what is primarily a legal question irrelevant considerations of a political nature.

3

Columbia University
in the City of New York

The University includes the following :

Columbia College, founded in 1754, and **Barnard College,** founded in 1889, offering to men and women, respectively, programs of study which may be begun either in September or February and which lead normally in from three to four years to the degree of Bachelor of Arts. The program of study in Columbia College makes it possible for a qualified student to satisfy the requirements for both the bachelor's degree and a professional degree in law, medicine, mining, engineering, chemistry, or architecture in six years.

The non-professional graduate Faculties of **Political Science, Philosophy** and **Pure Science,** offering advanced programs of study and investigation leading to the degrees of Master of Arts and Doctor of Philosophy.

The Professional Schools of :

Law, established in 1858, offering courses leading to the degrees of Bachelor of Laws, Master of Laws and Doctor of Law.

Medicine. The College of Physicians and Surgeons, established in 1807, offering courses leading to the degree of Doctor of Medicine.

Mines, founded in 1863, offering courses leading to the degrees of Engineer of Mines and Metallurgical Engineer.

Chemistry and Engineering, set apart from School of Mines in 1896, offering courses leading to degrees in Civil, Electrical, Mechanical, Chemical and Industrial Engineering.

Teachers College, founded in 1888, offering in its School of Education courses leading to appropriate diplomas and the degree of Bachelor of Science in Education ; in its School of Practical Arts courses leading to the degree of Bachelor of Science in Practical Arts ; and in both faculties courses leading to the degrees of Master of Arts and Master of Science.

Architecture, offering a program of indeterminate length leading to the degrees of Bachelor of Architecture and Master of Science.

Journalism, founded in 1912, offering courses leading to the degrees of Bachelor of Literature in Journalism and Master of Science.

Business, founded in 1916, offering courses in business training leading to the degrees of Bachelor of Science and Master of Science.

Dentistry, founded in 1917, offering courses leading to the degrees of Doctor of Dental Surgery.

Pharmacy. The New York College of Pharmacy, founded in 1831, offering courses leading to the degrees of Pharmaceutical Chemist, Bachelor of Science in Pharmacy and Doctor of Pharmacy.

In the **Summer Session** the University offers courses giving both general and professional training which may be taken either with or without regard to an academic degree or diploma.

Through its system of **University Extension** the University offers many courses of study to persons unable otherwise to receive academic training.

Home Study courses carrying no academic credit are offered to persons unable to attend courses conducted at the University.

The Institute of Arts and Sciences provides lectures, concerts, readings and recitals—approximately two hundred and fifty in number—in a single season.

The price of the University Catalogue is twenty-five cents postpaid. Detailed information regarding the work in any department will be furnished without charge upon application to the *Secretary of Columbia University,* New York, N. Y.

To Appear in June, 1925

Opium as an International Problem

The Geneva Conferences

BY

W. W. WILLOUGHBY

Counsellor and Expert to the Chinese Delegation at the
Geneva Conferences

Octavo. About 500 pages. Price about $4.00

This volume, in the nature of a semi-official report, presents, in a comprehensive manner, the fact leading up to the calling of the two Opium Conferences at Geneva, the discussions had in those Conferences and the results reached. The work will be indispensable to all those interested in combating, by international co-operative action, the widespread evils resulting from the abuse of opium and other narcotic habit-forming drugs. To students of international relations the volume will be of especial interest, giving as it does a detailed account of Conferences held under the auspices of the League of Nations and in which the United States Government was officially represented.

The mode of presentation is similar to that followed by Professor Willoughby in the account which he has given of the Washington Conference in his volume "China at the Conference."

The Johns Hopkins Press

Baltimore, Maryland

COLUMBIA UNIVERSITY PRESS BOOKS

LAW AND ITS ADMINISTRATION. By HARLAN F. STONE, Attorney General of the United States. Pp. vii+232. $2.50.

CONSTITUTIONAL GOVERNMENT IN THE UNITED STATES. By WOODROW WILSON, late President of the United States. Pp. vii + 236. $2.50.

OUR CHIEF MAGISTRATE AND HIS POWERS. By WILLIAM HOWARD TAFT, Chief Justice of the Supreme Court. Pp. vii + 165. $2.25.

CONSTITUTIONAL POWER AND WORLD AFFAIRS. By GEORGE SUTHERLAND, former United States Senator from Utah. Pp. vii + 202. $2.50.

WORLD ORGANIZATION AS AFFECTED BY THE NATURE OF THE MODERN STATE. By DAVID JAYNE HILL, late American Ambassador to Germany. Pp. ix + 214. $2.50.

THE GENIUS OF THE COMMON LAW. By SIR FREDERICK POLLOCK. Pp. vii + 141. $2.50.

THE MECHANICS OF LAW MAKING. By COURTENAY ILBERT, formerly Clerk of the House of Commons. Pp. viii + 209. $2.50.

AMERICAN CITY PROGRESS AND THE LAW. By HOWARD LEE MCBAIN, Eaton Professor of Municipal Science and Administration in Columbia University. Pp. viii+ 269. $2.25.

THE CANADIAN CONSTITUTION IN FORM AND IN FACT. By WILLIAM RENWICK RIDDELL, Chief Justice of the Supreme Court of Ontario. Pp. ix + 77. $1.60.

THE EQUALITY OF STATES. By JULIUS GOEBEL, Jr., Associate in International Law in Columbia University. Pp. viii + 89. $2.00.

THE AMERICAN COLONIES IN THE EIGHTEENTH CENTURY. By HERBERT LEVI OSGOOD, late Professor of History in Columbia University. In four volumes, 8vo, cloth. 550 pages each. $5.50 per volume; $20.00 per set.

THE PURPOSE OF HISTORY. By FREDERICK J. E. WOODBRIDGE, Dean of the Graduate Faculties in Columbia University. Pp. 89. $1.50.

RECENT CHANGES IN AMERICAN CONSTITUTIONAL THEORY. By JOHN W. BURGESS, Emeritus Professor of Political Science and Constitutional Law in Columbia University. Pp. xi + 115. $1.75.

BISMARK AND GERMAN UNITY. By MUNROE SMITH, Emeritus Bryce Professor of European History in Columbia University. Pp. xiv+188. Third revised edition. $2.75.

THE LEAGUE OF NATIONS AND MISCELLANEOUS ADDRESSES. By WILLIAM D. GUTHRIE, Member of the New York Bar. Pp. ix + 383. $2.50.

MARXISM VERSUS SOCIALISM. By VLADIMIR G. SIMKHOVITCH, Professor of Economic History in Columbia University. Pp. xvi + 298. $2.50.

Records of Civilization : Sources and Studies

HELLENIC CIVILIZATION. By G. W. BOTSFORD and E. G. SIHLER. Pp. xiii+719. $4.50.

THE HISTORY OF THE FRANKS. By GREGORY, Bishop of Tours. Translated by ERNEST BREHAUT. Pp. xxv + 283. Map. $3.50.

THE BOOK OF THE POPES (Liber Pontificalis). Translated by LOUISE ROPES LOOMIS. Pp. xxii + 169. $2.85.

AN INTRODUCTION TO THE HISTORY OF HISTORY. By JAMES T. SHOTWELL, Professor of History in Columbia University. Pp. xii + 339. $4.50.

THE LITERATURE OF THE OLD TESTAMENT IN ITS HISTORICAL DEVELOPMENT. By JULIUS A. BEWER, Professor in Union Theological Seminary. Pp. xiv+ 452. $3.00.

A GUIDE TO THE PRINTED MATERIALS FOR ENGLISH SOCIAL AND ECONOMIC HISTORY, 1750-1850. By JUDITH B. WILLIAMS. In press.

THE ECONOMIC INTERPRETATION OF HISTORY. By EDWIN R. A. SELIGMAN, McVikar Professor of Political Economy in Columbia University. Pp. ix + 166. Second edition, revised. $2.50.

THE SHIFTING AND INCIDENCE OF TAXATION. By EDWIN R. A. SELIGMAN. Pp. xii + 431. Fourth edition. $4.50.

THE CURRENCY PROBLEM. Pp. xxvii + 170. Paper. $1.90.

THE FEDERAL INCOME TAX. Edited by ROBERT HAIG, Professor of Business Organization in Columbia University. Pp. xii + 271. $3.25.

COLUMBIA UNIVERSITY PRESS
Columbia University   **New York**

The Academy of Political Science in the City of New York

The Academy of Political Science, founded in 1880, is composed of men and women interested in political, economic and social questions. Members receive the Political Science Quarterly, the Proceedings of the Academy, the Annual Record of Political Events and invitations to meetings. The annual dues are five dollars. Address The Academy of Political Science, Columbia University, New York.

POLITICAL SCIENCE QUARTERLY

Managing Editor

PARKER T. MOON

The Political Science Quarterly is the official organ of the Academy and is devoted to politics, economics and public law. It follows the most important movements of foreign politics, international relations and questions of present interest in the United States. Its attitude is non-partisan, every article is signed and expresses simply the personal view of the writer.

The Record of Political Events, published annually in January is a concisely arranged summary of the year's events throughout the entire world.

PROCEEDINGS OF THE ACADEMY OF POLITICAL SCIENCE

The Proceedings are issued semi-annually by the Academy as a record of its activities and as a means of giving detailed treatment to special subjects of importance. Recent issues are: Law and Justice, American Economic Policies, Wealth and Taxation. Price $1.50 each in paper covers. A full list of the numbers thus far issued will be sent on request. Address Academy of Political Science, Columbia University, New York.

Studies in History, Economics and Public Law

edited by

Faculty of Political Science of Columbia University

VOLUME X, 1898-99. 409 pp. Price, cloth, $3.50.

1. [26] Sympathetic Strikes and Sympathetic Lockouts.
By FRED S. HALL, Ph.D. Price, $1.00.
2. [27] *Rhode Island and the Formation of the Union.
By FRANK GREENE BATES, Ph.D. Price, $1.50.
3. [28]. Centralized Administration of Liquor Laws in the American Commonwealths.
By CLEMENT MOORE LACEY SITES, Ph.D. Price, $1.00.

VOLUME XI, 1899. 495 pp. Price, cloth, 4.00; paper covers, $3.50.

[29] The Growth of Cities.
By ADNA FERRIN WEBER Ph.D.

VOLUME XII, 1899-1900. 586 pp. Price, cloth, $4.00.

1. [30] History and Functions of Central Labor Unions.
By WILLIAM MAXWELL BURKE, Ph.D. Price, $1.00.
2. [31.] Colonial Immigration Laws.
By EDWARD EMERSON PROPER, A.M. Price, 75 cents.
3. [32] History of Military Pension Legislation in the United States.
By WILLIAM HENRY GLASSON, Ph.D. Price, $1.00.
4. [33] History of the Theory of Sovereignty since Rousseau.
By CHARLES E. MERRIAM, Jr., Ph.D. Price, $1.50.

VOLUME XIII, 1901. 570 pp. Price, cloth, $4.00.

1. [34] The Legal Property Relations of Married Parties.
By ISIDOR LOEB, Ph.D. Price, $1.50.
2. [35] Political Nativism in New York State.
By LOUIS DOW SCISCO, Ph.D. Price, $2.00.
3. [36] The Reconstruction of Georgia. By EDWIN C. WOOLLEY, Ph.D. Price, $1.00.

VOLUME XIV, 1901-1902. 576 pp. Price, cloth, $4.00.

1. [37] Loyalism in New York during the American Revolution.
By ALEXANDER CLARENCE FLICK, Ph.D. Price, $2.00.
2. [38] The Economic Theory of Risk and Insurance.
By ALLAN H. WILLETT, Ph.D. Price, $1.50.
3. [39] The Eastern Question: A Study in Diplomacy.
By STEPHEN P. H. DUGGAN. Ph.D. Price, $1.00.

VOLUME XV, 1902. 427 pp. Price, cloth, $3.50; Paper covers, $3.00.

[40] Crime in Its Relation to Social Progress. By ARTHUR CLEVELAND HALL, Ph.D.

VOLUME XVI, 1902-1903. 547 pp. Price, cloth, $4.00.

1. [41] The Past and Present of Commerce in Japan.
By YETARO KINOSITA, Ph.D. Price, $1.50.
2. [42] The Employment of Women in the Clothing Trade.
By MABEL HURD WILLET, Ph.D. Price, $1.50.
3. [43] The Centralization of Administration in Ohio.
By SAMUEL P. ORTH, Ph.D. Price, $1.50.

VOLUME XVII, 1903. 635 pp. Price, cloth, $4.00.

1. [44] *Centralizing Tendencies in the Administration of Indiana.
By WILLIAM A. RAWLES, Ph.D. Price, $2.50.
2. [45] Principles of Justice in Taxation. By STEPHEN F. WESTON, Ph.D. Price, $2.00.

VOLUME XVIII, 1903. 753 pp. Price, cloth, $4.50.

1. [46] The Administration of Iowa. By HAROLD MARTIN BOWMAN, Ph.D. Price, $1.50.
2. [47] Turgot and the Six Edicts. By ROBERT P. SHEPHERD, Ph.D. Price, $1.50.
3. [48] Hanover and Prussia, 1795-1803. By GUY STANTON FORD, Ph.D. Price, $2.00.

VOLUME XIX, 1903-1905. 588 pp. Price, cloth, $4.00.

1. [49] Josiah Tucker, Economist. By WALTER ERNEST CLARK, Ph.D. Price, $1.50.
2. [50] History and Criticism of the Labor Theory of Value in English Political Economy.
By ALBERT C. WHITAKER, Ph.D. Price, $1.50.
3. [51] Trade Unions and the Law in New York.
By GEORGE GORHAM GROAT, Ph.D. Price, $1.00.

VOLUME XX, 1904. 514 pp. Price, cloth. $3.50.

1. [52] The Office of the Justice of the Peace in England.
By CHARLES AUSTIN BEARD, Ph.D. Price, $1.50.
2. [53] A History of Military Government in Newly Acquired Territory of the United States. By DAVID Y. THOMAS, Ph.D. Price, $2.00.

VOLUME XXI, 1904. 746 pp. Price, cloth, $4.50.

1. [54] *Treaties, their Making and Enforcement.
By SAMUEL B. CRANDALL, Ph.D. Price, $1.50.
2. [55] The Sociology of a New York City Block.
By THOMAS JESSE JONES, Ph.D. Price, $1.00.
3. [56] Pre-Malthusian Doctrines of Population.
By CHARLES E. STANGELAND, Ph.D. Price, $2.50.

VOLUME XLVII, 1912. 544 pp. Price, cloth, $4.00.

1. [118] The Politics of Michigan, 1865-1878,
By HARRIETTE M. DILLA, Ph.D. Price, $2.00.
2. [119] *The United States Beet Sugar Industry and the Tariff.
By ROY G. BLAKEY, Ph.D. Price, $2.00.

VOLUME XLVIII, 1912. 493 pp. Price, cloth, $4.00.

1. [120] Isidor of Seville. By ERNEST BREHAUT, Ph. D. Price, $2.00.
2. [121] Progress and Uniformity in Child-Labor Legislation.
By WILLIAM FIELDING OGBURN, Ph.D. Price, $1.75.

VOLUME XLIX, 1912. 592 pp. Price, cloth, $4.50.

1. [122] British Radicalism 1791-1797. By WALTER PHELPS HALL. Price, $2.00.
2. [123] A Comparative Study of the Law of Corporations.
By ARTHUR K. KUHN, Ph.D. Price, $1.50.
3. [124] *The Negro at Work in New York City.
By GEORGE E. HAYNES, Ph.D. Price, $1.25.

VOLUME L, 1911. 481 pp. Price, cloth, $4.00.

1. [125] *The Spirit of Chinese Philanthropy. [By YAI YUE TSU, Ph.D. Price, $1.00.
2. [126] *The Alien in China. By VI. KYUIN WELLINGTON KOO, Ph.D. Price, $2.50.

VOLUME LI, 1912. 4to. Atlas. Price: cloth, $1.50; paper covers, $1.00.

1. [127] The Sale of Liquor in the South.
By LEONARD S. BLAKEY, Ph.D.

VOLUME LII, 1912. 489 pp. Price, cloth, $4.00.

1. [128] *Provincial and Local Taxation in Canada.
By SOLOMON VINEBERG, Ph.D. Price, $1.50.
2. [129] *The Distribution of Income.
By FRANK HATCH STREIGHTOFF, Ph.D. Price, $1.50.
3. [130] *The Finances of Vermont. By FREDERICK A. WOOD, Ph.D. Price, $1.00.

VOLUME LIII, 1913. 789 pp. Price, cloth, $4.50; paper, $4.00.

[131] The Civil War and Reconstruction in Florida. By W. W. DAVIS, Ph.D.

VOLUME LIV, 1913. 604 pp. Price, cloth, $4.50.

1. [132] *Privileges and Immunities of Citizens of the United States.
By ARNOLD JOHNSON LIEN, Ph.D. (Out of print.)
2. [133] The Supreme Court and Unconstitutional Legislation.
By BLAINE FREE MOORE, Ph.D. Price, $1.00.
3. [134] *Indian Slavery in Colonial Times within the Present Limits of the
United States. By ALMON WHEELER LAUBER, Ph.D. Price, $3.00.

VOLUME LV, 1913. 665 pp. Price, cloth, $4.50.

1. [135] *A Political History of the State of New York.
By HOMER A. STEBBINS, Ph.D. Price, $4.00.
2. [136] *The Early Persecutions of the Christians.
By LEON H. CANFIELD, Ph.D. Price, $1.50.

VOLUME LVI, 1913. 406 pp. Price, cloth, $3.50.

1. [137] Speculation on the New York Stock Exchange, 1904-1907.
By ALGERNON ASHBURNER OSBORNE. Price, $1.50.
2. [138] The Policy of the United States towards Industrial Monopoly.
By OSWALD WHITMAN KNAUTH, Ph.D. Price, $2.00.

VOLUME LVII, 1914. 670 pp. Price, cloth, $4.50.

1. [139] *The Civil Service of Great Britain.
By ROBERT MOSES, Ph.D. Price, $2.00.
2. [140] The Financial History of New York State.
By DON C. SOWERS. Price, $2.50.

VOLUME LVIII, 1914. 684 pp. Price, cloth, $4.50; paper, $4.00.

[141] Reconstruction in North Carolina.
By J. G. DE ROULHAC HAMILTON, Ph.D.

VOLUME LIX, 1914. 625 pp. Price, cloth, $4.50.

1. [142] The Development of Modern Turkey by means of its Press.
By AHMED EMIN, Ph.D. Price, $1.00.
2. [143] The System of Taxation in China, 1614-1911.
By SHAO-KWAN CHEN, Ph.D. Price, $1.00.
3. [144] The Currency Problem in China. By WEN PIN WEI, Ph.D. Price, $1.25.
4. [145] *Jewish Immigration to the United States.
By SAMUEL JOSEPH, Ph.D. Price, $1.50.

VOLUME LX. 1914. 516 pp. Price, cloth, $4.00.

1. [146] *Constantine the Great and Christianity.
   By CHRISTOPHER BUSH COLEMAN, Ph.D.   Price, $2.00.
2. [147] The Establishment of Christianity and the Proscription of Paganism.   By MAUD ALINE HUTTMAN, Ph.D.   Price, $2.00.

VOLUME LXI. 1914. 496 pp. Price, cloth, $4.00.

1. [148] *The Railway Conductors: A Study in Organized Labor.
   By EDWIN CLYDE ROBBINS.   Price, $1.50.
2. [149] *The Finances of the City of New York.
   By YIN-CH'U MA, Ph.D.   Price, $2.50.

VOLUME LXII. 1914. 414 pp. Price, cloth, $3.50.

[150] The Journal of the Joint Committee of Fifteen on Reconstruction.
39th Congress, 1865—1867.   By BENJAMIN B. KENDRICK, Ph.D.   Price, $3.00.

VOLUME LXIII. 1914. 561 pp. Price, cloth, $4.00.

1. [151] Emile Durkheim's Contribution to Sociological Theory.
   By CHARLES ELMER GEHLKE, Ph.D.   Price, $1.50.
2. [152] The Nationalization of Railways in Japan.
   By TOSHIHARU WATARAI, Ph.D.   Price, $1.25.
3. [153] Population: A Study in Malthusianism.
   By WARREN S. THOMPSON, Ph.D.   Price, $1.75.

VOLUME LXIV. 1915. 646 pp. Price, cloth, $4.50.

1. [154] *Reconstruction in Georgia.   By C. MILDRED THOMPSON, Ph.D.   Price, 3.00.
2. [155] *The Review of American Colonial Legislation by the King in Council.   By ELMER BEECHER RUSSELL, Ph.D.   Price, $1.75.

VOLUME LXV. 1915. 524 pp. Price, cloth, $4.00.

1. [156] *The Sovereign Council of New France
   By RAYMOND DU BOIS CAHALL, Ph.D.   Price, $2.25.
2. [157] *Scientific Management (3rd. ed. 1922).
   By HORACE B. DRURY, Ph.D,   Price, $2.00,

VOLUME LXVI. 1915. 655 pp. Price, cloth, $4.50.

1. [158] *The Recognition Policy of the United States.
   By JULIUS GOEBEL, JR., Ph.D.   Price, $2.00.
2. [159] Railway Problems in China.   By CHIH HSU, Ph.D.   (Out of print.)
3. [160] *The Boxer Rebellion.   By PAUL H. CLEMENTS, Ph.D.   Price, $2.00.

VOLUME LXVII. 1916. 538 pp. Price, cloth, $4.00.

1. [161] *Russian Sociology.   By JULIUS F. HECKER, Ph.D.   Price, $2.50.
2. [162] State Regulation of Railroads in the South.
   By MAXWELL FERGUSON, A. M., LL.B.   Price, $1.75.

VOLUME LXVIII. 1916, 1924. 815 pp.   (In two parts separately bound.)
Price, $7.00.

1. [163] *The Origins of the Islamic State.   By PHILIP K. HITTI, Ph.D.   Price, $4.00.
2. [163A] *The Origins of the Islamic State.   Part II.
   By F. C. MURGOTTEN, Ph.D.   Price, $3.00.

VOLUME LXIX. 1916. 489 pp. Price, cloth, $4.00.

1. [164] Railway Monopoly and Rate Regulation.
   By ROBERT J. MCFALL, Ph.D.   Price, $2.00.
2. [165] The Butter Industry in the United States.
   By EDWARD WIBST, Ph.D.   Price, $2.00,

VOLUME LXX. 1916. 540 pp. Price, cloth, $4.50.

[166] Mohammedan Theories of Finance
   By NICOLAS P. AGHNIDES, Ph.D.   Price, $4.00.

VOLUME LXXI. 1916. 476 pp. Price, cloth, $4.00.

1. [167] The Commerce of Louisiana during the French Regime, 1699—1763.
   By N. M. MILLER SURREY, Ph.D.   Price, $3.50.

VOLUME LXXII. 1916. 542 pp. Price, cloth, $4.50.

1. [168] American Men of Letters: Their Nature and Nurture.
   By EDWIN LEAVITT CLARKE, Ph.D.   Price, $1.50.
2. [169] The Tariff Problem in China.   By CHIN CHU, Ph.D.   Price, $1.50.
3. [170] The Marketing of Perishable Food Products.
   By A. B. Adams, Ph.D.   (Out of print)

VOLUME LXXIII. 1917. 616 pp. Price, cloth, $4.50.

1. [171] *The Social and Economic Aspects of the Chartist Movement.
By FRANK F. ROSENBLATT, Ph.D. Price, $2.00.
2. [172] *The Decline of the Chartist Movement.
By PRESTON WILLIAM SLOSSON, Ph.D. Price, $2.00.
3. [173] Chartism and the Churches. By H. U. FAULKNER, Ph.D. Price, $1.25.

VOLUME LXXIV. 1917. 546 pp. Price, cloth, $4.50.

1. [174] The Rise of Ecclesiastical Control in Quebec.
By WALTER A. RIDDELL, Ph.D. Price, $1.75.
2. [175] Political Opinion in Massachusetts during the Civil War and Reconstruction. By EDITH ELLEN WARE, Ph.D. Price, $1.75.
3. [176] Collective Bargaining in the Lithographic Industry.
By H. E. HOAGLAND, Ph.D. Price, $1.00.

VOLUME LXXV. 1917. 410 pp. Price, cloth, $4.00.

An extra-illustrated and bound volume is published at $5.00.
1. [177] New York as an Eighteenth Century Municipality. Prior to 1731.
By ARTHUR EVERETT PETERSON, Ph.D. Price, $2.00
2. [178] New York as an Eighteenth Century Municipality. 1731-1776.
By GEORGE WILLIAM EDWARDS, Ph.D. Price, $2.00.

VOLUME LXXVI. 1917. 489 pp. Price, cloth, $4.00.

1. [179] *Economic and Social History of Chowan County, North Carolina.
By W. SCOTT BOYCE, Ph.D. Price, $2.50.
2. [180] Separation of State and Local Revenues in the United States.
By MABEL NEWCOMER, Ph.D. Price, $1.75.

VOLUME LXXVII. 1917. 473 pp. Price, cloth, $4.00.

[181] American Civil Church Law. By CARL ZOLLMANN, LL.B. Price, $3.50.

VOLUME LXXVIII. 1917. 647 pp. Price, cloth, $4.50.

[182] The Colonial Merchants and the American Revolution.
By ARTHUR MEIER SCHLESINGER, Ph.D. Price, $4.00.

VOLUME LXXIX. 1917-1918. 535 pp. Price, cloth, $4.50.

1. [183] Contemporary Theories of Unemployment and Unemployment Relief. By FREDERICK C. MILLS, Ph.D. Price, $1.50.
2. [184] The French Assembly of 1848 and American Constitutional Doctrine. By EUGENE NEWTON CURTIS, Ph.D. Price, $3.00.

VOLUME LXXX. 1918. 448 pp. Price, cloth, $4.00.

1. [185] *Valuation and Rate Making. By ROBERT L. HALE, Ph.D. Price, $1.50.
2. [186] The Enclosure of Open Fields in England.
By HARRIET BRADLEY, Ph.D. Price, $1.25.
3. [187] The Land Tax in China. By H. L. HUANG, Ph.D. Price, $1.50.

VOLUME LXXXI. 1918. 601 pp. Price, cloth $4.50.

1. [188] Social Life in Rome in the Time of Plautus and Terence.
By GEORGIA W. LEFFINGWELL, Ph.D. Price, $1.25.
2. [189] *Australian Social Development.
By CLARENCE H. NORTHCOTT, Ph.D. Price, $2.50.
3. [190] *Factory Statistics and Industrial Fatigue.
By PHILIP S. FLORENCE, Ph.D. Price, $1.25.

VOLUME LXXXII. 1918-1919. 576 pp. Price, cloth, $4.50.

1. [191] New England and the Bavarian Illuminati.
By VERNON STAUFFER, PH.D. Price, $3.00.
2. [192] Resale Price Maintenance. By CLAUDIUS T. MURCHISON, Ph.D. Price, $1.50.

VOLUME LXXXIII. 1919. 432 pp. Price, cloth, $4.00.

[193] The I. W. W. Second Edition, 1920. By PAUL F. BRISSENDEN, Ph.D. Price, $3.50.

VOLUME LXXXIV. 1919. 534 pp. Price, cloth, $4.50

1. [194] The Royal Government in Virginia, 1624-1775.
By PERCY SCOTT FLIPPIN, Ph.D. Price, $3.00.
2. [195] Hellenic Conceptions of Peace. By WALLACE E. CALDWELL, Ph.D. Price, $1.25.

VOLUME LXXXV. 1919. 450 pp. Price, cloth, $4.00.

1. [196] The Religious Policy of the Bavarian Government during the Napoleonic Period. By CHESTER P. HIGBY, Ph.D. Price, $3.00.
2. [197] Public Debts of China. By F. H. HUANG, Ph.D. Price, $1.00.

VOLUME CXIII. 1924. 551 pp. Price, cloth, $6.50.

1. [252] The Humane Movement in the United States. 1910-1922.
By WILLIAM J. SHULTZ. Ph.D. Price, $3.50.
2. [253] Farmers and Workers in American Politics.
By STUART A. RICE, Ph.D. Price, $2.50.

VOLUME CXIV. 1924. 607 pp. Price, cloth, $6.50.

1. [254] *The Bank of North Dakota: an Experiment in Agrarian Banking.
By ALVIN S. TOSTLEBE, Ph.D. Price, $2.25.
2. [255] *A New American Commercial Policy.
By WALLACE MCCLURE, Ph.D. Price, $4.00.

VOLUME CXV. 1924-25. 583 pp. Price, cloth, $6.50.

1. [256] *Frances Wright.   By WILLIAM RANDALL WATERMAN, Ph.D. Price, $2.75.
2. [257] Tory Democracy.   By WILLIAM J. WILKINSON, Ph.D. Price, $3.50.

VOLUME CXVI. 1924-25. 667 pp. Price, cloth, $7.00.

1. [258] The Labor Policy of the United States Steel Corporation.
By CHARLES A. GULICK, JR., Ph.D. Price, $2.00.
2. [259] Protective Labor Legislation.
By ELIZABETH FAULKNER BAKER, Ph.D. Price, $4.50.

VOLUME CXVII. 1925. 489 pp. Price, cloth, $5.50.

1. [260] The Roman Colonate.   By ROTH CLAUSING, Ph.D. Price, $3.50.
2. [261] The Introduction of Adam Smith's Doctrines into Germany.
By CARL WILLIAM HASEK, Ph.D. Price, $1.50.

VOLUME CXVIII. 1925. 515 pp. Price, cloth, $6.00.

1. [262] Impressment of American Seamen.
By J. F. ZIMMERMAN, Ph.D. Price, $3.00.
2. [263] Extraterritoriality: its Rise and Decline.
By SHIH SHUN LIU, Ph.D. Price, $2.50.

VOLUME CXIX. 1925.

1. [264] Guillaume de Greef: The Social Theory of an Early Syndicalist.
By DOROTHY WOLFF DOUGLAS. (In press).
2. [265] Social Cleavages in Texas.   By WESTON JOSEPH MCCONNELL. (In press).

The price for each separate monograph is for paper-covered copies; separate monographs marked with an asterisk, (*), can be supplied bound in cloth, for 75c. additional. All prices are net.

The set of 114 volumes, covering monographs 1-263, is offered, bound, for $470; except that Volumes II, III, IV, VII, XXXIV, LXVI and LXXII can be supplied only in part, Volume II, Nos. 1 and 2, Volume III, Nos. 1 and 2, Volume IV, Nos. 2 and 3, Volume VII, No. 2, Volume XXXIV, No. 3, Volume XLVI, No. 1, Volume LIV, No. 1, Volume LXVI, No. 2 and Volume LXXII, No. 3 being out of print. Volumes II, III, and IV, as described in the last sentence, and Volumes I and XXV can now be supplied only in connection with complete sets, but the separate monographs of each of these volumes are available unless marked *"not sold separately"*

For further information, apply to

LONGMANS, GREEN & CO., 55 Fifth Avenue, New York.
P. S. KING & SON, Ltd., Orchard House, Westminster, London